THE CAMBRIDGE COMPANION TO

# BIBLICAL INTERPRETATION

This book provides the first complete guide for students to the
present state of biblical studies. The twenty-one specially commissioned chapters are written by established scholars from North
America and Britain, and represent both traditional and contemporary points of view. The chapters in Part one cover all the methods
and approaches currently practised in the academic study of the
Bible, while those in Part two examine the major categories of books
in the Bible from the perspective of recent scholarship – e.g. historical books of the Old Testament, Gospels, prophetic literature. Major
issues raised are: the relation of modern 'critical' study of the Bible to
'pre-critical' and 'post-critical' approaches; the place of history in the
study of the Bible; feminist, liberationist and New Historicist concerns; the relation of Christian and Jewish scholarship; and recent
interest in the Bible as literature.

John Barton is Oriel and Laing Professor of the Interpretation of
Holy Scripture, University of Oxford.

CAMBRIDGE COMPANIONS TO RELIGION
A series of companions to major topics and key figures in
theology and religious studies. Each volume will contain specially
commissioned essays by international scholars which provide
an accessible and stimulating introduction to the subject for new
readers and non-specialists.

*Titles in the series*

THE CAMBRIDGE COMPANION TO CHRISTIAN DOCTRINE
edited by Colin Gunton
ISBN 0521 47118 4 hardback
ISBN 0521 47695 x paperback

*Forthcoming*

THE CAMBRIDGE COMPANION TO LIBERATION THEOLOGY
edited by Christopher Rowland
ISBN 0521 46144 8 hardback
ISBN 0521 46707 1 paperback

THE CAMBRIDGE COMPANION TO DIETRICH BONHOEFFER
edited by John De Gruchy
ISBN 0521 58258 x hardback
ISBN 0521 58781 6 paperback

THE CAMBRIDGE COMPANION TO KARL BARTH
edited by John Webster
ISBN 0521 58476 0 hardback
ISBN 0521 58560 0 paperback

THE CAMBRIDGE COMPANION TO

# BIBLICAL INTERPRETATION

Edited by John Barton

CAMBRIDGE
UNIVERSITY PRESS

PUBLISHED BY THE PRESS SYNDICATE OF THE UNIVERSITY OF CAMBRIDGE
The Pitt Building, Trumpington Street, Cambridge CB2 1RP, United Kingdom

CAMBRIDGE UNIVERSITY PRESS
The Edinburgh Building, Cambridge CB2 2RU, UK
40 West 20th Street, New York, NY 10011–4211, USA
10 Stamford Road, Oakleigh, Melbourne 3166, Australia

First published 1998
Reprinted 1999

Printed in the United Kingdom at the University Press, Cambridge

Typeset in FF Celeste using QuarkXPress

*A catalogue record for this book is available from
the British Library*

*Library of Congress cataloguing in publication data*

The Cambridge companion to biblical interpretation / edited by John Barton
   p.  cm. – (Cambridge companions to religion)
Includes index.
ISBN 0 521 48144 9 (hardback) – ISBN 0 521 48593 2 (paperback)
1. Bible–Criticism, interpretation, etc.   I. Barton, John, 1948– .
II. Series.
BS511.2.C35   1998
220.6'1–dc21   97-27945   CIP

ISBN 0 521 48144 9 hardback
ISBN 0 521 48593 2 paperback

CP

# Contents

# Notes on contributors

ROBERT ALTER is Class of 1937 Professor of Hebrew and Comparative Literature at the University of California at Berkeley. He has written extensively on the novel, on modern Hebrew literature and on literary aspects of the Bible. Among his books on the Bible are *The Art of Biblical Narrative* (1981), *The Art of Biblical Poetry* (1985), and *Genesis: Translation and Commentary* (1996).

JOHN ASHTON is an Emeritus Fellow of Wolfson College, Oxford. Until 1996 he taught New Testament Studies at the University of Oxford. He is the author of the highly acclaimed *Understanding the Fourth Gospel* (1991) and *Studying John* (1994).

JOHN BARTON is Oriel and Laing Professor of the Interpretation of Holy Scripture in the University of Oxford. His books include *Reading the Old Testament: Method in Biblical Study* (1984, 2nd edition, 1996); *Oracles of God: Perceptions of Ancient Prophecy in Israel after the Exile* (1986); *People of the Book? The Authority of the Bible in Christianity* (1988); and *The Spirit and the Letter: Studies in the Biblical Canon* (1997).

JOSEPH BLENKINSOPP was born and educated in England but is a long-time resident of the United States. He has taught at several institutions in Britain and the US and is currently John A. O'Brien Professor of Biblical Studies at the University of Notre Dame, Indiana, USA. His most recent publications are: *A History of Prophecy in Israel* (1996); *Sage, Priest, Prophet: Religious and Intellectual Leadership in Ancient Israel* (1995); and *Wisdom and Law in the Old Testament. The Ordering of Life in Israel and Early Judaism* (1995).

ROBERT P. CARROLL is Professor of Hebrew Bible and Semitic Studies in the University of Glasgow. His publications include *When Prophecy Failed* (1986); *Jeremiah: a Commentary* (1986); *Wolf in the Sheepfold* (1991; 1997); and, edited with Stephen Prickett, the World's Classics, *The Bible: Authorised King James Version* (1997).

JAMES DUNN took his first degrees (MA BD) at Glasgow and his PhD at Cambridge, where he was also awarded a DD for his commentary on Romans. After teaching at the University of Nottingham for twelve years he was appointed to the University of Durham, where he holds the Lightfoot Chair of Divinity. His recent publications include: *The Acts of the Apostles* (TPI, 1996); *Epistles to the Colossians and to Philemon* (1996); *New Testament Guides: 1 Corinthians* (1995); with A. M. Suggate, *A Fresh Look at the Old Doctrine of Justification by Faith* (1993, 1994); and *The Theology of Paul's Letter to the Galatians* (1993).

TIM GORRINGE is Reader in Contextual Theology at St Andrews University. Among his recent books are *Capital and the Kingdom: Theological Ethics and Economic Order* (Orbis, 1994); *God's Just Vengeance: Crime, Violence and the Rhetoric of Salvation* (1996); and *The Sign of Love: Reflections on the Eucharist* (1997).

DAVID JASPER is Reader in Literature and Theology and Vice-Dean of Divinity at the University of Glasgow. Since 1991 he has been Director of the Centre for the Study of Literature and Theology. From 1987 to 1997 he was Senior Editor of the journal *Literature and Theology*. His most recent books are *Rhetoric, Power and Community* (1993) and *Readings in the Canon of Scripture* (1995).

WILLIAM JOHNSTONE has been Professor of Hebrew and Semitic Languages in the University of Aberdeen since 1980. Among his recent publications are *Exodus* (Old Testament Guides, 1990) and a two-volume commentary on Chronicles, *1 & 2 Chronicles* (1997); in 1995 he edited a collection of essays on William Robertson Smith (*William Robertson Smith: Essays in Reassessment*).

ANN LOADES is Professor of Divinity at the University of Durham. She edited the journal *Theology* for six years, and recently edited two books with Professor David Brown: *The Sense of the Sacramental* (1995) and *Christ the Sacramental Word* (1996). Her most recent publication is *Evelyn Underhill* (1997).

ROBERT MORGAN is Reader in New Testament Theology and fellow of Linacre College, Oxford. He is author (with John Barton) of *Biblical Interpretation* (1988), and of *Romans* (1995).

PHEME PERKINS is Professor of Theology (New Testament) at Boston College. She has served as President of the Catholic Biblical Association of America and President of the New England Region of the American Academy of Religion. Her most recent books include *Jesus as Teacher* (1991); *Gnosticism and the New Testament* (1993); *1 & 2 Peter, James and Jude* (1994); the commentary on Mark in the *New Interpreter's Bible* volume VIII (1995) and *Ephesians* (1997). She is presently working on commentaries on the pastoral epistles and Galatians.

STEPHEN PRICKETT is Regius Professor of English Language and Literature at the University of Glasgow. He has also held the Chair of English at the Australian National University in Canberra, and taught at the Universities of Sussex, Minnesota, and Smith College, Massachusetts. Among his books on Romanticism, Victorian studies, and literature and theology, are: *Romanticism and Religion: the Tradition of Coleridge and Wordsworth in the Victorian Church* (1976); *The Romantics* (ed. 1981); *Words and the Word: Language, Poetics and Biblical Interpretation* (1986); *Reading the Text: Biblical Criticism and Literary Theory* (ed. 1991); *The Bible* (with Robert Barnes, 1991); and *Origins of Narrative: the Romantic Appropriation of the Bible* (1996). Most recently he wrote the preface to the new World's Classics Bible (1997).

IAIN PROVAN is Marshall Sheppard Professor of Biblical Studies at Regent College, Vancouver. His publications include *Hezekiah and the Books of Kings* (1988); *Lamentations* (1991); *1 and 2 Kings* (1995); and *1 & 2 Kings* (Old Testament Guides, 1997).

STEFAN C. REIF is Director of the Genizah Research Unit and Head of the Oriental Division at Cambridge University Library. He teaches Hebrew and Jewish studies in the Faculties of Oriental Studies and Divinity at Cambridge and has published widely in these fields, particularly on Jewish liturgy and the Cairo Genizah. His most recent two volumes, both published by Cambridge University Press, are *Judaism and Hebrew Prayer* (1993), which is a survey of Jewish liturgical history, and *Hebrew Manuscripts at Cambridge University Library* (1997), in which he describes Cambridge's rich collection of over 1,000 Hebrew codices. He is currently working on two books about the Genizah Collection and has just completed a year in Israel as a Professorial Fellow of the Institute for Advanced Studies at the Hebrew University of Jerusalem.

ANTHONY THISELTON is Professor of Christian Theology and Head of the Department of Theology in the University of Nottingham. He is also Canon Theologian of Leicester Cathedral. His publications include: *The Two Horizons* (1980) and also in Korean (1990); *New Horizons in Hermeneutics. The Theology and Practice of Transforming Biblical Reading* (1992, reprinted 1994); and *Interpreting God and the Postmodern Self: on Meaning, Manipulation and Promise* (1995). He serves on the Editorial Boards of *Biblical Interpretation* and *Ex Auditu*; on the Church of England Doctrine Commission and its General Synod, and on the Human Fertilisation and Embryology Authority.

JAMES C. VANDERKAM is Professor of Hebrew Scriptures in the Department of Theology at the University of Notre Dame, Indiana. He is a member of the team of scholars who are editing the unpublished Dead Sea Scrolls and is serving as Consulting Editor for six volumes in the series *Discoveries in the Judaean Desert*. He is the author of *The Dead Sea Scrolls Today* (1994); *Enoch: A Man for All Generations* (1995); and has co-edited *The Jewish Apocalyptic Heritage in Early Christianity* (1996). He is one of the two editors-in-chief of the *Encyclopedia of the Dead Sea Scrolls* (forthcoming).

KEITH W. WHITELAM is Professor of Religious Studies and Head of Department at the University of Stirling. He is author of *The Invention of Ancient Israel: the Silencing of Palestinian History* (1996); *The Emergence of Early Israel in Historical*

*Perspective* (with Robert B. Coote, 1987); *The Just King: Monarchical Judicial Authority in Ancient Israel* (1979) and a number of articles on Israelite and Palestinian history in specialist journals.

ROBERT R. WILSON is Hoober Professor of Religious Studies and Professor of Old Testament at Yale University. He is the author of *Genealogy and History in the Biblical World* (1977); *Prophecy and Society in Ancient Israel* (1980); and *Sociological Approaches to the Old Testament* (1984). In addition he has contributed numerous articles to journals and reference works on biblical prophecy, law and historiography.

FRANCES YOUNG is Edward Cadbury Professor of Theology and Pro-Vice-Chancellor of the University of Birmingham. Her research interests are in early Christian theology and biblical interpretation, and in contemporary spirituality and pastoral questions. Her recent publications include *The Theology of the Pastoral Letters* (1994); *Dare We Speak of God in Public?* (1994); and *Biblical Exegesis and the Formation of Christian Culture* (1997).

# Glossary

**Achaemenids**  the dynasty that ruled in Persia from 553 to 330 B C, ending with the conquest of Persia by Alexander the Great

**aggadah**  Jewish teaching on non-legal matters (sometimes **haggadah**)

**allegory**  a text in which the meaning is presented symbolically

**androcentric**  male-centred

**angelophany**  the appearance on earth of an angelic being

**anglophone**  English-speaking

**apocalypticism**  movement of thought concerned with the revelation of heavenly secrets, often in coded form: the secrets frequently concern the end of the present age

**aspect**  in grammar, the way the action of a verb is internally organized, as opposed to tense, which concerns the time of its occurrence. Thus 'I go' and 'I went' are differences of tense, but 'I go', 'I am going' and 'I do go' are differences of aspect.

**canonical criticism**  a style of biblical interpretation which seeks to respect the canonical status of the text, usually through a synchronic interpretation

**Christology**  theories about the nature of Christ

**composite**  of a text, composed from several discrete sources

**cosmology**  theory about the origin and nature of the universe

**cultural relativism**  the belief that there are no absolute values or truths valid across all cultures

**deconstruction**  an attempt to show how texts 'subvert' themselves by undermining their own presuppositions (see chapter 4)

**diachronic**  concerned with historical change; thus a diachronic study of a text is interested in the stages by which the text came into being, as contrasted with a **synchronic** concern

**dissonance theory**  a sociological theory about the reaction of societies whose hopes and expectations are not fulfilled

**docetism**  theory that Christ was not really human but only appeared so

**Enlightenment**  intellectual movement of the seventeenth and eighteenth centuries characterized by belief in reason

**eschatology**  theories about the end of the world or of the present age, or more generally about the purposive course of history

**exegesis**  interpretation, esp. through exact philological study

**fictive**  fictitious

**fundamentalism**  the belief that everything in the Bible is true, usually allied to an evangelical system of doctrine

**genetic**  concerned with origins

**halakhah**  Jewish teaching on matters of conduct (adj. **halakhic**)

**hermeneutical circle**  the fact that the parts of a text can only be understood in the light of the whole, yet the whole can only be understood through the parts

**hermeneutics**  the science or art of interpretation, formulating general rules about the meaning of texts; sometimes as **a hermeneutic**, a particular interpretative technique

**Hexateuch** the **Pentateuch** plus Joshua

**historical-critical method, historical criticism** the attempt to analyse texts in their historical context (see chapter 1)

**holistic reading** a reading which seeks to interpret biblical texts exactly as they stand – as finished wholes – rather than seeing them as made up of pre-existing components

**intertextuality** the mutual relationship among texts within a given corpus of literature

*koinonia* fellowship

**liberation theology** system of thought and action which asserts that God is on the side of the powerless

**mantic** connected with prophecy

**Massoretic text** the standard text of the Hebrew Bible established by the **Massoretes** in the seventh and eighth centuries A D

**midrash** Jewish commentary on Scripture

**modernism** (1) synonym of **modernity**; (2) esp. in Catholic thought, attempt to apply an Enlightenment appeal to reason to faith and dogma

**modernity** movement of thought in aesthetics marked by belief in rationality, order and progress

**narratology** the study and theory of narrative texts

**natural theology** branch of theology concerned with what can be known of God without divine revelation

**New Historicism** a style of historiography which attends to the bias in our sources, especially where this tends against the interests of oppressed groups (see chapter 4)

**parallelism** primary technique of Hebrew verse, whereby the meaning of a line is repeated by using synonyms: 'he who dwells under the defence of the Most High / abides under the shadow of the Almighty' (Psalm 91:1)

**Pentateuch** the five books of Moses – Genesis, Exodus, Leviticus, Numbers and Deuteronomy

**pesher** commentary on Scripture concerned with fulfilment of the text at the present day; esp. found in the Dead Sea Scrolls and the New Testament

**poetics** study of literary techniques as forming a system

**polysemous** having many meanings

**postmodernism** originally an architectural term, postmodernism denotes a movement of thought which suspects all large-scale explanatory schemes and delights in parody and pastiche (see chapter 4)

**poststructuralism** movement which extended and also criticized structuralism by showing that the meaning of texts is indeterminate

**pseudepigraphic, pseudonymous** of texts, attributed to someone other than their true author

**Q**  a hypothetical document thought to have been drawn on by Matthew and Luke, and accounting for resemblances between them

**reader-response criticism**  style of literary criticism that stresses the role of the reader in not only perceiving but contributing to the meaning of a text

**reception**  what texts have been taken to mean

**redaction**  editing; **redaction criticism** study of the way biblical books were edited

**Second Temple period**  the time after the rebuilding of the Temple in Jerusalem in *c.* 530 BC; often used of the later part of this period, from 300 BC or so

**Seleucids**  dynasty founded by Seleucus Nicator, one of Alexander the Great's generals, which ruled over Syria-Palestine from 311 to 65 BC

*sophia*  wisdom

**speech-act theory**  linguistic theory concerned with the use of speech to perform actions, e.g. naming, blessing, promising

**structural linguistics**  the **synchronic** study of language as a structure of interrelated parts, as opposed to historical linguistics

**structuralism**  linguistic, literary or cultural analysis that finds meaning in the way a text or a culture is ordered, and in the contrasts between its parts

**synchronic**  concerned with the state of something at a given moment; thus a synchronic study of a text is interested in the interrelation of the parts with each other in its present form, as contrasted with a **diachronic** concern

*synecdoche*  figure of speech in which a part represents the whole

**Synoptic Gospels**  Matthew, Mark and Luke

**Synoptic Problem**  the question how the interrelationships among the Synoptic Gospels are to be explained

**Talmud**  massive compilation of Jewish teaching published in fifth century AD and existing in two editions, Babylonian and Palestinian

**Tenakh**  Jewish acronym for Scripture: the Law, the Prophets and the Writings (Torah, Nebiim, Ketubim); also **Tanak, Tanakh**

**Tetrateuch**  the first four books of the **Pentateuch**

**The Twelve**  the twelve 'Minor Prophets' (a title common in Judaism)

**theophany**  an appearance of God on earth

**Torah**  the Jewish Law or teaching, conceived of as contained in the Pentateuch and in oral traditions deriving from it

**tradition history**  attempt to discover the way in which various historical traditions developed in the telling

**typology**  drawing parallels between people or events in different periods, e.g. Jesus and Moses

**womanism**  movement of thought among non-white women corresponding to white feminism

# Introduction

After two thousand years, can there still be anything left to discover about the Bible? People who work in biblical studies are used to being asked this question. One answer – a true one – is that there is still primary research to be conducted, because the discoveries of modern times (such as the Dead Sea Scrolls) have increased our access to the world in which the Bible came into being; archaeology is continually revealing more about the physical realities of life in the biblical world; and fresh linguistic evidence sheds new light on the meaning of biblical texts. New information justifies fresh investigation.

But ancient texts require not only research, but also interpretation. When we have as accurate a text of the biblical books as can be secured, and as much knowledge as research makes available, we are still faced with the question: what does the Bible mean? This question can never be answered once and for all, not because the Bible changes, but because it takes two for meaning to be perceived: the text and its interpreter. In every age interpreters ask different questions, and so different aspects of the text's meaning emerge. The task of interpretation, unlike that of research, is never finished even in principle.

This book offers the reader a progress report on biblical interpretation in the 1990s. Biblical studies have been in turmoil throughout the last ten years, revealing that what seemed in the 1970s and 1980s to be a time of sharp controversies was really quite placid and conciliatory by comparison. The turmoil concerns less the interpretation of any given biblical book than the methods that ought to be employed in studying them all. Almost everyone who writes about biblical studies today talks in terms of a 'new paradigm' for reading the text – a shift from an interest in political history and the historical meaning of the Bible to a social-historical, sociological, literary or postmodern style of reading. At the same time, as readers will notice in many of the chapters below, interpreters are often at pains to claim that their new paradigm is not new at all, but the restoration of an older method which the intervening ascendancy of the 'historical-critical method' had temporarily effaced. Thus there is a perception among many biblical scholars that the newest approaches are also a restoration of something very old: for post-structuralist read precritical.

The first section of this book (chapters 1–11) accordingly surveys the present ferment over the aims and methods that students of the Bible should adopt. My own chapter (chapter 1) concentrates on the 'paradigm shift' itself, noting (what is undeniable) that the style of biblical studies has changed radically in the last decade or so, but at the same time asking whether the 'historical-critical method' (itself something of a misnomer to describe a complex set of attitudes and questions) may not have been falsely demonized in the process. When this book was being planned, some advisers suggested that there should be no chapter on historical criticism at all, since it was now entirely *passé*. Against this I have tried to show that 'historical' critics raised (and raise) issues that should still be on the agenda for the student of the Bible, and which will not go away.

The paradox that the newest methods hark back to the oldest is particularly clear in David Jasper's study of literary criticism of the Bible (chapter 2). He argues that recent literary approaches often draw on the vast resources of precritical exegesis (Jewish and Christian) to revive insights into the text lost through historical criticism. In particular, he illustrates the current concern for 'holistic' readings, in which biblical books are read just as they stand and without asking the questions about earlier sources and editions that characterized the historical interest in the text. This concern he traces back to precritical interpretation which, he argues, was similarly holistic in its interests.

The four chapters that follow deal with various styles of interpretation concerned with the location of biblical texts in a particular society – and of their readers in a different one. Keith Whitelam (chapter 3) discusses sociological and anthropological study of the Bible. This, as he says, goes back in essence at least two hundred years, but has gained vastly in depth and intensity over the last ten years or so in both Old and New Testament study. As now conceived it does not only treat the Bible as evidence for the social setting of ancient Israel and the early Church, but also examines the historical and modern contexts within which the biblical books were and are read.

Robert Carroll (chapter 4) traces a variety of positions that can be identified on the current intellectual map: poststructuralism, New Historicism and postmodernism. He too shows that even the most recent of such movements join hands in some ways with precritical interpretation, seeing historical criticism as the common enemy – and 'my enemy's enemy is my friend'.

New Historicism, which concentrates on the social setting in which history happens and is interpreted, has in fact produced some conclusions which, at least in Old Testament study, contribute also to 'historical-critical' enquiry, notably by redating much of the Old Testament to the Hellenistic age, only a couple of centuries before the Christian era. Its theoretical base, however, is 'ideology criticism', and its practical effect of redating texts is something of a side issue.

Political reading, according to Tim Gorringe (chapter 5), is also nothing new: the Church, for example, always saw the Bible as having a political message, at least until Luther drove a wedge between Christian and political life. But in its modern form it depends on Marx's insight that knowledge is socially situated, insisting that we should ask not just what the text meant or means, but who is reading the text and with what interests. Only then can the Bible be an instrument of social and political change rather than a means of entrenching the *status quo*.

One particular example of a political concern in reading the Bible has been the burgeoning feminist interest of the last few years. Ann Loades (chapter 6) shows how feminist attitudes to the Bible have polarized. Some feminists (e.g. Phyllis Trible) regard the Bible as a basically sound document which needs to be rescued from false androcentric interpreters; others (e.g. Mary Daly) think that the roots of patriarchy in modern society lie very largely in the Bible itself, whose androcentrism has if anything been underestimated. Feminists of the second kind can alert the reader to problematic elements in the Bible which can be overlooked by other kinds of political, anthropological and postmodern interpreters, whose work often has the practical effect of making the Bible easier to accept than it is on a historical-critical reading. Feminist interpreters of this kind are in many ways allies of the historical critics.

The art of interpretation – hermeneutics – has itself been the subject of much profound study in the modern period, beginning with Friedrich Schleiermacher. Anthony Thiselton (chapter 7) provides a detailed and searching account of modern hermeneutical theory, and shows how it has been the basis for many of the movements already surveyed in this volume through its destruction of the 'hermeneutics of innocence' – in other words, by showing that interpreters are themselves *situated*, not in the position of neutral observers.

Most students of the Bible have had theological (or religious) interests: they have wanted to understand the Bible, not as merely a historical document, but as the 'words of life'. Robert Morgan (chapter 8) provides a historical survey of the theological use of Scripture in Christian thought, stressing, like most of the contributors, the importance of the interpreter in the quest for religious meaning.

In describing the state of biblical studies above, I distinguished between interpretation and research. This is a rough-and-ready distinction, but it does serve to indicate to the reader that this volume does not provide, for example, a guide to biblical archaeology or to the Dead Sea Scrolls. However, one area of primary research that impinges very closely on interpretation is the contribution of philology and linguistics, particularly where the Old Testament is concerned. William Johnstone (chapter 9) describes and evaluates the linguistic contribution to our understanding of the Bible, showing how here too there has been a shift to a concern with the present form of the text rather than with the history of biblical languages (he illustrates this from the Sheffield *Dictionary of Classical Hebrew*). He himself defends a continued interest in historical ('diachronic') philology as a valid tool alongside the 'synchronic' concerns of contemporary linguistics.

Stefan Reif (chapter 10) comments on the whole scene of biblical studies from a Jewish perspective. He sees the 'biblical studies' taught in most theological centres as shot through with Christian attitudes, not least the assumption that the 'Old Testament' is fulfilled only in the New Testament and not legitimately continued in Judaism. He also regards 'biblical criticism' as a Christian phenomenon, explaining thereby why it was seldom adopted enthusiastically by Jewish scholars and is now fairly generally rejected in Jewish circles. It is perhaps worth noting how many of the contributors to this volume share many of his perceptions of biblical criticism, and would be sympathetic to traditional Jewish ways of reading Scripture: my own chapter is probably the only one to defend the type of biblical criticism he finds objectionable! It remains true that biblical study of the kind that goes on in theology departments remains more prominently a Christian than a Jewish activity, and that the reasons for this deserve to be more openly discussed than they are. Christian scholars need to listen much more closely to what Jewish scholars have to say about the books which are a shared heritage.

Finally in this first part we turn from interpretation of the Bible to its reception (not that the two can be sharply distinguished). In his chapter (chapter 11) Stephen Prickett examines, with the aid of several specific examples, what literature and art in the West have done with the Bible. He suggests intriguingly that from the study of the Bible in literature and art we can not only learn about past interpretations, but also be spurred on to new and more subtle interpretations of our own.

In the second part of the volume each group or genre of texts is surveyed. The aim here is twofold: to inform the reader as to what is generally thought about the books in question, and to illustrate some of the methods described in chapters 1–11. It may be helpful to highlight a few points.

The current debate about the respective merits of 'holistic' (or 'synchronic') and 'historical' (or 'diachronic') study of texts is focused most clearly in John Ashton's study of John's Gospel (chapter 17), where he takes as a salient example of what scholarship has been doing with this Gospel the story of Jesus and the woman at the well (John 4). He distinguishes 'smooth' readings, i.e. readings where it is taken as a given that the text forms a unity and contains no evidence of dislocations or inconsistencies, and 'rough' readings where this is not the case. 'Rough' readings have traditionally resulted in hypotheses about the history of the composition of the text, that is, they have pointed scholars in a diachronic direction. As Ashton shows, 'smooth' readings are in the ascendant at the moment – but he points to reasons why we should not smooth over difficulties in the text through a doctrinaire commitment to synchronic approaches. There are also interesting reflections on this issue in Joseph Blenkinsopp's chapter on the Pentateuch (chapter 12), where the newer 'paradigm' is more clearly in evidence but there is still respect for the old questions.

Another recent tendency is the treatment of the 'historical' books of the Old Testament, and (to a lesser extent, perhaps) the Gospels and Acts as 'story' rather than history – carefully crafted narrative whose literary and theological effect does not depend on its closeness to the historical 'facts'. This is commented on in Iain Provan's chapter (chapter 13), with reference to various holistic styles of reading and to the ideological criticism which has led to radical redatings of the material (see above under New Historicism). It can also be seen in Pheme Perkins's chapter on the Synoptic Gospels and Acts (chapter 16), which highlights the results of redaction criticism, where interest centres on what the evangelists have done with the sources at their disposal in order to tell the story of Jesus in a particular and distinctive way.

The continuing vigour of more traditional biblical criticism can be seen in James Dunn's chapter on the Pauline Letters (chapter 18) and Frances Young's on the non-Paulines (chapter 19), as well as in those on apocalyptic by James VanderKam (chapter 20) and on the prophetic books by Robert Wilson (chapter 14). All these chapters provide readers with an up-to-date account of the historical background and development of the biblical books in question, as well as their contents and importance in the Bible as a whole.

Finally, Robert Alter's chapter on the poetic and wisdom books (chapter 15) identifies one area where there has been a particularly high degree of activity in the last twenty years or so: the identification and description of Hebrew verse. Despite two hundred years of research, the principles of Hebrew poetry are still not fully understood. Alter's survey, with carefully worked examples, brings the reader close to such consensus as there now is in a field fraught with controversy.

Biblical studies today is as far as possible from the stereotype with which we began, a sterile discipline which has lasted too long already. On the contrary, it is an exciting field in which the rate of change is now probably faster than it has ever been. The hope of all the contributors to this volume is that it will both inform readers about the current state of biblical scholarship, and also stimulate them to join in a fascinating and rewarding study.

**Part one**

*Lines of approach*

# 1 Historical-critical approaches

JOHN BARTON

Historical criticism, also known as the historical-critical method, was the dominant approach in the academic study of the Bible from the mid-nineteenth century until a generation ago. In the English-speaking world it is now under a cloud. There is much talk of a 'paradigm shift' away from historical methods and towards 'text-immanent' interpretation which is not concerned with the historical context and meaning of texts; it is widely felt that historical criticism is now itself of largely historical (or 'academic'!) interest (see Barton, *The Future of Old Testament Study*; Keck, 'Will the Historical-Critical Method Survive?'; Watson, *Text, Church and World*). It is still practised, however, by a large number of scholars even in the English-speaking world, and by many more in areas where German is the main language of scholarship.

What is historical criticism? Unfortunately its definition is almost as controversial as its desirability. It may be helpful to begin by identifying the features which many students of the Bible now find objectionable in the historical-critical method, before trying to refine our definition by seeing what can be said in its defence. We shall outline four features normally said to be central to historical-critical study of the Bible.

## GENETIC QUESTIONS

Historical critics, it is usually said, are interested in *genetic* questions about the biblical text. They ask when and by whom books were written; what was their intended readership; and, in the case of many biblical books, what were the stages by which they came into being – for it is historical criticism to which we owe the suggestion that many books are composite, put together out of a number of originally separate source documents. Often the finished product seems to be of less interest to such critics than the underlying sources.

Thus, in the case of the Pentateuch, historical-critical approaches generated the hypothesis that Genesis–Deuteronomy should be read, not as five discrete books, but as the interweaving of four separate, older sources (see chapter 12 on the Pentateuch; also Whybray, *The Making of the Pentateuch*; Nicholson, *The Pentateuch in the Twentieth Century*). Once they had established the existence of these sources, Pentateuchal critics took little further interest in the Pentateuch as it now stands. Even where they asked about the theology of the work, they took this to mean the four separate theological outlooks of the sources J, E, D and P, and made no attempt to integrate these into any larger whole. To the question 'What is the Pentateuch?' they answered 'The amalgam of J, E, D and P': thus a question potentially about the *nature* of the work was given an exclusively genetic answer, an answer couched purely in terms of the work's *origin*. Much the same would be true for the Synoptic Gospels, where historical criticism concentrated on the 'Synoptic Problem': how are the overlaps and divergences among the three Synoptic Gospels to be accounted for, and how far can we reconstruct the process by which the Gospels as we now have them were compiled? (On the Synoptic Problem see the classic textbook, Streeter, *The Four Gospels*, and the annotated bibliography by Longstaff and Thomas, *The Synoptic Problem*.) It could be said that historical criticism addressed itself almost entirely to the question of how we came to have the Bible, and when it had solved this problem, saw little else for the biblical scholar to do.

### ORIGINAL MEANING

Because of its concern for the history and prehistory of the text, historical criticism tended (it may be said) to be interested in the 'original' meaning of the text, what it had meant to its first readers, and not what it might mean to a modern reader. Very sophisticated philological and linguistic studies could be brought to bear on obscure texts, in order to establish what the original author could have meant in his own historical period. Institutions such as the lawcourt in Israel (cf. Köhler, *Hebrew Man*) or services for worship in the early Church might be reconstructed in order to discover what the texts that belonged in those contexts had meant in their own time. A term such as 'justice' might turn out to involve concepts quite different from ours, when it occurred in the Psalms or in Paul's epistles. The concern was always to place texts in their historical context, and to argue that we misunderstand them if we take them to mean something they could not have meant for their first readers – indeed, most historical critics regarded this as obvious. The original meaning was the true meaning, and the main task of biblical scholars was to get back to this meaning, and to eliminate the false meanings that unhistorical readers thought they had found in the text. Thus when in Philippians 1:1 we read in the Authorized Version of 'bishops and deacons', a historical critic would point out that these terms did not mean what they later came to mean, as titles for two levels in the developed church hierarchy of later times, but referred to quite different officials in the early Pauline churches. This made it illicit to appeal to such a text in support of Catholic church order, for example (see Beare, *A Commentary on the Epistle to the Philippians*, for an elementary statement of this point).

### HISTORICAL RECONSTRUCTIONS

Historical criticism was also concerned with history in the straightforward sense of the term – not only the historical context of words and meanings, or the historical development of texts, but what happened in the past. In the nineteenth century a major influence on great biblical critics such as W. M. L. de Wette, Julius Wellhausen and D. F. Strauss was the burgeoning discipline of historical writing in the German-speaking world. Scholars such as Theodor Mommsen and Leopold von Ranke set themselves the task of writing, for the first time, a properly critical history of the classical world, by going back to the original sources and refusing to accept what ancient writers said at face value. In the same way, biblical historians subjected the historical books of the Old Testament, the Gospels, and Acts to a critical scrutiny that asked what *really* happened – as opposed to what the (far from impartial) writers of those books believed (or wanted their readers to believe) had happened. Similarly, source-analysis of the Gospels had as one of its aims the recovery of the earliest sayings of Jesus and the original stories about him. This would make it possible to reconstruct a genuine history of his life and times, rather than simply retelling the story as the Gospels present it. And Wellhausen called his examination of the Pentateuchal sources and their themes *Prolegomena to the History of Israel*: sorting out the order and historical implications of the four Pentateuchal sources was the necessary precondition to writing a critical history of Israel (which, however, never got written).

### DISINTERESTED SCHOLARSHIP

Perhaps most important of all, historical criticism was meant to be value-neutral, or disinterested. It tried, so far as possible, to approach the text without prejudice, and to ask not what it meant 'for me', but simply what it meant. Against any 'pious' reading, a historical-critical enquiry is guided by a desire to discover the facts as they actually are, as in Ranke's famous dictum that the historian's task is to establish the facts about the past 'as it actually was' (*wie es eigentlich gewesen*). For the historical critic, the 'holiness' attributed by Christians to the biblical books might be the reason why people studied them in the first place, but it certainly did not give them any kind of diplomatic immunity once the historian had them in his hands. The historical critic's calling was to be a neutral observer, rescinding from any kind of faith-commitment in order to get at the truth. This might result in accounts of Jesus, the early Church or ancient Israel wildly at variance with the accounts of them given by the biblical writers: Strauss and Wellhausen both lost their theological chairs because of the revisionist character of their historical reconstructions (see Morgan, *Biblical Interpretation*). But both felt they must follow where the truth led, and not be silent about what they saw as the real facts which the biblical writers had suppressed or distorted.

All these characteristics – but especially the last, the belief in scholarship's ability to arrive at objective truth – are commonly seen nowadays as part of the legacy of the Enlightenment. It is, indeed, from the Enlightenment onwards that historical biblical criticism seems to have become a dominant force in the academic world, bringing it into a more or less uncomfortable relationship with traditional theology. In England, the publication of Thomas Hobbes's *Leviathan* in 1651 brought a critical understanding of the Bible to the attention of the reading public for the first time, and it was followed by many works stemming mostly from the deist tradition and perceived, correctly, as hostile to an orthodox theological position about the Bible. Such works were united by a refusal to let the traditional religious authority of Scripture dictate the conclusions to which historical investigators might come: they were in the literal sense 'free-thinking'.

Since the heyday of historical biblical criticism, which lasted into the post-war years, many alternative approaches have arisen, and are surveyed in the rest of this volume. In many cases they are predicated on the conviction that historical criticism, even if useful and important in its own day, rested on a series of mistakes; and, as indicated above, many scholars argue that there needs to be what is called a 'paradigm shift', that is, a complete mental realignment, resulting in styles of biblical study and interpretation that avoid the traps which historical critics fell into.

Perhaps the central accusation against the historical-critical method that one hears nowadays concerns its Enlightenment origins. The neutral, scientific pursuit of truth by a disinterested scholar has been shown (it is said) to be bankrupt. The presence of the observer makes a difference to all scientific experiments, and in the same way the concerns of the investigator colour, even determine, historical reconstructions. No-one is really 'disinterested'; everyone has an axe to grind. We should therefore abandon the pretence of academic neutrality, and accept that our biblical study serves some interest or other. For example, it may serve our Christian commitment as members of the Church, and there is no reason why we should be embarrassed about that, for in acknowledging it we are at least being honest about our commitment – unlike historical critics, who are pretending to be neutral but thus smuggle in their commitments under cover of dark. (This case is argued with great skill in Watson, *Text, Church and World.*) A postmodernist position, especially, legitimates scholars in being candid about the ends they wish their enquiries to serve, and encourages them not to imagine that they can serve simply 'truth' – an entity that does not exist in its own right, but only within some intellectual system or other.

Such a shift would also affect our other three points. It would make the exclusive concern for 'original' or 'historical' meanings in texts pointless as well as impractical; for why should it matter to us (except perhaps as a kind of harmless hobby) what texts meant when they were first written? Why should this meaning enjoy any privileges above all the other meanings the text has been taken to have throughout its history? This in turn would render the genetic interest of historical critics largely irrelevant. It would also mean that the quest for historical reconstruction is a fruitless quest, since even to pursue it is to assume that objective historical facts can be recovered, which is an illusion. From a postmodern perspective, the historical-critical method is just a piece of self-deception, and biblical scholars would be advised to turn to more fruitful approaches.

There are two issues here. One is the validity of a postmodern attack on the pursuit of objective truth. This is an enormous subject in its own right, but this is not the best place to discuss it. It will be clear already from the tone of my discussion that I do not by any means believe that the case has been made, and therefore think the argument in favour of the recommended 'paradigm shift' needs to be made much more rigorous before it will command assent. But the other issue is the nature of historical criticism itself. The account given above (into which I have tried to insert 'it is said', 'so people say', and so on) certainly does seem to invite the postmodernist response in many ways. But my own suspicion is that 'historical criticism' is thus defined in order to invite this response, and that the definition does not correspond to the historical-critical method as one actually encounters it in practice. This has in turn two aspects: the detailed interests which 'historical critics' have had; and the theory of historical criticism they have worked with.

(1) If we survey the past hundred years of 'historical criticism', we can see that it has a number of features which are puzzling in the light of its alleged concerns, as described above.

Studies of the Pentateuch or the Gospels which have taken an interest in the sources of these texts and how they have been combined to produce the books we now have can be called 'historical' in the sense that they are what is nowadays called 'diachronic'. They are concerned with the development of the texts through time, rather than with the finished product just as we encounter it. It is also true that some 'historical' critics have been interested in source-analysis of the biblical text because of an overarching concern with writing history – Wellhausen is a case in point. But the general impression an ordinary historian is likely to form after reading books dubbed 'historical-critical' by theologians is that they are predominantly *literary* in their interests. The primary motivation behind both Pentateuchal and Synoptic criticism was the desire to untangle the complex interrelationships within and between complex texts. It is common nowadays to contrast historical with literary criticism and to regard the former as markedly 'unliterary' in character. But this is because 'literary' criticism nowadays is notably unhistorical, with an enormous emphasis on 'synchronic' reading of texts exactly as they lie before us. A few generations ago much 'literary' criticism was just as diachronic as the work of most biblical interpreters. To call what biblical critics did until thirty or so years ago 'historical-critical' makes it sound as though they had a choice whether to work diachronically or synchronically, and consciously chose the former. But this is anachronistic. Biblical critics applied to biblical documents the kind of detailed analysis which anyone engaged in 'literary' studies at the time would have been likely to engage in, asking questions about the origins and development of the text, the intentions of its author or authors and its connection with other, similar texts. It is in the sophistication of their literary analysis that most so-called 'historical' critics excelled. When they turned to write history in the normal sense of the term their efforts were usually far less sophisticated, being often guided by theological assumptions or even by a tendency to paraphrase the biblical text (very obvious in Bright, *History of Israel*).

Furthermore, even the diachronic concerns of traditional critics can be exaggerated. On the whole these appear patchily. In studying the Pentateuch, critics of the historical-critical persuasion certainly did engage in detailed analysis of earlier stages of the text, though (as just remarked) this would at the time have been regarded as a perfectly normal interest for a *literary* critic. But the study of the wisdom literature, for example, has seldom been very 'historical'. Gerhard von Rad's *Wisdom in Israel* lacks almost any concern for dating the material or tracing 'historical' developments within it, and the average commentary on Job, for example, has always been a commentary on the 'final form' of the book, or at most has allowed for a few 'additions' to a mostly unified book. Genetic concerns have been comparatively uncommon in the study of Paul's epistles, which the majority of commentators interpret as self-contained theological works, despite the fact that correlations between them and Paul's career as it can be established from the epistles and Acts together have also been made (see classically Knox, *Chapters in a Life of Paul*). Most interpretation of Paul has until recently been more open to the criticism that it studies him in a historical vacuum than that it is excessively historical in its interests (cf. Sanders, *Paul and Palestinian Judaism* and *Paul, the Law, and the Jewish People*).

Moreover, the allegation that 'historical-critical' scholarship has been indifferent to the contemporary relevance of the biblical text and 'antiquarian' in its concerns can be made plausible only by concentrating on a few extreme cases: Pentateuchal critics who reduced the books of Moses to sixty-five separate documents, or Gospel critics who reconstructed a Jesus no Christian could possibly be attracted to. The vast majority of biblical interpreters until very recently have been religious believers. Many have worked in ecclesiastically supported colleges and faculties, and most have been intensely interested in the religious relevance of their exegetical work. E. P. Sanders's trenchant criticisms of most scholars who have written on Jesus and Paul show that their reconstructions have normally been heavily influenced by their religious beliefs: by the need to show the uniqueness of Jesus, or the essentially Lutheran character of Paul's teaching.

The neutrality at which historical criticism aims, so far from having been taken to the point where the Bible is no longer the Church's book, has hardly ever gone far enough to pose any kind of threat to most believers. The accusation that historical criticism has neglected the contemporary application of the Bible is a useful ploy to make other approaches seem attractive, but is historically on very weak ground. The reverse could be argued: that criticism has scarcely ever been historical enough, that it has usually been far too influenced by commitments lying outside scholarly detachment. A single example: if one compares Wellhausen's reconstruction of Israel in the Old Testament period with that of John Bright or even Siegfried Herrmann, one has the impression that there has been a slow back-pedalling, from a sharply focused and very critical approach in the late nineteenth century to a far more bland and accepting attitude towards the biblical materials in the mid twentieth. To suggest that biblical study became increasingly 'historical-critical' during that period, so that a fresh paradigm is needed to make biblical study relevant to the concerns of religious believers, is to argue in the face of the evidence.

(2) A larger question can be asked about historical criticism. What was its overall aim or philosophy? The usual perception today is that historical criticism derives from the Enlightenment, and that its practices belong to 'modernity' – a rationalistic approach committed to an ideal of neutral, universal truth attainable by 'scientific' procedures, in the general sense of 'scientific' which corresponds to German *wissenschaftlich* and denotes an objective search for independently existing reality. It would be foolish to deny historical criticism's debt to the Enlightenment. Nevertheless it is possible to attempt a revisionist account which makes some of today's attitudes towards it seem less plausible.

There is a tradition in German scholarship of tracing the origins of historical criticism not to the Enlightenment but to the Reformation. Rather than speak of 'the historical-critical method', it may be argued, we should speak simply of 'biblical criticism', for the connection with history is (as suggested above) at best partial and occasional (see Barr, 'Bibelkritik' and *Holy Scripture*). The idea of reading the Bible critically is not derived from an interest in history, even though in the nineteenth century there was a (contingent) alliance between the two concerns; it is linked with the Reformation insistence on the authority of the Bible, read freely, over the Church. Christian believers, according to Reformation principles, have the right to ask whether the Bible really means what the Church says it means. In that sentence lies the whole development of biblical criticism in germ. Faced with an ecclesiastical interpretation of this or that text, the biblical critic does not automatically accept that the magisterium of the Church guarantees that the meaning proposed is the true one, but reserves the right to apply rational principles of criticism. Chief among these will be to ask whether the proposed meaning was possible at the time the text was written: did a given term have the range of meanings being put forward? The example from Philippians 1 above illustrates this well: were there 'bishops' and 'deacons' in the sixteenth-century sense in Paul's day? This is certainly a historical question; but it derives from a question about language usage, about the meaning of such terms as *episkopos* and *diakonos* in New Testament times and thus about what the text 'really' means.

An effect of postmodernism has been to banish the expression 'really means' to outer darkness, and consequently to brand any style of academic enquiry for which it is still regarded as usable as hopelessly naive and outmoded. But we should not necessarily be swayed by that. In all sorts of contexts we operate quite uncomplicatedly with the idea that words have definite meanings, and postmodernists do the same when they read everyday texts: instruction booklets that come with household equipment, legal documents, personal letters conveying information, shopping lists or cookery books. In asking what a text really means or actually says, and being open to the possibility that this is not what the Church, or tradition, or the individual thinks or wishes it says or would like to make it say, biblical critics were trying to let the text speak through the stifling wrappings of interpretation with which it had been surrounded. This led, inevitably, to historical reconstruction, textual analysis and the whole range of so-called 'historical-critical' enquiry. The proliferation of historical-critical writings has threatened, of course, to become simply a fresh set of wrappings with the same effect, and it is understandable that people should feel that it is time to begin again. But the underlying motivation of 'historical' criticism is to free the text to speak. Where it has failed to do this, that is, in my judgement, because it has continued to be too hidebound by tradition and by the expectations of the wider religious community; and the cure is more criticism, not less.

Biblical criticism so understood is concerned with the 'plain sense' or 'natural sense' of the text. It is usually harmless to describe this as the 'historical' or 'original' sense, meaning 'what the writer meant by the text'. But strictly speaking these are not exactly the same. Where we do not know who wrote the text or what he or she meant by it, we may still be able to say that the text 'could mean A' or 'could not mean B' on the basis of our knowledge of the language in which the text is written. This is indeed a 'historical' point in the sense that it concerns the language, Hebrew or Greek or Aramaic, at some particular stage in its history; but not in the sense of 'historical' usually understood today, in which the 'historical' critic is assumed to be locked into seeking past meanings when present ones are what is needed. So-called 'historical criticism' has the task of telling the reader what biblical texts can or cannot mean, not merely what they did or did not mean; to say of this or that interpretation, 'No, the text cannot possibly mean that, because the words it uses will not bear that meaning.' This is potentially an enormously iconoclastic movement, because it refuses to allow people to mean anything they like by their sacred texts. So far from this movement having had its day in the churches, it has scarcely even arrived there. The world of academic biblical interpretation is already trying to move people on from a position whose strength they have by no means yet grasped, and to offer instead allegedly new modes of exegesis which will allow a place of refuge within safe 'interpretive communities' of faith to those who do not wish to be challenged by the biblical text, despite the place of honour they claim to give it.

What are the prospects for historical-critical approaches? Our answer to this will depend on what definition we prefer for 'historical criticism', the one usually current or the 'revisionist' definition just attempted. If we identify 'historical-critical' approaches along the lines of our fourfold definition above, then it must be said that in spite of the pressure for new paradigms a great deal of historical-critical study continues to be undertaken. Pentateuchal studies are as active, and as intricate, as ever: the massive work of Erhard Blum (*Studien zur Komposition des Pentateuch*) is proof enough that some scholars still want to know how the Pentateuch came into being. (For a similarly genetic approach to the historical books, see Auld, *Kings Without Privilege*.) The Synoptic Problem, similarly, continues to attract detailed attention. The history of ancient Israel and of the early Church are flourishing fields, and although the former at least is finding highly radical and novel solutions (cf. Davies, *In Search of 'Ancient Israel'* and Lemche, *Early Israel*), the means of study used to discover them is undeniably historical-critical. Even the reception history of biblical texts, a burgeoning and exciting field of study, requires historical criticism – the fact that it is concerned with what texts were later taken to mean rather than with what they originally meant does not make it any the less a historical investigation.

None of this suggests that historical critics are an endangered species; nor does it present any good reasons why they should be regarded by proponents of new paradigms as lost souls beyond redemption. Biblical studies have always involved bitter feuds – most academic fields do – but there seems little reason for a rift to run precisely between 'synchronic' and 'diachronic' approaches. All the more is this true if we depart from customary usage and speak, in the revisionist way outlined earlier, of 'biblical criticism' rather than 'the historical-critical method'. According to that way of speaking, it is not the 'historical' (diachronic) element that is the defining characteristic of biblical criticism, but its 'critical' character: its emphasis on asking free questions about the meaning of texts unconstrained by alleged authorities – whether the authority of Christian or Jewish tradition, the authority of current ecclesiastical structures or the authority of received academic opinion.

The point is that no-one may legislate as to what questions the reader of Scripture is allowed to ask, or declare that certain questions ('synchronic' or 'diachronic') shall be deemed 'uninteresting' or unimportant. This sense of freedom, which ultimately inherits both Reformation and Enlightenment insights, is opposed to the establishment of 'official' methods which interpreters are 'permitted' to use. Some proponents of new paradigms are correct in thinking that the international body of biblical scholars (sometimes quaintly referred to as 'the Guild') tends to canonize particular approaches from time to time, and that adherence to 'historical criticism' has in some times and places been a prerequisite for getting an academic job. The evil of this situation will not be purged by making it instead into an absolute bar. Both diachronic and synchronic issues can be handled in a spirit of criticism, asking questions that present themselves to intelligent and enquiring minds, or parroted in the belief that they will please the examiners – or interviewers. It is a shame to an academic discipline if the latter course becomes the norm; and the cure is not to defend this or that method as ideologically pure, but to revive a true spirit of criticism, for which there is no such thing as ideological purity, only open-mindedness and honesty.

## Further reading

Auld, A. G., *Kings Without Privilege: David and Moses in the Story of the Bible's Kings*, Edinburgh, 1994.

Barr, J., 'Bibelkritik als theologische Aufklärung', in T. Rendtorff (ed.), *Glaube und Toleranz: Das theologische Erbe der Aufklärung*, Gütersloh, 1982, pp. 30–42.

*Holy Scripture: Canon, Authority, Criticism*, Oxford, 1983.

Barton, J., *The Future of Old Testament Study*, Oxford, 1993.

Beare, F. W., *A Commentary on the Epistle to the Philippians*, London, 1959.

Blum, E., *Studien zur Komposition des Pentateuch*, Berlin, 1990.

Bright, J., *History of Israel*, London, 1960; several subsequent editions.

Davies, P. R., *In Search of 'Ancient Israel'*, Sheffield, 1992.

Herrmann, S., *A History of Israel in Old Testament Times*, London, 1975.

Keck, L. E., 'Will the Historical-Critical Method Survive?', in R. A. Spencer (ed.),

*Orientation by Disorientation: Studies in Literary Criticism and Biblical Literary Criticism*, Pittsburgh Theological Monographs 35, 1980, pp. 115–27.

Knox, J., *Chapters in a Life of Paul*, London, 1989 (first published 1950).

Köhler, L., *Hebrew Man*, London, 1956 (=*Der hebräische Mensch*, Tübingen, 1953).

Lemche, N.-P., *Early Israel: Anthropological and Historical Studies on the Israelite Society before the Monarchy*, Supplements to *Vetus Testamentum* 37, Leiden, 1985.

Longstaff, T. R. W., and P. A. Thomas, *The Synoptic Problem: A Bibliography, 1716–1988*, New Gospel Studies 4, Macon, GA, 1988.

Morgan, R. with J. Barton, *Biblical Interpretation,* Oxford Bible series, Oxford, 1988.

Nicholson, E. W., *The Pentateuch in the Twentieth Century*, Oxford, 1998.

Sanders, E. P., *Paul and Palestinian Judaism: A Comparison of Patterns of Religion*, London, 1977.

*Paul, the Law, and the Jewish People*, Philadelphia, 1985.

Streeter, B. H., *The Four Gospels: A Study of Origins*, London and New York, 1924.

Von Rad, G., *Wisdom in Israel*, London: SCM Press, 1972 (=*Weisheit in Israel*, Neukirchen-Vluyn, 1970).

Watson, F., *Text, Church and World: Biblical Interpretation in Theological Perspective*, Edinburgh, 1994.

Wellhausen, J., *Prolegomena to the History of Israel*, Edinburgh 1885 (=*Prolegomena zur Geschichte Israels*, Marburg, 1883 – a revised edition of *Geschichte Israels I.* Marburg, 1878).

Whybray, R. N., *The Making of the Pentateuch*, Sheffield, 1987.

# 2 Literary readings of the Bible

DAVID JASPER

The twentieth century has seen a growing fascination with the Bible 'as literature', with an accompanying persistent sense of theological unease, apart from the obvious recognition that it is a collection of 'literary' texts having, in common with other literature, narratives, poems, epistles and so on. In 1935 T. S. Eliot suggested that when the Bible is discussed as 'literature' then its 'literary' influence is at an end, for it is far more than that. For T. R. Henn more recently, however, the phrase 'the Bible as literature' suggests a manner of approach to the reading of Scripture, and therefore also a means of assessment, one lightened of theology. As C. S. Lewis earlier wrote of the Authorized Version, 'it is very generally implied that those who have rejected its theological pretensions nevertheless continue to enjoy it as a treasure-house of English prose'.[1]

However, the modern discipline of 'literary criticism' has developed largely out of ancient traditions of biblical interpretation, and the uneasy separation of literary readings of the Bible from supposedly more substantial theological or religious readings is a contemporary, or at least post-Romantic phenomenon subsequent upon the almost universal claims of the principles of historical criticism in scriptural interpretation.[2] Ancient Jewish hermeneutics comprised four overlapping methods of reading – Literalist, Midrashic, Pesher and Allegorical.[3] These acknowledge the complexity of the act of reading between 'intrinsic' approaches which draw from within the text itself and 'extrinsic' approaches drawing from perspectives not derived from the text.

Within the canon of Scripture itself, in both Hebrew and Christian Bibles, an intricate pattern of cross-referencing establishes a web of inter-textuality which promotes what modern literary critics from T. S. Eliot to Harold Bloom and Julia Kristeva have variously examined, that is the intrinsic relationships between and within the texts of literature. In the Bible not only does this establish a theological as well as a literary coherence between the books of the canon,[4] but it also makes possible a particular view of 'history', as, for example, in the first two chapters of St Matthew's Gospel, where the 'historical evidence' for the birth narratives lies precisely in the literature of the Hebrew Bible, understood as 'history' because these events were exactly what the writings of prophecy announced would happen.[5]

The typological understanding of the New Testament, assuming that anticipations of Christ appear throughout the literature of the Old Testament, begins in the earliest strata of Christian literature and remains hugely important in English literature, particularly of the seventeenth century, but also in the Victorian period, with profound effects upon the secular culture of the time.[6]

We see, then, that the literary form of the Bible as a whole, and the ancient hermeneutical strategies applied to it, have evoked principles of literary interpretation which have remained extremely important for literature even when biblical criticism itself has abandoned them for more 'historical' or 'scientific' forms of reading. More particularly, specific literary forms within Scripture, such as mashal or parable, have survived through Western literature to the present day,[7] and continue to prompt forms of literary reading which have themselves returned to the biblical parables to reinterpret them 'as literature'.[8]

Finally, the formation of the canon of the Bible, both Jewish and Christian, and early debates about the canon surrounding such figures as Marcion (d. *c.*160 CE) have recently become important for the project of 'canonical criticism', associated especially with two scholars, Brevard S. Childs and J. A. Sanders, which, though still within the broad school of 'historical criticism', provides what Robert Morgan has described as 'a witness to the theological necessity of a more literary approach to the Bible'.[9]

In this very brief introduction we suggest how the Bible, both as a whole and in its specific literary elements and genres, has continued to interact with Western literature, even within its theological purposes, and to be a fundamental resource for 'literary readings' and critical approaches which biblical criticism itself has often neglected, particularly in the last two hundred years. It was at the end of the eighteenth century, under the scrutiny of Enlightenment reason, that the Bible became subject to the systematic critical attention of a complex approach to reading known as the 'historical-critical'. Ultimately rationalist, this effected a broad separation between biblical criticism and other forms of literary criticism which remains in place largely to the present time; a *Gletscherwall*[10] ('glacial-moraine') dividing biblical studies from the reading of other literature. Thus we now have the odd and rather artificial category of 'literary readings' of the Bible entering through the back door of biblical scholarship.

An early and spirited example of a 'literary' wariness of biblical criticism is to be found in S. T. Coleridge's marginal notes to Johann Gottfried Eichhorn's great *Einleitung ins Alte Testament* (1780–83), with their repeated comment that the German scholar fails to understand the language of poetic imagination. For example, Eichhorn dismisses Ezekiel's vision of the chariot (Ezekiel 1:15–21) as *blosse Einkleidung, blosse poetische Dichtungen* ('mere drapery, mere poetic fiction'), and exchangeable for other poetic images in the mind of another poet. To this Coleridge retorts:

> It perplexes me to understand how a Man of Eichhorn's Sense, Learning, and Acquaintance with Psychology could form, or attach belief to, so cold-blooded an hypothesis. That in Ezechiel's Visions Ideas or Spiritual Entities are presented in visual Symbols, I never doubted; but as little can I doubt, that such Symbols did present themselves to Ezechiel in Visions – and by a Law closely connected with, if not contained in, that by which sensations are organized into Images and mental sounds in our ordinary sleep.[11]

To Coleridge, in other words, Ezekiel's visions are *real*, and he accuses Eichhorn of allegorizing poetry too fully in a historical sense, or else dismissing the poetry of Scripture as 'mere poetic garnish'. What Eichhorn fails to appreciate is the universal poetic imagination, synchronically present in the Bible (particularly) and also in all great poetic genius, above all Shakespeare. In both the Bible and Shakespeare there is 'that unity or total impression'[12] which Eichhorn's criticism tends to disintegrate into fragments as it fails to recognize poetic language as irreducible, organic and emerging from the inspired imagination as the vehicle which, like the wheels of Ezekiel's chariot, carries (for us) the divine truths with which it is consubstantial.[13]

Coleridge remained, in many ways, a solitary voice through much of the nineteenth century. Biblical criticism was diverted, first, by the publication in 1835 of D. F. Strauss's *Das Leben Jesu* with its disembodied Hegelian idealism, focusing attention on the historical and theological claims of Christian belief through its mythical interpretation of the Gospel stories. Second, the nineteenth century remained fixed in historical readings of Scripture. According to Albert Schweitzer the influence of H. S. Reimarus (1694–1768) was particularly powerful, felt as late as Johannes Weiss's *Die Predigt Jesu vom Reiche Gottes* (1892) which Schweitzer described as a 'vindication, a rehabilitation, of Reimarus as a historical thinker'.[14] This perspective was encouraged, among other things, by the development of archaeology, resulting in a criticism which Robert Alter has dubbed 'excavative' – 'either literally, with the archaeologist's spade and reference to its findings, or with a variety of analytic tools intended to uncover the original meanings of biblical words, the life situations in which specific texts were used, the sundry sources from which longer texts were assembled'.[15] Such readings are historical not inasmuch as they record history – understood broadly in the modern sense of the word – but as they arise from a particular historical context.[16]

The nineteenth century, and most biblical criticism since, was more interested in the *context* within which the Bible was written and has been understood than the actual *text* of Scripture and its immediate interaction with the reader. In his book *The Use and Abuse of the Bible* (1976), Dennis Nineham examines the huge, and perhaps unbridgeable gap between the cultures which conceived the texts of Scripture and our own culture, and dismisses the idea of 'the Bible considered simply as literature'.[17] Despite critical objections, however, the Bible continued to be read 'as literature' in an ongoing textual response to its 'textuality' apart from the historical and theological problems posed by nineteenth-century critics, particularly in Germany. The naive Galilean peasant of Ernest Renan's *La Vie de Jésus* (1863), stripped of the supernatural and the miraculous, is hardly the product of a scholarly theological investigation, but an immediate and imaginative response to the Jesus of the Gospels which broke all the rules of scholarship and brought Jesus 'alive' for Renan's many readers. In Schweitzer's words:

> Renan's work marked an epoch, not for the Catholic world only, but for
> general literature . . . He offered his readers a Jesus who was alive, whom
> he, with his artistic imagination, had met under the blue heaven of
> Galilee, and whose lineaments his inspired pencil had seized. Men's
> attention was arrested, and they thought to see Jesus, because Renan
> had the skill to make them see blue skies, seas of waving corn, distant
> mountains, gleaming lilies, in a landscape with the Lake of Gennesaret
> for its centre, and hear with him in the whispering of the reeds the
> eternal melody of the Sermon on the Mount.[18]

With all its romanticism and theological inadequacy, Renan's work was enormously influential and simply dismissed the hermeneutical problems of cultural relativism and historical distance: literature feeds upon the reader's imagination, and Renan foreshadows subsequent 'literary readings' by linking the biblical texts with the narratives, stories and lyrics of other literature.[19] The reader is confronted immediately by the text and its dramatic characters – and it is not without significance that Renan was enormously influential on the Greek novelist Nikos Kazantzakis, particularly when he was writing the controversial *Last Temptation of Christ* (1959).

Literary readings of the Bible hover between the imaginative and poetic, and the academic. That is why, in spite of the development of the language and science of literary theory, they have never quite been taken seriously by biblical criticism emerging out of the demands of historical critical methods and theology. There is an *uncritical* dimension, which is nonetheless rigorous, expressed with characteristic energy by D. H. Lawrence as he seeks to define his vocation as an artist: 'I always feel as if I should be naked for the fire of Almighty God to go through me – and it's rather an awful feeling.'[20] Translated into the realm of biblical interpretation, the sense of awe is consciously sustained in the critical work of Austin Farrer, particularly in *The Glass of Vision* (1948, on the prophets), *A Rebirth of Images* (1944, on Revelation) and *St Matthew and St Mark* (1954). Farrer was a biblical critic whose effect on the literary reading of the Bible has been enormous, particularly through the more recent work of the literary critic, Frank Kermode.

Farrer's Bampton Lectures, published as *The Glass of Vision*, were subjected to two major critical attacks, one theological by H. D. Lewis in his book *Our Experience of God* (1959), and one literary by Dame Helen Gardner in *The Limits of Literary Criticism* (1956).[21] Farrer's response is, significantly, in the readerly tradition of Coleridge. For if Lewis subsumes poetry into theology, and Gardner separates the two, maintaining an absolute distinction between the historical Jesus and our own time, Farrer sustains a delicate polarity between the two, both moving under a control of images which are in time and yet also eternal – diachronic and synchronic. The imagination draws together the ancient literature of the Scriptures, their tradition of theological reading and the response of the contemporary reader to the structure of the text, in a single moment of vision and inspiration. Kermode, who once grouped Farrer with Claude Lévi-Strauss and Roland Barthes as a 'structuralist', reflects sadly upon Farrer's exile from the academy of biblical scholars:

> As to Farrer, his work was rejected by the establishment and eventually
> by himself, largely because it was so literary. The institution knew
> intuitively that such literary elaboration, such emphasis on elements
> that must be called fictive, was unacceptable because damaging to what
> remained of the idea that the gospel narratives were still, in some

measure, transparent upon history . . . [Farrer] assumes that there is an enigmatic narrative concealed in the manifest one.[22]

Farrer, the devout Christian, and Kermode, the sceptical critic, so different in many ways, join in acknowledging the critical necessity of recognizing the 'fictive' element in Scripture, and the need to respond to the literary 'structure' of works like Mark's Gospel, so that they are read as a whole – much as one would read a novel – and not disintegrated into brief pericopes or fragments. Thus, in his important book, *The Genesis of Secrecy*, Kermode (as Coleridge had done before him) reads the Bible in the context of a wider literature from Kafka, Joyce and Pynchon to Henry Green.

Long before Kermode's work, D. H. Lawrence had described the Bible as 'a great confused novel'.[23] More academically, and more recently, critics like Robert Alter and Gabriel Josipovici have analysed biblical narratives with techniques used by literary criticism to read prose fiction.[24] To do this is not necessarily to abandon the traditional concerns of the biblical critic. On the contrary, Alter's reading of Genesis 38, the story of Judah and Tamar, suggests that it is a carefully constructed part of a larger, coherent narrative, the story of Joseph – an insight already to be found in Thomas Mann's huge novel *Joseph und seine Brüder* (1933–43) – and not just a fragment in a patchwork stitched together by an inept editor. But also, Alter and Josipovici release these ancient texts and their characters to be responded to with an immediacy and freedom often denied to 'sacred texts', weighed down by theological preconception or prejudice. Josipovici's response was that the Bible

> seemed much quirkier, funnier, quieter than I expected . . . it contained narratives which seemed, even in translation, as I first read them, far fresher and more 'modern' than any of the prize-winning novels rolling off the presses.[25]

These literary readings of the Bible claim to 'take the varnish off'[26] texts which have been coated by centuries of religious reading and theological interpretation. The implication, of course, is that they will return us to a pristine purity of reading which is also immediate, alongside other great literature from Aeschylus to Dante and Shakespeare. Nor has this enterprise been limited to biblical narratives. Biblical poetry has been examined by scholars like Alter and James L. Kugel[27] in the tradition of Robert Lowth (1710–87) who, in his *De Sacra Poesi Hebraeorum Praelectiones Academicae* (1775), claimed to have rediscovered the ancient art of 'parallelism' in the

Hebrew Scriptures, so that, once again, we might read Scripture in its original poetic form, and understand its poetry as did its authors and first readers.

By focusing upon *text* rather than *context*, these literary readings of the Bible claim to overcome the hermeneutical problem of the 'two horizons', that is, the gap between the ancient text and the modern reader. By concentrating on the literary qualities of the biblical texts, the reader encounters with new immediacy their power and mystery. Like all great texts of literature, they are seen as both historical *and* contemporary, as living within history. In their *Literary Guide to the Bible*, Alter and Kermode distinguish their task from what they call 'traditional historical scholarship'[28] and deny that their aims are theological. Instead, they situate themselves within the traditions of Western culture and as responding to a great achievement of 'written language'. Having established this, however, they limit themselves within the literary critical field, most specifically by neglecting 'deconstructionists and some feminist critics who seek to demonstrate that the text is necessarily divided against itself'.[29]

Putting aside for a moment this rather sweeping criticism, let us look more closely at a thread which has been running through this chapter. A major shift in literary theory in recent years has also been reflected in literary approaches to the Bible – that is, the change in focus of interest from the intention of the author and the original context of the writing, to the response of the reader in determining the meaning and significance of the text.[30] Immediately this concentrates attention upon the moment of reading rather than the moment of the text's origin as of primary importance. Although 'reader-response criticism' is complex and difficult to define, it is clear that its tendencies cut across the grain of a great deal in biblical studies.[31] To start with, concentrating upon the contemporary reader undercuts the historical emphasis of biblical studies. Attention is given to the individual in the act of reading, or to the 'interpretative community' of readers here and now. Second, there is an inevitable weakening of the status of the text itself, with the consequent fear of solipsism and relativism, most clearly demonstrated in Stanley Fish's celebrated essay 'Is There a Text in This Class?', with its anxious question from a student, 'I mean in this class do we believe in poems and things, or is it just us?'[32]

It would seem, therefore, that as literary readings of the Bible have drawn us away from an emphasis on context to a focus on the text itself, so gradually that text is in turn dissolved in the new and ever-contemporary context of the reader and the interpretative community. Questions then arise concerning the nature of authority as the 'sacred' text is subsumed under the conditions of all other literature. At this point a challenge is presented by a relatively new 'emancipatory' criticism in feminist readings of the Bible. Broadly speaking these have been given voice by the possibilities offered by literary readings – with their emphasis on the (woman) reader, their refusal to be constrained by history and tradition, and their challenge to (patriarchal) authority. In particular, what Josipovici calls the 'irresponsibility' of his own response to the Bible is echoed in a critic like Mieke Bal, whose readings of the Hebrew Bible, and especially of the Book of Judges[33] emerge variously from intertextual readings with such diffuse partners as Freud, the art of Rembrandt or feminist theory itself. Bal's readings are uncompromisingly political, as are those of her early feminist predecessor Elizabeth Cady Stanton in *The Woman's Bible* (1898). They are also based upon clear literary premises.

When Bal considers the Book of Judges she 'deals with the text as a whole . . . conceived of as one text'.[34] She then questions the text read as historiography inasmuch as this assumes a theology and imposes a coherence upon the book. This coherence, she argues, is actually imposed by the assumptions of a patriarchal tradition which elides and ignores certain elements in the text, usually those concerned with women. What she proposes to establish is a counter-coherence 'which is a deconstruction in its own right but also more than that'.[35] It emerges through a careful and highly imaginative interactive reading of the narratives of the text, playing games with it, arguing with its apparent assumptions, until violence is exposed in the arena of reading itself. Other feminist critics, such as Phyllis Trible, have followed the same path of reading, creatively interacting with texts such as Judges 11: 29–40 (the sacrifice of Jephthah's daughter) and Genesis 19:8 (Lot's offering of his daughters to the men of Sodom to protect a male guest) to expose 'the sin of patriarchy'.[36] Like Mieke Bal, Trible uses close literary readings to expose the processes of power and authority operative in a text from its origins, in its tradition and in the assumptions of its contemporary (male) readers. She claims that her feminist reading

> recognizes that, despite the word, authority centres in readers. They accord a document power even as they promote the intentionality of its authors . . . In the interaction of text and reader, the changing of the second component alters the meaning and power of the first.[37]

Feminist criticism, then, tends to follow the literary trend of focusing upon the reader and deconstructing the assumptions of traditional biblical critics by exercises in close reading which play with the biblical texts on their own terms, that is introducing characters, situations and possibilities in a 'fictive' game which takes utterly seriously the Bible 'as literature' and thus challenges it as an authoritative 'sacred text' within a patriarchal tradition. Bal, in particular, seems to be conscious of herself as a writer of narrative fiction, giving names to the nameless in the biblical narrative (for example, 'Bath' for Jephthah's daughter) and thereby violating the scriptural text which otherwise becomes the instrument of *her* violation through its ideological position.[38]

This deconstruction inherent in feminist readings of the Bible links them with the wider field of postmodern and poststructuralist biblical criticism which has been granted wider public attention by the publication of *The Postmodern Bible* (1995), written by 'the Bible and Culture Collective'. Despite the nervousness of Alter and Kermode that such readings 'seek only to demonstrate that "every text is divided against itself"',[39] postmodern readings of Scripture have frequently offered dazzling intertextual exercises which recognize that reading is an exchange between text and reader in a constant struggle which wounds even as it illuminates. In his book *Mark and Luke in Poststructuralist Perspectives*, Stephen D. Moore maintains:

> My main tactic is a simple one. I am eager to reply to the Gospels in kind, to write in a related idiom. Rather than take a jackhammer to the concrete, parabolic language of the Gospels, replacing graphic images with abstract categories, I prefer to respond to a pictographic text pictographically, to a narrative text narratively, producing a critical text that is a postmodern analogue of the premodern text that it purports to read.[40]

In Moore's hands, biblical criticism becomes a dramatic exercise in deconstructive readings, teasing the text through its layers of 'encrusted reading', exposing its potential for new and different readings, acknowledging that the text itself is, finally, only another reading of a reading, *ad infinitum*. Moore acknowledges his heavy dependence on Stanley Fish – indubitably a brilliant *reader* whether you agree with him or not – and reading Moore himself is less the cerebral exercise of thinking through words of more conservative biblical criticism, and more an exercise of thinking in and by words through a punning style more akin to Moore's fellow Irishman, James Joyce (whose *Finnegans Wake* is one of the greatest of all intertextual biblical 'readings') than what we normally expect of biblical scholarship and commentary.

Postmodern criticism is fascinated by the Bible, unable to escape the 'persistent presence of the religious as the constant frame, our frame of reference, of the deconstructionist case',[41] and committed to endless readings which expose the irreducible[42] edges, metaphors and tropes of the biblical texts. In the writings of Jacques Derrida the persistent theme of 'the lack' emerges as a lack within reason itself that demands the play of religion,[43] prompting a stream of readings of Scripture, and readings of readings (for example, Kierkegaard on Genesis 22: 1–18, the Binding of Isaac, often referred to by the Hebrew term 'Akedah')[44] in an endless struggle with the text which seems to encourage closure and conclusion, and then deconstruct conclusion in further readings. Derrida's brilliant and tireless exercises in literary readings emerge, it has been suggested, out of his background in Rabbinic thought[45] with its midrashic intertextuality and its sense of struggle within and for the text.

Another Jewish scholar, Geoffrey H. Hartman, has insisted that the literary study of the Bible, in a continuation of the conversations of the ancient rabbis, alone keeps alive the irreducible asymmetries and superfluities which constitute the mystery of a text like Genesis 32:1–22, the wrestling of Jacob at Peniel.[46] In Hartman's essay, 'The Struggle for the Text', we move from the fictive or fictional qualities of the Bible to its frictionality, that is its irritating qualities which drive us to scratch and read again, aware that there are traces left which never yield to the searches of the biblical scholars in history or indeed elsewhere. In his classic essay on the Akedah (Genesis 22:1–18), 'Odysseus' Scar',[47] Erich Auerbach distinguishes between Greek and Hebraic conceptions of reality, and of textuality. If in the Homeric text 'nothing must remain hidden and unexpressed', in the Biblical narrative the mystery is held 'fraught with background', full of gaps and omissions. With the rabbis we are reminded that the Bible resists closure and conclusion, its endless writing demanding an endless exercise of reading and rereading, writing and rewriting.

In his posthumously published *Confessions of an Inquiring Spirit*, Coleridge affirms that 'in the Bible there is more that finds me than I have experienced in all other books put together'. The last years of his life were spent in continual readings of the Bible against the background of a whole lifetime spent among books and as a poet. Coleridge's frustration with 'bibliolaters' and others who seemed to dissect the text of Scripture in order to kill its spirit, emerged from a sense that, although it is endlessly studied as an authoritative and even 'sacred' text, it is actually rarely read with the readerly attention given to other great literature, for him, particularly Shakespeare. T. S. Eliot was fearful for the Bible if read merely 'as literature'; Coleridge was convinced that the Bible was somehow different from all other literature, 'having proceeded from the Holy spirit', but that this very difference would be endlessly revealed in literary readings which acknowledge and respond to its poetry and its inspiration.

In this brief chapter it has been possible only to offer a cursory survey of 'literary readings' of the Bible over the last two hundred years or so. Much has, of necessity, been omitted, not least the enormous literature in poetry and fiction itself and, more recently, film, which has continually 'read' the Bible even as it has been read by it in the ongoing task of literature. Biblical figures from Samson and King David, to Mary Magdalen and, repeatedly, Jesus himself, have appeared as figures in 'fiction', sometimes in a spirit of quiet devotion, and at other times as characters offensive to those who love the Bible in their own way.

Reading the Bible will never be an easy task, and its peculiar relationship with our complex cultural and religious histories will always claim the necessary attention of scholars whose investigations demand the skills of the historian, the philologist and the theologian. But the Bible also is literature, often of the very highest order, much of it written by poets and writers who, though often enmeshed in the particular prejudices and preconceptions of their own cultures, continue to speak with a universal voice that responds to readings made with literary sensitivity and imagination, often prompting such readings even when the scholars would prefer to believe that other and different critical tools will better discern the mystery of its pages.

## Notes

1 See, for example, T. S. Eliot, 'Religion and Literature', 1935, in *Selected Essays*, 3rd edn (London, 1951); C. S. Lewis, 'The Impact of the Authorised Version', in *They Asked for a Paper*, pp. 26–50 (London, 1962); T. R. Henn, *The Bible as Literature* (London, 1970); John B. Gabel and Charles B. Wheeler, *The Bible as Literature: An Introduction* (Oxford, 1986); Robert Alter and Frank Kermode (eds.), *The Literary Guide to the Bible* (London, 1987).

2 See Stephen Prickett, *Words and 'The Word': Language, Poetics and Biblical Interpretation* (Cambridge, 1986), and *Origins of Narrative: The Romantic Appropriation of the Bible* (Cambridge, 1996).

3 See Werner G. Jeanrond, *Theological Hermeneutics: Development and Significance* (London, 1991), pp. 16–17.

4 See C. H. Dodd, *According to the Scriptures* (London, 1952); also Ruth ap Roberts, *The Biblical Web* (Ann Arbor, 1994).

5 See J. C. Fenton, *Saint Matthew*, The Pelican New Testament Commentaries (Harmondsworth, 1963), pp. 33–5.

6 See George P. Landow, *Victorian Types, Victorian Shadows: Biblical Typology in Victorian Literature, Art and Thought* (Boston, London and Henley, 1980).

7 Modern writers of parables include Dostoevsky, Kierkegaard, Kafka and Borges.

8 Literature on the parables is vast, and interpretation of the New Testament parables begins in the Gospels themselves (cf. Mark 4:14–20, an interpretation of the Parable of the Sower). David Stern, *Parables in Midrash* (Cambridge, MA, 1991) links the mashal with midrash and Rabbinic forms of biblical interpretation. C. H. Dodd's classic *The Parables of the Kingdom* (London, 1935) begins with a survey of parable interpretation from Augustine. More recent 'literary' readings are in John Dominic Crossan, *In Parables* (San Francisco, 1973); Sallie McFague, *Speaking in Parables* (Philadelphia, 1975); and Frank Kermode, *The Genesis of Secrecy: On the Interpretation of Narrative* (Cambridge, MA, 1979).

9 Robert Morgan with John Barton, *Biblical Interpretation*, Oxford Bible Series (Oxford, 1988), p. 214. See also David Jasper, *Readings in the Canon of Scripture* (Basingstoke and New York, 1995).

10 Hermann Usener, *Religionsgeschichtliche Untersuchungen* (Bonn, 1911). Written in 1888, and cited in Prickett, *Words and 'The Word'*, p. 1.

11 S. T. Coleridge, *Marginalia*, ed. George Whalley, *Collected Coleridge* (London and Princeton, 1979–), vol. II, p. 410.

12 Coleridge, *Confessions of an Inquiring Spirit*, 1840 (Philadelphia, 1988), p. 33.

13 See Coleridge, *The Statesman's Manual*, 1816, in *Lay Sermons*, ed. R. J. White, *Collected Coleridge*, vol. VI (London and Princeton, 1972), p. 29: 'a system of symbols, harmonious in themselves, and consubstantial with the truths, of which they are the *conductors.* These are the Wheels which Ezekiel beheld.'

14 Albert Schweitzer, *The Quest of the Historical Jesus*, 1906, trans. W. Montgomery (London, 1936). p. 23.

15 Robert Alter, *The Art of Biblical Narrative* (London and Sydney, 1981), p. 13.

16 See Christopher Tuckett, Introduction, *Reading the New Testament. Methods of Interpretation* (London, 1987).

17 Dennis Nineham, *The Use and Abuse of the Bible*, 1976 (London, 1978), p. 40.

18 Schweitzer, *The Quest of the Historical Jesus*, p. 181.

19 Such 'literary readings' have always been accused of flippancy and a lack of scholarly seriousness. Stephen Neil writes of Renan: 'Professing to work as an historian, he does not pursue with the needed seriousness the historical problems of the life of Christ' (*The Interpretation of the New Testament: 1861–1961*, 1964 (Oxford, 1966), p. 194).

20 Cited in George Steiner, *Tolstoy or Dostoevsky*, 1959 (Harmondsworth, 1967), p. 14.

21 Farrer defended himself in an article, 'Inspiration: Poetical and Divine', in F. F. Bruce (ed.), *Promise and Fulfilment* (Edinburgh, 1963), pp. 91–105. The debate is discussed in detail in my book *Coleridge as Poet and Religious Thinker* (London, 1985), pp. 145–53.

22 Kermode, *The Genesis of Secrecy*, pp. 63–4.

23 D. H. Lawrence, 'Why the Novel Matters', published posthumously in *Phoenix*, 1936. Reprinted in *Selected Literary Criticism*, ed. Anthony Beal (London, 1956), p. 195.

24 Alter, *The Art of Biblical Narrative*; Gabriel Josipovici, *The Book of God: A Response to the Bible* (New Haven and London, 1988).

25 Josipovici, *The Book of God*, p. x.

26 Harold Bloom, *The Book of J* (London, 1991), p. 44.

27 Robert Alter, *The Art of Biblical Poetry* (New York, 1985); James L. Kugel, *The Idea of Biblical Poetry* (New Haven and London, 1981).

28 Alter and Kermode (eds.), *The Literary Guide to the Bible*, p. 2.

29 *Ibid.*, p. 6.

30 See, generally, Francis Watson (ed.), *The Open Text: New Directions for Biblical Studies?* (London, 1993).

31 See further, Stanley E. Porter, 'Why Hasn't Reader-Response Criticism Caught on in New Testament Studies?', *Literature and Theology*, 4, 3 (1990), pp. 278–92.

32 Stanley Fish, *Is There a Text in This Class? The Authority of Interpretive Communities* (Cambridge, MA, 1980), p. 305.

33 Mieke Bal, *Lethal Love: Feminist Literary Readings of Biblical Love Stories* (Bloomington, 1987); *Murder and Difference* (Bloomington, 1988); *Death and Dissymmetry* (Chicago, 1988).

34 Bal, *Death and Dissymmetry*, p. 4.

35 *Ibid.*, p. 5.

36 Phyllis Trible, 'Treasures Old and New: Biblical Theology and the Challenge of Feminism', in Watson (ed.), *The Open Text*, p. 37. See also Trible, *God and the Rhetoric of Sexuality* (London, 1978), especially her fine reading of the Book of Ruth, pp. 166–99.

37 Trible, 'Treasures Old and New', pp. 48–9.

38 Bal, *Death and Dissymmetry*, p. 43.

39 *The Literary Guide to the Bible*, p. 35.

40 Stephen D. Moore, *Mark and Luke in Poststructuralist Perspectives* (New Haven and London, 1992), p. xviii. Moore's recent *Poststructuralism and the New Testament: Derrida and Foucault at the Foot of the Cross* (Minneapolis, 1994) is a more introductory text.

41 Valentine Cunningham, *In the Reading Gaol: Postmodernity, Texts and History* (Oxford, 1994), p. 366. In his final chapter, 'The Rabbins Take It Up One After Another', Cunningham explores the thesis that 'Biblical logocentricity is already deconstructionist'.

42 Austin Farrer wrote at length of the 'irreducible imagery' of the Bible, for example, *The Glass of Vision* (London, 1948), p. 94.

43 Jacques Derrida, *The Truth in Painting*, trans. Geoff Bennington and Ian McLeod (Chicago, 1987), pp. 53–6. See also Cunningham, *In the Reading Gaol*, p. 366.

44 See Derrida, *The Gift of Death*, trans. David Wills (Chicago, 1995), pp. 64–7. Also, Derrida, *Memoirs of the Blind: The Self-Portrait and Other Ruins*, trans. Pascale-Anne Brault and Michael Naas (Chicago, 1993), for readings of the blind Jacob, pp. 97–100, and Samson, pp. 104–10, and Saul/Paul, pp. 112–17.

45 See Susan A. Handelmann, *The Slayers of Moses. The Emergence of Rabbinic Interpretation in Modern Literary Theory* (Albany, 1982). Also, Daniel Boyarin, *Intertextuality and the Reading of Midrash* (Bloomington, 1990).

46 Geoffrey H. Hartman, 'The Struggle for the Text', in Geoffrey H. Hartman and Sanford Budick (eds.), *Midrash and Literature* (New Haven and London, 1986), pp. 3–18.

47 Erich Auerbach, *Mimesis: The Representation of Reality in Western Literature*, trans. Willard R. Trask (Princeton, 1974), pp. 3–23.

## Further reading

Alter, Robert and Frank Kermode (eds.), *The Literary Guide to the Bible*, London, 1987.

Alter, Robert, *The Art of Biblical Narrative*, London and Sydney, 1981.

Bal, Mieke, *Murder and Difference*, Bloomington, 1988.

Gabel, John B. and Charles B. Wheeler, *The Bible as Literature: An Introduction*, Oxford, 1986.

Hartman, Geoffrey H. and Sanford Budick (eds.), *Midrash and Literature*, New Haven and London, 1986.

Josipovici, Gabriel, *The Book of God: A Response to the Bible*, New Haven and London, 1988.

Kermode, Frank, *The Genesis of Secrecy: On the Interpretation of Narrative*, Cambridge, MA, 1979.

Moore, Stephen D., *Poststructuralism and the New Testament: Derrida and Foucault at the Foot of the Cross*, Minneapolis, 1994.

Watson, Francis (ed.), *The Open Text: New Directions for Biblical Studies?*, London 1993.

# 3 The social world of the Bible

KEITH W. WHITELAM

## THE QUEST FOR THE SOCIAL WORLD OF THE BIBLE

The quest for the social world of the Bible has been one of the major goals of biblical scholarship since the early nineteenth century. Travellers' reports from the Middle East of a culture radically different from that of the West, along with the increasing excitement of reports in the national press of archaeological discoveries in Palestine, captivated audiences across Europe and the USA. Such developments offered the prospect of revealing the world from which the Bible had emerged in the ancient past. Monumental works such as George Adam Smith's historical geography of Palestine brought alive an ancient landscape on which the biblical events were played out.[1] At the same time, biblical scholars were trying to reconstruct the history and social contexts out of which the Bible arose in order to understand a foundational text for Western culture. The critical methods which emerged were designed to date and locate the biblical texts, or their constituent parts, in specific historical contexts in order to reveal their meaning. The reconstruction of the history of ancient Israel, understood in its broadest terms as ranging from the early second millennium to the end of the first millennium BCE, and of the early Christian community in the first century CE was central to this enterprise. The pioneering work of William Robertson Smith, Sigmund Mowinckel, Julius Wellhausen, Johannes Pedersen, H. Wheeler Robinson, S. H. Hooke, Shirley Case Jackson, Albrecht Alt, William Foxwell Albright and Martin Noth, among many others, illustrates a concern with social organization and social setting, drawing on the emerging disciplines of sociology and anthropology, from the inception of modern biblical studies to its classic formulation in the twentieth century.[2] The burgeoning interest in 'the social world of ancient Israel' or 'the social world of early Christianity' from the 1970s onwards, at a critical moment in the history of modern biblical studies, was heir to this long tradition rather than a radical break with past scholarship. It represented an attempt to move beyond the literature of the Bible to understand the social, political and historical development of Palestine from the Bronze Age to the Roman period. These attempts to understand the multi-faceted aspects of societies associated with the development of the Bible, and their environments, by appeal to a wide range of social science disciplines formed part of the continuing quest for the social world of the Bible which had fired the imaginations of nineteenth-century scholars, travellers and readers.

It is remarkable that after two centuries or more this quest for the social world of the Bible continues and, in fact, is now more controversial than perhaps it has ever been. Despite the long tradition of utilization of insights from sociology and anthropology the increasing appeal to the social sciences by biblical scholars from the beginning of the 1970s has invariably been perceived as representing a new or, at least, distinctive phase in the quest. The widespread use, at the time, of such phrases as 'the sociological approach' or 'the sociological method' suggested that this was a new methodological departure in biblical studies in contrast with more traditional textual, philological and historical studies. The publication of George Mendenhall's seminal essay on 'The Hebrew Conquest of Palestine' in 1962 is usually acknowledged as providing the stimulus to this renewed dialogue in biblical studies with the social sciences. The pioneering works of George Mendenhall and Norman Gottwald on the history of early Israel were crucial in the early stages of this movement, drawing upon more recent anthropological and sociological studies to question many of the assumptions which had underpinned long accepted constructions of early Israelite history: in particular, the relationship of nomadism to sedentary and state societies and the nature of social and political organization and relationships within Palestine.[3] Similarly, New Testament scholars began to apply social scientific approaches and data in innovative ways to understanding the biblical texts within first century CE Palestine and the Mediterranean world.[4] Gottwald understood the 'sociological method', as he termed it, as providing the tools for reconstructing the whole social system of ancient Israel, including functions, roles, institutions, customs, norms, judicial and religious organization, military and political structures, and the material aspect of culture. He saw this as complementing traditional historical studies in order to 'reconstruct ancient Israel as a lived totality'.[5] However, he warned against the dangers of such an approach as being seen as a '"tacked on" adjunct to the customary privileged methods' so that it appeared as 'tangential and quixotic, as a problematic interloper'.[6] It is clear from such concerns that this movement in its early stages was considered by many to be on the radical fringes of the discipline: this was evident in the heated debates and exchanges in specialist journals and conferences at the time.

Although it might be said that such attempts to recover the social world of the Bible have moved increasingly from the radical fringes of the disci- pline closer to the mainstream, there remains considerable unease in many quarters. Thus Bengt Holmberg's detailed review of the important contribu- tions within New Testament studies is entitled *Sociology and the New Testament. An Appraisal.* Similarly, a recent collection of essays edited by Philip Esler, *Modelling Early Christianity. Social-scientific Studies of the New Testament in its Context*[7] provides a defensive justification for such approaches in contrast with dominant theological understandings of the New Testament literature. The main purpose for using anthropological models, it is claimed, is in order to expose the meaning of the texts in terms of the first-century Mediterranean cultural contexts in which they were ori- ginally produced. Esler argues that what distinguishes the work of contri- butors to the volume from that of others interested in these texts 'is that they consider it necessary explicitly to enlist the help from the social sciences, anthropology, sociology and social psychology in particular'.[8] Such inter- disciplinary approaches are designed to uncover the meaning of texts for the 'original audience' in order to facilitate the contemporary appropriation of New Testament texts by believing communities. A theological appreciation of the texts is closely identified with understanding the social contexts in which they were produced. In contrast, the direction of much recent work on the social world of ancient Israel has tended to draw a sharp distinction between historical reconstruction and theological understandings of the Hebrew Bible.

The increasing influences of what has become known variously as the 'sociological approach' or the use of 'social-scientific criticism' is illustrated in the various handbooks which adopt or discuss the application of such approaches.[9] The publication of a vast body of literature over the last quarter of a century illustrates that these concerns and approaches can no longer be dismissed as merely 'quixotic' or considered a 'tacked on interloper'. However, it is also clear that there remain considerable disagreements among scholars as to the applicability or even validity of such attempts to construct the social world of the Bible. Esler's claim that the primary motivation is to understand the original context and meanings of the New Testament literature is hardly distinctive since this has been the central impulse of the historical-critical method since the nineteenth century. However, the primary question which has emerged is how scholars might have access to the ancient past and the multifaceted social world of ancient Palestine and the Mediterranean. It is the pursuit of this question which has contributed to a series of significant shifts in understanding what actually constitutes the social world of the Bible, which periods are appropriate for investigation and how they might be investigated.

## THE BIBLE AND ITS SOCIAL WORLD

In order to understand the different directions which now characterize the new quest, it is important to understand the convergence of a series of influential trends whose combined force has transformed biblical studies in the latter part of the twentieth century. It was the result of the convergence of new intellectual currents in psychoanalysis, linguistics and philosophy which helped undermine the authority and the stability of established disciplines and their previously thought 'assured results'. The rise to prominence of newer literary studies within biblical studies was part of this general movement. The publication of Robert Alter's *The Art of Biblical Narrative* and David Gunn's *The Fate of King Saul* and *The Story of King David* had a profound effect on the way in which biblical narratives were read as artful constructions.[10] Thus the books of Samuel, for instance, were increasingly understood as skilful and serious literature rather than primary sources for the monarchy of Saul and David. Many biblical books which had previously been considered to be historical, in the sense that they preserved a reasonably accurate picture of the history of ancient Israel or later communities, became the subject of detailed literary treatments. Furthermore, developments in historical studies in general, allied to increasing archaeological data from the region, raised serious questions about the world of ancient Palestine and the Mediterranean as it had been understood. The result was a general disillusionment with previous historical studies, which were seen to be too limited in scope or theologically motivated. The search for the social world of the Bible since the nineteenth century had been closely identified with the history of Israel through to the first century CE. The gradual and ever-increasing erosion of this history, its increasing divorce from the biblical texts was the catalyst for fresh attempts to explore and reconstruct the social world of ancient Palestine and the Mediterranean world. The appeal to the social sciences was an attempt to recover the many aspects of society which were not mentioned in the texts but which formed an essential element in the social world from which they emerged. The appeal to archaeology, sociology and anthropology, in particular, was seen as addressing some of the deficiencies in the biblical texts as sources for their own social world. This was paralleled by an increasing interest in the social production of the biblical literature, its ideological aspects, the factional disputes which lay behind it and the social and political world it represented or reflected. The trends and directions in current research which constitute the new search for the social world of the Bible are much too varied a phenomenon to be categorized by a single phrase such as 'the sociological approach'.

It is ironic that the new search for the social world of the Bible, initiated by Mendenhall and Gottwald, has resulted in a redefinition of the 'biblical period' which has severely restricted its chronological limits. Earlier in the century, it was understood as stretching over two millennia from the early second millennium to the end of the first century CE. The impact of literary studies, which increasingly questioned the relationship of the complex of biblical narratives from Genesis to 2 Kings to history, has undermined confidence in the construction of vast periods of Israelite history. The result has been the loss of the Patriarchal and Conquest periods from many historical accounts and an increasingly fierce debate over the nature of the settlement and early monarchic periods. Ironically, therefore, the very search for the world of the Bible which informed many of these revisionist studies of the history of Israel has resulted in the removal of several centuries previously attributed to that world.[11] The conviction that the Hebrew Bible was the product of the Persian and Hellenistic periods has underpinned this radical shift. R. P. Carroll states baldly what many biblical scholars have been coming to accept for a long time: 'The Hebrew Bible is the product of the second Temple period. This ought to be an uncontentious statement, but I imagine some unreconstructed biblical scholars may wish to contest it in favour of a First Temple period origin for the Bible with some appendices from the time of the second Temple. While I can see that there *may* be something to be said for the view that the Bible contains fragments of material from before the collapse of the temple in the sixth century, the claim that the Bible *as we know it* (i.e. the fully redacted final form of the various books constituting it) comes from the Second Temple period seems to me ungainsayable.'[12] The implications of this conviction are highlighted by P. R. Davies when he writes of the 'desire to see the "biblical period" properly defined as the period in which the Bible was written – or, more correctly, when the literature in its "biblical" form was composed, since by its very nature, the Bible, being a collection of scriptures, was not *written*, but *ratified* by consent or decree or both (and thus, of course, the term "biblical authors" is also misleading)'.[13] The implication of this now widespread conviction, a return to the position of Wellhausen in many ways, is that if the Bible is the product of the Persian, Hellenistic and Roman periods, then the search for the social world of the Bible should be restricted to those periods.

The key problem which has emerged, and which dominates all attempts to understand the social world of the Bible, is the complex relationship between texts and their social worlds. The legacy of literary studies has been to undermine confidence in the assumption that the world of the texts coincided with the views of the past they portrayed. However, dating the final form of these texts to the Persian and Hellenistic periods or first-century Roman Palestine does not solve the problem of their relationship to the socio-historical backgrounds or ideological influences which shaped them. The methodological problems have multiplied and sharpened on how to investigate periods where there is insufficient (literary) evidence, particularly for the Late Bronze and Iron Ages, and how to bridge the gap between text and social reality in the Persian to Roman periods. The biblical traditions can no longer be understood as simple reflections of earlier historical reality. Rather they offer a valuable insight into perceptions of that reality from particular points of view at the time of the writers. This is not to suggest that such texts may not preserve some authentic memories and information about the past but these are increasingly difficult to assess. The relationship between the text and society is considerably more complex than the common binary opposition between literature and society, text and context. For example, the social practices presented in a text may not correspond to any such practices in reality: they may be an attempt to subvert current social practices. How far a text subverts the dominant or some other perception of reality or represents a dominant view depends on its relationship to other pieces of literature, monuments, artefacts, etc. that can reveal important comparative information about social attitudes or perceptions of reality. Many New Testament scholars, in particular, have appealed to the social sciences in order to try to understand the implications of key concepts in New Testament literature in terms of its wider social setting.[14] However, Carroll offers an important reminder of the inherent difficulties in such attempts to move from textual levels to social world.[15] It is ironic that as the focal point of the social world of the Bible has shifted from the Iron Age to Persian, it has become evident that very little is known about the social and historical background of the Second Temple period. It is for this reason that scholars appeal to social-scientific studies and data in order to try to make sense of the fragmentary and partial textual and artefactual data available. Carroll concludes that 'the gap between texts and the real world remains as unbridgeable as ever'.[16] However, the biblical texts offer access to the privileged conception of reality of a literate stratum of society revealing little or nothing of the 'sub-literate culture', to use Eric Hobsbawm's phrase, or the deep-seated movements of history. As such, the value of these texts as a source for the historian is not so much in terms of the past they purport to describe but as such an insight. They are important, therefore, as much for what they choose to leave out as for what they include. The multi-layered nature of the texts, their adaptability and vitality means that the historian needs to ask how they shaped and were shaped by their different contexts, what audiences they address, and what other possible constructions of the past they deny and thereby silence. The appeal to social scientific models and data drawn from social and cultural anthropology, sociology, economics, politics, archaeology or cultural studies has been instrumental in helping to uncover the social world of ancient Palestine and the Mediterranean.

## THE TRENDS IN RECENT SCHOLARSHIP

### History and society

One of the most important trends to emerge in recent years has been a more encompassing definition of the history of Palestine and the Mediterranean world. Much of 'biblical history' has concentrated on the aristocratic view of history paying little or no attention to the wider realities of the past by examining long-term patterns and trends in order to make sense of short-term events and individuals. Demography, settlement patterns, and economic trends are the most obvious indicators of the 'deep-seated' movements of history. Such a history cannot be based solely upon the written archives of the literate elite which are necessarily myopic of long-term trends and which also deny a voice in history to the vast majority of society. The new search for ancient Israel which has emerged in recent years has increasingly questioned the biblically inspired interpretation of archaeological data from surveys and excavations. Although the primary focus of discussion has concerned the location and identity of early Israel in the Late Bronze–Iron Age transition, it is this discussion which has done most to investigate the wider history of the region and the period and which has increasingly influenced understandings of the history of the region in the Persian, Hellenistic and Roman periods. The archaeological data covering the Late Bronze–Iron Age transition and the early Iron Age provide valuable information on the demography, settlement, economy and social organization of Palestinian society. The steadily accumulating weight of evidence illustrating the continuities in material culture between Late Bronze and early Iron Age sites has revealed that the settlement shift of the Late Bronze–Iron Age transition was part of a protracted process which needs to be understood in the context of the complex events and forces affecting the whole of the eastern Mediterranean over a century or more.[17] It has become increasingly evident that the transition period from Late Bronze–Iron 1 Age was not uniform or simultaneous throughout Palestine but was characterized by a complex process in which indigenous, Egyptian and Philistine cultures overlapped for certain periods.

The publication of surveys of the region has allowed the study of settlement history, demography, economy, social relations and political organization in ways that were previously not possible. The same type of investigation is gradually being extended to subsequent periods of the Iron Age, freeing the study of the region from the stranglehold of biblical historiography. The period of the united monarchy is experiencing a fundamental reassessment. Previous attempts to apply anthropological findings on state formation to the rise of the monarchy remained too closely wedded to the biblical traditions,[18] whereas recent studies have concluded that there is little evidence to support the assumption that a major state structure existed in the region prior to the eighth century BCE. Such a radical shift effectively removes what had been considered one of the most influential periods in the history of the region, the monarchies of David and Solomon, as the social and political location for the development of the biblical traditions.

In the past there was often an indecent haste to correlate archaeological findings with the biblical traditions, to identify a destruction level with some battle mentioned in the Bible, or to associate the fortification of a site with the building programme of some Judaean or Israelite king who is given a few verses in the Deuteronomistic history. Socio-environmental factors and the fluctuations in economic cycles have been ignored in favour of the seemingly easy option of accepting, or supplementing, the construction of the past offered by writers of the Hebrew Bible. The publication of archaeological surveys and data from excavations, allied to the literary readings of biblical texts, has contributed to an important shift in the investigation of the social world.

This reassessment of biblically based reconstructions is increasingly being applied to later Persian, Hellenistic and Roman periods.[19] We know, for instance, that the pastoral-nomadic element has been a constant in the social continuum of the region.[20] Yet this element of society does not form part of the self-perception of those responsible for the development of the traditions. While nomads may have been a constant in the history of the region, their part in the past, and so the present, has been silenced by the literate elite of the Second Temple period, or whoever is responsible for this construction of this past. Furthermore, these traditions tell us little or nothing of how these societies, or the region in general, were linked to the wider economy, whether Egyptian, Assyrian, Babylonian, Achaemenid, Hellenistic or Roman. Nor are they informative of demography, settlement patterns or economic trends, the best indicators of the deep-seated movements of history which provide the wider perspective from which to view the short-term trends that are the inevitable focus of our literary deposits.

Two recent studies on the economy of Palestine in the Iron Age and Herodian Period are illustrative of the new ways in which the social world of Palestine is being explored.[21] David Hopkins attempts to reconstruct the economy of late Iron-Age Jerusalem and its intersections with the wider regional economy. In the process, he highlights the methodological problems due to the fact that much economic behaviour is materially invisible or its material correlates are ephemeral. Similarly, biblical texts are unreliable and lack sufficient data to enable readers to understand economic reality. Hopkins reconstructs the intersecting set of economies which were determined, in large part, by the complex and fragmented landscape. His study illustrates the problems and prospects of newer attempts to understand the complex realities of the social world of Palestine which are ignored or obscured by the biblical texts. Similarly, Sean Freyne's attempt to recover the economy of Antipas's Galilee exposes the problems of trying to model ancient economies on the basis of partial evidence. The integration of archaeological data with literary evidence in conjunction with appeal to ethnography and social anthropology provides an important perspective on the deep-seated realities of history and the Gospel narratives. Freyne concludes that the radical nature of Jesus' social programme undermined the values of the market economy and the centrality of Jerusalem.

## Social location and ideology

Such attempts to reconstruct the economic and socio-environmental setting of the biblical traditions have been accompanied by another important trend in recent scholarship. This is the attempt to investigate the social locations and ideological conflicts and assumptions which have shaped the texts. The exploration of the social location of prophecy in the Hebrew Bible again illustrates the prospects and problems of exploring these aspects of the social world of the Bible. The use of cross-cultural parallels and ethnographical materials has done much to illuminate the nature of prophecy as a social and religious phenomenon in ancient society.[22] R. R. Wilson's study offers a new perspective on the nature and function of prophets as intermediaries, particularly central and peripheral intermediaries. T. W. Overholt draws extensively on ethnographic material, particularly from North America, to emphasize the social pressures which shape prophetic roles and performance. Similarly, P. D. Hanson's analysis of the development of apocalyptic literature and its social setting and function signals a growing interest in the different disputes embedded within and behind the development of the prophetic literature. R. P. Carroll's application, from psychology, of dissonance theory to the understanding of the development and adaptability of prophetic texts has provided a further important exploration of the social world of the biblical texts. This is paralleled in New Testament studies by G. Theissen's seminal attempts to reconstruct the social world of Palestinian and Pauline Christianity, which provided the inspiration and impetus for a wide-ranging and diverse exploration of the social location of early Christianity and the ideological shaping of New Testament literature. B. J. Malina's innovative application of cultural anthropology has been particularly influential in introducing the concepts of shame and honour as crucial aspects of the Mediterranean social world in which early Christians were integrated, and which offers an interesting and important perspective from which to view the New Testament texts. This has been followed by an appeal to and application of social-scientific theories of small group formation and development, sectarianism, conversion and deviance.[23] In all cases, contemporary models have been used to understand how and why Christianity spread throughout the Mediterranean world, its diversity and inner tensions, and the social norms embedded within the biblical texts.

Yet again the question of the relationship of the text to its social world becomes paramount; there is considerable disagreement on the dating of prophetic literature, the composition and identification of different sources in prophetic books, and the applicability or validity of contemporary models and data in understanding the social organization and norms of the ancient cultures from which the Bible emerged. The major objections to these developments have tended to focus on the problems of using different models, the lack of understanding or appreciation of the diversity and disputes within the modern social sciences, or the possibilities of 'historical sociology'.[24] However, the problematic relationship of texts to socio-historical context which informed the switch to the pursuit of the deep-seated realities of ancient Palestine is equally applicable to these attempts to explore the social world of the Bible. It is important to recognize the dangers, particularly the tendency to circular reasoning, in trying to extrapolate the social world of the Bible from the biblical texts themselves. The appreciation of the manifold problems in such an exercise appears to be less well developed in New Testament studies compared with parallel movements in the study of the Hebrew Bible.

### The social world of the Bible: modern scholarship and models

The social world of the Bible cannot simply be restricted to the periods when the biblical literature was composed and crystallized into the scriptures of Judaism and Christianity. It is also the world, or worlds, in which the Bible has been received and utilized since its formation through to the present day. The shifts in understanding the social world of ancient Palestine and the Mediterranean are closely tied to understanding the social location of modern biblical scholarship. This is a topic that has become increasingly important in recent years with a series of major studies on the development and socio-political setting of biblical studies and cognate disciplines in the modern period. A detailed analysis of the social and political contexts of the shifts which engulfed biblical studies remains to be done.[25] However, what is becoming increasingly clear is that the set of assumptions, particularly of the role of nation-states in the past or the evolutionary development of society, which informed scholarship from the nineteenth century onwards, no longer has the explanatory power it once had. The importance of the appeal to the social sciences and the methodological debates which have ensued have revealed the problems of modelling ancient societies. Despite concerns about the appropriateness of applying contemporary models to understanding ancient pasts, the appeal to social-scientific theories makes explicit, and therefore open to criticism and debate, the models and assumptions being used to explore the social world of the Bible. The problem where models have been implicit or masked in contemporary scholarship has been illustrated by the tremendous hold that evolutionary theory and the model of the nation state have imposed upon biblical studies in general.

Although the renewed dialogue between biblical studies and the social sciences has gradually moved from the radical fringes to an increasing centrality over the last quarter of a century, the realization of Gottwald's dream of reconstructing the social world of ancient Israel, or early Christianity, in its totality remains unfulfilled. It can hardly be denied that the series of important and interrelated developments in the pursuit of the deep-seated realities of the ancient past, the complexities of social organization or social norms embedded within and behind the biblical texts have provided fresh insights into the social world of the Bible. However, the methodological debates which have accompanied this new quest, including the social location of contemporary scholarship and the ways in which it has determined the search, mean that the search for the social world of the Bible remains, as for nineteenth- and early twentieth-century scholarship, a tantalizing prospect.

## Notes

1 G. A. Smith, The *Historical Geography of the Holy Land, Especially in Relation to the History of Israel and the Early Church* (London: Hodder and Stoughton, 1894).

2 There are numerous works which survey the development of this quest: J. Rogerson, *Anthropology and the Old Testament* (Oxford: Blackwell, 1978); A. D. H. Mayes, *The Old Testament in Sociological Perspective* (London: Marshall, Morgan, and Scott, 1989); B. Holmberg, *Sociology and the New Testament. An Appraisal* (Minneapolis: Fortress Press, 1990); N. K. Gottwald, 'Sociology of Ancient Israel', *Anchor Bible Dictionary*, ed. D. N. Freedman, vol. VI (New York: Doubleday, 1992), pp. 79–89; S. R. Garrett, 'Sociology of Early Christianity', *Anchor Bible Dictionary*, vol. VI, pp. 89–99.

3 G. E. Mendenhall, 'The Hebrew Conquest of Palestine', *Biblical Archaeologist* 25 (1962), pp. 66–87; *The Tenth Generation: The Origins of the Biblical Traditions* (Baltimore: Johns Hopkins Press, 1973); N. K. Gottwald, *The Tribes of Yahweh. A Sociology of the Religion of Liberated Israel, 1250–1050 BC* (London: SCM Press, 1979).

4 See D. Tidball, *An Introduction to the Sociology of the New Testament* (Exeter: Paternoster Press, 1983); J. H. Elliott, *What is Social Scientific Criticism?* (Minneapolis: Fortress Press, 1993); and Holmberg, *Sociology and the New Testament* for a discussion of ground-breaking works in New Testament studies.

5 N. K. Gottwald, 'Sociological Method in the Study of Ancient Israel', in M. J. Buss (ed.), *Encounter with the Text. Form and History in the Hebrew Bible* (Philadelphia: Fortress Press, 1979), p. 70.

6 *Ibid.*, p. 71.

7 P. Esler (ed.), *Modelling Early Christianity. Social-scientific Studies of the New Testament in its Context* (London: Routledge, 1995). B. Holmberg, *Sociology and the New Testament. An Appraisal* (Minneapolis: Fortress Press, 1990).

8 Esler, 'Models, Context and Kerygma in New Testament Interpretation', in Esler (ed.), *Modelling Early Christianity*, p. 3.

9 R. R. Wilson, *Sociological Approaches to the Old Testament* (Philadelphia: Fortress Press, 1984); Rogerson, *Anthropology and the Old Testament*; Mayes, *The Old Testament in Sociological Perspective*; R. E. Clements (ed.), *The World of Ancient Israel: Sociological, Anthropological and Political Perspectives*

(Cambridge: Cambridge University Press, 1989); Tidball, *An Introduction to the Sociology of the New Testament*; Elliot, *What is Social Scientific Criticism?*.

10 R. Alter, *The Art of Biblical Narrative* (London: Allen and Unwin, 1981); D. M. Gunn, *The Fate of King Saul: An Interpretation of a Biblical Story* (Sheffield: JSOT Press, 1980) and *The Story of King David: Genre and Interpretation* (Sheffield: JSOT Press, 1978).

11 G. W. Ahlström, *Who Were the Israelites?* (Winona Lake, MN: Eisenbrauns, 1991) and *The History of Ancient Palestine from the Palaeolithic Period to Alexander's Conquest* (Sheffield: JSOT Press, 1993); R. B. Coote and K. W. Whitelam, *The Emergence of Early Israel in Historical Perspective* (Sheffield: JSOT Press, 1979); N.-P. Lemche, *Early Israel: Anthropological and Historical Studies on the Israelite Society before the Monarchy* (Leiden: Brill, 1985); T. L. Thompson, *The Early History of the Israelite People: From the Written and Archaeological Sources* (Leiden: Brill, 1992); I. Finkelstein and N. Na'aman (eds.), *From Nomadism to Monarchy. Archaeological and Historical Aspects of Early Israel* (Jerusalem: Israel Exploration Society, 1994).

12 R. P. Carroll, 'Textual Strategies and Ideology in the Second Temple Period', in P. R. Davies (ed.), *Second Temple Studies 1. Persian Period* (Sheffield: JSOT Press, 1991), p. 108.

13 P. R. Davies, 'Sociology and the Second Temple', in Davies (ed.), *Second Temple Studies*, pp. 11–12.

14 Esler (ed.), *Modelling Early Christianity*; B. J. Malina, *The New Testament World* (London: SCM Press, 1983).

15 Carroll, 'Textual Strategies', p.109.

16 *Ibid.*, p. 124.

17 Coote and Whitelam, *Emergence;* I. Finkelstein, 'The Great Transformation: The "Conquest" of the Highland Frontiers and the Rise of the Territorial States', in T. E. Levy (ed.), *The Archaeology of Society in the Holy Land* (Leicester: Leicester University Press, 1995), pp. 434–65.

18 F. S. Frick, *The Formation of the State in Ancient Israel. A Survey of Models and Theories* (Sheffield: Almond Press, 1985); Coote and Whitelam, *Emergence*; C. Hauer, 'From Alt to Anthropology: The Rise of the Israelite State', *Journal for the Study of the Old Testament* 36 (1986), pp. 3–15; I. Finkelstein, 'The Emergence of the Israelite Monarchy: the Environmental and Socio-Economic Aspects', *Journal for the Study of the Old Testament* 44 (1989), pp. 43–74.

19 K. G. Hoglund, *Achaemenid Imperial Administration in Syria-Palestine and the Missions of Ezra and Nehemiah* (Philadelphia: Scholars Press, 1992); W. D. Davies and I. Finkelstein (eds.), *The Cambridge History of Judaism. Introduction: the Persian Period* (Cambridge; Cambridge University Press, 1984).

20 Lemche, *Early Israel.*

21 D. Hopkins, 'Bare Bones: Putting Flesh on the Economics of Ancient Israel', in V. Fritz and P. R. Davies (eds.), *The Origins of the Ancient Israelite States* (Sheffield: JSOT Press, 1996), pp. 121–39; S. Freyne 'Herodian Economics in

Galilee. Searching for a Suitable Model', in Esler (ed.), *Modelling Early Christianity*, pp. 23–46.

22  R. R. Wilson, *Prophecy and Society in Ancient Israel* (Philadelphia: Fortress Press, 1980); T. W. Overholt, *Channels of Prophecy: the Social Dynamics of Prophetic Activity* (Minneapolis: Fortress Press, 1989); R. P. Carroll, *When Prophecy Failed: Reactions and Responses to Failure in the Old Testament Prophetic Traditions* (London: SCM Press, 1979); G. Theissen, *The First Followers of Jesus: A Sociological Analysis of the Earliest Christianity* (London: SCM Press, 1978); P. D. Hanson, *The Dawn of Apocalyptic: The Historical and Sociological Roots of Jewish Apocalyptic Eschatology*, rev. edn (Philadelphia: Fortress Press, 1979 (first edition 1975)).

23  See the essays in Esler, *Modelling Early Christianity*, or L. M. White and O. L. Yarbrough (eds.), *The Social World of the First Christians. Essays in Honor of Wayne A. Meeks* (Minneapolis: Fortress Press, 1995).

24  C. Rodd, 'On Applying a Sociological Theory to Biblical Studies', *Journal for the Study of the Old Testament* 19 (1981), pp. 95–106; Garrett, 'Sociology of Early Christianity', pp. 89–99.

25  In particular, see B. Kuklick, *Puritans in Babylon: the Ancient Near East and American Intellectual Life, 1880–1930* (Princeton: Princeton University Press, 1996); K. W. Whitelam, *The Invention of Ancient Israel: the Silencing of Palestinian History* (London and New York: Routledge, 1996); W. H. C. Frend, *The Archaeology of Early Christianity: a History* (London: Geoffrey Chapman, 1996); M. T. Larsen, *The Conquest of Assyria: Excavations in an Antique Land* (Routledge: London, 1994); N. Silberman, *Digging for God and Country. Exploration in the Holy Land, 1799–1917* (New York: Doubleday, 1982) and *Between Past and Present. Archaeology, Ideology, and Nationalism in the Modern Middle East* (New York: Doubleday, 1989).

## Further reading

Carroll, R. P., *When Prophecy Failed: Reactions and Responses to Failure in the Old Testament Prophetic Traditions*, London: SCM Press, 1979.

Carter, C. E. and C. L. Meyers, *Community, Identity, and Ideology: Social Science Approaches to the Hebrew Bible*, Winona Lake, MN: Eisenbrauns, 1996.

Clements, R. E. (ed.), *The World of Ancient Israel: Sociological, Anthropological and Political Perspectives*, Cambridge: Cambridge University Press, 1989.

Elliott, J. H., *A Home for the Homeless: A Sociological Exegesis of 1 Peter, its Situation And Strategy*, Philadelphia: Fortress Press, 1981.

  *What is Social Scientific Criticism?*, Minneapolis: Fortress Press, 1993.

  *Social Scientific Criticism of the New Testament*, London: SPCK, 1995.

Esler, P. F., *The First Christians in their Social Worlds: Social-scientific Approaches to New Testament Interpretation*, London: Routledge, 1994.

Esler, P. F. (ed.), *Modelling Early Christianity. Social-scientific Studies of the New Testament in its Context*, London: Routledge, 1995.

Garrett, S. R., 'Sociology of Early Christianity', *Anchor Bible Dictionary*, vol. VI, Doubleday: New York, 1992, pp. 89–99.

Gottwald, N. K., 'Sociology of Ancient Israel', *Anchor Bible Dictionary*, vol. VI, Doubleday: New York, 1992, pp. 79–89.

Holmberg, B., *Sociology and the New Testament. An Appraisal*, Minneapolis: Fortress Press, 1990.

Horsley, R. A., *Galilee: History, Politics, People*, New York: Trinity Press International, 1995.

Horsley, R. A. and John S. Hanson, *Bandits, Prophets, and Messiahs: Popular Movements in the Time of Jesus*, New York: Winston Press, 1985.

Malina, B. J., *Christian Origins and Cultural Anthropology: Practical Models for Biblical Interpretation*, Louisville, KY: John Knox Press, 1986.

*The New Testament World: Insights from Cultural Anthropology*. Louisville, KY: Westminster/John Knox Press, 1993.

*The Social World of Jesus and the Gospels*, London: Routledge, 1996.

Malina, B. J. and John J. Pilch, *Biblical Social Values and Their Meaning: A Handbook*, Peabody, MA: Hendrickson Publishers, 1993.

Mayes, A. D. H., *The Old Testament in Sociological Perspective*, London: Marshall, Morgan, and Scott, 1989.

Moxnes, H., *The Economy of the Kingdom: Social Conflict and Economic Relations in Luke's Gospel*, Philadelphia: Fortress Press, 1988.

*Constructing Early Christian Families: Family as Social Reality and Metaphor*, London: Routledge, 1997.

Neyrey, J. H., *The Social World of Luke–Acts: Models for Interpretation*, Peabody, MA: Hendrickson Publishers, 1991.

Overholt, T. W., *Channels of Prophecy: the Social Dynamics of Prophetic Activity*, Minneapolis: Fortress Press, 1989.

Rogerson, J., *Anthropology and the Old Testament*, Oxford: Blackwell, 1978.

Theissen, G., *The First Followers of Jesus: A Sociological Analysis of the Earliest Christianity*, London: SCM Press, 1978.

*The Social Setting of Pauline Christianity: Essays on Corinth*, Edinburgh: T. & T. Clark, 1990.

Tidball, D., *An Introduction to the Sociology of the New Testament*, Exeter: Paternoster Press, 1983.

White, L. M. and O. L. Yarbrough (eds.), *The Social World of the First Christians. Essays in Honor of Wayne A. Meeks*, Minneapolis: Fortress Press, 1995.

Wilson, R. R., *Prophecy and Society in Ancient Israel*, Philadelphia: Fortress Press, 1980.

*Sociological Approaches to the Old Testament*, Philadelphia: Fortress Press, 1984.

# 4 Poststructuralist approaches
## New Historicism and postmodernism

ROBERT P. CARROLL

Poststructuralism is a convenient umbrella term for a wide range of different and differing theoretical approaches to architecture, the arts, literature, philosophy, cultural and textual studies characterized, among other things, by its dissent from the search for binary forms and its opposition to criticism and Enlightenment values. If structuralism had sought to overcome the text by the use of tightly structured analyses which forced texts to yield up *all* their secrets to a mathematically inscribed scrutiny, in biblical studies structural analysis quickly gave way to poststructuralist approaches to the text. A new generation of theory-driven scholars emerged after the 1960s determined to read themselves into the text and to construct reading strategies in the discipline of biblical studies which would reflect the points of view of their own reader-response approaches to the biblical text. Rejecting structuralism's obsession with discovering binary oppositions everywhere in the text, poststructuralism emphasized the instability of the signifier, especially in its deconstructive mode. This approach to reading texts meant that the text had no secrets to yield to the gaze of mathematically inclined readers. On the contrary, texts tended to become mirror images of the readers who assumed into their textual readings their own values as explicit modes and strategies for their reading processes. No longer were the concealed assumption of values or of the constructions of the self deemed to be adequate for all the reading operations entailed in the construction of meaning for indeterminate texts. These reading operations and the values judged to be inherent in them had to be carried out in accordance with the group values of the readers engaged in any and all reading strategies. Detailed accounts of such techniques as were being consciously employed in reading strategies were declared to be an integral and obligatory part of the task of reading the Bible. Such consciously acknowledged approaches to readers' responses to reading the biblical text helped to create a dimension of biblical studies which sought to transform the discipline from being in the (concealed) service of traditional Western cultural hegemonic values into serving newer values reflecting the theopolitical demands of various post-sixties social movements and political lobbies.

Poststructuralist approaches to the Bible not only permitted new avenues of theoretical readings to be explored, they also greatly assisted older and more reactionary theological values and practices to revamp themselves and to regroup for a concerted attack on the common enemy identified as the Enlightenment and historical-critical biblical scholarship. This principle of 'my enemy's enemy is my friend' allowed poststructuralism and biblical fundamentalism to bracket out the Enlightenment, to ward off the critical reading of the Bible and to seek to repristinate medieval approaches to biblical texts where allegory and non-rational modes of interpretation could once more flourish in biblical studies. While the historical-critical approach to reading the Bible continued to be dominant in the Academy (the universities of the West), newer ways of reading the text slowly moved in from the peripheries of scholarship to contest the middle ground (if not the high ground). As the millennium draws to a close these new approaches continue strongly to contest the territory once held securely by critical modernism. Both the fundamentalism inherent in premodern approaches to reading the Bible and in postmodernist rejections of critical rationality appear to have come together in equally trenchant dismissals of the Enlightenment project. While Western religious fundamentalism may itself be regarded as a postmodernist phenomenon, it would equally be true to say that much of what passes for postmodernist practice looks like a kind of neo-fundamentalism.[1]

Modernism, since the time of Baruch Spinoza, in reading the Hebrew Bible had dislodged from intellectual dominance certain traditional readings of the Bible which had formed a received mythology of the Bible: e.g., Moses as the author of the Pentateuch, David as author of the Psalms, single authored prophetic books, messianic predictions as the main mode of prophetic discourse and the preponderance of the miraculous in the biblical text. Postmodernist approaches to the Bible appeared to maintain this work begun under modernism, so may be deemed to have brought the modernist programme to full realization by extending it much further to its logical conclusions. At one level such postmodernism in Hebrew Bible studies might well be described as modernistic biblical studies becoming fully conscious of itself and implementing the Enlightenment project in the reading of the Bible. In so far as the new approaches to biblical historiography may be redefined as a form of New Historicism (or cultural poetics) in biblical studies, then we may read the current controversy about 'the invention of ancient Israel' as part and parcel of poststructuralist readings of the Bible. Such investigations of biblical historiography might be better defined as the search for a cultural history of the Bible or as a set of cultural materialist readings of the Bible, but I shall treat such readings here as being analogous to New Historicist approaches to the Hebrew Bible.

## NEW HISTORICISM

What new historicism does is to locate a crucial site of social contestation in the discursive realm, as the place where political and cultural dissensus and consensus are forged and re-forged. In doing so, such historicism restores literary works to their multiple historical contexts, asks how both literary and 'nonliterary' works are not only reflective but formative of their times and ours.
(Michael Bérubé, *Public Access*, p. 218)

New Historicism is essentially a turn away from theory and a movement in the direction of culture, history, politics, society and institutions as the social contexts of the production of texts. It represents what Louis Montrose has called 'a reciprocal concern with the historicity of texts and the textuality of history'.[2] By that neat chiastic phrase Montrose means 'the cultural specificity, the social embedment, of all modes of writing' (both the texts themselves and the texts which study such texts) and, acknowledging the fact that we cannot have access 'to a full and authentic past, a lived material existence, unmediated by the surviving textual traces of the society in question', we must recognize that all 'such textual histories necessarily but always incompletely constitute in their narrative and rhetorical forms the "History" to which they offer access' (following Hayden White). While there is formally no real pursuit of New Historicist approaches to texts currently operating in biblical studies, I will treat the various attempts at a cultural history of the Bible embedded in recent major works on biblical historiography as coming within the ambience of New Historicism. It seems to me that the intense interest aroused among professional biblical scholars by the controversy surrounding the newer readings of the Bible as 'history' and biblical historiography as a reflection of social activities of a period much later than normally believed to be the case by mainstream biblical scholars constitutes the beginnings of an emergent New Historicism in biblical studies.

Since the Second World War there has been a subgenre of Hebrew Bible studies devoted to the production of 'histories of ancient Israel'. This branch of biblical studies has involved paraphrasing the biblical text in conjunction with accounts of the latest archaeological discoveries as are deemed relevant to the Bible and the realignment of the biblical narrative with a historiography partly derived from other ancient Near-Eastern documents, artefacts and material remains. Following the dictates of the Enlightenment the historical, in terms of a critical retrieval of the past, was seen as the dominant element to be sought for in the biblical narratives and the historiographies constructed by these 'histories of ancient Israel' reflect a compromise between the textual narratives and modernist theories of history. Such constructions have often stayed far too close to the biblical text to be genuinely historiographical studies, so have given the impression of being a modernistic adjustment of the text and a retelling of the narrative in keeping with modern values (e.g., the exclusion of the miraculous, the modification of large numbers etc). As such they began to give way in the seventies to a more radical critique which subjected both biblical text and the archaeological material remains to severe critical analysis. That is, though the writing of such 'histories of ancient Israel' continued without abatement, but with growing sophistication, alternative voices could be heard arguing for very different ways of reading the biblical text and especially in conjunction with different readings of the archaeological remains unearthed in the Near East.

The first serious attack on the consensus of approach to the writing of such histories appeared in Thomas L. Thompson's book on the so-called patriarchs, *The Historicity of the Patriarchal Narratives: The Quest for the Historical Abraham*. This work has been continued ever since by Thompson in many more writings, especially in his *Early History of the Israelite People: From the Written and Archaeological Sources*.[3] The work of Niels Peter Lemche parallels that of Thompson, especially his books *Early Israel: Anthropological and Historical Studies on the Israelite Society Before the Monarchy* and *Ancient Israel: A New History of Israelite Society*.[4] Equally important has been the continuing work of John Van Seters, whose cumulative publications constitute a formidable body of work contributing to laying the foundations of a New Historicist approach to reading the Hebrew Bible, especially his seminal books *Abraham in History and Tradition* and *In Search of History: Historiography in the Ancient World and the Origins of Biblical History*.[5] To these large-scale works must be added the minor but important book by Philip Davies *In Search of 'Ancient Israel'*.[6] The presence of inverted commas around the phrase 'ancient Israel' underlines the fact that such a term as 'ancient Israel' is judged as representing a construction of modern biblical scholarship. Of considerable importance is Gosta Ahlström's *The History of Ancient Palestine from the Palaeolithic Period to Alexander's*

*Conquest* because it has turned attention from the focus on the biblical narrative and shifted it to the larger dimensions of the ancient territory of Palestine (a more modern name which carries the trace of the Philistines).[7] More recently Keith Whitelam has taken up these two specific aspects of the New Historicist approaches to reading the Bible and in his *The Invention of Ancient Israel: The Silencing of Palestinian History* has argued for strong connections between the activity of the construction of 'Ancient Israel' histories and the silencing of Palestinian history.[8]

In these newer 'histories of ancient Israel' or 'histories of "ancient Israel"' (following Davies) or even 'histories of Palestine' (following Ahlström and Whitelam) the biblical narratives have been read as textual productions of a period much later than normally claimed for them, even by modernist biblical scholarship. Now the Hebrew Bible begins to look more like a product from the Persian or, more especially, the Greek period than from the earlier Assyrian or Babylonian periods. Written in retrospect it is seen as having become the ideological literature of the post-imperial period and as reflecting a variety of values, including diaspora matters. Whatever status may be granted to some of the historical elements embedded in the biblical narratives themselves (a much disputed point among historians of the Bible), the overall production of the literature is now postdated by perhaps a millennium from what used to be thought to have been the case in biblical studies. This redating of the production of the literature has allowed for a serious *Ideologiekritik* (another formidable poststructuralist approach to reading the Bible) to be undertaken of biblical literature.[9] No longer inscribed as a value-free work, the Bible is now seen as the construction of a writing elite in the Persian or Greek period who represented themselves as the heirs of ancient traditions of land acquisition and of a temple guild in Jerusalem. The New Historicist approaches to the reading of the biblical literature have contributed greatly to a retuning of the historical dimensions detected in the text and to a rethinking of the literature as a reflection of the times in which it was written rather than as evidence for what is supposed to be represented within the text itself.

Questions about whether the biblical text contains any references to the world outside itself tend in postmodernist thought to be sidetracked because such referentiality is deemed irrelevant in postmodern theory. But the New Historians who have been reconstructing the history of 'ancient Israel' would not deny the possibility of such referentiality. However, they would challenge the belief in an ancient Israelite monopoly of truth in the representation of its own historiography and they would seek to correct this mistaken belief by introducing a balancing focus on what is left out of the biblical text, what is silenced by it and also on what the material remains may be said to indicate in relation to that text. New Historicist approaches to the Bible seek to redress history in favour of the silenced and repressed of (somebody else's) history, usually the wretched of the earth. For the Bible is now taken to represent a congeries of historiographical writings which isolate, exclude, repress and misrepresent as much as they may be deemed to advocate. New Historicism has as one of its aims the reinscription of the repressed and excluded, the inclusion of the excluded and the breaking of the silences which have lasted since the documents in the Bible were written and ultimately incorporated into the various collections of books we now call the Bible.[10]

Larger questions are also entailed in the approaches of these very different writers on biblical historiography. They do not form a school or even a unified approach. What they have in common is a rejection of the conventional approaches of biblical scholars to the reading of the Bible as history *simpliciter* and a fundamental questioning of the kind of historiography represented both by the writings in the Bible and by those contemporary biblical historians whose books may be regarded as the continuation of the biblical narratives by other means. But each writer has a very distinctive approach of his or her own to the issues of historiography and the Bible. For example, for Whitelam the continued search for the mythical (or constructed) 'ancient Israel', that is the quest to situate the so-called ancient Israel(ites) in history, is also a continued and sustained refusal to take Palestinian history seriously: 'Palestinian history has been silenced by an entity which in literary terms is extremely small' (Whitelam, *The Invention of Ancient Israel*, p. 220). It is for him a form of 'retrojective imperialism' which collaborates in the dispossession of the Palestinians of their own and ancient history. Current events in the Middle East where the Palestinians are oppressed and without a state of their own obviously play a strong part in shaping Whitelam's approach to reading the scholarship of biblical historiography. There is also a very strong influence of the writings of Edward Said on Whitelam's thinking, especially Said's notion of 'Orientalist discourse'.[11] But even Whitelam is not seeking to write 'a history of Palestine' as such. What he is doing in his writings is to reflect on the discursive operations involved in the continued production of 'histories of Israel' and how such activities reinscribe what is going on in the world at large today. That is one of the most characteristic features of New Historicism – it 'asks how both literary and "nonliterary" works are not only reflective but formative of their times and ours' (Bérubé, *Public Access*).

Thompson's concerns, on the other hand, while similar to some of Whitelam's, also reflect rather different interests, approaches and methods. For him the Bible, containing fragments of memory of the past, is constituted by a cumulative, collected tradition coming from the Persian period which is essentially folkloristic in its essence and which reflects a constructed entity called Israel:

> The concept of a *benei Israel*: a people and an ethnicity, bound in union and by ties of family and common descent, possessing a common past and oriented towards a common futuristic religious goal, is a reflection of no sociopolitical entity of the historical state of Israel of the Assyrian period, nor is it an entirely realistic refraction of the post-state Persian period in which the biblical tradition took its shape as a cohering self understanding of *Palestine*'s population. It rather has its origin and finds its meaning within the development of the tradition and within the utopian religious perceptions that the tradition created, rather than within the real world of the past that the tradition restructured in terms of a coherent ethnicity and religion.
>
> (Thompson, *Early History of the Israelite People*, p. 422; emphasis original)

The operative notion here is of 'ancient Israel' as an imagined community which is represented by the writers, whose work is to be found in the Bible, as having lived in an imagined past (cf. Benedict Anderson, *Imagined Communities*). Most of the writers subsumed under the New Historicist label would hardly disagree with such a broad brushstroke approach to reading the biblical narratives, but they would differ in their view of whether the Bible was the product of the Persian or of the Greek period. It would generally be recognized that part of the function of such a construction by the biblical writers would undoubtedly be 'the legitimation and justification of the present' (cf. Whitelam, *The Invention of Ancient Israel*, p. 22).

In collecting all these different writers into the single category of 'New Historicism in biblical studies' I am taking the liberty of minimizing their differences and grouping them in a way with which they themselves might well be less than happy. If New Historicism is to be understood as 'cultural poetics' (Stephen Greenblatt's preferred description), then it might be a useful practice to gather all these diverse and discrete historians together under the general rubric of 'cultural poetics in contemporary Biblical Studies'.[12] This kind of poetics (or New Historicism) takes a number of different approaches to reading both the biblical text and all the ways in which it has been read by subsequent readers. It includes a strong focus on the material conditions of the text's production and a close scrutiny of omissions, alternative explanations and treatment of other relevant material. Where poststructuralism has tended to textualize history and to treat the Bible as simply text, New Historicism retains the older focus on history characteristic of the Enlightenment. It also seeks to construct a cultural poetics of the Bible (including a poetics of biblical culture) giving due weight to history as to literature, with perhaps a favouring of history over literature. Yet both the categories of history and of literature when used in relation to the Bible are equally in need of interpretation, so the old-fashioned category of hermeneutics remains as ever the fundamentally necessary approach to any reading of the Bible (whatever the intellectual basis of that approach). New Historicism or cultural poetics is another form of that ancient practice of hermeneutics, but now practised in a (post)modern key. In many ways it is also very resistant to the wilder forms of postmodern theory with their rejection of the possibility or desirability of the critical retrieval of the past.[13]

### POSTMODERNISM

Postmodernity may be conceived of as modernity conscious of its true nature – *modernity for itself.* The most conspicuous features of the postmodern condition: institutionalized pluralism, variety, contingency and ambivalence – have been all turned out by modern society in ever increasing volumes; yet they were seen as signs of failure rather than success, as evidence of the unsufficiency of efforts so far, at a time when the institutions of modernity, faithfully replicated by the modern mentality, struggled for *universality, homogeneity, monotony* and *clarity.* The postmodern condition can be therefore described, on the one hand, as modernity emancipated from false consciousness; on the other hand, as a new type of social condition marked by the overt institutionalization of the characteristics which modernity – in its designs and managerial practices – set about to eliminate and, failing that, tried to conceal.
(Zygmunt Bauman, *Intimations of Postmodernity*, pp. 187–8; emphases original)

The study of the Bible from postmodernist points of view is in its infancy in biblical studies, with the exception of Stephen Moore's sophisticated work on postmodern readings of the Gospels and New Testament Studies.[14] Most of the postmodern approaches to the Bible which have appeared in recent years have been themselves selective combinations of poststructuralist readings driven by ideologies of gender, race and egalitarianism. The one comprehensive volume which has appeared, incorporating the Bible into a postmodernist set of approaches to reading the Bible, *The Postmodern Bible* produced by the Bible and Culture Collective, illustrates some of these ideological positions very well.[15] This book represents all the different approaches which seem to have been excluded by what is generally known as modernistic readings of the Bible. If awareness of pluralism is one of the more distinctive features ascribed to postmodernity (Bauman, *Intimations of Postmodernity*, p. 102), then this volume itself is a very good representative example of such postmodernity, dealing as it does with a wide spectrum of poststructuralist (and other) approaches. It includes chapters on reading the Bible from the points of view of reader-response, structuralist and narratological, poststructuralist, rhetorical, psychoanalytic, feminist and womanist, and ideological criticism. The book's summary chapters on this varied mixture of approaches are good exemplary expositions of the theoretical sophistication involved in postmodernist ways of reading the Bible.

It has to be admitted, however, that there are strong tendencies in the different approaches of the writers and in the overall tone of the book indicative of an authoritarian nature which suggests that the writers are making a serious bid for intellectual hegemony in the Guild of Biblical Studies in the next century.[16] As postmodernism is represented in the book it seems to have a highly authoritarian and totalizing ideology of its own (made up of so many parts race and gender and so many parts egalitarianism), in which its enemies, liberal and historical-critical study of the Bible, are denounced mercilessly and damned throughout the book. In this highly partisan account of a postmodern smorgasbord approach to reading the Bible are gathered some of the main tenets of anti-Enlightenment and anti-historical criticism. It is difficult to see how all the approaches can be said to be postmodernist as such because rhetorical criticism, feminism and psychoanalysis (apart from the inevitable postmodernist obsession with the Lacanian deformations of Freudian psychoanalysis) are not in themselves necessarily approaches which either decentre the subject or reflect postmodernist ideologies. It is possible to see how they may all be used to denigrate Enlightenment values and practices. They can apparently be marshalled against a common enemy, the modernist reading of texts from a centred subject's (akin to Kant's thinking subject) search for objective, intentioned meaning in texts. The gods of postmodernism are other than the gods of modernism when it comes to reading the Bible. The writers of *The Postmodern Bible* swear by and follow after Louis Althusser, Roland Barthes, Jonathan Culler, Jacques Derrida, Terry Eagleton, Michel Foucault, Gerard Genette, not to mention Mieke Bal, Fredric Jameson and Julia Kristeva, so little criticism of these gods will be found in these readings of postmodernist theory as applied to the Bible. Conspicuously absent from the book is the usual poststructuralist high elevation of playfulness and irony as ways of reading texts. A collection of books as varied as those in the Bible must be an open invitation to the playful and ironic readings of postmodernist theory, so *The Postmodern Bible* is a rather disappointing book as a practical exemplar of the strengths of post-modernism. In what should have been a wonderful opportunity for a cele-bration of the sheer carnivalesque of the Bible, the Collective have only succeeded in being didactic as well as deadly dull.[17]

As a book it is however an excellent introduction to postmodern theor-etical approaches to different ways of reading the Bible. Yet by its own lights *The Postmodern Bible* quickly and easily deconstructs itself: ten white, privi-leged academics denounce white academicism! Itself lacking black writers (of either gender) and womanist writers (black feminist women), the Collective discusses and advocates black and womanist readings of the Bible. It sounds very much like the false consciousness of modernism easily adopted and practised by postmodernist writers themselves. Its advocacy of popular readings of the Bible is undermined by its own lack of popular writers in the Collective and by its production of a complex, non-popular book requiring considerable intellectual sophistication on the part of its readers in order to understand it. Insisting on the open acknowledgement of individual personal political and ideological commitments the writers them-selves are able to hide their own personal and political baggage behind the anonymity afforded by being part of a collective. Anonymity and collectivity are ideal modes for concealment, masking whatever may be imagined to be going on in the publication itself. Just as women are coming more and more to the fore as public activists in the Guild of Biblical Studies, the women in the Collective are anonymized by the procedures of collective authorship. In many ways, the book illustrates the fundamental *doubleplusgood duckspeak* of postmodernism which will undoubtedly provide a field day of criticism for the many modernist biblical scholars who will welcome the opportunity to get back at the flawed praxis of postmodernism by exposing the defects of postmodernist ideologies as reading strategies in biblical studies.

A further grave defect of *The Postmodern Bible* is its lack of any sustained readings of actual biblical texts. Too much theory and far too little text render the book opaque rather than illuminating. On the other hand, some of the real strengths of poststructuralist readings of the Bible can be seen in books which make good use of postmodern theory in application to specific biblical narratives. For example, Hugh White's *Narration and Discourse in the Book of Genesis*, Hugh Pyper's *David as Reader: 2 Samuel 12: 1–15 and the Poetics of Fatherhood*, David Rutledge's *Reading Marginally: Feminism, Deconstruction and the Bible* and Yvonne Sherwood's *The Prostitute and the Prophet: Hosea's Marriage in Literary-Theoretical Perspective* all use theory in the most sophisticated ways to illuminate their readings of the Bible.[18] The application of postmodernist theories to specific biblical texts allows readers to determine for themselves how such theories help in the construction of meaning for the text and also engage readers in such interpretative praxis. The subtleties of the text are combined with perceptive uses of theory to create first-rate readings of well-known texts. Taken as examples of postmodern readings at their best, these books invite readers to share in the task of constructing meaning for the texts under scrutiny and offer readings which are immensely thought-provoking and illustrative of how theory can be consciously used by readers to explore the textualities of the Bible.

White sets out a functional theory of narrative, arising out of his own work with speech-act theory, using the work of Edmund Ortigues on semiotics and in conjunction with the writings of Eugenio Coseriu, Emile Benveniste, Julia Kristeva, Lubomir Dolezel and Michael Bakhtin. This may be far too much theory for the average Anglo-American biblical critic, but when White applies his theoretical analyses to the Genesis narratives he produces a most dynamic, integrated reading of the biblical stories in relation to narrative types which will open the eyes of readers to the immense subtleties of the textual constructions in the Bible. Pyper's reading of Nathan's parable is a splendid exposition of what is entailed in the reading process. The notion of David as reader serves to make contemporary readers aware of their own status 'as subject and object of acts of reading, of interpretation, of judgment' (Pyper, *David as Reader*, p. 215). Rutledge provides a fine introduction to the complexities of Derridean deconstructive thought and how they may be adjudged to contribute to a suitable set of strategies for a feminist hermeneutics. Applied to a reading of Genesis 2:4b–3:24 (Rutledge, *Reading Marginally*, pp. 180–214) his approach uncovers the rhetoric of sexuality in the narrative and exposes the Garden of Eden as 'the disturbed dream of patriarchy, at once representing the highest degree of patriarchal power, and troubled by a nervous awareness of its own contingent foundations' (p. 202). Sherwood's reading of Hosea 1–3 includes a semiotic analysis of the text, a deconstructive reading of it ('Derrida among the Prophets') and a feminist analysis. Her analyses are dense and brilliant, providing a thick description of the text of Hosea 1–3, of its historical reception and of its deconstructive reception in contemporary biblical scholarship:

> On one level a text from the eighth century BCE and the contemporary critical context are structured by the same hierarchy. However, like the perception of sex and violence, this hierarchy is both affirmed and deconstructed by current critical trends. The assumption that man perceives and defines his world neutrally and objectively is besieged not only by feminist criticism (the contrary views of the 'non-ego'), but by post-modern, materialist and psychoanalytic re-definitions of the thinking subject. The subject is redefined not as one who observes with detachment but as one who is *subjected* to the defining pressures of his or her environment. (Sherwood, *The Prostitute and the Prophet*, p. 322)

What all these books have in common is a sophisticated blending of modernist and postmodernist approaches to reading texts which demonstrates the great power of the newer ways of reading the Bible according to the developing canons of contemporary literary criticism. They effect a marriage between modernity and postmodernity which gives birth to the reader as active subject in the construction of meaning in the reading process. Their concerns are other than the old-fashioned ones of finding objective meanings in texts which may then be imposed on all readers in authoritarian modes. They represent modernity come to maturity in reading the Bible in postmodern ways. In many ways they also represent one of the most important features of the future of biblical studies: the rescue of the Bible from its ecclesiastical and academic captivities in hermeneutic forms which have grown sclerotic over the centuries. In my opinion they are also representative of some of the best work now being done in biblical studies.

CONCLUSION

Some forms of postmodern approach to biblical readings would insist on an egalitarian relationship between competing interpretations whereby everybody's point of view must be respected and acknowledged as equal to everybody else's point of view – every woman will do right in her own eyes (a good biblical trope).[19] Thus even a reconstituted South African apartheid-driven reading of the Bible would stand on all fours with post-Bakhtinian dialogical, post-Lacanian psychoanalytical and post-Derridean deconstructive readings. The future will be a paradise of different readings with none privileged and all equally valid: the modernistic lion will lie down with the postmodernist lamb, the Marxist bear will eat straw with the capitalist goat, the pre/postmodernist fundamentalist sheep will safely trade biblical proof-texts with the modernist wolf and the ecclesiastical dove will dwell in peace with the academic serpent. It will be a veritable paradise of (non)aggressive differing-but-equal biblical readings in which every man and every woman will sit under their own vine and fig tree undisturbed by any point of view alien to themselves. The Enlightenment rupture between medievalism and postmodernity will be healed by a return to a future of uncompetitive diverse readings. Readers of the Bible will also be able to move from community to community as and when they please, choosing the reading communities which suit their current needs best. A veritable reading utopia will have dawned and the old hierarchies and hegemonies of historical-critical biblical studies will have gone for ever.

Yet like all utopias this utopia may find itself deconstructed by advancing fundamentalistic revivalisms which will insist on empowering some readings over others.[20] The Enlightenment project may yet prove to be not as dead as many postmodernists proclaim it to be and certain modernistic values (reason, truth, universal liberation) may reassert themselves in order to sort out the sheep from the goats among the uncompeting different readings. New Historicist readings will insist on certain values accompanying all readings – slavery is wrong, oppression is to be resisted, etc. – in the construction of any cultural poetics of the Bible and contemporary readings of it.[21] Postmodernity may be conceived of as modernity becoming conscious of its true nature – *modernity for itself*[22] – and as such becoming emancipated from false consciousness. In this account of the matter not all readings will be valued as having the same worth as readings which resist oppression and domination or which seek to encourage the practising of liberty and critical reasoning. The future of biblical studies looks bright but rather confusing. While postmodernism may fail to (re)build the 'original' Tower of Babel, it may well produce the erased Bible – B̶I̶B̶L̶E. On the other hand, New Historicist and other modernistic approaches (whether postmodern or otherwise) will contribute strongly to a brave new world of kaleidoscopic biblical readings.

## Notes

1 On fundamentalism as a postmodernist phenomenon see Fredric Jameson, *Postmodernism, or, the Logic of Late Capitalism* (London and New York: Verso, 1991), pp. 376–91; Martyn Percy, *Words, Wonders and Power: Understanding Contemporary Christian Fundamentalism and Revivalism* (London: SPCK, 1996), pp. 147–55; Zygmunt Bauman, *Postmodernity and its Discontents* (Oxford: Polity Press, 1997), pp. 165–85.

2 Louis A. Montrose, 'Professing the Renaissance: The Poetics and Politics of Culture', in H. Aram Veeser (ed.), *The New Historicism* (New York and London: Routledge, 1989), p. 20.

3 Thomas L. Thompson, *The Historicity of the Patriarchal Narratives: The Quest for the Historical Abraham*, Beiheft zur *Zeitschrift für die alttestamentliche Wissenschaft*, 133 (Berlin: de Gruyter, 1974); *Early History of the Israelite People: From the Written and Archaeological Sources*, Studies in the History of the Ancient Near East 4 (Leiden: Brill, 1992).

4 Niels-Peter Lemche, *Early Israel: Anthropological and Historical Studies on the Israelite Society Before the Monarchy*, *Vetus Testamentum* Supplement 37 (Leiden: Brill, 1985); *Ancient Israel: A New History of Israelite Society*, The Biblical Seminar 5 (Sheffield: JSOT Press, 1991).

5 John Van Seters, *Abraham in History and Tradition* (New Haven and London: Yale University Press, 1975); *In Search of History: Historiography in the Ancient World and the Origins of Biblical History* (New Haven and London: Yale University Press, 1983).

6 Philip R. Davies, *In Search of 'Ancient Israel'*, *Journal for the Study of the Old Testament Supplements* 148 (Sheffield: JSOT Press, 1992; 2nd edn, 1995).

7 Gosta Ahlström, *The History of Ancient Palestine from the Palaeolithic Period to Alexander's Conquest* (Sheffield: JSOT Press, 1993).

8 Keith W. Whitelam, *The Invention of Ancient Israel: The Silencing of Palestinian History* (London and New York: Routledge, 1996).

9 There is as yet no comprehensive work devoted to analysing the Bible in terms of *Ideologiekritik*, but see David Jobling and Tina Pippin (eds.), *Ideological Criticism of Biblical Texts*, *Semeia* 59 (Atlanta, GA: Scholars Press, 1992); Tina Pippin, 'Ideology, Ideological Criticism, and the Bible', *Currents in Research: Biblical Studies* 4 (1996), pp. 51–78; and the articles on 'The Bible and Ideology' by Robert P. Carroll in the *Journal of Northwest Semitic Languages*: 'As Seeing the Invisible: Ideologies in Bible Translation', 19 (1993), pp. 79–93; 'On Representation in the Bible: An *Ideologiekritik* Approach', 20/2 (1994), pp. 1–15; 'An Infinity of Traces: On Making an Inventory of Our Ideological Holdings. An Introduction to *Ideologiekritik* in Biblical Studies', 21/2 (1995), pp. 25–43; 'Jeremiah, Intertextuality and *Ideologiekritik*', 22/1 (1996), pp. 15–34.

10 See for example the topos of the 'empty land' in the Bible as analysed by Hans M. Barstad, *The Myth of the Empty Land: A Study in the History and Archaeology*

*of Judah During the 'Exilic' Period*, Symbolae Osloenses Fasc. Suppl. XXVIII
(Oslo: Scandinavian University Press, 1996); and Robert P. Carroll, 'The Myth
of the Empty Land', in *Ideological Criticism of Biblical Texts, Semeia* 59
(Atlanta, GA: Scholars Press, 1992), pp. 79–93.

11 See Edward W. Said, *Orientalism: Western Conceptions of the Orient* (London:
Routledge & Kegan Paul, 1978; Harmondsworth: Penguin Books, 1991);
*Culture and Imperialism* (London: Chatto & Windus, 1993).

12 See the chapters on 'Towards a Poetics of Culture' and 'Resonance and Wonder'
in Stephen J. Greenblatt, *Learning to Curse: Essays in Early Modern Culture*
(New York and London: Routledge, 1990), pp. 146–83.

13 For critical discussion of and disagreement with many of the works discussed
in the section on New Historicism in biblical studies see William G. Dever,
' "Will the Real Early Israel Please Stand Up?" Archaeology and Israelite
Historiography: Part I', *Bulletin of the American Schools for Oriental Research*
297 (1995), pp. 61–80; ' "Will the Real Early Israel Please Stand Up?" Part II:
Archaeology and the Religions of Ancient Israel', *Bulletin of the American
Schools for Oriental Research* 298 (1995), pp. 37–58; Iain W. Provan,
'Ideologies, Literary and Critical: Reflections on Recent Writing on the
History of Israel', *Journal of Biblical Literature* 114 (1995), pp. 585–606 (with
critical responses from Thompson and Davies on pp. 683–705).

14 See Stephen D. Moore, *Literary Criticism and the Gospels: The Theoretical
Challenge* (New Haven and London: Yale University Press, 1989); *Mark and
Luke in Poststructuralist Perspectives* (New Haven and London: Yale University
Press, 1992); *Poststructuralism and the New Testament: Derrida and Foucault
at the Foot of the Cross* (Minneapolis: Augsburg Fortress, 1994).

15 Elizabeth A. Castelli, Stephen D. Moore, Gary A. Phillips, Regina M. Schwarz
(eds.), *The Postmodern Bible* (New Haven and London: Yale University Press,
1995).

16 Something of the authoritarian attitude of postmodernist writers may be
detected in the prescriptions laid down by Gary Phillips in his article 'Exegesis
as Critical Praxis: Reclaiming History and Text from a Postmodern
Perspective', in Gary A. Phillips (ed.), *Poststructural Criticism and the Bible:
Text/History/Discourse, Semeia* 51 (Atlanta, GA: Scholars Press, 1990),
pp. 33–6.

17 For other introductions to postmodernist approaches to the Bible see Edgar
V. McKnight, *Postmodern Use of the Bible: The Emergence of Reader-Oriented
Criticism* (Nashville: Abingdon Press, 1988); Phillips (ed.), *Poststructural
Criticism and the Bible*; David Jobling and Stephen D. Moore (eds.),
*Poststructuralism as Exegesis, Semeia* 54 (Atlanta, GA: Scholars Press, 1992).

18 Hugh C. White, *Narration and Discourse in the Book of Genesis* (Cambridge:
Cambridge University Press, 1991); Hugh S. Pyper, *David as Reader: 2 Samuel
12: 1–15 and the Poetics of Fatherhood*, Biblical Interpretation series 23
(Leiden: Brill, 1996); David Rutledge, *Reading Marginally: Feminism,
Deconstruction and the Bible*, Biblical Interpretation series 21 (Leiden: Brill,

1996); Yvonne Sherwood, *The Prostitute and the Prophet: Hosea's Marriage in Literary-Theological Perspective*, Gender, Culture, Theory 2 (Sheffield: Sheffield Academic Press, 1996).

19 The most extreme form of this point of view is to be found in the work of the structuralist critic Daniel Patte; see his *Ethics of Biblical Interpretation: A Reevaluation* (Louisville, KY: Westminster/John Knox, 1995); 'Acknowledging the Contextual Character of Male, European-American Critical Exegesis: An Androcritical Perspective', in Fernando F. Segovia and Mary Ann Tolbert (eds.), *Reading from this Place* vol. 1, *Social Location and Biblical Interpretation in the United States* (Minneapolis: Fortress Press, 1995), pp. 35–73.

20 It would require a further and different article to analyse the possible impact of fundamentalist readings of the Bible in the future. Fundamentalism as I understand it in this chapter is more than adequately analysed in Paul Boyer, *When Time Shall Be No More: Prophecy Belief in Modern American Culture* (Cambridge, MA and London: The Belknap Press of Harvard University Press, 1992); Bruce B. Lawrence, *Defenders of God: The Fundamentalist Revolt Against the Modern Age* (London and New York: I. B. Tauris, 1990); Charles B. Strozier, *Apocalypse: On the Psychology of Fundamentalism in America* (Boston: Beacon Press, 1994); and Percy, *Words, Wonder and Power*.

21 Such a necessarily critical reading of the Bible is an inevitable consequence of seeking to engage in *ethical readings* of the Bible. See the writings of Stephen Greenblatt for an exemplary practice of this kind of ethical rejection of vicious values embodied in or reflected by texts.

22 Zygmunt Bauman, *Culture as Praxis* (London: Routledge & Kegan Paul, 1973); cf. Bauman, *Intimations of Postmodernity* (London and New York: Routledge, 1992), p. 187.

## Further reading

Anderson, Benedict, *Imagined Communities: Reflections on the Origin and Spread of Nationalism*, London and New York: Verso, 1991; revised edn.

Bauman, Zygmunt, *Intimations of Postmodernity*, London and New York: Routledge, 1992.

*Postmodernity and its Discontents*, Oxford: Polity Press, 1997.

Berman, Marshall, *All That Is Solid Melts Into Air: The Experience of Modernity*, New York: Simon & Schuster, 1982; London: Verso, 1983.

Bérubé, Michael, *Public Access: Literary Theory and American Cultural Politics*, London and New York: Verso, 1994.

Carroll, Robert P., 'Clio and Canons: In Search of a Cultural Poetics of the Hebrew Bible', in Moore, *The New Historicism* (see below), pp. 300–23.

Docherty, Thomas, *After Theory*, Edinburgh: Edinburgh University Press, 1996.

Docherty, Thomas (ed.), *Postmodernism: A Reader*, New York and London: Harvester/Wheatsheaf, 1993.

Greenblatt, Stephen J., *Learning to Curse: Essays in Early Modern Culture*, New York and London: 1990.

   *Renaissance Self-Fashioning: From More to Shakespeare*, Chicago and London: University of Chicago Press, 1980.

   *Shakespearean Negotiations: The Circulation of Social Energy*, Oxford: Clarendon Press, 1988.

Harris, Marvin, *Cultural Materialism: The Struggle for a Science of Culture*, New York: Vintage Books, 1980.

Harvey, David, *The Condition of Postmodernity: An Enquiry into the Origins of Cultural Change*, Cambridge, MA and Oxford: Blackwell, 1990.

Hutcheon, Linda, *A Poetics of Postmodernism: History, Theory, Fiction*, New York and London: Routledge, 1988.

Jameson, Fredric, *Postmodernism, or, The Cultural Logic of Late Capitalism*, London and New York: Verso, 1991.

Jencks, Charles, *What is Postmodernism?*, 4th edn, London: Academy Editions, 1996.

Leitch, Vincent B., *Deconstructive Criticism: An Advanced Introduction*, London: Hutchinson, 1983.

Lyotard, Jean-François, *The Postmodern Condition: A Report on Knowledge*, Minneapolis: University of Minnesota Press, 1980.

   *Toward the Postmodern*, Atlantic Highlands, NJ: Humanities Press, 1993.

Moore, Stephen D. (ed), 'The New Historicism', *Biblicial Interpretation* 5/4 (1997).

O'Neill, John, *The Poverty of Postmodernism*, London and New York: Routledge, 1995.

Veeser, H. Aram (ed.), *The New Historicism*, New York and London: Routledge, 1989.

   *The New Historicism Reader*, New York and London: Routledge, 1994.

Waugh, Patricia (ed.), *Postmodernism: A Reader*, London: Edward Arnold, 1992.

White, Hayden, *Tropics of Discourse: Essays in Cultural Criticism*, Baltimore and London: Johns Hopkins University Press, 1978.

Zurbrugg, Nicholas, *The Parameters of Postmodernism*, London: Routledge, 1993.

# 5 Political readings of Scripture

TIM GORRINGE

It is often suggested that 'political readings' of Scripture are a recent invention, more especially of Marxist or leftist thought. That Scripture did not bear on human life together, on the 'polis', would however have sounded very strange to most Christians before the end of the eighteenth century, as a moment's reflection on the political involvement of the Byzantine and medieval Church will show.[1] Martin Luther's two-kingdom doctrine, which taught that the Church and the state occupied two quite different spheres of responsibility, and which was very much a response to his own political situation, paved the way for the privatization of religion, especially in pietism. Luther himself, however, did not hesitate to draw the most brutal political consequences from Scripture.[2] Where sixteenth- and seventeenth-century Protestantism read the whole Bible as the word of God, pietism focused on the New Testament, and the soul's relation to Jesus. The political context of the Old Testament was thereby lost to view. By 1790, in his *Reflections on the Revolution in France*, Edmund Burke is telling us that politics and the pulpit 'have little agreement', a foretaste of countless angry protests when church leaders have criticized political policies.[3] The rise of the *wissenschaftlich* approach in religion in the newly reorganized German universities at the beginning of the nineteenth century brought to biblical study the need for academic detachment. Exegesis had to stand above the political fray to be truly scientific. Max Weber's advocacy of 'disinterested science' is the apotheosis of this movement. Pietist and rationalist sources come together in the neo-Marcionitism of Adolf von Harnack, who disdained the primitive material of the Old Testament, and took from the New a simple ethical religion of the fatherhood of God and the brotherhood of man which was above politics. The Gospel, he said, proclaims a 'holy indifference' with regard to worldly problems.[4] Taken together, these very disparate factors help explain why the overtly political exegesis which appeared throughout the Christian world in the 1970s seemed so novel and why it was so often accused of 'lack of balance' and 'subjectivity'. In fact, the older tradition of 'political' reading of Scripture never died out, though the new style had very distinct roots and causes. I shall comment briefly on the ancient tradition before turning to the new.

## TRADITIONAL POLITICAL READINGS OF SCRIPTURE

A favourite Victorian hymn alludes to Elijah's encounter with Yahweh on Horeb (1 Kings 19), and pleads 'breathe through the heats of our desire . . . O still small voice of calm'. Its author, J. G. Whittier, has helped generations to forget that the 'still small voice' in question set in motion two palace revolutions and a slaughter of the ideologically unsound!

No reader of the Old Testament can miss its political content, whether in its history of kings and palace revolutions, its law codes or its prophetic critique of injustice. As Norman Cohn famously showed, apocalyptic material fired revolutionary movements from the book of Daniel onwards.[5] Daniel started life as a document of resistance to the Seleucid empire and was a key text for radical figures such as Thomas Muenzer or Gerard Winstanley. Even the wisdom literature, in the shape of the comments on wage labour in Ecclesiasticus 34, inspired Bartolomeo de las Casas' great protest against slave labour in Latin America.

Throughout the history of the Church Christians have interpreted their political situation quite directly in relation to the Old Testament story, a method Clodovis Boff calls the 'correspondence of terms'.[6] One or two examples will have to do duty for a theme which could be more or less endlessly illustrated. Eusebius, in the fourth century, hails Constantine as the 'new Solomon', and understands Constantine's great programme of church building as fulfilling Solomon's intentions in building the Temple. Cromwell justifies his massacre of Catholics in Drogheda and Wexford by appealing to the slaughter of the Amalekites in 1 Samuel 15. Simon Schama has shown how the Old Testament provided the framework within which the Dutch leaders in seventeenth-century Holland understood themselves, a tradition continued by the Boers in the Great Trek.[7] Later still their descendants used Scripture to defend apartheid. Highly ambivalent though these appeals to Scripture are I think that we can say, nevertheless, that when Nicaraguan peasants make explicit connections between their situation and that of the Gospels they are continuing a tradition which, for good or ill, runs right through Christian history.[8] Richard Bauckham is therefore right to characterize the 'political readings' of the past thirty years as 'a return to normality'.[9]

James Barr calls this traditional appeal to Scripture the 'theocratic model', as it rests on the belief that we have in Scripture a divinely revealed account of the way society ought to be governed. As he points out, for most of Christian history this involved belief that monarchy was divinely ordered, a belief which suppressed the very ambivalent feelings of the Old Testament witness towards that institution. He is further sceptical of the use of Scripture in the cause of both social reform and of liberation, a theme to which I shall return.[10]

The overt political context of the great bulk of Old Testament writing made it a natural resource for those with social and political concerns. It is often pointed out that one reason why the New Testament is, by contrast, thought to be 'non-political' is that in the first century Israel was no longer a sovereign state, and so questions of law and social and political formation are not foregrounded in the same way. True though this is, it has not deterred Christians through the ages from making a wide variety of political claims with direct reference to the New Testament. Like the book of Daniel, Revelation has had a fundamental significance for millenarian protest movements. The political significance of Revelation 18, the tremendous attack on a Rome which traffics in human souls, is quite inescapable. When contemporary commentators such as A. Boesak or C. Rowland highlight the book's political significance, therefore, they are not innovating but joining the historical mainstream. On the other side of the coin, Romans 13 and Jesus' 'Render to Caesar' (Mark 12:17 and parallels in the other Synoptic Gospels) are still invoked time and again by status quo politicians.

At this stage it is sufficient to note that the Bible has in fact consistently been used as a court of political appeal, and that it has been so used in defence of a wide variety of positions. What is it which marks off this traditional political use of Scripture from the political readings of the past thirty years? In a word, it is the difference made by the advent of sociology.

## EXEGESIS AND THE SOCIOLOGY OF KNOWLEDGE

'It is not consciousness that determines life, but life that determines consciousness.' So Karl Marx, in *The German Ideology,* written in 1845–6, but not published until 1932. It was Marx who first established that all knowledge is socially situated, and intelligible only in relation to this situation. These ideas were developed by Karl Mannheim, who coined the phrase 'the sociology of knowledge', and more recently by Jürgen Habermas.[11] The sociology of knowledge establishes that what we write, as authors, or what we understand, as readers, is profoundly influenced by the society in which we live and our place in it. Exegesis which takes account of these factors will therefore ask of the text, of the commentary and of the reader questions about the type of society they come from, their class allegiance and where they stand in relation to the conflicts of their society. These questions automatically generate a 'political' reading of Scripture, though what type of politics emerges is another matter.

To some extent the perceptions of the sociology of knowledge are in tune with the more familiar idea that the reader always brings a 'pre-understanding' to the text. Rudolf Bultmann made this point forcibly in his 1950 essay on hermeneutics.[12] As he took his ideas from Heidegger, however, and seems never to have read Mannheim, the discussion of hermeneutics remained for twenty years tied to existentialism and its highly individualistic view of life. Such perspectives were congenial to the idealism of a great deal of New Testament work. R. P. Martin's important study of the 'Christ hymn' of Philippians 2:5ff., for example, reviews countless theories but never once considers that the word 'doulos' (slave) in the passage might have had an immediate sociological relevance in Paul's context. The index, which is a compendium of theological and historical-critical theories, mentions neither slaves nor slavery![13] Exegeses informed by the sociology of knowledge develop a very different reading, understanding the hymn as advocating a society not based on domination.[14]

In asking questions about social class and social interest the sociology of knowledge generates a 'hermeneutics of suspicion' which has been profoundly important for liberation theology. As Juan Luis Segundo sets it out, our experience of reality (for example, the experience of oppression) raises questions about the dominant understanding of reality, an understanding reflected in the prevalent interpretation of Scripture. Such questions lead to a new way of reading Scripture which in turn leads to a new understanding of reality. It ought perhaps to be remarked that 'reality' here means 'social reality'. The sociology of knowledge calls into question the existence of any timeless or non-context-related metaphysic or ontology.[15]

We have seen how the issue of slavery is absent from Martin's reading of Philippians. In a more sinister way, the anti-Semitic bias of some of the contributors to the *Theologisches Wörterbuch zum Neuen Testament*, including Kittel himself, is now well established.[16] The context of the production of the *Wörterbuch* makes clear that anti-Semitism is not a harmless private prejudice but a very significant political issue. The perceptions generated by the sociology of knowledge, therefore, whilst not political in the sense of inculcating a political programme, *always situate exegesis in its political context and as such can be profoundly illuminating.*

## SOCIOLOGICAL ANALYSIS AND POLITICAL READINGS

As soon as biblical exegesis became 'scientific' the new disciplines of social anthropology, social science and sociology, all of which emerged between the late eighteenth and the mid nineteenth century, began to be applied to the interpretation of Scripture. Over the century from 1860 to 1960 many important studies contributed to our understanding of prophecy, sacral kingship, ancient law codes and tribal federations, whilst Ernst Troeltsch's work on sects began the much slower process of serious sociological study of the New Testament. This work paved the way for the full-blown sociological analyses of the past thirty years associated with Norman Gottwald, Fernando Belo, Michel Clévenot and Ched Myers.

The subtitle of Norman Gottwald's great study *The Tribes of Yahweh* – 'A sociology of liberated Israel' – makes the impact of sociology plain. Gottwald acknowledges his debt to Durkheim, Weber and Marx, as well as to scholars such as George Mendenhall who, from the perspective of social science, had anticipated the main lines of his conclusions. As in sociology in general, different approaches generate a different politics. Gerd Theissen's eclectic appeal to Talcott Parsons and Weber in his work on the New Testament produces a picture of wandering charismatics, rooted in the socio-economic conditions of first-century Palestine, to whom the radical ethic of the Synoptic Gospels is uniquely applicable.[17] The more Marxist approach of Gottwald, Belo or Myers, however, discerns an account of class struggle in Scripture, and an account of property, which still challenges our present. Thus Gottwald uses sociological tools to argue that pre-conquest Israel was, for a period of around two hundred years, an egalitarian society. In his view a society based on egalitarian relations provided the 'leading edge' in bringing Israelite Yahwism into being, which then in turn sustained egalitarian social relations.[18] Since the realization of social equality is one of the major goals of socialism it is hardly surprising that Gottwald's argument has been seized on by liberation theology.

To develop a political reading of Judges is not, perhaps, surprising. Given the Western Christian consensus of the past two hundred years, that the Gospels are 'non-political', the recent reading of Mark as a 'political gospel' represents more of a challenge. Just as Gottwald builds on the work of earlier scholars, so Myers builds on the work of Belo and Clévenot and it is his commentary on Mark, *Binding the Strong Man*, which I shall consider.[19]

Like Belo, Myers's work appeals not only to sociology but to recent literary theory, especially structuralism. He takes from the latter a critique of historical criticism as severing any direct connection between the reader and the text. For historical criticism it is the pre-textual reality (for example, 'the historical Jesus') which is the most important thing. Whilst by no means indifferent to such questions Myers wants to insist that the text is not a window on to the past but reflects a complex and rich life of its own. The insights of cultural anthropology are especially important in helping us apprehend this life. These teach us that every society has symbol systems which reproduce social power through codes of hierarchy and purity, legitimated through various types of 'mythic discourse'. In every society, Myers claims, there is a 'war of myths' and part of the task of reading a text is to see where it stands in that process (we might compare Edward Said's reading of *Mansfield Park* in *Culture and Imperialism*[20]). These insights lead us to understand Mark as the product of an early Christian discipleship community in its war of myths with the dominant social order and its political adversaries.

Sociological insights help us to get a picture of the various groups and class alignments of first-century Palestine. This analysis is well established, with the exception, perhaps, of the emphasis on forms of popular dissent. What leads to the impression that Myers offers a 'more political' reading than other commentators is that, like Gottwald, he draws more on Marx, who highlights the role of class conflict, than on Durkheim and Weber, who minimize it. Even so, the 'politics' which emerges from his reading is no left-wing caricature. He situates Mark amongst the various competing ideologies of the day. These were those of the ruling power, the *pax Romana*, an ideology which masked brutal repression; of the collaborative ruling class, the Sadducees; the reformist ideology of the Pharisees, the strongest competitor to Mark's community; and the ideology of the Essenes, who were both reformist and escapist. Myers could have mentioned here the Zealots, who were certainly attracted by the Jesus movement, and who represented what we might call a 'militarist nationalism'. By contrast Mark's Jesus (whom Mark takes as a paradigm for his community) is non-reformist, politically engaged, opposing both the Roman presence and the authority of the Jewish aristocracy. In Myers's view the Gospel emerges at that moment between the first and second sieges of Jerusalem when people are compelled to 'choose sides' and take part in the great struggle against Rome. From Mark's point of view the military means and the restorationist ends are both counte-revolutionary. What Jesus had in view was much more far-reaching – essentially a new kind of human community, not based on violence, debt or exclusion.

To illustrate how this 'political' reading works I shall look at Myers's treatment of three incidents not normally understood as 'political' at all. The first is the inaugural exorcism in Capernaum (Mark 1:21–8). This is usually read as 'demanding a religious decision' (Dennis Nineham), or 'demonstrating the authority of Jesus' (Eduard Schweizer).[21] On Myers's reading however Jesus here moves to the heart of first-century Jewish sacred space and time. The demons who cry out do so on behalf of the scribal aristocracy whose social role and power Jesus is threatening. The exorcism is an act of confrontation in the war of myths.

Secondly we can take the puzzling little story about binding the strong man, from which Myers takes the name of his book, which follows the allegation that Jesus casts out demons through Beelzebub (Mark 3:20–5). Nineham tells us that the passage shows us that it was 'sin of the most grievous kind' which brought Jesus to the cross. For Schweizer its significance is that 'man should take courage to live in the presence of the almighty God and under his promise'. For Myers these verses represent the climax of Jesus' first 'campaign', and reveal the stark polarization he has brought about. When the ruling class feels its hegemony threatened it neutralizes its critics by identifying them with the cultural arch-demon – just as critics of United States policy are invariably labelled 'communist'. Jesus intends the overthrow of the 'strong man' – the scribal establishment represented by the demon. Jesus' words about 'blasphemy against the Holy Spirit' are a way of saying that what is not pardonable is to turn real human liberation into something odious.

As a final example we can look at Myers's treatment of the story which attracted much sentimental Victorian representation – 'Suffer the children'.[22] To understand this story Myers turns to contemporary work on violence against children, which shows that children bear the brunt of violence in the family. Children are picked out by Jesus not because they are so wide-eyed and adorable, or so docile, but because they are on the extreme margins of society, really non-persons. In saying that we can only enter the kingdom as children Mark/Jesus is saying that the practice of non-violence must extend to the building blocks of human community.

How new is Myers's project? It will be clear to anyone familiar with church history that his understanding of the Gospel stands in broad continuity with the Anabaptist tradition, one of whose most cogent contemporary spokesmen, John Howard Yoder, has also written on 'the politics of Jesus'.[23] It is also true that, just as the writers of the nineteenth-century 'Lives of Jesus' saw their own faces at the bottom of the well of Christian history, so Myers's

Jesus closely resembles a member of the discipleship group of which he is a part. This should not surprise us, nor does it call his reading into question. We saw that readings according to the 'correspondence of terms' make a direct connection between Jesus' situation and their own. There are criticisms of this method to which I now turn, but it remains true that there are some situations (for example, those likely to lead to jail and death by torture for siding with the poor) which are much closer to the situation of Jesus than others (for example, working in the groves of academe). That the former situation is likely to lead to a more insightful reading of the text than the latter does not seem, to me, far-fetched.

## REINVENTING BIBLE STUDY

Twentieth-century biblical exegesis has for the most part involved a split between the reading of the congregation and that of the academy. The various forms of Bible study notes available to Christian congregations in Europe are mostly framed within the 'hermeneutics of privatism'. Their aim is to deepen devotion to the Saviour and they resolutely avoid political questions. The commentaries of the academy, on the other hand, have raised historical-critical questions which aim at the reconstruction of the text, situating it within the history of ideas, and testing its historical accuracy (was Luke a good historian?). Though their tenor is very different from devotional works they too avoid political questions. That these two approaches provide the dominant models for reading of Scripture explains why the approaches which derived from Latin American base communities seem so novel.

Base communities mushroomed throughout Latin America in the 1960s and 1970s and most included the practice of reading Scripture within the context of discussion of immediate social and political problems. Very often a priest trained in the academy was present, but he did not lead the discussion. A good deal of reflection has emerged from this practice as to how Scripture is to be interpreted. At its simplest, as represented for example in Ernesto Cardenal's *The Gospel in Solentiname*, it has assumed the 'correspondence of terms'. Realizing that this method fails to do justice to the complexities of the text Clodovis Boff has proposed replacing this simple correlation with what he calls a 'correspondence of relationships'. This begins from a recognition of the results of twentieth-century critical work, namely that the texts are the witness of faith rather than historical records, and then relates the witness of the first-century CE, or fifth-century BCE, faith community to the faith community of the present. Both are politically situated, and the assumption is that we can be stimulated to appropriate response in our situation by reflecting on the response of the earlier community. Boff appeals to Gerhard von Rad to argue that this method is true to the way Scripture itself is constituted, for the documents in our Bible are the product of a continuous creative appropriation of tradition.

Differences and similarities between this mode of Bible study and both pietist and academic forms are clear enough. Where pietist forms are intended to strengthen the soul's relation with God this asks first and foremost how the text bears on the political and social situation. Where academic forms have often been a variant of studies in ancient history this is concerned primarily about the text's contemporary significance. As Carlos Mesters puts it: 'the principal objective of reading the Bible is not to interpret the Bible but to interpret life with the help of the Bible'.[24] Where both have tended to be individualist this is necessarily an affair of the community. At the same time there are real connections. Cardenal's Bible studies are the products of a community which believes that Jesus is the incarnate, risen and ascended Lord, who encounters us both in the eucharist and in the struggle for justice. Whilst recognizing that everything is political the members of this community do not think that politics is everything. And Cardenal will often introduce material which relates to the historical background to see that exegesis does not become simply free flight. Historical work provides a control on liberation exegesis just as it does on the older patristic method of allegorizing the text.

## CAN THERE BE NON-POLITICAL EXEGESIS?

'There has never been a document of culture which was not at one and the same time a document of barbarism.' This thesis of Walter Benjamin's on the philosophy of history prompts Fredric Jameson to observe that all works of class history are 'profoundly ideological', and have a vested interest in and functional relationship to social formations based on violence and exploitation.[25] Whilst such a perception underwrites the work of Gottwald, Belo and Myers it has to be said that the vast majority of biblical scholars would not recognize it as a necessary or valid presupposition. It is, as Jameson says, a 'hard saying'. The most profound reason for rejecting the view that all that we do has a political dimension is the deeply ingrained prejudice that there is a private sphere in our lives which has nothing whatever to do with the public sphere. Some of the reasons for the growth of such a view are set out in the introduction to this chapter. We would need to add to those the growing importance of the idea of autonomy, from 1780 onwards, which is the ideological correlate of the Industrial Revolution and the advent of both the anonymous city and the anonymous workplace. In these conditions the private sphere seemed the only guarantee of the survival of precious values. The doctrine that the significance of the death of Christ is primarily the removal of my sin, and cannot have 'political' significance is a version of this.

The notion that there is an intrinsically private area to life has, nevertheless, been challenged, especially by feminism with its slogan that 'the personal is the political'.[26] This slogan formalizes the perception that our 'private' attitudes structure what we do in our life together. Perusal of pornographic magazines may take place in solitude but impacts on the way in which men in the polis, or community, treat women in the polis. It is, therefore, a political act. That the personal is the political, then, only spells out Aristotle's ancient observation that human beings are political animals, that is that they are, willy nilly, obliged to depend on others and structure a common life. This means that the Bible cannot be read in private any more than any other text because all that we do bears on our life together. Edward Said's reading of *Mansfield Park*, mentioned earlier, attempts precisely the 'restoration of the greatest cultural monuments' by 'a passionate and partisan assessment of everything that is oppressive in them', which Jameson demands. The need to recognize the link between culture and barbarism is a fundamental aspect of the hermeneutic task which applies as much to biblical study as to anything else. Phyllis Trible's *Texts of Terror* attempts such a restoration with regard to some of the most terrible texts of the Hebrew Bible.[27] 'Purely scientific', 'strictly a-political' works, descriptions which would probably be applied to most non-devotional biblical commentaries in the present century, also play their part in the reproduction of relations of power. To recognize the political dimension of all that we do is not to ask that every work of scholarship be a manifesto. It is simply to recognize, make explicit and take responsibility for our common life. To put it in the jargon of biblical scholarship, it is the fact of *koinonia* which makes our biblical work, with all else, inescapably political.

## IS SCRIPTURE POLITICALLY POLYVALENT?

'The story of Naboth', wrote Ambrose, in the middle of the fourth century, 'ancient though it may be, is of perennial application. Daily the rich and prosperous covet other people's goods, daily they endeavour to dispossess the humble, robbing the poor of their possessions . . . every day some Naboth is done to death, every day the poor are murdered.'[28] From the undoubted fact that Scripture has been used to justify all sorts of polities James Barr urges caution against claims that it supports social reform or liberation. He in fact discerns six distinct approaches to politics in Scripture, and argues that most political views which have appealed to Scripture are only partly in agreement with it, or agree with only a thin segment of it. Whilst Ambrose's rhetoric is echoed time and again throughout the Church's history, Barr objects that the prophets were not reformers but conservatives, insisting on a traditional morality. The prophets did not make practical suggestions for change in the structure of society, and the reformist idea that such change is necessary if justice is to be done is lacking in them.[29] To this charge we have to reply that social reformers such as William Cobbett or William Morris also thought they were appealing to a traditional morality, idealized in much the same way as Amos or Micah's may have been. Both contributed far more in terms of ethical critique of injustice, through the education of desire, than through proposing alternative structures. The prophets of Israel are the great teachers of such ethical critique, now widely recognized as an essential part of a radical agenda.[30]

Barr likewise maintains that liberation is not the true theme of the exodus narrative, but rather the destruction of the Egyptians and the migration to a new land. This, however, is not how Deuteronomy appears to see it, as there the memory of slavery in Egypt has a critical significance for present social policy (Deuteronomy 6:21 and often).

With the exception of Revelation it is still widely believed that the New Testament is politically quietist. Many would agree with Barr in finding that Jesus opts for political neutrality and refuses 'to align God with the partisan struggles of men'.[31] The proximity of such accounts to right-wing apologetic such as Digby Anderson's, on the one hand, and the profoundly political reading of the Synoptic Gospels in John Chrysostom's homilies on the other, puts us on our guard.[32] There is a prima facie oddity about this view given that Jesus is tried before a Roman governor and dies a death reserved for slaves or rebels, that he criticizes Herod, who had put John the Baptist to death, and that some of the letters of Paul were written from Roman jails. Paul's arrest is unlikely to have been on the grounds of civil law, and criminal charges almost certainly alleged a threat to the state. Whilst most standard work on Paul, if it thinks of his political views at all, mentions only Romans 13, and the failure to critique slavery, Walter Wink's three-volume study of the language of 'the powers' has shown that the underlying perceptions of the Pauline corpus may be far more profoundly political than is usually perceived.[33] Wink argues that this language, far from representing a primitive world view, is actually a way of talking of the interiority of political structures, created by God, and therefore good, but fallen and in need of redemption.

An old German Jesuit, who had lived through Nazism, once told me that the only political slogan to take from Scripture was 'be sober, be watchful' (1 Peter 4:7). One can sympathize. Noting the way the Bible has been used to justify reactionary policies, John Barton concludes that the danger of hearing from the Bible what we want to hear is simply too great, and he therefore prefers not to justify political systems by appeals to biblical models.[34] I would, however, wish to argue that the Bible is not simply political in the sense outlined in my second section, but that there is a *nisus* within it which takes sides with the poor against the rich, the oppressed against the oppressors, which demands justice, and which understands justice as respecting the fact that all people are made in the image of God, and that all are sisters and brothers of the Son of Man. This claim would rest on the hermeneutic significance of Jesus' story for the whole of the biblical narrative, on Jesus' commitment to the marginalized, his teaching about service and greatness, on the fact of his crucifixion by Roman power and the way the theme of service and death is interpreted by Paul in passages such as 1 Corinthians 1–3, and Philippians 2.5ff. To read the Bible in this way is not to support just one political programme, but it does on the other hand rule out a great many. Perhaps what we should learn from the conflict of political interpretations is not just caution, but more the need for an adequate hermeneutic, which takes social and ideological factors into account as well as formal ones. Of course, this is to take sides in a very long-running argument, but the need to take sides, I would argue, is also palpably clear in our text. In his contest with the Baal prophets, the prelude to his flight to Horeb, it was this that Elijah demanded!

## Notes

1  Tertullian asks rhetorically, 'What has the church to do with the "res publica"?' (*Apology* 38), but he is hardly a-political. His refusal of legitimacy to the imperial cult and to military service had profound political consequences.

2  Consider the appeals to Scripture in *Against the Robbing and Murdering Hordes of Peasants*, for instance, in *Luther's Works*, ed. H. J. Grimm, H. T. Lehmann,

H. C. Oswald and J. J. Pelikan (Minneapolis: Fortress Press, 1967), vol. XLVI, pp. 49ff. 'A prince must remember that according to Romans 13:4 he is God's minister and the servant of his wrath and that the sword has been given him to use against such people. If he does not fulfil the duties of his office by punishing some and protecting others, he commits as great a sin before God as when someone who has not been given the sword commits murder.'

3 Cf. the protests in D. Anderson (ed.), *The Kindness that Kills* (London: SPCK, 1984).

4 A. von Harnack, quoted in E. Bammel and C. F. D. Moule, *Jesus and the Politics of His Day* (Cambridge: Cambridge University Press, 1984), p. 27.

5 N. Cohn, *The Pursuit of the Millennium* (London: Secker & Warburg, 1957).

6 C. Boff, *Theology and Praxis* (Maryknoll, NY: Orbis, 1987), pp. 142f.

7 S. Schama, *The Embarrassment of Riches* (London: Fontana, 1987).

8 E. Cardenal, *The Gospel in Solentiname* (London: Search Press, 1977).

9 R. Bauckham, *The Bible in Politics: How to Read the Bible Politically* (London: SPCK, 1989), p. 1.

10 J. Barr, 'The Bible as a Political Document', in *Explorations in Theology vol 7* (London: SCM Press, 1980), p. 109.

11 K. Mannheim, *Ideology and Utopia* (London: Kegan Paul, 1936), ch. 5; J. Habermas, *Knowledge and Human Interests* (London: Heinemann, 1972).

12 R. Bultmann, 'The Problem of Hermeneutics', in S. Ogden (ed.), *New Testament and Mythology and Other Basic Writings* (London: SCM Press, 1985).

13 R. P. Martin, *Carmen Christi Philippians ii 5–11 in Recent Interpretation and in the Setting of Early Christian Worship* (Cambridge: Cambridge University Press, 1967).

14 B. Wielenga, *Biblical Perspectives on Labour* (Madurai: Tamilnadu Theological Seminary, 1982).

15 J. L. Segundo, *The Liberation of Theology* (Maryknoll, NY: Orbis, 1976), p. 9.

16 G. Kittel (ed.), *Theologisches Wörterbuch zum Neuen Testament* (Stuttgart: W. Kohlhammer, 1933–73). See the chapter on Kittel in R. Eriksen, *Theologians under Hitler* (New Haven: Yale University Press, 1985), esp. pp. 50ff. and cf. the remarks on *Wörterbuch* articles in E. P. Sanders, *Paul and Palestinian Judaism* (London: SCM Press, 1977), pp. 42n., 225ff.

17 G. Theissen, *Sociology of Early Palestinian Christianity* (Philadelphia: Fortress Press, 1977).

18 N. Gottwald, *The Tribes of Yahweh* (London: Fortress Press, 1979), p. 643.

19 C. Myers, *Binding the Strong Man* (Maryknoll, NY: Orbis, 1988).

20 E. W. Said, *Culture and Imperialism* (London: Vintage, 1994), pp. 100ff.

21 See D. Nineham, *The Gospel of St Mark* (Harmondsworth: Penguin, 1963), pp. 74f.; E. Schweizer, *The Good News According to Mark* (London: SPCK, 1970), pp. 49f.

22 See the treatment of this episode in Mrs J. Luke's hymn, 'I think, when I read that sweet story of old', and the countless illustrations in 'Children's bibles'.

23 J. Howard Yoder, *The Politics of Jesus* (Grand Rapids, MI: Eerdmans, 1972).

24  C. Mesters, 'Como se faz Teologia hoje no Brasil?', quoted in C. Rowland and M. Corner, *Liberating Exegesis* (London: SPCK, 1990), p. 39.

25  F. Jameson, *The Political Unconscious: Narrative as a Socially Symbolic Act* (London and New York: Routledge, 1989), p. 299.

26  See for example Iris Marion Young, 'Impartiality and the Civic Public' in S. Benhabib and D. Cornell (eds.), *Feminism as Critique* (Cambridge: Polity Press, 1987).

27  P. Trible, *Texts of Terror: Literary-Feminist Readings of Biblical Narratives* (Philadelphia: Fortress Press, 1984).

28  Ambrose, *On Naboth*, in P. Phan (ed.), *Message of the Fathers of the Church: Social Thought* (Wilmington, Delaware: Glazier, 1984).

29  Barr, 'The Bible as a Political Document', pp. 100f.

30  Cf. R. Kothari, 'Environment, Technology and Ethics', in J. R. and J. E. Engel (eds.), *Ethics of Environment and Development* (London: Belhaven, 1990).

31  Barr, 'The Bible as a Political Document', p. 97.

32  Cf. D. Anderson, *The Kindness that Kills*.

33  W. Wink, *Naming the Powers* (Philadelphia: Fortress Press, 1984); *Unmasking the Powers* (Philadelphia: Fortress Press, 1986); *Engaging the Powers* (Philadelphia: Fortress Press, 1992).

34  J. Barton, *What is the Bible?* (London: SPCK, 1991), p. 120.

## Further reading

Bauckham, R., *The Bible in Politics: How to Read the Bible Politically,* London: SPCK, 1989.

Gottwald, N., *The Tribes of Yahweh,* London: SCM Press, 1979.

(ed.), *The Bible and Liberation,* Maryknoll, NY: Orbis, 1983.

Myers, C., *Binding the Strong Man,* Maryknoll, NY: Orbis, 1988.

Rowland, C. and M. Corner, *Liberating Exegesis,* London: SPCK, 1990.

Wink, W., *Engaging the Powers,* Philadelphia: Fortress Press, 1992.

Yoder, J. Howard, *The Politics of Jesus,* Grand Rapids, MI: Eerdmans, 1972.

# 6 Feminist interpretation

ANN LOADES

'It might be interesting to speculate upon the probable length of a "depatriar-chalized Bible". Perhaps there would be enough salvageable material to com-prise an interesting pamphlet.'[1] Thus Mary Daly in 1973, sharply engaged with feminist interpretation in its early stages. Roughly twenty-five years later, feminist interpretation flourishes whether inside or outside the aca-demic community where there are feminists qualified and interested enough to engage in it, with some of it undertaken by Jewish and Christian writers together, focusing on women and the gender symbolism of the Hebrew Bible.[2] This chapter, however, engages with feminist Christian interpreta-tion of the Bible as a whole (with some reference to the Apocrypha). Feminist interpretation is here understood as presupposing that the Bible is still read and heard and preached as an authoritative text in communities of belief and worship. And 'authoritative' here means that by using reason, imagination, historical insight, reflection on human experience and whatever other resources we can muster, the Bible somehow mediates to us a God who enables human beings to be most fully themselves. And there's the rub, for feminists at least. Mary Daly's sharp comment has its point. For the biblical text and the uses to which it has been put have arguably not mediated to women the possibility to be most fully themselves. At this juncture, therefore, we need to consider 'feminism' before proceeding further, because it is feminism which has been and remains most profoundly concerned with the full humanity of women.

There is and can be no one thing meant by 'feminism' any more than there is one thing meant by 'Christian' or 'theology' or 'interpretation', and feminist Christian theological interpretation is inevitably as diverse as Christian theological interpretation, but with a particular 'edge' to it. A femi-nist need not, of course, be female by sex, which to some may be a matter of surprise. But a feminist will seek change for the better in terms of justice for women, and this requires detailed, unremitting attention to women's perspectives. Such attention is needed to dislodge the androcentrism which defines males and their experience as the normal or neutral standard and females and their experience as a variation on or even deviation from that norm. The 'patriarchy' of Mary Daly's quotation is simply 'father-rule', that is, the perspective of some powerful males over some other males, and over most women and children. That perspective needs to be changed in favour of one more humanly inclusive, and the shift is inextricably connected with issues of power-sharing, and hence of the basics of justice. In so far as the Bible legitimates patriarchy (and it would be hard to argue that it has nothing to do with such legitimization) feminists must necessarily engage with it.

White feminists have been brought sharply to task for presuming to speak for 'womanist'/African American, 'mujerista'/Hispanic and Far East Asian women theologians,[3] so feminist interpretation is perhaps particularly sensitive to the complexities of race and class and economic status as well as the impact of gender for interpretation. But gender relations in their biological, social and cultural complexity distinguish feminist interpretation across race and class boundaries. The fascination and difficulty of preoccupation with gender lies not simply in how human beings relate to one another, but with how such relationship affects their relationship to God, and how God may be mediated to them. Issues about justice to women and the gender symbolism used for God are entangled with one another more clearly in some examples more than others but need scrupulously careful attention at all times. And it is arguable that men as well as women suffer spiritual and other forms of damage when the symbolism is false or mistaken. Feminist interpretation is therefore at root a theological task, and some feminists become exasperated with what appear to be quite intractable texts. So Mary Daly again: 'We do not wish to be redeemed by a god, to be adopted as sons, or to have the spirit of a god's son artificially injected into our hearts, crying "father".'[4] This chapter assumes a willingness to continue to struggle, but in full consciousness of the very real difficulties to be encountered. Feminist interpretation proceeds, however, on the assumption that all stand to gain by it, not just women.

In 1973 Mary Daly's target was Phyllis Trible and we turn to her work as an example of someone whose engagement with the Bible is largely positive. It is worth noting that feminist interpretation began to flourish not simply in reaction to those, such as Mary Daly, whose feminism has taken them out of their churches, but at a time when new possibilities in interpretation were developing in any case. Feminist interpretation flowered into new life when a text could be treated as a whole literary unit, rather than dissolved into bits. And new tools were available to engage with a text. So, for instance, Phyllis

Trible's method is derived from rhetorical criticism. 'How the text speaks and what it says belong together in the discovery of what it is', she writes. The work of other feminist interpreters uses speech-act theory, or reader-response criticism, or whatever seems to be helpful from appropriate human disciplines. Phyllis Trible's method, as with some other feminist interpreters, is basically at the service of her creative imagination, employed in the hope that the biblical text will so to speak yield a usable past. Others are by no means so confident. They may well think either that such a past cannot be identified, or if it can it is of doubtful value to illuminate gender relationships and symbolism for God in the present or future of our churches and those societies still imbued with biblical values.

It is undoubtedly important to test Phyllis Trible's approach to the limits, for no one should assume in advance just what a new reading of a text may or may not yield to us. Feminists need every resource they can identify, and biblical texts may yet be found to be among those resources, though at present, few non-religious feminists would suppose anything of the kind. Since women as biblical interpreters are relative newcomers on the scene (given their very recent access to theological education) those who hope to sustain their commitment to the religious traditions which have nourished them will especially value Phyllis Trible's exegesis. *God and the Rhetoric of Sexuality*[5] is therefore one particularly constructive response to Mary Daly's insistence that the Christian tradition is irredeemably damaging to women. There can be no doubt that the use of biblical texts has sustained convictions about women's inferiority and therefore necessary subordination to men, but there may be resources in the biblical texts themselves to challenge those convictions. Critique and evaluation of Genesis chapters two and three are of much importance here.[6] In Phyllis Trible's work, male and female life originates with God. 'Dust of the earth and rib of the earth creature are but raw materials for God's creative activity' and sexual differentiation owes its origin to that creativity. The woman of the story is a 'helper', indeed, but that is a word also used of the God who creates and saves us. She 'corresponds' to the man in full companionship, and it is she who is competent to discuss theology with the serpent. The love scene that went awry in these chapters is redeemed in the love lyrics of the Song of Songs, with God as it were withdrawing as the lovers rediscover themselves. Thus Phyllis Trible finds meaning within these and other biblical texts to help regenerate renewed relationships between women and men. She and other feminist interpreters are obviously partial to certain possible meanings and emphases within the Bible, for the sake of present-day, lived reality and community. So she provides us with an example of a feminist interpreter who seeks the connections between text and the context of the interpreter, not as an afterthought as it were, but as integral to the very process of interpretation itself. And there is no attempt to conceal the influence of such an interest in relationships between women and men on the interpreter.[7] Rather, declaring one's interest is regarded as a merit in feminist interpretation.

Of special theological importance is Phyllis Trible's second chapter in which she tracks the journey of a single metaphor (womb/compassion) which highlights female/feminine related imagery for God, metaphor which is reality-depicting as much as any language for God may be. The importance of her work here can hardly be overestimated, given the extent to which the Christian tradition displays considerable unease about the association of the female/feminine with the godlike and divine. This is so notwithstanding the theological rule-of-thumb to the effect that God transcends both sex and gender. In addition, given that God is ultimately incomprehensible, it could be said that the mystery of the divine being positively demands a variety of names. Any and each of these could then act as a corrective against the tendency of any particular one to become 'fixed' in such a way as to foster idolatry. Phyllis Trible's exegesis is concerned to get us to attend to easily overlooked associations of the divine with the female/feminine. Deuteronomy 32:18, for instance, uses two metaphors for God. One is 'rock' and the other is derived from the labour pains of birth, as in the RSV translation, 'You were unmindful of the rock that begot you / and you forgot the God who gave you birth.' Yet it is the rock image which has been repeatedly used in the past. Most important is that Phyllis Trible has forced us to attend to the text of Isaiah in a new way.[8] With feminist interpretation we learn that God's 'womb-love' not only goes beyond that of a human mother whose love may fail, but that the metaphor of God as mother can be direct and explicit. Of the texts she discusses, Isaiah 42:14 is much to the point: 'Like a travailing woman I will groan, I will pant. I will gasp at the same time', which is to say that God suffers for human kind as does a woman giving birth. This is not to say that feminist interpretation does not value the language of divine Fatherhood, given its notes of intimacy and accessibility as well as of righteousness (e.g. John 17:25–6)[9] but the language of divine 'mothering' needs to be honoured also, no less than the lives of human mothers.

Feminist interpretation has also highlighted the importance of reassessing the women who appear in the biblical text, since here feminist interpretation has produced original and perceptive work on such topics as the status of women in the ancient Near East and in Israel, as well as attending to stories in which women are the major focus of attention, for good or ill. Feminist interpretation of the stories of Susanna, Judith, Esther and Ruth is one place to start.[10] Another is to imagine and think through the relationship between Sarah and Hagar[11] and to engage in sympathetic interpretation of Sarah in her relationship with her son, Isaac. Her husband, Abraham, is prepared to sacrifice their son in obedience to God, although Isaac is the child of divine promise. Carol Delaney believes the meaning of the story of the binding of Isaac to lie in the establishment of father-right, the foundation of patriarchy.[12] The story thus functions to establish the authority of God the Father, omnipresent though invisible, legitimating a patriarchal way of life, displacing the value of women as mothers. Some of the most perceptive material about Sarah, however, is to be found not in modern feminist interpretation, but in homilies from the eastern Mediterranean of the fourth to sixth centuries, and the most moving treatment of Sarah's ordeal can be found in Jewish exegesis of that time. For example, and to quote briefly: 'If only I were an eagle, or had the speed of a turtle-dove, so that I might go and behold that place where my only child, my beloved was sacrificed, that I might see the place of his ashes, and see the site of his binding, and bring back a little of his blood to be comforted by its smell.' Deeply engaged and sympathetic engagement with biblical texts is not solely the achievement of feminist interpretation in the modern age.[13]

With the story of Sarah we are on the verge of having to address yet a third of Phyllis Trible's targets of attention. Having said that her approach is fundamentally positive, that is, concerned with the Bible as mediating salvation for both women and men, it must be added that she has not shirked the horrors of some texts such as those concerned with the death of Jephthah's daughter and the unnamed concubine of Judges 19. *Texts of Terror: Literary-Feminist Readings of Biblical Narratives*[14] speaks powerfully of slavery and exile (Hagar), of rape and murder, and of the sacrificial killing of a daughter by her father. Feminist interpretation finds resonance between such texts and the experiences of women and children of our own time. Thus, for instance, the story of the rape of Tamar by Amnon (2 Samuel 13) has taken on a life of its own in the context of protest at violence against women.[15] Will God aid and abet oppressors, or simply be absent from the plight of the victims? And who is finally responsible for the possibility of such horror? Mieke Bal[16] for one has released the virgins, wives, mothers and the blessed though lethal women of the Book of Judges from the confines of 'salvation history' by being rightly hypersensitive to the power of language to construct texts themselves as instruments of violation of female bodies. What is possible in imagination is possible in action – hence the danger implicit in the texts. Isaac, for instance, at least has a name and an identity and lives. Jephthah's daughter remains nameless, and her death is brutally indicated in that her father 'did with her according to his vow which he had vowed' (Judges 11:39). Occasionally, women resist. Thus the Rizpah of 2 Samuel 3, a violated concubine, defended the slaughtered bodies of her own sons and the sons of Michal from predators until David was forced to bury them, having turned them over alive for killing to the enemies of Saul's house.

Whose interest can or could such texts possibly serve? Danna Nolan Fewell and David Gunn[17] send feminist interpreters on a hunt for the male subject who finds his identity in opposition to the alien female. They practise reading in defiance of the apparent disposition of the text, hunting for women not just with speaking parts and walk-on parts, but even for those with no parts at all but whose necessary presence is missed. They make the attempt to read Genesis to Kings as a story of women, in other words. And, crucially again for theology, they explore the extent to which as a male character, God is a manifestation of the male subject. Their point is that unless the character of God is subject to the same kind of critical scrutiny as that of the other characters in the texts, there is an aspect of reading which is being avoided, and must be undertaken. It is arguable that how God is symbolized represents certain social norms and reinvigorates them, having a return effect on male self-perception and on men's perception of women. Are we indeed left with 'a pervasive subjectivity that is constructed on the back of woman as Other'?[18] Those who want to attempt to side-step such painful theological questions for the moment may wish to follow Cheryl Exum's tactics in *Fragmented Women. Feminist (Sub)versions of Biblical Narratives*.[19] She treats the Bible as a cultural artefact and not as a religious object, as profoundly androcentric, and one in which women are often made to speak and act against their own interests. Patriarchy is found to have difficulties in justifying its subjugation of 'others' but some women learn to resist. But readers also need to learn to resist their own ways of reading the text that further violate women characters. So now it is the gender-interests of interpreters too which come under scrutiny. We need to see Bathsheba, for instance, as the victim of a rape, Delilah being threatened and bribed into doing the Philistines' work for them. Only feminist interpretation can begin to restore the dignity of women as those who can be trusted, cannot be easily manipulated, or intimidated, and who may not be viewed as so dangerous that their sexuality needs to be kept under male control. Cheryl Exum's *Plotted, Shot and Painted. Cultural Representations of Biblical Women*[20] makes another shift in evaluating gender bias in interpretation. What different claims do biblical texts make upon female and male readers, for instance, and what happens when visual images (painting, film) are added to the mix? The female body positioned as an object of male desire again impinges on our own social problems. And what are we to make of 'prophetic pornography', that is, of the texts where God appears as the subject, and the object of his sexual violence is personified Israel/Judah/Jerusalem? Even as a cultural artefact, it is impossible to avoid the recognition that certain texts raise theological problems, and this of course is in complete contrast with Phyllis Trible's positive and constructive emphasis on the importance of 'mother' metaphors for God. Ambivalent and contradictory evaluations of male–female relationships have important consequences for our theology. In principle, there is no reason why honesty about this should be an achievement of feminist interpretation, but such an achievement it seems to be.

So far, we have concentrated on 'Old Testament' texts, and it needs to be emphasized that Christian feminist interpreters need to 'read' Deborah, Miriam, Jael, Ruth, Esther (and Judith in the Apocrypha[21]) together with Jewish feminists to avoid the infection of anti-Semitism in interpretation. There is certainly no justification for seeing Jewish as distinct from Christian women pictured in negative terms, nor for supposing that the devaluation of women can be attributed to Judaism rather than to the Christian inheritance. It is the Bible as a whole which needs the kind of feminist scrutiny we have already indicated. The New Testament itself is hardly free of evidence of threatened or covert violence against women. The most obvious example is that of the woman taken in adultery (John 8:1–11) when juxtaposed and illuminated with reports of the stoning of an Iranian woman in 1990 as in Luise Schottroff's *Lydia's Impatient Sisters. A Feminist Social History of Early Christianity*.[22] We might add that the Christian tradition is replete with examples of the devaluation of women in certain ways (for instance the development of the figure of Mary of Magdala as a prostitute) such that they are vulnerable to intimidation if not actually to death-threats. A text such as the 'household code' of 1 Peter 3 has certainly been associated with physical intimidation.

Both in this book, and in *Let the Oppressed Go Free*,[23] we find in Luise Schottroff's work another emphasis in feminist interpretation, that is, attention to social history, oppressive structures and the possibility of their transformation. A transformed feminist consciousness requires attention to fundamentally important aspects of life such as the relationship between work and money, and the impact of illness on people's lives when they have absolutely no other resources than their wages. The possibility of resistance becomes central to liberation from demeaning circumstances, not least for women and children. So placing biblical texts in socio-economic context by no means relegates them to the past, but aligns them with the present in such a way as to generate severe and justifiable social criticism. What, for instance, does the 'Jesus tradition' have to offer to the working world of women who are prostitutes?[24] Out of such social criticism, however, comes Luise Schottroff's theological claim that 'revelation' can mean that God's action becomes visible in the work women do to keep life going. Her feminist interpretation yields many illuminating comments, for instance on the bleak poverty of those villages from which itinerant female and male prophets might emerge, and on the way in which the work of both slave and free is rendered invisible by being attributed to their masters. These latter may become instrumental in keeping others not only unemployed and poor, but treated as if they had brought their predicament upon themselves. Philippians 2.2–11 becomes a 'resistance' text which in its turn provokes resistance to the very text itself. As the confession of poor women and men and of female and male slaves, with whom Christ was identified, these groups of human beings may in turn be strengthened by him to co-operate in their own liberation.

Luise Schottroff also brings us close to the world of the rural household, in which the hands of women at work become visible, as they are in work on the land, in trade, textile production, fishing and street-vending. The parable of the woman searching for a lost coin has its origin in the situation of the landless, where women must provide food for themselves and their children, and for those too old to work. This they do either by their own paid work (in the course of which it takes them twice as long to earn the same amount as it would a man) or by supplementing the lamentable wages of a poverty-stricken husband. New light is thus shed on the persistence of the stubborn widow's confrontation with a judge who refused to attend to the plight of someone robbed of the economic foundation of her life. And how different does a woman's response need to be to the threat of intimidation described in Matthew 5:39–41? Painful too are the 'woes' to women in the eschatological passages of the Gospels when related to what we know of the wartime behaviour of 'freeborn' men in their time and ours. We are confronted with the ultimate defiance of a woman who slaughters her own child in protest against the marauding soldiers of her 'own' side. And one can see afresh how the poverty-stricken women prophets of the harbour-city of Corinth, for example, might well take heart from the text we know as the 'Magnificat', attributed to another poverty-stricken countrywoman.[25]

The most outstanding contribution to feminist interpretation of the New Testament, however, is undoubtedly the work of Elisabeth Schüssler-Fiorenza, first woman President of the Society of Biblical Literature. *In Memory of Her. A Feminist Theological Reconstruction of Christian Origins*[26] is a landmark in feminist interpretation. For her, revelation and authority are found in the lives of those such as poor and oppressed women whose cause God has adopted (though perhaps we need to add, so far as we know). This sounds like a clue taken from liberation theology, but is in fact a sense of 'liberation' virtually invented rather than appropriated by feminist interpreters, since liberation theology as a movement has hardly begun to focus explicitly on the plight of women, despite its preoccupation with the poor, who are predominantly female. For Elisabeth Schüssler-Fiorenza, feminist interpretation involves working from the perspective of the oppressed, who may also find strength in addressing their oppression and in resisting it – the point we have already met in Luise Schottroff's work. Women's strength and power does not simply stand over against biblical texts, but opens up ways of reading them that are creative, and which will enable readers to overcome the ambivalence of the Christian tradition towards women. Central to *In Memory of Her* is the assumption that women as church may claim Jesus and the praxis of the earliest church as a prototype of their own history, open to future transformation. The past does not lie behind us as an archetype to which we must conform, but at its best it is a prototype, even when fully recovered. Not only symbolism and metaphor for God are in principle open to reconfiguration, but inevitably, ecclesiology and ministry. Feminist interpreters attend increasingly to many possible implications of their work, not least for the sake of sustaining their own deep commitment to Christianity and the Church.

*In Memory of Her* has a remarkable introduction, by way of reconsidering the story in Mark's Gospel of the woman who in a prophetic sign-action anoints Jesus' head. In spite of Jesus' words that wherever the gospel is preached, what she had done would be told in memory of her, neither her name nor more details of her story have become gospel knowledge. Elisabeth Schüssler-Fiorenza, however, insists that the gospel cannot be proclaimed if the women disciples and what they have done are not remembered. Early Christian history needs thorough reconstruction as women's history, and the biblical text is by no means coterminous with human reality and history. She rejects, therefore, not just patriarchal violence against and subordination of women but the near-eradication of women from historical and theological consciousness. It is a tricky business to recover those whose traces have been almost erased, but she endeavours to recover from the text all the clues that may articulate women's struggles for liberation, and challenges at every possible point those who relegate women to marginal status in church and theology. Her method depends on an egalitarian vision hardly characteristic of Christianity as we have known it in experience, whatever its aspirations. In recovering the past as inclusively human history, she also helps to make clear what it is like to embody a somewhat confused and confusing partially feminist consciousness within oppressive boundaries.

Her hope is clearly that by paying attention to the movement initiated by Jesus of Nazareth and the women and men associated with him we can find resources for change to mutual acknowledgement of the full dignity and worth of all human persons. It may be, indeed, that her hope for the future leads her to find more in the early Christian movement than can justifiably be claimed. The reason for her search is that those for whom these texts are important and who cannot see them as merely 'prototypical' in the relationships they depict or in the metaphors for God they deploy use them as 'authority' for their refusal to negotiate feminist critique of the Church. It may well be that there never was a time when women were visible and vocal and authoritative in the Church, and that the changes women seek cannot be warranted by biblical texts. For Elisabeth Schüssler-Fiorenza, however, both sexes were indispensable to the early missionary activities of the 'Jesus-movement', and its attempt to make its way in a slave-owning society living by certain household codes. It is not to be denied that such codes have had, and may still have, their uses in some contexts. It is the contention of *In Memory of Her* that limitation of women's roles, despite the lived experience of some of the alternatives originally offered them, gradually restricted again what they could do in the religious as well as the social context. Faithful representation of the discipleship and apostolic leadership of women is important in encouraging women to continue in their efforts to appropriate Jesus' practice of love and service, so that they too may be seen as the image and body of Christ. It must be obvious that in this mode of feminist interpretation the biblical texts cannot be treated as alone giving us clues as to how to make sense of our world, since it is women's struggle for justice which has provoked such an attempt to reconstruct the past as is to be found in *In Memory of Her*. Feminist interpretation here recognizes authority only in that which summons women to become most fully themselves.

A very important section of *In Memory of Her* is headed 'The Sophia-God of Jesus and the discipleship of women' and it is inevitable and appropriate that feminist interpretation of the New Testament should turn its attention to Christology. The notion of 'Sophia-God' is important to express the gracious goodness in the divine by selective use of Jewish 'wisdom' theology, which arguably used elements of 'goddess' language to speak of God, and made possible Jesus' invitation to women to become his disciples. At least one recent feminist interpreter is far less confident than Elisabeth Schüssler-Fiorenza was (at any rate in 1983) about the weight to be given to the 'wisdom' traditions in a feminist interpreted biblical Christology. Judith E. McKinlay's reading of John's Gospel,[27] in line with the wisdom tradition, suggests that its 'wisdom' theme expresses not the feminine-divine, but the final stage of a very long process of the masculinization of wisdom. As with feminist interpretation of the texts of the Hebrew Bible, therefore, one needs to attend to the ways in which the feminine dimension of the divine has been overcome by its masculinization. Traces of the feminine dimension may cling to the Jesus of the Gospel, but 'wisdom' is never quite voiced with her invitations to water, food and wine, all representing the life we are urged to choose and invited to take.

By the 1990s Elisabeth Schüssler-Fiorenza had also introduced the term 'kyriarchy' (master-rule) into currency to replace 'patriarchy', with 'kyrio-centrism' meaning the framework which legitimates and is legitimated by certain social structures and systems of domination. In *Miriam's Child, Sophia's Prophet*[28] she turns her attention to Jesus' execution and the theology of the cross. Feminist interpretation of Scripture and of doctrine is deeply critical of traditions which urge the willing suffering of violence, even when such suffering is allegedly redemptive, since it always serves kyriarchal interests. Using form-criticism in the interests of feminist interpretation, she displays the extent to which Scripture theologizes and christologizes suffering and victimization, as early Christians sought to find meaning in Jesus' execution. Such early accounts employ a diversity of formulas to make sense of what had happened, and feminist christological discourse in our own time is best understood as another 'religious-political rhetorical practice', in much the same way as those early formulations. The language seeks to give value to a dehumanized non-person, and to reconstitute the dignity, agency and memory of those killed. Resurrection then means a political and real vindication of struggle for a world free of injustice. Reading with the same principle as was operative in *In Memory of Her*, it is to be assumed that women actively shaped early Christian meaning-giving unless it can be proved otherwise. It is then striking that women in particular are ascribed a leading role in the stories of Jesus' suffering, death and resurrection. Of particular importance is the future-orientated empty-tomb proclamation of Jesus as the vindicated

Resurrected one, 'ahead of us'. The Gospel attributed to 'Matthew' combines traditions of the empty tomb narrative and the legitimating claim of 'having seen the Resurrected One' with a primary place given to the women witnesses. Feminist discourses on suffering and the cross thus need to position themselves within the 'open space' of the empty tomb and the open-ended 'road to Galilee' to experience and proclaim divine and life-enhancing power.

After this rapid survey, a fitting conclusion may be to urge attention to the claim associated with feminist interpretation, that not only is it a stimulating way of reading texts, but also has great potential both for persuading us to look differently at our relationships, and also, and more importantly, to re-symbolize God. There is, however, still some considerable distance to go before it is practised as so integral to strategies of interpretation that it is no longer distinguishable as a separate genre.

## Notes

1 M. Daly, *Beyond God the Father* (Boston, MA: Beacon Press, 1973), p. 205; cf. A. Loades, 'Beyond God the Father', in A. Linzey and P. Wexler (eds.), *Fundamentalism and Tolerance* (London: Bellew, 1991).

2 E.g. C. Buchmann and C. Spiegel (eds.), *Out of the Garden* (London: Pandora, 1994).

3 E.g. M. P. Aquino (ed.), *Our Cry for Life* (Maryknoll, NY: Orbis, 1995); C. J. Sanders (ed.), *Living the Intersection* (Minneapolis: Fortress Press, 1995); H. Kinukawa, *Women and Jesus in Mark* (Maryknoll, NY: Orbis, 1994).

4 M. Daly, *Pure Lust* (London: Women's Press, 1984), p. 9.

5 *God and the Rhetoric of Sexuality* (London: SCM Press, 1978).

6 See G. Lloyd, *The Man of Reason.'Male' and 'Female' in Western Philosophy* (London: Routledge, 1984/93).

7 E.g. A. Brenner (ed.), *A Feminist Companion to Genesis* (Sheffield: Sheffield Academic Press, 1993).

8 See also 'Women and Isaiah', in J. F. A. Sawyer, *The Fifth Gospel. Isaiah in the History of Christianity* (Cambridge: Cambridge University Press, 1996); and K. P. Darr, *Isaiah's Vision and the Family of God* (Louisville, KY: Westminster/ John Knox, 1994).

9 J. Martin Soskice, 'Can a Feminist call God Father?', in A. F. Kimel (ed.), *Speaking the Christian God* (Grand Rapids, MI: Eerdmans, 1992).

10 E.g. A. Lacocque, *The Feminine Unconventional* (Minneapolis: Fortress Press, 1990).

11 K. P. Darr, *Far More Precious than Jewels* (Louisville, KY: Westminster/John Knox, 1991).

12 C. Delaney, 'The Legacy of Abraham', in M. Bal (ed.), *Anti-Covenant* (Sheffield: Sheffield Academic Press, 1989).

13 S. Brock, 'Reading Between the Lines', in L. J. Archer et al. (eds.), *Women in Ancient Societies* (London: Macmillan, 1994).

14 *Texts of Terror: Literary-Feminist Readings of Biblical Narratives* (London: SCM Press, 1984).

15 P. Cooper-White, *The Cry of Tamar* (Minneapolis: Fortress Press, 1995).

16 M. Bal, *Death and Dissymmetry* (Chicago and London: University of Chicago Press, 1988).

17 D. Nolan Fewell and D. M. Gunn, *Gender, Power and Promise* (Nashville: Abingdon Press, 1993).

18 *Ibid.*, p. 116. See also R. Weems, *Battered Love* (Minneapolis: Fortress Press, 1995).

19 *Fragmented Women, Feminist (Sub)versions of Biblical Narratives, Journal for the Study of the Old Testament Supplements* 163 (Sheffield: JSOT Press, 1993).

20 *Plotted, Shot and Painted. Cultural Representations of Biblical Women* (Sheffield: Sheffield Academic Press, 1996).

21 E.g. T. Craven, 'Tradition and Convention in the Book of Judith', in A. Loades (ed.), *Feminist Theology. A Reader* (London: SPCK, 1990/96).

22 *Lydia's Impatient Sisters. A Feminist Social History of Early Christianity* (London: SCM Press, 1995).

23 *Let the Oppressed Go Free* (Louisville, KY: Westminster/John Knox Press, 1991).

24 M. Davies, 'On Prostitution', in M. D. Carroll et al. (eds.), *The Bible in Human Society* (Sheffield: Sheffield Academic Press, 1995).

25 See also A. Clark Wire, *The Corinthian Women Prophets* (Minneapolis: Fortress Press, 1990); K. J. Torjesen, *When Women were Priests* (San Francisco: Harper San Francisco, 1993); F. M. Gillman, *Women who Knew Paul* (Collegeville, MN: Liturgical Press, 1992).

26 *In Memory of Her. A Feminist Theological Reconstruction of Christian Origins* (New York: Crossroads, 1983).

27 J. E. McKinlay, *Gendering the Host* (Sheffield: Sheffield Academic Press, 1996).

28 *Miriam's Child, Sophia's Prophet* (London: SCM Press, 1994).

## Further reading

Exum, C., *Fragmented Women. Feminist (Sub)versions of Biblical Narratives, Journal for the Study of the Old Testament Supplements* 163, Sheffield: JSOT Press, 1993.
*Plotted, Shot and Painted. Cultural Representations of Biblical Women*, Sheffield: Sheffield Academic Press, 1996.

Newsom, C. A. and S. H. Ringe (eds.), *The Woman's Bible Commentary*, London: SPCK, 1992, includes essays on each book of the Bible and the Apocrypha, and on early extra-canonical writings, and valuable bibliographies.

Schottroff, L., *Lydia's Impatient Sisters. A Feminist Social History of Early Christianity*, London: SCM Press, 1995.

*Let the Oppressed Go Free*, Louisville, K Y: Westminster/John Knox Press, 1991.

Schüssler-Fiorenza, E., *In Memory of Her. A Feminist Theological Reconstruction of Christian Origins*, New York: Crossroads, 1983.

*Miriam's Child, Sophia's Prophet*, London: SCM Press, 1994.

Schüssler-Fiorenza, E. (ed.), *Searching the Scriptures. Volume One. A Feminist Introduction*, New York: Crossroad/London: SCM Press, 1993/4) and *Searching the Scriptures. Volume Two. A Feminist Commentary*, New York: Crossroad/London: SCM Press, 1994/5).

Trible, P., *God and the Rhetoric of Sexuality*, London: SCM Press, 1978.

*Texts of Terror: Literary-Feminist Readings of Biblical Narratives*, London: SCM Press, 1984.

# 7 Biblical studies and theoretical hermeneutics

ANTHONY THISELTON

Hermeneutics entails critical reflection on the basis, nature and goals of reading, interpreting and understanding communicative acts and processes. This characteristically concerns the understanding of texts, especially biblical or literary texts, or those of another era or culture. However, it also includes reflection on the nature of understanding human actions, sign-systems, visual data, institutions, artefacts or other aspects of life. In biblical studies it applies traditionally to the interpretation of texts, but also the interweaving of language and life both within the horizon of the text and within the horizons of traditions and the modern reader.

It remains helpful to distinguish hermeneutics as critical and theoretical reflection on these processes from the actual work of interpreting and understanding as a first-order activity. Often writers speak loosely of someone's 'hermeneutic' when they discuss only how they go about the task rather than their reasons for doing so and their reflection on what is at issue in the process. The decisive foundation of theoretical hermeneutics as a modern discipline occurred with the work of Friedrich Schleiermacher over the first thirty years of the nineteenth century. All the same, scattered building blocks for modern theory emerge at regular intervals from the ancient world to the post-Reformation period up to Schleiermacher. These might be regarded as constituting the prehistory of theoretical hermeneutics, in the modern sense of the term.

## THE PRE-HISTORY OF THEORETICAL HERMENEUTICS BEFORE SCHLEIERMACHER

Plato and the Stoics debated the status of allegorical interpretations of Homer and Hesiod. But these debates belonged to an agenda which concerned issues other than the specific nature of interpretation. Similarly, Plato's discussion of artistic productions as 'copies of copies of Ideas' in *Ion* and the *Republic* x constituted part of his theory of Forms.

Aristotle, by contrast, considers the nature of 'emplotment' and the communicative processes which it generates as an aspect of hermeneutical theory in his *Poetics*. As Paul Ricoeur points out, we are indebted to Aristotle for the notion that narrative plot draws together otherwise apparently isolated actions into an action-orientated purposive 'whole' (*teleios . . . holēs*) which lends it coherence and intelligibility for the audience.[1] Equally, he is perhaps the first to formulate a theory of audience or reader effects, examining the goals and consequences of tragic plot for readers or audience. His work *On Interpretation* remains less useful for hermeneutics, since his main concern is about the logic and rhetoric of propositions. In biblical studies the significance of Aristotle's work regained recognition only with the advent of narrative theory and reader-response criticism in biblical hermeneutics around the later 1970s.

The biblical writings themselves offer many examples of interpretative processes, but few, if any, theoretical aspects. The nearest is perhaps the two-way principle in Luke that both texts illuminate the present while present circumstances may also illuminate texts (Luke 24: 27, 32), and Paul's insistence on Christology as a hermeneutic principle or key (2 Corinthians 3: 15, 16). In rabbinic traditions, the so-called seven rules of Hillel offer rough guidelines about the extensions of texts to new situations. These are hardly hermeneutical theory, but as a building block place recontextualization and intertextuality on an agenda which awaited explication.

Among the Church Fathers, perhaps only Origen (*c.* 185–254) consciously formulated a theory of hermeneutics, examining interactions between levels of meaning, and purposes of interpretation in relation to different methods and tasks.[2] For the most part, even the significant work of Irenaeus and others tended to reflect polemical situations which in part substantiate Schleiermacher's incisive diagnosis that 'hermeneutics' was usually drawn in as a court of appeal to try to validate some prior understanding, or some prior tradition of understanding, rather than to initiate understanding. It arose when problems of '*mis*understanding' occurred, rather than to explore what it might be to understand.[3] Thus the discussion about tradition and interpretation in Irenaeus arises because texts, as he saw it, became distorted and 'garbled' within the frame brought by his gnostic opponents.[4] However, he places an important theoretical issue on the agenda.

The medieval tradition expanded questions about levels of meaning and theories of signs. But the discussion took a new turn with the polemical context of the Reformation. In the face of Erasmus's hesitancy about whether biblical interpretation remained too problematic and complex to allow a basis for action, in 1525 Martin Luther asserted its 'clarity'. But this is in no way to short-cut his appreciation of problems of interpretation. Their debate partially anticipated the postmodern question of contextual relativism: can 'interpretation' ever yield firm enough ground for ethics or action outside some predetermined tradition of reading?[5] In his *Institutes* (1536–9) John Calvin endorsed the widespread patristic understanding of the Bible as the word of God, but insisted that, 'like a nurse', God accommodated revelation to the specificities of time, place and given human capacities, as God had also done in the incarnation.[6] He also called into question Melanchthon's method of interpreting the Bible by first identifying its *loci* or 'leading themes', on the ground that a running historical and contextual reading should determine first what counted as leading themes.[7] That this implies theory can be seen from Heinrich Bullinger's insistence in the same period (1538) that while contextual details (*causa, locus, occasio, tempus, instrumentum, modus*) shape our understanding of the text, our judgements about these equally depend on how we understand where the whole argument leads. Thus he offers a proto-version of the hermeneutical circle, which would be formulated by F. Ast, and refined by Schleiermacher.

William Tyndale and J. M. Chladenius provide two further examples of approaches which only later attain a theoretical role. Tyndale's treatise *Pathway into the Holy Scriptures* might count today as an exposition of speech-act theory in biblical studies before its time. Scripture, he declares, performs actions: it wounds, heals, drives to despair, liberates, commands and above all promises.[8] He is clear that this focus on action stands at the heart of the matter. In 1742 Chladenius argued that all interpretations of the Bible depend on 'viewpoint' (*Sehe-Punkt*) which leaves the interpreter to construe what cannot immediately be seen from a limited historical vantage-point.[9] In modern theory Wolfgang Iser's work rests on R. Ingarden's theory of perception, in accordance with which the reader 'fills in gaps' which are presupposed as part of an active response to the text.[10] This heralds ahead of its time the entry of reader-response theory into biblical studies, especially for reading the parables of Jesus.

## THE FOUNDING OF MODERN THEORETICAL HERMENEUTICS SCHLEIERMACHER AND DILTHEY

Friedrich Schleiermacher (1768–1834) established hermeneutics as a modern discipline in its own right. He combined a theory of language as a system with a theory of interpersonal communication as a particular process of understanding. The sophistication of his work is widely underrated. His drive towards theoretical reflection owed little or nothing to rationalism, but stemmed from his deep appreciation of the revolution brought about by Immanuel Kant's transcendental method of philosophy. Where Kant's predecessors had asked how we know or how we reason, Kant asked on what basis we know or reason, and explored the nature and boundaries of knowledge and reason. Similarly Schleiermacher considered that questions about whether this or that interpretation has validity were premature until we had examined the basis, nature and limits of human understanding, whether of a text or of another person. In 1805 and 1809–10 he sketched out a series of *Aphorisms* in hermeneutics, and produced his *Compendium* on hermeneutics in 1819. He added further notes in 1828 and 1832–3, and delivered his *Academy Addresses* on hermeneutics in 1829.

Schleiermacher criticized previous approaches for being 'entirely mechanical', as if merely to observe 'rules' guaranteed understanding.[11] This may represent a necessary condition as part of linguistic or 'grammatical' hermeneutics, but never a sufficient condition. Interpretation is an 'art'.[12] Those who had appealed to hermeneutics as a 'regional' discipline to validate some understanding supposedly reached already on some other ground failed to see that 'in interpretation it is essential that one be able to step out of one's own frame of mind into that of the author'.[13] This constitutes the interpersonal dimension, in contrast to the 'grammatical' or 'technical' axis, which Schleiermacher unfortunately termed 'the psychological', giving rise to misunderstandings which stemmed from Wilhelm Dilthey's exposition of his work.[14] Strikingly anticipating Ferdinand de Saussure a century before the latter's work, Schleiermacher argued that understanding entails a dialectical appreciation both of 'the communality of thought . . . the totality of language' (cf. Saussure's *la langue* or language-system) and 'every act of speaking . . . the speaker's thoughts' (cf. Saussure's *la parole,* as the act of speech).[15]

Very loosely, the comparative, more mechanical, more 'masculine' quality of criticism addresses issues of language and genre concerning which some so-called 'rules' may apply; but a more creative, more intuitive or suprarational 'feminine' capacity of perception is needed to recover the unique and holistic in interpersonal understanding. Neither task is 'higher'; both are essential.[16] If either appears 'higher' this arises from issues of strategy alone in how we approach a text, and the sequence of questions asked. But the process of understanding is lengthy and always subject to correction or expansion. For only 'a complete knowledge of the language' coupled with 'complete knowledge of the person' could bring the process to completion;

meanwhile 'it is necessary to move back and forth between the grammatical and psychological sides'.[17]

It has often been mistakenly assumed that Schleiermacher collapses the task into exploring mental processes of intention, or commits the so-called genetic fallacy of equating meaning with origins. But, as I have argued elsewhere, like Dilthey and the later Ludwig Wittgenstein and John Searle, he sees the currency of meaning as grounded in public life. Hence he insists on the importance of 'New Testament authors in their time and place'.[18] 'Each text was addressed to specific people.'[19] But the task does not end with identifying historical specificity. The task is 'to understand the text at first as well as, and then even better than, its author ... The task is infinite.'[20] Here Schleiermacher takes up his well-known notion of 'the hermeneutical circle': 'Each part can be understood only out of the whole to which it belongs, and vice versa ... Only in the case of insignificant texts are we satisfied with what we understand on first reading.'[21] For subsequent readings correct and refine the prior agenda of questions, or 'pre-understanding' (*Vorverständnis*) which we bring to the text in order to acquire a deeper understanding of it. The interpreter may even come 'to transform himself'.[22] The text in this respect produces 'effects'.[23]

Schleiermacher's intellectual successor in hermeneutics was Wilhelm Dilthey (1833–1911). In Dilthey the theoretical aspect becomes still more clearly pronounced. He aimed to formulate a universal theory of human understanding, based on a critique of historical reason as profound and influential as Kant's critiques of pure reason and of practical reason. In the light of the debates which followed Hegel's formulations concerning historical reason, Dilthey placed 'life' (*Leben*) and 'lived experience' (*Erlebnis*) at the centre, where Locke, Hume and Kant had spoken of sensations, ideas or concepts. Hermeneutics, as against rationalist, empiricist or critical theories of knowledge, Dilthey urged, restored blood to the veins of the human subject.[24] Interactive historical understanding becomes objectified in institutions, and invites the enquirers to pay attention equally to the general and the particular, to the universal and the unique. Here 'understanding' (*Verstehen*) differs decisively from 'knowledge' and especially from 'explanation'. In his *Einleitung in die Geisteswissenschaften* (1883) Dilthey made this contrast foundational for the different methods of the natural sciences (*Naturwissenschaften*) and 'human' sciences (*Geisteswissenschaften*).

In his incisive work *Understanding and Explanation*, Karl-Otto Apel traces this 'E–V' controversy, as he terms it (i.e. *Erklärung*, explanation, vs. *Verstehen*, understanding) from Dilthey and Max Weber through

Wittgenstein, Peter Winch and G. H. von Wright, to Hans-Georg Gadamer and Jürgen Habermas.[25] The contrast remains fundamental for Emilio Betti, is developed and modified by Habermas and Ricoeur, and is anathema to Gadamer. I have suggested elsewhere that it bears some relation to the use of Dilthey in Rudolf Bultmann's hermeneutics of the New Testament, where it encourages his dualism between history, law, myth and descriptive report (*Erklärung*) and faith, gospel, kerygma and personal address (*Verstehen*), although Martin Heidegger and neo-Kantian philosophy also widen this dualism.[26] Dilthey argued that the *Verstehen* of interpersonal relations between an I and a thou can become objectified through social institutions and historical habituation. On this basis a 'science' of human studies may be founded on the hermeneutical category of understanding. In his essay on hermeneutics of 1900 Dilthey writes: 'Our actions always presuppose understanding of other people ... empathy with the mental life of others. Indeed philology and history rest on the assumption that the understanding (*Verstehen*) of the unique can be made objective ... Only by comparing myself with others and becoming conscious of how I differ from them can I experience my own individuality.'[27]

Dilthey's hermeneutics contain weaknesses as well as certain strengths, as indeed remains the case also with Schleiermacher. These will begin to emerge in the next section.

### IS HERMENEUTICS A THEORETICAL DISCIPLINE?
### BETTI, BULTMANN OR GADAMER?

Hans-Georg Gadamer (b. 1900) for many years Professor of Philosophy at Heidelberg and a former pupil of Heidegger, has received wide recognition as perhaps the most influential hermeneutical theorist of the twentieth century. His *magnum opus*, *Truth and Method*, first appeared in German in 1960 (revised English translation based on fifth German edition, 1989).[28] But Gadamer *opposes* 'method' to truth. The whole notion of 'method', he believes, stems from following the rationalism of Descartes, rather than the older, more historical, tradition of Vico and others, and reached its climax in the Enlightenment glorification of the sciences as methods of 'mastering' truth.[29] This merely transposed 'truth' into a passive object, shaped and construed, as Kant perceived, by prior categorizations which the human subject imposed upon it. Thereby it reductively distorted truth. To substitute *technē* for the cumulative wisdom of communities and traditions on which truth had made some impact was to turn the project of understanding upside down.[30] Following his teacher, Heidegger, he urged that the subject-matter of truth must address the human subject on its own terms, not on terms laid down in advance by the enquirer. Hence hermeneutics has in its goal not the formulation of methodological theory, in Dilthey's sense, but the 'coming-to-speech' of the subject-matter of truth (*das Zur-Sprache-Kommen der Sache selbst*).[31]

Does this mean that, after all, Gadamer does not expound a theory of hermeneutics, or even that he is hostile to theory? He does indeed attack theory if by 'theory' we mean the kind of methodological foundation which Dilthey attempted to construct, and which is represented in the twentieth century more rigorously by Emilio Betti. At the same time, he expresses profound respect for Betti's work. He agrees with Betti that, as he expressed it as recently as 1991, hermeneutics concerns 'an Other ... to whom we are bound in the reciprocation of language and life'.[32]

Emilio Betti (1890–1968) founded an Institute of Hermeneutics in Rome in 1955, and in the same year produced his massive *Teoria generale della interpretazione*, of which a German version, *Allgemeine Auslegungslehre der Geisteswissenschaften*, appeared in 1967.[33] His thesis that hermeneutics provides the theoretical methodology for all of the humanities and social sciences finds expression in the title of his work *Die Hermeneutik als allgemeine Methodik der Geisteswissenschaften* (1962).[34] Since Betti's major work predated that of Gadamer, his main target is Heidegger, but in subsequent dialogue Betti accuses Gadamer of collapsing hermeneutics into a phenomenology that can offer no objective criteria for 'valid' interpretation, while Gadamer replies that he describes 'what is' rather than some prior notion of what ought to be or should be.[35]

In America E. D. Hirsch presses Betti's case against Gadamer.[36] But Betti remains more careful and rigorous than Hirsch in avoiding reducing hermeneutics to *techné*. Betti sees hermeneutics more broadly and deeply as the general or universal foundation for all human studies, not least because, since he shares with Schleiermacher the view that processes of understanding are virtually infinite and always corrigible, hermeneutics calls for patience, tolerance, reciprocity and 'listening' to the Other. Above all, it nurtures respect for the otherness of the Other. Betti and Gadamer are at one in questioning the centrality of the self as that which 'knows' other selves only on its own terms, rather than on the terms of the Other.

Rudolf Bultmann (1884–1976) has achieved an enormous influence in biblical studies, and, like Betti, has engaged in dialogue with Dilthey and with Heidegger. But his own hermeneutical theory betrays a supreme paradox.

As an heir to radical nineteenth-century Lutheranism, to Kierkegaard's emphasis on the will, and to Wilhelm Herrmann's antipathy to doctrine, Bultmann's exposition of the net impact of the Christian kerygma is voluntarist, existential and profoundly anti-theoretical, even anti-intellectual if not anti-rational. Yet he employs a complex network of theory drawn from neo-Kantianism, from Dilthey and R. P. Collingwood, and from Hans Jonas and Heidegger, his colleagues at Marburg, to serve as a basis for his anti-theoretical interpretation of the New Testament.[37] Faith is sheer venture. Hence on one side Bultmann engages in the work of historical reconstruction, notably in his early work *The History of the Synoptic Tradition*. Yet faith does not depend on the reliability of historical reports: 'I calmly let the Fires burn ... "Christ after the flesh" is no concern of ours. How things looked in the heart of Jesus I do not know and do not want to know.'[38] Strictly, for Bultmann historical reconstruction offers only a phenomenology of the faith-responses of early communities (apart from the bare 'fact' of Jesus). But this is not kerygma; it is not the goal of 'understanding' in the sense of hermeneutical engagement with the New Testament texts.

Bultmann agrees with Schleiermacher and Dilthey that 'Exegesis is a work of personal art (*der persönlichen Kunst*) ... intensified by a thorough-going communion with the author.'[39] Hence 'the "most subjective" [*subjectivste*] interpretation is the "most objective" [*objectivste*], that is, only those who are stirred by the question of their own existence [*Existenz*] can hear the claim which the text makes'.[40] But the 'claim' and 'address' of the kerygma are wrapped up in 'mythological' clothing: texts appear to describe or to report supernatural occurrences when their intended function is not descriptive but existential. He writes: 'Myth should be interpreted not cosmologically but anthropologically, or better still existentially.'[41] In a further essay he explains:

> The restatement of mythology is a requirement of faith itself. For faith needs to be emancipated from its association with every world-view expressed in objective terms ... Our radical attempt to demythologise the New Testament is in fact a perfect parallel to St Paul's and Luther's doctrine of justification by faith alone ... It destroys every false security ... security can be found only by abandoning all security.[42]

Bultmann's theory of hermeneutics does often assist the interpreter in coming to terms with 'the point' of descriptive language which may serve some further purpose. For example, language about creation and the last judgement functions not primarily to satisfy curiosity by describing past or future events as such, but to call readers to responsibility as creaturely stewards of the earth who are accountable for their attitudes and actions. But such language cannot be translated solely into existential address comprehensively and without remainder, as if the descriptive aspects were merely a strategy without content. Indeed Bultmann operates with a remarkably simplistic philosophy of language, as if all communication were *either* descriptive *or* expressive *or* voluntarist-existential. The tradition of speech-act theory from J. L. Austin to John Searle suggests that directive, self-involving language often presupposes that certain states of affairs are the case; while work from the later Wittgenstein to Jacques Derrida underlines that language operates at various levels often simultaneously.

Gadamer offers a much more profound and influential account of hermeneutics. But can it be called a theory? We have noted that he replies to Betti, 'Fundamentally I am *not proposing a method*; I am describing *what is the case*.'[43] But is phenomenology (for example in Edmund Husserl) not a theory, or description (for example, in the later Wittgenstein) not a method of approach? Gadamer's major point, like that of Wittgenstein, is that only as part of the very process of understanding can we tell in each case, and not in advance, what counts as an act or process of understanding. Gadamer stands in the tradition of Hegel and of Heidegger, and traces what he regards as the mixed success of Romanticist hermeneutics from Schleiermacher through Dilthey as it rightly disestablished the drive of Enlightenment rationalism to 'master' truth by 'method', but failed to subject the consciousness of the individual interpreter to a sufficiently radical critique. Tracing the most positive aspects of hermeneutics from Johann Gustav Droysen and Dilthey through Graf Yorck and Heidegger to his own work, he comments as recently as 1991: 'Subjectivity and self-consciousness ... lost their primacy. Now instead, there is an Other.'[44]

The models of play, art and celebration clarify what is central for Gadamer. He writes, 'Play does not have its being in the player's consciousness or attitude, but on the contrary play draws him into its dominion ... The player experiences the game as a reality that surpasses him.'[45] A game would not be a game if every player followed the same 'correct' routine of identical moves, with a predictable and identical outcome on each occasion.[46] What counts as 'a correct presentation' (*Darstellung*) of a theatrical play or recreational game is 'highly flexible and relative'.[47] Hence in a festival 'its *celebration* [is] *sui generis* ... A festival exists only in being celebrated', and what is appropriate depends on its time and place within an expanding tradition.[48] One of his most reliable commentators, Joel C. Weinsheimer, succinctly comments: 'There is such freedom that no game is ever played twice identically, and for all this variety it is still the one game.'[49]

In biblical studies Gadamer's work has at the very least shaken to its foundations 'the hermeneutics of innocence' of traditional Enlightenment thought. It provides the theoretical and philosophical groundwork for the view expressed by Robert Morgan and John Barton that what count as criteria in interpretation depend, among other things, on the goal proposed for this or that process of interpretation.[50] It has also succeeded in showing the importance of the history of text-reception, as worked out, for example, by Gadamer's pupil Hans Jauss.[51] In the New Testament hermeneutics of Ernst Fuchs, Gadamer's work provides a theoretical basis for his notion of a 'projected world' in parable and narrative.[52] Within this 'world', as in Heidegger's 'worldhood' and in Gadamer's 'game' or art, eventful actualizations may operate at a pre-conscious level in such a way as to lead to transformations of attitude which run deeper than 'didactic' concepts. In America this perspective of Fuchs and Gadamer had been explored in New Testament studies by Robert W. Funk.[53]

### THE CLIMAX OF MULTIDISCIPLINARY THEORY
### RICOEUR ON DECEPTION AND CREATIVE UNDERSTANDING

In an interview in the *Frankfurter Allgemeine* in October 1989, Gadamer insisted that his early work on dialectic in Plato held even more importance for him than his *Truth and Method*.[54] The open-endedness of question and conversation, he explained, alone avoided the possibility of manipulation, which assertions encouraged. Political propaganda and deceptive, manipulative ways of 'imposing one's beliefs' upon another, or the Other, represent another dimension of the 'mastery' imposed by 'method' in science. Robert Sullivan shows how this antipathy to propaganda was bound up with Gadamer's suspicion of the Nazi regime.[55]

Paul Ricoeur (b. 1913) has formulated a sophisticated theory of hermeneutics which addresses, on one side, the need for suspicion and the problem of deception and manipulation, and on the other side a programme for the creative retrieval of understanding, especially on the basis of projected narrative-worlds and the creative opening of new 'possibility'. His work remains directly relevant to biblical studies, although he writes as a multi-disciplinary philosopher for whom the Bible is a source of faith but not a major part of his professional concerns.

Ricoeur presses numerous disciplines into the service of hermeneutical theory: theories of the will and action; phenomenology, psychoanalysis, structuralism and semiotics; and linguistics and theories of metaphor, symbol and narrative. His greatest genius, however, is to share with Gadamer the task of dethroning the self as the centre of the stage from Descartes to later modernity, while resisting the postmodern reduction of so decentring the self that it becomes a mere amalgam of imposed role-performances rather than an active, responsible, accountable agent whose life has purpose, continuity and destiny. This emerges in his splendid climactic work *Oneself as Another* (French edition 1990, English edition 1992).[56]

Ricoeur's interest in a hermeneutic of the self began with work under his teacher Gabriel Marcel, for whom selves were never mere statistics or case-numbers, but named persons with existential identity. During the war years Ricoeur became a prisoner in Germany, and there engaged closely with the work of Karl Jaspers, Husserl and Heidegger. In his earliest phase of writing, his work on the human will and experiences of alienation found expression in his writings *Fallible Man* and *The Symbolism of Evil* (French edition, 1960; English edition, 1967). Ricoeur notes that this work constantly brought to his attention 'double-meaning' expressions, in which evil or guilt might be expressed as stain, blot, burden, bondage or estrangement. He writes, 'To interpret is to understand a double meaning.'[57] Hence, 'I had to introduce a hermeneutical dimension into reflective thought.'[58]

Since persons are fallible and all capable of self-deception as well as of deceiving others, *suspicion* is demanded to understand double-meanings. Here Ricoeur appeals positively to the 'three great masters of suspicion', namely Karl Marx, Friedrich Nietzsche and Sigmund Freud. Nietzsche, for example 'interpreted' the text 'the salvation of the soul' as disguised code for 'the world revolves round me'.[59] The truth-claim 'God forgiveth him that repenteth' is for Nietzsche a disguised power-claim: 'forgiveth him that submitteth himself to the priest'.[60] Ricoeur, however, finds the most constructive model of suspicion in Freud's interpretation of dreams. Freud believed that in the dream-as-dreamed ('dream-content' or 'dream-account') the self disguises wishes which may be too painful for the conscious mind to accept and face. Hence when one level of meaning is repressed, what is recounted to the psychoanalyst is a distorted, 'scrambled' version, involving displacement, condensation and other protective strategies.[61] Psychoanalytical hermeneutics comes into play because 'the subject is never the subject one thinks it is'.[62]

Ricoeur does not accept Freud's mechanistic, causal world view, which he shows goes hand in hand with Freud's use of causal or economic metaphors. Nevertheless, like Dilthey and Apel and contrary to Gadamer, he recognizes the place of 'explanation' alongside 'understanding'. The former provides 'a hermeneutic of suspicion'; the latter, 'a hermeneutic of retrieval'. Hence in a very important succinct summary of his central concern, he observes: 'Hermeneutics seem to me to be animated by this double motivation: willingness to suspect, willingness to listen.'[63] Ricoeur speaks of faith in this context. Idols must be destroyed, but this may generate 'faith that has undergone criticism, postcritical faith . . . a second naïveté'.[64]

This has direct relevance to biblical studies. The axis of suspicion encourages *Ideologiekritik* of the text and suspicion concerning the vested interests of the interpreter and the interpreter's community-traditions. What subtexts lie beneath both the biblical text and the interpreter's goals, methods and conclusions? We begin to travel the road of social and ideological critique of 'interest' explored further by Habermas, as well as issues of manipulation and power exposed by Michel Foucault and others.

Nevertheless Ricoeur's most brilliant work stands on the side of retrieval and creative understanding. In particular, he sees symbol as giving rise to thought, especially at the level of word; metaphor interactively creates understanding at the level of sentence or statement; narrative projects a 'world' which belongs to a stable frame of temporal continuity in which disparate elements acquire coherence and intelligibility through 'plot'. His superb exposition of narrative plot comes especially in his three-volume *Time and Narrative*. The self discovers temporal continuity and coherence in the emplotment of narrative, where, as in Aristotle, isolated or seemingly random actions achieve coherence as part of a single, larger, action, and the discontinuities of time, to which Augustine drew attention, assume a medium of 'human' time in which memory (past), attention (present) and hope (future) offer not the abstract intelligibility of logic, but the temporal logic of purposive life.[65] 'The dynamic of emplotment is to me the key to the relation between time and narrative.'[66]

Ricoeur has a special interest in Job. In Job 42:1–6 divine transcendence and hiddenness cannot be transcribed by speech; nevertheless Job also yields the wonder that God does *speak*, speaking not *about* Job, but *to* Job.[67] Alongside the narrative and wisdom modes, which Ricoeur especially considers as worthy of wider hermeneutical attention, the prophetic address from God to humankind (whether or not in indirect terms) operates with the hymnic mode of human address to God (especially in the Psalms) and the familiar prescriptive mode of texts of law or spiritual direction. No single revelatory mode and no single model of hermeneutics can be allowed to eclipse the resources of the others.

Ricoeur's hermeneutics have to this extent encouraged the hermeneutical pluralism of goals and models which characterize the post-Gadamerian period. But it remains clear from *Time and Narrative* and *Oneself as Another* that Ricoeur does not wish hermeneutics to collapse into a diversity that loses its overall coherence and sense of direction. He resists the postmodern turn of Roland Barthes and Jacques Derrida, even if he appreciates their concerns in the context of intellectual life in the Paris of the late 1960s and 1970s, and shares some of them. The greatness of Gadamer and especially Ricoeur lies in their capacity to address the distrust and suspicions of postmodern contextualism while insisting that life and truth also offer much more.

## RETROSPECT AND PROSPECT: FOUR SELECTIVE ASSESSMENTS

(1) Our discussion has underlined, first, the need for a multi-disciplinary approach to hermeneutics, as exemplified, but not exemplified exhaustively, in Ricoeur. Schleiermacher rightly saw that hermeneutics could not perform a creative and genuinely critical function if it remained a service discipline for particular traditions of theology. But his bold and valid attempt to establish the subject as an 'art of thinking' based on a transcendental critique nevertheless lacked adequate resources for sufficient self-criticism. He fell prey to Kantian notions of the centrality of the human subject, and shared too many Romanticist assumptions about the priority of experience over texts or doctrines as residues from creative experience. Gadamer, even if perhaps too ruthlessly, exposes these weaknesses. By contrast, Ricoeur draws on so many diverse critical disciplines as to remain aware of the limitations and biases of each.

(2) As against Gadamer and postmodern approaches, the work of Paul Ricoeur shows that it is possible to appreciate a wide plurality of hermeneutical approaches without subscribing to a pluralism of world views. Thus his use of Freud's psychoanalytic of suspicion in no way carries with it an endorsement of his mechanistic world view. Ricoeur points out that Freud's very drawing of metaphors from economics and physical science predisposes him towards such a world view, which Ricoeur rejects as inadequate and ill-founded. Recently Francis Watson has rightly warned us that the strenuous efforts of hermeneutical theorists to expose the inadequacy of merely causal explanations of life and texts has failed to shift the prejudices of those biblical scholars who regard secular pluralism as value-free and Christian theology as value-laden.[68] Theology, he rightly insists, cannot be excluded from biblical interpretation. Watson's appreciation of

postmodernity makes his warnings and appeal all the more convincing.[69] To destroy idols and to learn to listen does not mean to disengage from theology. In another work I have argued that the very opposite is the case.[70]

(3) We have not had space to explore in this discussion the potential of speech-act theory for biblical interpretation. Some explanations remain shallow and disappointing, but others hold out the promise of new advances. J. G. du Plessis explores speech-act theory with reference to G. N. Leech's pragmatics; Dietmar Neufeld approaches 1 John on this basis; I have attempted to show some implications of speech-act theory for New Testament Christology.[71] More remains to be explored in this area. It offers not only a convincing approach to language, but also coheres closely, as Tyndale urged, with the functions, effects and presuppositions of biblical texts.

(4) Lack of space necessitated our omitting a full discussion of Jürgen Habermas (b. 1929). In his early work Habermas explored the role of 'interests', broadly in the sense of vested interests, as one determining factor for what is deemed to count as knowledge or understanding in given social contexts.[72] In dialogue with Gadamer and Ricoeur in the 1970s he rejects a positivist or supposedly value-neutral view of social science.[73]

The struggle against manipulative interpretation has become probably the most urgent project of hermeneutics, as the mood of postmodernity, even if not its substance, invades cultures, institutions, politics, society, religions and churches. We note how in religious traditions, smaller groups break off from mainline churches initially to experience new freedom and a greater sense of corporate self-identity. But rapidly the new freedoms become routinized into new institutional constraints and power-structures. Domination and authoritarianism on the part of a new leadership become self-sustaining because all the criteria for biblical interpretation and expected life-styles have become internal to the group. The biblical writings come to be used manipulatively to validate the new power structures. The same phenomenon occurs in other parts of society. If, with Ricoeur, we have to turn to 'masters of suspicion', the work, but not the world view, of Nietzsche, Foucault and Derrida may play a part in the struggle against manipulative interpretation.[74] Habermas rightly places these issues on the agenda, even if we cannot subscribe to his proposals as a whole. The issue of manipulation becomes even more central for hermeneutics with the rise of liberation theologies, feminist hermeneutics and postmodern approaches to texts. But these are discussed elsewhere in this volume.

## Notes

1 Aristotle, *Poetics* (Oxford: Oxford University Press, 1968), 50b, pp. 23–4. See further Paul Ricoeur, *Time and Narrative*, 3 vols. (Chicago and London: Chicago University Press, 1984–8), vol. I, pp. 31–51.

2 Origen, *de Principiis* IV: 1.

3 Friedrich Schleiermacher, *Hermeneutics: The Handwritten Manuscripts,* ed. H. Kimmerle (Missoula: Scholars Press and American Academy of Religion, 1977), p. 49 (Aphorism 49), and more especially pp. 110–13.

4 Irenaeus, *Adversus Haereses* I: 8:1; cf 8:1–5 and II: 28:1–3.

5 Martin Luther, *On the Bondage of the Will* (Edinburgh: T. & T. Clark, 1957), pp. 66–7, 71, 125–9; and Desiderius Erasmus, *The Praise of Folly* (Chicago: Pickard, 1946), p. 84; cf. the discussions in Richard H. Popkin, *The History of Scepticism from Erasmus to Spinoza* (Berkeley: University of California Press, 1979), pp. 1–17; F. Beisser, *Claritas Scripturae bei Martin Luther* (Göttingen: Vandenhoeck & Ruprecht, 1966); and Anthony C. Thiselton, *New Horizons in Hermeneutics: the Theory and Practice of Transforming Biblical Reading* (London: HarperCollins and Grand Rapids, MI: Zondervan, 1992), pp. 179–90.

6 John Calvin, *Institutes of the Christian Religion*, 2 vols. (Edinburgh: T. & T. Clark, 1957), vol. I: 13:1.

7 *Ibid.*, vol. III: 17:14 and vol. IV: 16:13; cf. especially T. H. L. Parker, *Calvin's New Testament Commentaries* (London: SCM Press, 1971), pp. 32–4; and on H. Bullinger, pp. 38–40.

8 William Tyndale, 'Pathway into the Holy Scriptures', in *Doctrinal Treatises and Introductions to Different Portions of the Holy Scriptures* (Cambridge: Parker Society edn, 1848), esp. pp. 3–13.

9 J. M. Chladenius, *Einleitung zur richtigen Auslegung vernünftiger Reden und Schriften* (rpt. Düsseldorf: Stern, 1969 (1742)), section 194.

10 Wolfgang Iser, *The Act of Reading: a Theory of Aesthetic Response* (Baltimore and London: Johns Hopkins University Press, 1978 and 1980).

11 Schleiermacher, *Hermeneutics*, p. 175; cf. p. 49 (Aphorism 49), and pp. 176–95, on F. Wolf.

12 *Ibid.*, 176.

13 *Ibid.*, p. 42 (Aphorism 8). On the lack of 'general hermeneutics', cf. p. 95.

14 *Ibid.*, pp. 99 and 103. The misunderstanding is corrected by H. Kimmerle both in his 'Foreword' (pp. 19–40) and in his 'Hermeneutical Theory on Ontological Hermeneutics', *Journal for Theology and the Church: 4, History and Hermeneutic* (Tübingen: Mohr and New York: Harper & Row, 1967), pp. 107–21; and also in Thiselton, *New Horizons in Hermeneutics*, pp. 223–5 and 558–61; cf. also pp. 104–36.

15 Schleiermacher, *Hermeneutics*, p. 97.

16 *Ibid.*, p. 99.

17 *Ibid.*, p. 100.

18 *Ibid.*, p. 104; cf. Thiselton, *New Horizons in Hermeneutics*, pp. 223–5 and pp. 558–61.

19 Schleiermacher, *Hermeneutics*, p. 107.

20 *Ibid.*, p. 112.

21 *Ibid.*, p. 113; cf. also p. 148, and especially pp. 195–6 in the *Second Academy Address*.

22 *Ibid.*, p. 150.

23 *Ibid.*, p. 151.

24 Wilhelm Dilthey, *Gesammelte Schriften*, 12 vols. (Leipzig and Berlin: Teubner, 1962), vol v, p. 4; cf. vol. i, pp. xvii and 217. Dilthey's key essay of 1900, 'The Development of Hermeneutics', is available in English in H. P. Rickman (ed.), *Dilthey: Selected Writings* (Cambridge: Cambridge University Press, 1976), pp. 246–63, and also in David Klemm (ed.), *Hermeneutical Inquiry, vol. i, The Interpretation of Texts* (Atlanta: Scholars Press, 1986), pp. 93–106.

25 Karl-Otto Apel, *Understanding and Explanation. A Transcendental-Pragmatic Perspective* (Cambridge, MA and London: MIT Press, 1984), esp. pp. 1–82 and 243–50, but throughout.

26 Bultmann's dualisms and their relation to Dilthey find some discussion in Anthony C. Thiselton, *The Two Horizons: New Testament Hermeneutics and Philosophical Description with Special Reference to Heidegger, Bultmann, Gadamer and Wittgenstein* (Exeter and Carlisle: Paternoster Press and Grand Rapids, MI: Eerdmans, 1980), pp. 205–92, esp. pp. 212–18, 234–40 and 245–51.

27 Wilhelm Dilthey, 'The Development of Hermeneutics', in Rickman, *Dilthey*, p. 246 and Klemm, *Hermeneutical Inquiry*, p. 93.

28 Hans-Georg Gadamer, *Truth and Method* (2nd rev. edn from 5th German edn, London: Sheed & Ward, 1989). (An earlier 1975 English translation is from the 2nd German edn of 1965.)

29 *Ibid.*, pp. xxi–xxxviii, 3–34 and 277–307 (1975 edn pp. xi–xxvi, 5–33, and 245–74).

30 *Ibid.*, pp. 307–41 (1975 edn pp. 274–305).

31 *Ibid.*, p. 379 (1975 edn p. 341); *German Wahrheit und Methode* (2nd edn, Mohr: Tübingen, 1965), p. 360; cf. p. 379, and see whole section pp. 362–79 and 389–405 (1975 edn 325–41 and 357–66).

32 Hans-Georg Gadamer, 'Foreword' to Jean Grondin, *Introduction to Philosophical Hermeneutics* (New Haven and London: Yale University Press, 1994), (German, 1991).

33 Emilio Betti, *Teoria generale della interpretazione*, 2 vols. (Milan: Giuffrè, 1955; new edn with additional MS notes, 1990); Germ edn, *Allgemeine Auslegungslehre der Geisteswissenschaften* (Tübingen: Mohr, 1967).

34 Emilio Betti, *Die Hermeneutik als allgemeine Methodik der Geisteswissenschaften* (Tübingen: Mohr, 1962).

35 Gadamer's response appears in 'Supplement i' to the 2nd – 5th edns of *Truth and Method* (esp. pp. 510–17; 2nd Germ edn, pp. 482–8) and the 'Afterword' of the 1989 edn, pp. 554–9.

36 E. D. Hirsch Jr, *Validity in Interpretation* (New Haven and London: Yale University Press, 1967) and *The Aims of Interpretation* (Chicago: Chicago University Press, 1976), esp. pp. 1–13 and 17–49.

37 Expounded in detail in Thiselton, *The Two Horizons*, pp. 205–92.

38 Rudolf Bultmann, *Faith and Understanding,* vol. i, (London: SCM Press, 1969), p. 132.

39 Rudolf Bultmann, *Essays Philosophical and Theological* (London: SCM Press, 1955), p. 238; German *Glauben und Verstehen*, 4 vols. (Tübingen: Mohr, 1964–5), vol. ii, p. 215.

40 *Ibid.*, p. 256; German edn, p. 230.

41 Rudolf Bultmann's programmatic essay in Hans-Werner Bartsch (ed.), *Kerygma and Myth*, 2 vols. (London: SPCK, 1964 and 1962), vol. i, p. 10.

42 *Ibid.*, pp. 210–11.

43 Gadamer, *Truth and Method*, p. 512 (his italics); (1975 edn, p. 465; German edn, p. 183).

44 Gadamer 'Foreword' to J. Grondin, *Introduction to Philosophical Hermeneutics*, p. x, in comparison with *Truth and Method* pp. 212–18 (Droysen), pp. 218–42 (Dilthey), pp. 242–54 (Yorck), pp. 254–64 (Heidegger) and pp. 265–379 (the central part of his work).

45 Gadamer, *Truth and Method*, p. 109.

46 *Ibid.*, p. 118.

47 *Ibid.*, p. 119.

48 *Ibid.*, pp. 123–4.

49 Joel C. Weinsheimer, *Gadamer's Hermeneutics* (New Haven and London: Yale University Press, 1985), p. 104.

50 Robert Morgan (with John Barton), *Biblical Interpretation* (Oxford: Oxford University Press, 1988), pp. 5–15 (esp. p. 8), 167–200 (esp. pp. 184–9) and 267–96 (esp. p. 287).

51 Hans R. Jauss, *Toward an Aesthetic of Reception* (Minneapolis: University of Minnesota Press 1982). Cf. also Robert C. Holub, *Reception Theory. A Critical Introduction* (London and New York: Methuen, 1984).

52 Ernst Fuchs, *Hermeneutik* (4th edn, Tübingen: Mohr, 1970); *Studies of the Historical Jesus* (London: SCM Press, 1964); 'The New Testament and the Hermeneutical Problem', in J. M. Robinson and J. B. Cobb, Jr (eds.), *New Frontiers in Theology: ii, The New Hermeneutic* (New York: Harper & Row, 1964), pp. 111–45.

53 Robert W. Funk, *Language, Hermeneutic and Word of God* (New York: Harper & Row, 1966).

54 Gadamer's interview is translated as 'Gadamer on Gadamer', in Hugh J. Silverman (ed.), *Gadamer and Hermeneutics* (New York and London: Routledge, 1991), pp. 13–19. See also Hans-Georg Gadamer, *Dialogue and Dialectic. Eight Studies on Plato* (New Haven: Yale University Press, 1980).

55 Robert R. Sullivan, *Political Hermeneutics. The Early Thinking of Hans-Georg*

*Gadamer* (University Park: Pennsylvania State University Press, 1989), esp.
pp. 171–81.

56 Paul Ricoeur, *Oneself as Another* (Chicago: University of Chicago Press, 1992).

57 Paul Ricoeur, *Freud and Philosophy. An Essay in Interpretation* (New Haven and
London: Yale University Press, 1970), p. 8.

58 Paul Ricoeur, *The Rule of Metaphor. Multidisciplinary Studies of the Creation
of Meaning in Language* (London: Routledge & Kegan Paul, 1978), p. 317.

59 Friedrich Nietzsche, *Complete Works*, 18 vols. (London: Allen & Unwin,
1909–13), vol. xvi, *The Antichrist*, p. 186, aphorism 43.

60 *Ibid.*, p. 161, aphorism 26.

61 Ricoeur, *Freud and Philosophy*, p. 93.

62 *Ibid.*, p. 420.

63 *Ibid.*, p. 27.

64 *Ibid.*, p. 28.

65 Ricoeur, *Time and Narrative*, vol. i, pp. 5–51.

66 *Ibid.*, p. 53.

67 Paul Ricoeur, *The Conflict of Interpretations* (Evanston, IL: Northwestern
University Press, 1974), p. 461, and *Essays on Biblical Interpretation* (London:
SPCK, 1981), pp. 86–9.

68 Francis Watson, *Text, Church and World. Biblical Interpretation in Theological
Perspective* (Edinburgh: T. & T. Clark, 1994), pp. 1–14.

69 *Ibid.*, pp. 79–154.

70 Anthony C. Thiselton, *Interpreting God and the Postmodern Self. On Meaning,
Manipulation and Promise* (Edinburgh: T. & T. Clark and Grand Rapids, MI:
Eerdmans, 1995).

71 J. G. du Plessis, 'Speech-Act Theory: Speech-Act Theory and New Testament
Interpretation with Special Reference to G. N. Leech's Pragmatic Principles',
in P. J. Hartin and J. H. Petzer (eds.), *Text and Interpretation. New Approaches in
the Criticism of the New Testament* (Leiden: Brill, 1991), pp. 129–42; Dietmar
Neufeld, *Reconceiving Texts as Speech Acts. An Analysis of 1 John*, Biblical
Interpretation series, 7 (Leiden: Brill, 1994); and Thiselton, *New Horizons in
Hermeneutics*, pp. 283–307, and 'Luke's Christology, Speech-Act Theory, and
the Problem of Dualism in Christology after Kant', in Joel B. Green and M.
Turner (eds.), *Jesus of Nazareth. Lord and Christ* (Carlisle: Paternoster Press
and Grand Rapids, MI: Eerdmans, 1994), pp. 453–72.

72 J. Habermas, *Knowledge and Human Interests* (Boston: Beacon Press, 1971;
2nd edn, London: Heinemann, 1978).

73 J. Habermas, *Zur Logik der Sozialwissenschaften* (5th edn, Frankfurt:
Suhrkamp, 1982); and *Legitimation Crisis* (Boston: Beacon Press, 1975).

74 Cf. Thiselton, *Interpreting God and the Postmodern Self*, pp. 3–45 and 121–64.

## Further reading

Gadamer, Hans-Georg, *Truth and Method*, 2nd English edn, London: Sheed and Ward, 1989, rpt. 1991.

Jeanrond, Werner, *Theological Hermeneutics*, London: Macmillan, 1991.

Mueller-Vollmer, Kurt (ed.), *The Hermeneutics Reader*, Oxford: Blackwell, 1986.

Ricoeur, Paul, *Essays on Biblical Interpretation*, London: SPCK, 1981.

*Time and Narrative*, 3 vols., Chicago and London: Chicago University Press, 1984–8.

Thiselton, Anthony C., *The Two Horizons*, Exeter: Paternoster and Grand Rapids, MI: Eerdmans, 1980.

*New Horizons in Hermeneutics*, London: HarperCollins, 1992, rpt. Carlisle: Paternoster, 1995.

Watson, Francis, *Text, Church and World*, Edinburgh: T. & T. Clark, 1994.

# 8 The Bible and Christian theology

ROBERT MORGAN

The character and contents of the Bible have shaped the ways in which it has been interpreted. They have not, however, exercised total control. The different aims and interests of its readers have also been influential, and this chapter will consider the most far-reaching of these. The terms of our title could be reversed to 'Christian theology and the Bible', indicating that the primary focus will be on the subjects who read, not the object that is read. The Bible has never of itself given birth to theology. Even its most heavily theological parts contribute to the ongoing task of Christian theology only by being interpreted in quite particular ways. Christians seek to understand their faith in part through their thoughtful engagement with the biblical texts. What they are doing needs explanation as much as the texts that they are reading. This Companion introduces to a wider audience not only the Bible but some of those who interpret it.

Biblical interpretation has generally been dominated by religious interests. Not all these, however, are theological. That category embraces different levels of sophistication, but properly refers to the intellectual process of articulating a religious belief and practice by relating an authoritative religious tradition to contemporary knowledge and experience, and vice versa.

The importance of this theology for some believers arises from their instinct that the authenticity of their religious position depends in some way on its truth. Arguments about the truth of the Bible have seldom done justice to the elusive quality of religious truth, but they represent a sound instinct, and one which has stimulated rigorous historical and linguistic analysis as well as theological reflection. The latter does not depend on biblical scholarship and some of it may look naive to biblical specialists, but its restless enquiry as to the truth of the gospel distinguishes it from other religious uses of these texts. These less rigorous uses of Scripture are more pervasive. The Bible has over centuries projected a world and underwritten a view of human life for millions whose knowledge of it has been highly selective and largely derivative. Even today the Bible still echoes powerfully in common prayer and liturgy, and faintly in the wider culture, for many who scarcely understand more than what is necessary to absorb from selected passages the religious and moral instruction, motivation and sanctions that guide Christian faith and life.

More than that is intended by 'theology'. The word has undergone shifts in meaning as the disciplined reflection on religious faith has waxed and waned in Western culture. From a 'talk of God or the gods' originally associated with ancient Greek religion and myth its credit rose in Christian discourse to refer to a rational talk of God closely related to philosophy. In a world where the Bible was assumed to contain and bear witness to divine revelation, but human reason also thought capable of making some true judgements about God and the world, this led to a distinction between 'natural' and 'revealed' theology. That broke down in the modern world as talk of God was squeezed out of non-religious contexts and restricted to religious discourse, normally that of some specific tradition. This restriction has not destroyed its public character. It is still based on experience available to all, and still aims to make true assertions by relating its tradition to the present state of knowledge. However, this specificity does demand separate treatments of the Bible in Judaism and in Christian theology, even though the Hebrew Bible is Scripture in both religions. Abstracting from the particulars of Christianity and Judaism would lose what is theologically most important in each. The restriction of what follows to *Christian* theology is demanded by limitations of space and competence, but is also intended to express respect for the integrity of Judaism which has too often been misrepresented by interpreters more familiar with Christianity.

The dependence of Christian theology on the alleged revelation of God in Jesus Christ is the key to its close relationship to the Bible and explains why this relationship is different in the case of the Old Testament and the New. The latter contains the primary witnesses to the founding events of Christianity, but these were interpreted as the decisive revelation of God only through an already existing religious faith and tradition, rooted in a scripture. What the followers of Jesus came to call the Old Testament identifies their God as God of Abraham, Isaac and Jacob. They say that when read aright (i.e. in a Christian way) it points to the fulfilment of God's saving work in Christ. Their selective reading of these scriptures often criticizes parts of that witness as no longer appropriate to the time of fulfilment, but the whole Hebrew Bible (and initially its Greek translation and expansion) were retained as inspired Scripture and have remained indispensable religious tradition for Christians as for Jews. The New Testament witness to the life, death and resurrection of Jesus as the decisive eschatological revelation of God is also indispensable religious tradition and was soon accepted as equally inspired Scripture. As witness to the fulfilment it became the measure of earlier prophecy; both testaments, read in a Christian theological relationship, became the measure or canon (rule) of subsequent developments.

It is this indispensability of the biblical witness as a whole to the knowledge of God in Christ which has led believers to speak of the Bible as itself revelation, or 'word of God'. This metaphor, encouraged by prophetic oracles introduced by the formula, 'Thus says the Lord', has in turn generated the misunderstanding of the Bible as divine oracles, and theology as a deduction of doctrinal truths from revealed data. But that was never an accurate representation of Christian theological appeals to Scripture. Those who thought in such terms were themselves working within the context of the Church's faith, clarifying their belief with the help of Scripture, but never deriving their own faith-statements from the Bible alone or direct. The sixteenth-century Protestant Reformers' 'sola scriptura' was momentous, but only a momentous proposal about the right ordering of authorities. The witness of Scripture was not to be suppressed by subsequent tradition, especially not by the contemporary magisterium, or teaching office of the Catholic Church. Clearly not, because the Fathers had themselves intended only to interpret Scripture, and the conciliar definitions had marked out the direction of Christian scriptural interpretation. Even the contemporary magisterium was supposed to be continuing the witness of Scripture, not overriding it. Popes and bishops who contradicted the theologically clear witness of Scripture were to be criticized and if necessary repudiated.

Both the Christian scriptures and Christian theology function in an ecclesial context where they are read as bearing witness to the revelation of God in Christ. The two terms of our title thus presuppose that third term. The claim to revelation lies behind both the derivative products and determines their relationship to one another. The different ways in which the revelation of God in Christ has been understood have resulted in different perceptions of the Bible in Christian theology, but this larger context of Christian faith-responses to the revelation of God in Christ is the key to the use of the Bible in theology. Unreflective direct transference of biblical language into contemporary Christian discourse is sometimes powerful and sometimes banal, but it is never *theology*, unless it illuminates for faith the revelation to which Christian theological interpreters presuppose that the Bible bears witness. This is what Karl Barth called *Sachexegese*.

Critical theology also preserves the modern theologian's freedom to disagree in the name of the gospel with the letter of Scripture. This is what Rudolf Bultmann called *Sachkritik*. That dialectic between Scripture and the gospel, in which Scripture is necessary for the mediation of revelation but is not itself identified with revelation (except in a derivative sense) is apparent throughout the history of theological interpretation of the Bible. Successive interpretations of Scripture are designed to understand the Christian message better and to persuade its hearers or readers to appropriate it in their lives. They preserve the Church's sense that the ultimate subject of Scripture is beyond all human history and calculation, and at the same time draw on whatever literary or historical methods and insights are currently available. These instruments, drawn from the contemporary intellectual milieu, may subvert previously treasured theological convictions. Traditional readings of Scripture are, after all, tradition not revelation.

The dependence of both the Bible and theology upon a prior revelation of God, and the denial that theology consists simply in deductions from the Bible, can be confirmed by recalling that Christian theology antedated the Christian Bible. The beginnings of Christian theology can be traced within the New Testament to a period before it was described as either 'Christian' or 'theology'. Those who first confessed the crucified and risen Jesus Messiah and Lord remained Jews. They interpreted their experience of Jesus during his ministry and after his death in the language of his own and their own Jewish scriptures and other Jewish traditions. However rudimentary, their choice of confessional language itself required theological thought. The powerful rhetoric of Paul's letters goes further, including moral argument and some critical theological reflection and argument in defence of his missionary practice. Paul's refusal to impose the marks of Jewish identity on Gentiles separated his Gentile mission from the synagogue. If the Lord Jesus was decisive for their relationship to God, the Torah was not, however much of it they nevertheless observed.

Paul constructed from his Bible, notably from the story of Abraham and passages from the prophets and psalms, an argument in support of what on the basis of his missionary experience he thought was right. This form of theological persuasion remains paradigmatic even today, when methods of exegesis and assumptions about the Bible have changed. A generation after Paul other messianic Jews were expelled from the synagogue, partly on account of their christological belief. The Johannine community responded by drawing the boundaries even more sharply, developing theological convictions that were repugnant to Jewish sensibilities. Sharing the same scripture could not prevent divisions when a new principle of interpretation emerged among those who acknowledged Jesus as Messiah, Lord and Son of God. A disruption of fellowship and division of religious community followed. Those whose worship of God was now decisively reshaped by their experience of Jesus and the Spirit in Christian communities read their Jewish scriptures afresh. They read the law and especially the prophets and psalms in new ways in the light of a perceived fulfilment. However valuable for moral instruction, and necessary for theological construction many of the traditions in their God-given scriptures remained, neither the Hebrew Bible nor its Greek translation and enlargement were now the decisive factors in their new covenantal relationship to God. Memories of Jesus, inter-pretations of his death and celebration of his vindication became more important to them, and some treasured apostolic instruction provided resources for their Christian life and thought.

By the end of the first century Paul's epistles were being collected and one or more Gospels being read. New writings were being composed which would jostle with Paul and the four Gospels for recognition as Christian Scripture alongside the Septuagint. The formation of a New Testament was a slow process, not complete until the fourth century, but the main lines were clear by the time of Irenaeus (*c.*180). This Catholic canon took shape as the second-century Church excluded as heretical unacceptable versions of its religion, based partly on strange interpretations of Paul and John, which assimilated the gospel to oriental syncretism. These 'gnostic' systems drove a wedge between the creation of the world by a Demiurge, and salvation by knowledge or 'gnosis' revealed by a divine envoy or revealer. More danger-ous because religiously powerful was Marcion's equally dualistic and non-Jewish selective reading of Paul, and his formation around 140 A D of a small New Testament canon consisting of a Gospel of Luke and collection of ten Pauline epistles, both severely edited by major excisions.

In the struggle with these heresies most of the New Testament canon was accepted, and this then defined the broad parameters of Catholic ortho-doxy. It was itself a product of respect for tradition, ecclesiastical use and theological discrimination. When later theology found its sources and norms in Scripture it acknowledged not an alien rule but a pattern of faith which was already guiding its interpretation of the gospel. The old and new scriptures were already being read in ecclesial contexts and so interpreted in the light of that sense of what already constituted Christian faith and life. In response to challenges judged incompatible with the ancient scriptures and apostolic tradition, this rule of faith was made explicit. Most decisively, the authority to define and defend the pattern of Christian truth devolved upon an episcopal leadership authenticated by its standing in an apostolic succession and able to provide a visible focus for unity more stable and lasting than the philosophical schools of Valentinus and Basilides, or the charismatic enthusiasm of the Montanist schism. The dangerously ambiguous writings of Paul and John were made safe in the Catholic and apostolic framework, best exemplified by Luke–Acts, and by being placed alongside the more ecclesiastical Pastoral, Johannine and other Catholic epistles.

However incomplete, the Christian Bible as a theological achievement and hermeneutical programme is visible in the great work of Irenaeus, *Against Heresies*. The theological effect of combining the Jewish scriptures with an emerging New Testament was to contradict all gnostic heresies by representing the unity of creation and redemption in the biblical history of salvation. Those parts of the Old Testament found embarrassing or no longer relevant in this time of fulfilment could be allegorized and the whole Scripture retained by the church. As in Luke's theology, the essential components of Christian belief were articulated in a narrative account of God's gracious and saving plan from the creation, through Israel's history to Christ, and on into the time of the Church, until the end. This pattern was summarized in the Old Roman Creed, the chief ancestor of the so-called Apostles' Creed, another broadly Lucan document.

The biblical theology of Irenaeus was neither a speculative engagement with the philosophical ideas of the day nor an attempt to answer rational objections and defend the truth of Christian belief. The first task was to reaffirm, against the speculative gnostic systems of the day, the fundamental shape of the Christian system of symbols, based on a Scripture interpreted along the lines of the rule of faith. The beginnings of a more philosophical theology were already apparent in the Logos Christology of the second-century Apologists, especially Justin Martyr, a convert from Platonism who addressed his political and intellectual 'defences' of Christianity to the ruling elite in Rome. The early third-century successors of these Apologists, Clement of Alexandria, and Tertullian the father of Latin theology, made better use of the New Testament, but it took the genius of Origen to synthesize the Bible, Greek philosophy and mystical spirituality, and give to Greek theology its distinctive character. Subsequent patristic, medieval, humanist and even some contemporary theology and biblical interpretation are foreshadowed here. And the greater part of this first truly systematic theologian's writing (most of it now lost) consisted in biblical exposition. He drew the essentials of his saving 'knowledge' from the Bible, and some of the inconsistencies in his philosophical theology can be explained as the result of this fidelity to Scripture.

The allegorical interpretation which Origen, like Philo the Alexandrian Jew, applied to the Bible appears subjective and wholly arbitrary to anyone schooled in a more historical approach to texts. However, it offered the Christian Platonist a method by which the Spirit-inspired interpreter might penetrate to the spiritual meaning of Scripture, and Origen combined it with a critical exegesis which would be borrowed and imitated in Greek and Latin for centuries. Even his allegorical method invites reassessment in a generation that is abandoning the fantasy of coming to a knowledge of God by critical historical study and is open to the possibilities of more imaginative readings of religious texts.

Not only the liturgical, devotional and moral life of the Church, but also its theology, have always been sustained by biblical exposition. The decisive debates of Greek patristic theology did not hinge on the biblical texts marshalled by opposing schools, but they were fuelled by a determination to do justice to the biblical witness as a whole. The word *homoousion* by which the Nicene fathers excluded the subordinationism of Arius is not biblical, and the reservations felt about it on that score are an indicator of normal expectations. In *De Synodis*, therefore, Athanasius is at pains to argue that the term is true to the sense of Scripture. The main theological question addressed by the Greek theologians was how to speak religiously of Christ without endangering Judaeo-Christian monotheism. When the experience of salvation in the Church and sacrament was thought to demand the confession of his full divinity, that was considered not a novelty but a clarification with the conceptual tools available in Greek philosophy, of what had always been believed everywhere by all orthodox Christians. It led to a trinitarian doctrine of God adumbrated by the New Testament triadic formulae in Matthew 28:19, and 2 Corinthians 13:10, and looser formulations such as 2 Corinthians 1:18–22, 1 Peter 1:3–12. It was then hard to think of Jesus as divine without falling into docetism; this danger was also addressed and his true humanity reaffirmed. These parameters of orthodox theology were discussed in several theological proposals, fixed in the classical dogmatic formulae, and are summarized in the Church's doctrines of the Trinity and Incarnation. They correspond to the belief of all the New Testament witnesses that in having to do with the crucified and risen Lord Jesus they were having to do with God.

Later theology thought itself bound to this central religious conviction by means of the dogmatic formulae which defined the shape of orthodoxy.

When reality was understood in terms of Greek philosophy, it was not possible to speak of the reality of God without drawing on this language, nor of Jesus as himself the decisive saving revelation of God without these formulae. An age and culture which generally believed that God could be known by reason thought that its philosophical language could epitomize Christian belief in a way that would be true to the biblical witness and could guide subsequent Christian interpretation of the Bible.

Western theology adopted and developed the Greek achievement but made its own distinctive elaborations on the human condition and salvation. Augustine's readings of St Paul proved a potent brew. His Catholic (anti-Donatist) understanding of the Church and his Pauline (anti-Pelagian) theology of grace informed medieval views of salvation through the sacraments, and his doctrine of predestination (drawn especially from Romans 9) was revived by the sixteenth-century Reformers. Paul and Augustine stand behind all subsequent arguments about justification and fed most theories of atonement from Anselm and Abelard into seventeenth-century Protestant scholasticism and beyond. Through Augustine even social and political thought in the West has owed much to what the inspired apostle was thought to have intended.

With Anselm and later medieval scholasticism a new style of university theology based on the use of Aristotelian dialectic replaced the older monastic reflection on Scripture. But St Thomas Aquinas and others were friars and masters of the 'sacred page' before they were makers of systematic theology, and the liturgical reading of Scripture continued to inform their thinking and provide the raw material of their theologies. The philosophical bent of this kind of theology provoked several reactions which appealed to Scripture. These were facilitated by humanist scholarship, translations into the vernacular and the invention of printing, until finally new biblically based theologies transformed and splintered the Western Church in the sixteenth-century Reformations.

Protestant theology was bound into a new dependence on Scripture by its repudiation of the Catholic magisterium. It inherited the tradition of the ancient Church, but in principle subjected all tradition (as *norma normata*) to the test of Scripture (as *norma normans*), and accepted as necessary to salvation only doctrines found in Scripture. Its relative freedom from ecclesiastical control made further divisions inevitable, but Scripture was still read within a traditional Christian doctrinal framework. The new impetus to biblical study has remained a feature of Protestantism, but when in the wake of Lutheran and Calvinist reform the Protestant theological faculties of German and Swiss universities developed their new dogmatics, Aristotle was again an indispensable resource.

The first reactions against this new and seemingly arid scholasticism appeared in seventeenth-century pietism, a forerunner of the evangelical revival in England. This recovery of the heart gave prominence to devotional reading of the Bible and led to a new biblical theology which was impatient with the schematism of dogmatics. It was nevertheless a modern movement and included a rational element which found expression in textual criticism of the New Testament (e.g. Bengel). In eighteenth-century Enlightenment Germany it coalesced with the new rationalist criticism of orthodox belief. This came to Germany in the main from such English free-thinkers as the deists John Toland and Matthew Tindal, Anthony Collins, Thomas Chubb and Thomas Morgan, but as their criticisms were absorbed and synthesized by Hermann Samuel Reimarus, so the possibilities they held out for constructive revision of Christian theology were built into a new biblical criticism by such notable 'neologians' as Johann Salomo Semler and Johann David Michaelis. Modern liberal theology has many of its roots here. These enemies of dogma and advocates of reasonable religion were dependent on the Bible for their radical revisions of Christian belief, but also independent. They freed the teaching of Jesus from its biblical context and credal frame of reference, reinterpreting it according to modern convictions.

Debates between orthodox restatements of Christian belief which take account of modern knowledge while remaining in clear continuity with the tradition, and those which propose more drastic revision, have dominated religious thought in the West since the eighteenth century. Throughout this period the theological argument has been stimulated by and interwoven with the emergence and development of a new critical study of the Bible. This has been dominated by historical and literary methods which both discredited theories of biblical inerrancy and dismantled orthodox dogmatics. The progress of modern science and philosophy threw doubt on the biblical miracles, chronology, and creation narratives. The literary sensitivity of modern readers opened up a new appreciation of its poetry and myth, and the scepticism of much modern historical enquiry eroded all the biblical narratives.

Subjecting the gospel story to these kinds of analysis destroyed older ways of reading them and substituted a human historical figure for the incarnate Lord of Christian faith. This was no longer orthodox Christology, but it was still dependent on the Bible for historical source material, and it was still arguably Christian. Most of the theological scholars involved were still convinced Christians working in ecclesial contexts which officially retained the classical Christian belief of the older Protestantism. Neo-Protestantism was a numerically small part of nineteenth-century Christianity, but its dissolution of classical Christianity was in tune with a modern culture increasingly at odds with the churches, and its attempts at reconstruction were calculated to appeal to much that was best in a society becoming post-Christian. Large sections of the Christian churches, including official Roman Catholicism, responded to modernity by refusing to engage with some of its legitimate challenges. Liberal Protestantism at its best was more truthful, but sacrificed much that the New Testament writers and subsequent Christians have generally considered essential to their faith.

Karl Barth's reaction against Protestant liberalism has dominated twentieth-century theology and is still in the process of being critically assimilated. Its many strands include a reaffirmation, under the conditions of modernity, of the Reformers' sense of the biblical witness and its centrality to any Christian theology. The human character of Scripture is generally acknowledged outside fundamentalist circles, but opinions remain divided about what that means in practice. The ancient world views of the biblical writers cannot be imposed on modern Christians, and yet religious belief is so bound up with a person's understanding of reality that marking off what can be eliminated and what must be retained is distorting. The tradition as a whole has to be received and interpreted critically, acknowledging that it is no more than tradition, yet trusting that it does and may again become the medium or occasion of divine revelation for some who receive its witness.

The Bible is central to Christian theology because its indispensable traditions are involved in whatever accounts of God's revelation in Christ are elaborated. As a historical phenomenon the Christian religion is entirely dependent on tradition, but all traditions are human and fallible. Theology therefore scrutinizes them and marginalizes some, as it mediates the Christian message as truthfully as it can. It aims to be both faithful to what the tradition as a whole has been seeking to express and also alert to changing situations which require constantly new formulations. By privileging some of its earliest traditions and retaining the scriptures of its religious matrix the Church has made engagement with these Old and New Testament writings central to its interpretative task. Gerhard Ebeling called church history 'the history of the interpretation of scripture'. If that is understood broadly to include its performance in many million lives lived out of the gospel heard from Scripture, it is no exaggeration. Theological interpretation of Scripture guides and informs Christian moral and spiritual practice no less than belief.

The theological relationship of Scripture to tradition is a relationship of some early traditions to all that have followed and been remembered, bad and good. The relationship of Scripture to revelation is less clear and more dialectical. Barth wrote of 'the three-fold form of the Word of God' (*Church Dogmatics* 1,1 para. 4). Strictly speaking only the Word Incarnate, the cruci-fied and risen Lord Jesus, is for Christians the decisive revelation of God. However, God can be known only through this revelation in Christ being mediated in the word of Christian proclamation which is itself dependent on the written word of the biblical witness. The derivative words of Scripture and preaching therefore belong to the operations of Christian revelation too.

Most theologians would agree with Barth that this revelation of God in Christ cannot be grasped directly, like a piece of this-worldly knowledge. It is not available to historical research or to metaphysical speculation. On the other hand, by committing themselves to God as mediated by endlessly unfolding faith-pictures of a particular person, Christians are exposed to the risks which that contingency entails. They cannot eschew an interest in what historians say about Jesus, however trivial this may be for religious faith. So long as it is Jesus of Nazareth that they confess as their risen Lord the ques-tion of the historical Jesus remains on their theological agenda, whatever uncertain and varied answers it receives.

Barth and Bultmann vetoed the historicism which had given modern historical research controlling shares in theology. Following Kierkegaard, and Martin Kähler's corrective emphasis upon the kerygmatic aspect of revelation ('the real Christ is the preached Christ') they minimized faith's need of past history, locating the revelation event in the present moment in which proclamation is obediently heard. Both this aspect of reception, which Bultmann went on to explicate with the help of philosophical categories describing human existence, and the new attention to the biblical text (rather than the history reconstructed from these sources) pointed towards the new literary paradigms which have been gaining ground in Christian theology over the past twenty years. The narrative expanse of Barth's *Church Dogmatics* has proved to be *the* theological monument of the century, restoring 'the strange new world of the Bible' to the centre of much theological endeavour from the conservative 'biblical theology' movement to the latest experi-ments of postmodernism. Bultmann's more stringent exegesis has had less influence outside the professional world of New Testament scholarship, but its achievement in combining the most rigorous critical scholarship with a committed (if anaemic) theology remains the best model for a theologically interested and interesting biblical study. Its Lutheran emphasis on hearing the word (and being transformed) has some affinity both with recent reader-response approaches to the biblical literature and with speech-act theory.

Christian theological interpretation of Scripture has always taken seriously both the biblical texts themselves and their transformative impact upon faithful readers. Even nineteenth-century historicist readings were usually suffused with an idealist philosophy of history which allowed some historians to believe that their rational investigations traced something of the Universal Spirit that Christians call God (a powerful misreading of John 4:24). Their procedures were public and more methodically controlled than Origen's, but they had more in common with his spiritual exegesis than the gulf between his allegorical interpretation and their historical exegesis might suggest. Both ancient and modern exegetes allowed their interest in the question of God to affect their biblical interpretation in ways that most historians would today consider unprofessional. It is this uncoupling of the historian's craft from larger philosophical and theological commitments following the decline of idealism which has led recent theology to loosen the bond with historical scholarship, while insisting on the necessity of this in its proper (subordinate) place.

Origen's genius continues to influence spiritual exegesis in Roman Catholic and Orthodox theology. It also established early in the Church's history a truly critical (though not historical) exegesis, and so the literal sense of Scripture which he himself undervalued but which has guided most university theology, medieval and Reformation and modern. In contrast to preaching, where the imagination has always been allowed more space, Christian doctrine depends upon the literal sense. Its assimilation of modern historical exegesis, with its new techniques and powerful methods, is one form of this commitment, even if not the only one. When its alliance with nineteenth-century idealist theological partners faded a new partnership with kerygmatic and existentialist theology flourished briefly in Germany, despite widespread opposition and distrust. The theological maelstrom of the 1920s contained the potential for relating in different ways to a variety of new cultural currents but these were not much explored until the late 1960s. European and North American theological exegesis remained remarkably stable and the churches relatively unchanged as Western society at large moved further from its Judaeo-Christian roots and values. In the final quarter of the present century the cultural rivers have burst their tradition-shaped banks in a bewildering variety of directions and cultural artefacts like the Bible are read in a corresponding variety of ways. How many of these are of interest to Christian theology remains an open question, but as intellectuals theologians are bound to be more hospitable to new ideas than are most other participants in a religious tradition.

The sheer diversity of hypotheses available within the historical-critical paradigm of modern biblical research had already undermined the hopes of ecumenical leaders that this might provide answers to some of the questions of contemporary Christian theology. Gradually it opened the minds of both theologians and biblical scholars to the possibilities of alternative reading strategies. Most Western theologians today continue to insist that since the Bible is a collection (or two) of ancient texts, historical exegesis based on linguistic competence and some understanding of their original contexts remains an indispensable guide to their meanings, and provides some controls against arbitrary readings.

Such controls are necessary if texts are ever to guide the life of communities. Whether rational controls can ever be adequate when our Enlightenment ideas of a universally valid rationality have been effectively challenged is, however, doubtful, and in practice successful communities have usually imposed other controls on valid interpretation, such as some measure of agreement with a tradition of interpretation and/or subjection to some authoritative institution or person, with all the dangers of manipulation and misuse of power which that implies. Even post-liberal theologies, in discovering points of contact with premodern interpretative practices, are vulnerable to these unattractive aspects of ecclesiastical control.

Within the Christian Church the tradition of freedom, stemming from Jesus himself, to challenge authority has allowed biblical interpreters remarkable scope to search the scriptures and discover new meanings. This has made biblical study a pace-maker of theological change, especially in modern Protestantism, and since the mid twentieth century in Roman Catholicism too. The recent explosion of biblical study into a bewildering variety of literary possibilities is likely to weaken its revolutionary potential and indirectly support the *status quo*. It requires a strong belief in rationality for biblical scholarship and interpretation to speak with a sufficiently strong common voice to achieve institutional change.

Recent trends do not suggest that biblical scholarship alone will ever change the world. There is little evidence that it ever did. Biblical interpretation has always involved more than biblical scholarship, however crucial within it the role of the latter has sometimes been, both in breaking up hard dogmatic ground and opening minds to new possibilities. The seeds of change have usually come from outside the religious community and the task of theology has been to test them by reference to Scripture and tradition as well as experience, and to relate them to new readings of Scripture which will inspire and motivate those who expect somehow to draw their life's meaning, or at least to nourish it, from these wells.

The emergence of narrative theologies, and their symbiosis with recent literary study of the Bible, indicate a renewed sense of the value of tradition and the necessity of stories in shaping our personal and communal identities. Within the still dominant historical paradigm of biblical scholarship recent social-scientific studies of the texts and the histories behind the texts proffer similar suggestions for interpreting our own situations with the help of these precious resources. The more socially and politically engaged theologies of recent years owe much to the liberation from dogmatic and ecclesiastical conservatism effected by biblical criticism. Marx's debt to David Friedrich Strauss and Bruno Bauer bore late fruit. Even the liberation theologies of Latin America were partly the product of Western universities. The importance for biblical interpretation (and vice versa) of the feminist liberation theology which persuaded many Christians in the West that discipleship is a partnership of equals is now widely accepted. It needed a campaign on their own doorsteps before the emancipating pressures stemming from the Enlightenment woke some Christians from their dogmatic slumbers and alerted them to values within their own tradition (including tolerance) and new priorities in the cultivation of Christian life in community.

The roles of the Bible in this ongoing history of Christian theology are less changed than seemed to be the case in the heyday of modernity. A new age which broke with and often despised tradition had less use for the Bible than predecessors who had invested it with near-absolute authority. But a millennium earlier, in the dark ages, it was the monastic bearers of tradition who, largely through their *lectio continua* of Scripture, preserved much of value from the ancient world and made possible a Renaissance. For that process to be repeated the continued close reading of the Bible in faith-communities remains essential, whatever its cultural spin-offs in the now fragile world of humanistic learning and the shallower world of mass communication. It will be mainly out of religious contexts, that is from faithful responses to God who is known and loved through being mediated by the interpretation of texts bearing witness to a Gospel, that new theological experiments can be expected to interpret the experience of the less comfortable future now dawning.

## Further reading

Adam, A. K. M., *Making Sense of New Testament Theology,* Macon, GA: Mercer,
    1995.

*The Cambridge History of the Bible*, 3 vols., Cambridge: Cambridge University Press,
    1963–70.

Campenhausen, H. von, *The Formation of the Christian Bible,* London: A. & C. Black,
    1972.

Frei, H., *The Eclipse of Biblical Narrative*, New Haven: Yale University Press, 1974.

Jeanrond, W., *Text and Interpretation as Categories of Theological Thinking*, Dublin:
    Gill and Macmillan, 1988.

Kelsey, D., *The Uses of Scripture in Recent Theology*, Philadelphia: Fortress Press and
    London: SCM Press, 1975.

Morgan, R., with J. Barton, *Biblical Interpretation*, Oxford: Oxford University Press,
    1988.

Perdue, L. G., *The Collapse of History: Reconstructing Old Testament Theology*,
    Minneapolis: Fortress Press, 1994.

Stroup, G. W., *The Promise of Narrative Theology*, Atlanta: John Knox Press, 1981.

Thiselton, A. C., *New Horizons in Hermeneutics*, London: HarperCollins, 1992.

Tracy, D., *The Analogical Imagination*, London: SCM Press, 1980.

# 9 Biblical study and linguistics

WILLIAM JOHNSTONE

Linguistics as the 'science of language' is concerned not just with the description of individual languages in and for themselves (though these provide essential data) but with abstract and general questions that arise from language as a universal human phenomenon. The theoretical issues involved in the study of language and of the processes in the mind and in the environment which enable learning and communication have many ramifications, psychological, sociological and philosophical.

The Bible, as a library of literary works written in three original languages, Hebrew, Aramaic and Greek, and translated in whole or in part into some 2,000 'receptor' languages, inevitably raises questions posed by linguistics at both the practical and the theoretical levels. Most biblical interpreters approach these questions pragmatically. They are concerned with a range of practical tasks and it is through the effort to discharge these tasks that they are most likely to encounter the underlying theoretical issues. For example, the problems involved in translation, one of the most challenging areas of linguistic theory and practice, are inescapable already in New Testament interpretation, for the version of the Hebrew Scriptures largely presupposed in the New Testament is already a translation, the Greek Septuagint from the second century BCE. And, since no-one is a native speaker of classical Hebrew, imperial Aramaic or *koinē* Greek, the problems of translation from 'source' to 'receptor' language confront the interpreter of the Bible at every turn as the attempt is made to transpose words and content out of the original language into the idioms of the interpreter's everyday speech. Formally or informally, on paper or just in the mind, the anglophone has to convey in English what the text of the original says and it is that process which marks the definitive stage in the decision about the meaning of what is written in the ancient language.

The task is not unique to biblical studies. An instructive example of the problems attending the transfer of meaning from one culture to another is the experience of Sir George Grey, sent by the British Government in 1845 to

become governor-in-chief of New Zealand. In order to deal with the Maoris'
grievances Grey felt it necessary to learn their language. As a virtual pioneer,
he had first to compile his own dictionary and his own grammar of the Maori
language. But even then, to his surprise, he found that he could still only very
imperfectly understand what was being said to him.

> Soon . . . a new and quite unexpected difficulty presented itself . . .
> [The] chiefs, either in their speeches to me, or in their letters, frequently
> quoted, in explanation of their views and intentions, fragments of
> ancient poems or proverbs, or made allusions which rested on an
> ancient system of mythology . . . Only one thing could . . . be done, and
> that was to acquaint myself with the ancient language of the country,
> to collect its traditional poems and legends, to induce their priests to
> impart to me their mythology, and to study their proverbs.[1]

Grey's experience plots well the stages of linguistic competence, from the
acquisition of mere words and the description of grammatical constructions
to the perception of their function in creating a web of discourse that has
both historical and contemporary reference, in order to convey a complete
culture. In a word, he was practising socio-semiotics – the study of the conventions of signs, including the signs of language, used by a community –
arguably the fundamental principle of modern Bible – or any – translation,[2]
a good century before the term was invented! To give an example nearer
home: it is one thing to mumble a few words in schoolchild French in the
local *boulangerie*; it is quite another to attempt a conversation with Parisians.
Unless one knows what they are talking about, one cannot understand what
they are saying.

Four areas of immediate practical concern call for discussion: (1) words:
the establishment of meaning; the lexicon; (2) the connection between
words to make statements: grammar and syntax; (3) learning the language
in the first place: applied linguistics; (4) the transmission of meaning from
one culture to another: translation.

(1) Grey at least had the advantage of native speakers and interpreters
to help him, but how does one know what the words of an ancient dead language mean? Fortunately, we are not the first in the field. There is a tradition
of meaning passed down by generations of scholars; they have transmitted
from earliest times orally and in writing inherited views of what words in
passages mean. We have monuments to medieval Hebrew scholarship in,
for instance, Rabbi David Kimchi's *Book of Roots*.[3] For the most part this
inherited lore is the working hypothesis, which has operated successfully, in

a general way, in innumerable commentaries and translations. And once we have reached a certain plateau of competence in the language we do not sit with our nose in the dictionary – any more than we do in English for the odd unfamiliar word or usage – but are guided by the expectations aroused by experience and context to what seems to be a reasonable approximation to the sense of a passage. But at the level of scientific lexicography, it might be said that the task of scholarship is to take this tradition of meaning as the opening hypothesis and to assess it critically. The question is how to go about this task of critical appraisal.

To control traditional understandings of meaning 'scientifically', two main sets of external criteria have conventionally been applied in Hebrew lexicography in modern times: the witness of the ancient translations of the Bible to the tradition of meaning; and the evidence from the Semitic languages cognate to biblical Hebrew. The ancient translations of the Scriptures into Greek, Latin, Syriac and so on, dating back for two millennia or so, are invaluable testimony to the tradition of understanding of the original in early receptor languages. But in many ways their evidence is difficult to evaluate. Can one be really sure that they are reliable witnesses to the meaning of a text, particularly of an obscure text? Quite apart from uncertainties of the transmission of the original biblical text, which is a problem for all methods of interpretation, there is uncertainty about the history of the transmission of the text of these versions themselves. Even more to the point, one cannot be sure whether the text of the Scriptures from which they were translating is identical with the accepted text available to us (the publication of the Dead Sea Scrolls, for instance, is opening up vast new areas for discussion of textual matters). Even if it is, can we be sure that they are translating accurately, and not paraphrasing, or even just guessing at the meaning? This evidence is too voluminous and too problematical to be deployed consistently in the large lexica (though there would be a case for even larger lexica that did!; the dawning electronic age with its CD-ROMs may well facilitate that) and is on the whole appealed to with due caution only for rare or obscure words.

The appeal to Hebrew's sister Semitic languages has made a much wider appearance in the standard lexica in the task of establishing 'scientifically' the meaning of words. This has been the tradition in Hebrew lexicography especially since the nineteenth century and it is still operative today in two of the major lexica of biblical Hebrew in current use, *A Hebrew and English Lexicon of the Old Testament*, edited by F. Brown, G. R. Driver and C. A. Briggs ('BDB'),[4] now more than a century old in its earliest parts, and, in its various guises, the post-Second World War *Hebräisches und aramäisches Lexikon zum Alten Testament*, initially edited by L. Koehler and W. Baumgartner ('HAL').[5] The method is now under serious challenge on grounds of modern linguistics itself.

The approach in these works is termed 'comparative historical linguistics'.[6] An important witness to the history and development of meaning is thought to be the study of etymology – the origins of a word and the way its uses have ramified through time. Since Hebrew is not an isolated language but belongs to the wider circle of Semitic languages, it is fascinating to see how words of common stock have been applied at different times and in different ways in the cognate languages. Stimulus to the study of the comparative historical linguistics of the Semitic languages has arisen from the quite sensational epigraphical discoveries which have been made in the last two centuries, pre-eminently Akkadian in the nineteenth and Ugaritic in the twentieth. In an area where the corpus of texts is relatively small, any new discovery gives a vantage point from which 'established' knowledge can be re-examined.

The founding father of the method, first applied to 'Indo-European' languages, is recognized to be Sir William Jones (1746–94). The method is both comparative and diachronic: the similarities between 'Indo-European' languages must be evidence of common ancestry, 'Proto-Indo-European'. It is the task of the historical linguist to trace back the histories of these sister languages to their common parent and to compare the evolution of meaning in these different branches. By analogy, the search for the 'original Semitic language' was on (the comparable founding father of Semitic lexicography is Wilhelm Gesenius, 1786–1842) and Arabic with its 'primitive' inflections soon became the firm favourite as the primary witness to what that original language must have looked like.

It is hardly surprising that BDB, emanating from the same press as the *Oxford English Dictionary* (originally called *A New English Dictionary on Historical Principles* in the agreement of 1879 between the Philological Society and Oxford University Press), Liddell and Scott's *Greek-English Lexicon* (1843 and later editions) and Lewis and Short's *A Latin Dictionary* (1890), and edited by well-trained classicists, should be based on similar comparative and historical principles. The editors brought their expectations with them, applied techniques familiar to them and equally wished to commend their field to the general world of scholarship. BDB is almost as imposing externally as its Greek and Latin sisters.

The method has been tried to the limits of possibility. The problem is that we do not have nearly enough data to carry through the task. The relative dating of the biblical sources alone is fraught with uncertainty and, therefore, controversy. The attempt to eke out the Hebraic evidence by appeal to other languages of the same group adds much data, the relevance of which is, however, highly problematical: it assumes some kind of parallel development in the unfolding of meaning in the related languages. The application has at times been undisciplined and impressionistic, and, because of the vastness of the field, dictionary orientated, rather than a careful tracing of sense in the individual languages.[7]

The danger has been that a legitimate inquiry and an acknowledged method of discussing rare cases have been exalted into a principle; thence have flowed complaints about 'coining a new Hebrew vocabulary by means of an uncritical use of Ugaritic or another Semitic language'.[8] M. J. Dahood's commentary on Psalms, storehouse of many insights as it is, is a well-known example.[9]

But meantime an attack in principle on comparative historical linguistics as a means of establishing the meaning of words in contemporary discourse has been launched from a different approach to linguistics, referred to as 'structural linguistics'. If 1786 (the year of W. Jones's pioneering lecture to the 'Asiatick Society' in Calcutta) may be recognized as the birth of historical linguistics, then the course on general linguistics by the Swiss linguist Ferdinand de Saussure (1857–1913) in 1910–11[10] marks the birth of structural linguistics. Saussure's famous analogy between language and the game of chess makes the point (R. Harris, *F. de Saussure*, p. 23, cf. pp. 87f., 108). The chess pieces are bound by a system: they have a conventional set of moves on a conventional board. The variety of possible moves that can be made is myriad and depends on the skill of the players. External questions like what material the pieces are made of are irrelevant. Still further, one can meaningfully describe the state of play at any move within the game; the history of moves within the game up to that point can no longer affect the present interrelationship of the pieces. The outcome of the match depends on the current move. So, by analogy, it is with language. The force and the function of words come from their current interrelation with one another in the present system, not from their historic force and function at any previous stage.

The crux in Saussure's account, it seems to me, is the question of how 'value' is assigned. Using his analogy of the 8.45 train from Geneva to Paris (R. Harris, p. 107) one can say, 'I come to work every morning by the same train.' What makes the train 'the same' is not the driver or the rolling-stock, but its place in the network: the fact that it is not the earlier train or the later train or a train by another route. Thus what makes for the 'value' of a word is not its intrinsic sense but the fact that it is not the other words in a sentence ('In the language itself, there are only differences', Saussure as in R. Harris, p. 118). Thus in the chess analogy, the knight, for example, is kept in 'value'/'equilibrium' only by its relation to the other pieces (pp. 108f.).

An enterprise which seeks self-consciously to apply 'the principles of modern linguistics' understood in Saussurian terms is the *Dictionary of Classical Hebrew*, edited by D. J. A. Clines ('DCH').[11] The meaning of a word is not established by etymology, by tracing its history *diachronically* back through time, to some hypothetical original meaning and then understanding how that original meaning has developed and changed, perhaps in the light of an assumed similar development of the same root in cognate Semitic languages. Rather, meanings of words are established *synchronically*: language is a system; it is only in relation to other words in the current state of the evolution of the language as an overall structure that the individual word functions.

The corpus of texts in DCH is widened beyond the Hebrew Bible to include Ben Sira, the Dead Sea Scrolls and inscriptions: that in itself makes the publication of great value, since it draws together all the known material on 'Classical Hebrew' in one convenient collection. More controversially, that material is treated as a 'single phase'. The approach is based on what is there rather than on reconstructions; in this respect, it matches recent developments in other areas of the study of the Hebrew Bible, e.g., 'final form' literary studies, 'canonical criticism'.

The meaning of a word is not something that it bears within itself by virtue of its evolution from its ancestors; it arises from its interrelationships in the contemporary system of the language. Thus, the first statement under an entry in DCH is termed the 'gloss', merely an initial orientation. The main entry then lists the occurrences of the word in the corpus within a double set of synchronic relationships: context ('syntagmatic' relationship) and semantic field ('paradigmatic' relationship).

There is, thus, no listing of cognates in other Semitic languages, for that is 'strictly irrelevant to the Hebrew language', least of all in privileged position at the head of the entry as in BDB and HAL.[12] This point is perhaps taken a little too far. In an area where the evidence is on all hands acknowledged to be restricted we need all the help we can get. There must be a difference in the process of understanding an ancient, 'dead', written language, which is only a torso of the whole, and a modern living one, where, at the very least, interrogation can take place between contemporaries. It might be argued that all understanding of language is a matter of hypothesis-forming: the hearer/reader picks out the familiar in what is being said, pre-eminently individual words, generally with external referents, which bring baggage with them from other contexts, diachronic as well as synchronic. It is this prior knowledge which enables the reader to get a 'sight' on what is now being stated and to begin to form expectations, even if these expectations have to be validated or invalidated from the current discourse (cf. Aitchison, p. 88: 'the meaning of words tells us quite a lot about the meaning of sentences, since sentences are individual words linked together by means of the syntax'). It is in no small measure the restrictedness and unsatisfactoriness, real or imagined, of the contexts in the corpus of classical Hebrew which have impelled scholars to incorporate the comparative data as hypotheses to be validated or invalidated by the Hebrew Bible itself. This process may operate both for common and for rare words. Thus – to stick to examples covered by the published first volume of DCH – the common verb ʾamara in Arabic means most frequently 'to command'; this presents the hypothesis that at least somewhere in Hebrew, where the cognate verb is most frequently defined as 'to say', it might have the same meaning. In fact, such a meaning is recognized by DCH, but there is an added sense of conviction about the validity of the hypothesis in the light of the Arabic usage. In the case of a rare word like 'Ariel' the reader may feel bereft of reference to the 'Moabite Stone' or to possible Akkadian cognates, which at least give some plausible angles on the meaning.[13] The fact that there were lively cultural contacts between ancient Israel and contemporary Moab and Assyria suggests that Hebrew should not be hermetically sealed off as a self-contained system: foreign loan-words, fully or only partly domesticated, may have been just as much part of the language.

A further useful – even indispensable – contribution of comparative linguistics is the identification of homonyms (cf., e.g., English 'bear', an animal, a verb 'to carry', even a crop in the fields, each with a different etymology). As is well-known, the Hebrew 'alphabet' has only twenty-two letters; Arabic has twenty-eight and Ugaritic thirty (there are different ways of counting each!). The larger number of consonants in the longer Semitic alphabets are funnelled into the shorter Hebrew, inevitably producing identical-looking roots which are, however, clearly to be distinguished historically. This is particularly the case in the strong gutturals and the sibilants: e.g., the Hebrew ḥṣr. The fact that an odd assortment of Hebrew words with contradictory meanings, e.g., ḥāṣîr; 'grass', ḥāṣēr, 'courtyard'; ḥāṣēr, 'unwalled settlement', can all appear to share the same consonants is explicable from the fact that they come from different stems, in this case no fewer than three still visible in Arabic (*ḵḏr*, *ḥzr* and *ḥḍr*, respectively).[14] Once again, the observation of such parallels provides, at the very least, a hypothesis for the disentangling of meanings. Now it might be argued that the English speaker knows very well from context without any help from etymology which 'bear' might be meant, and why should it be any different for Hebrew? But in dealing with the Bible we are not native speakers of a modern language; a recognition of diverse backgrounds aids identification and understanding – not to say memorization – of vocabulary. Further, under-standing of what a word once was and may now no longer be is as helpful in control of meaning (and much easier to remember) as, say, the antonyms with which it is found in this or that context.

As a 'structural linguistics' dictionary, the listing of synonyms and antonyms is also another important feature of DCH. It is by this means that words are related 'paradigmatically' in their semantic fields.[15] Here there is made available a bird's-eye view of the range of associations of a word in Hebrew. But once again, as is freely acknowledged, the dictionary cannot do everything: the possible interconnections extend in limitless fashion (Clines, Introduction to vol. I of DCH, 1993, p. 21). Thus in the list of synonyms of the verb *'āsaph* 'gather', for example, the verb *qāhal* 'congre-gate', which is integral, say, to the semantic field of the Chronicler's presenta-tion of 'all-Israel' (1 Chronicles 13:5; 15:3, etc.), is not given.

(2) There have been comparable developments in the grammatical description of Hebrew. As once the historical dictionary was matched by the 'comparative grammar of the Semitic languages',[16] so now diachronic and comparative interests in grammar and syntax have given way to synchronic description within the language itself as a self-contained system. The aim is to describe uninflected Hebrew in its own terms rather than in those of inflected Arabic (not to mention Latin and Greek).[17]

Hebrew is a 'configurational' language, i.e., it depends, like English, on word order to show the interrelationship of words in the sentence (Arabic, by contrast – and Greek – signals also by case-endings the relationship of words to one another). Thus 'constituent analysis' rather than the signals given by case-endings enables the structure of sentences in Hebrew to be analysed and the interrelation of elements plotted (for the terms see Aitchison, *Teach Yourself Linguistics*, pp. 61f.). Hence, it is argued, in the grammatical description of the Hebrew noun the term 'case' should be abandoned, for hardly any case endings are shown in Hebrew; 'the noun in Hebrew fulfils its various grammatical roles by syntactic means ... and is sufficiently identified in terms of subject or object or of an adjectival or adverbial function'.[18] Thus, terms using 'case', like 'adverbial accusative', borrowed from Arabic, should be dropped from the description of Hebrew: it is sufficient to talk of a noun's 'adverbial function'.[19]

Equally problematical, it is argued, is the use of the term 'tense' in relation to the Hebrew verb. Hebrew verbs 'do not locate an event or situation *in* time, leaving that to the context, but view them in their relation *to* time, i.e., whether they are punctual or iterative, complete or still going on, etc.'[20] Thus the term 'aspect' is to be preferred to 'tense'. The *vav*-consecutive is not a 'tense' but the bearer of the narrative, the 'on-line' story; the other 'tense' introduces circumstantial clauses and other 'off-line' data.[21]

As in the discussion of the 'synchronic' dictionary above, so in this context I think it is still possible to defend a comparative and diachronic approach, however speculative that may be. It is precisely because it is speculative that it can be creative in formulating hypotheses about the formation of Hebrew words and sentences. I have argued elsewhere that it is possible that there are in Hebrew quite unsuspected uses of, e.g., the passive participle of the derived conjugations of the verb, the dual, and the construct and 'genitive', which only come to light if Arabic is used heuristically.[22] There are some commonplace idioms in Arabic, too, such as the use of the verbal noun, and the co-ordination of imperatives to express the conditional, which are less well-recognized in Hebrew (the latter especially prints through to the New Testament: the injunction, 'be angry but do not sin' (Ephesians 4:26 RSV), is not intended as an encouragement to anger!). At least Arabic helps to identify a function, even if that function has to be differently described, in terms more appropriate to Hebrew (just as many people have had the experience that it was only when they tried to learn the grammar of inflected Latin or German that they began to understand the grammar of uninflected English).

Structural linguistics is, as its name implies, concerned with language as a system of interconnected words. Such a system is capable of analysis into its component parts (for the analysis of sentence patterns, see Aitchison, *Teach Yourself Linguistics*, pp. 63–77). A potentially highly significant application of structural linguistics is in connection with the computerized analysis of texts. By morphological tagging, texts become machine-readable and so analysable by mechanical means. One of the most influential undertakings in this field is that associated with the 'Werkgroep Informatica' begun in 1977 in the Theology Faculty of the Free University of Amsterdam, the ultimate aim of which is a fundamental appreciation of the linguistic rules and mechanisms which govern the syntax of the Hebrew Bible. Already a system has been evolved for encoding the individual words – or 'lexemes' – of the entire text of BHS.[23] The next stage will be to show how this data can be used at more elaborate levels of syntactical analysis. A sample of the kind of work that can be expected is the subtle analysis of the syntax of Solomon's prayer by E. Talstra, one of the leaders of the same school.[24]

There is space to refer to the final two practical dimensions of biblical linguistics – language learning and translation – only briefly: in any case, at this point it becomes no longer a matter of the passive consultation of secondary resources – the lexicon and the grammar – but of acquiring and using practical skills at first hand. One can only learn to cycle by getting on the bicycle.

(3) Language teaching and learning are often referred to as 'applied linguistics'. In this connection a teaching grammar which seeks to apply the insights and principles of structural linguistics merits attention. This is J. F. A. Sawyer's *A Modern Introduction to Biblical Hebrew*.[25] The book is written for the needs of the 'non-linguist', but also partly with an eye to 'contribute something to the wider field of Hebrew and Semitic linguistics' (p. v). True to the interest in structural linguistics, 'the starting-point is always the sentence, and words are thus analysed ... only in actual contexts'. Further, 'all comparative philology and historical linguistics ... are "optional extras" excluded from the main part of the grammar' (pp. v,vii).

A longer theoretical discussion is provided in Appendix B (pp. 163–73) where the stress, e.g., on arranging 'vocabulary in "fields" (sets of terms of related meaning)', 'the analysis of meaning-relations such as synonymy and opposition', and the view that 'the meaning of a term is to a large extent dependent on ... context' are closely reflected in the aims stated in DCH. Further, as regards etymology, 'although clearly it is probable that all words containing the same root have at one time had a semantic element in common, how important that element is varies so widely from one word to another and from one context to another, that the "root-meaning" as a starting-point for semantic description is at best inadequate, at worst totally misleading' (pp. 168f.).

Whether in the event the grammar is effective for the initial learner is not the point: for students at any stage who wish to orient themselves in a practical way with regard to structural linguistics the work provides a highly accessible introduction.

(4) Translation, as it happens, brings us into contact, if in modified form, with the third major phase in the history of general linguistics, that

marked by the dominant figure of the post-Second World War period, the American scholar Noam Chomsky.[26]

The theory of translation has been succinctly expressed by E. A. Nida and C. R. Taber, in terms of 'dynamic [now 'functional'] equivalence'.[27] The aim of a translation is to 'transport' the message of an original text into a receptor language in such a way that the response of hearer or reader is in every respect essentially the same as that of the original receptors.

In order to attain this goal, the text of the original has first to be 'back transformed'. This 'back transformation' is defined in terms approximating Chomsky's 'transformational grammar': 'the surface structure of a discourse is analyzed ... into its underlying kernels'. These kernels are the fundamental structural elements within the sentence, the nouns, verbs, adjectives and adverbs, and the morphemes that specify the interrelationship between these parts of speech. Any language has only a limited number of types of kernel; Nida and Taber reckon six to twelve. These kernels are transferred from source language to the receptor language. There they are to undergo 'forward transformation'. Nida and Taber, *The Theory and Practice of Translation*, pp. 33–55, provide numerous examples from the New Testament of the process and exercises to give the reader practice in carrying out the process. E.g., the Authorized Version of Ephesians 2:8 offers a translation of the Greek text which merely reproduces the structure of the Greek in an inadequately literal, 'formal equivalent' way: 'For by grace ye are saved through faith; and that not of yourselves: it is the gift of God: not of works, lest any man should boast.' In Nida and Taber's view, this text has to be broken down into its 'kernels', which formulated in literary dress appear as, 'God showed his grace to you, and in this way he saved you through your trusting in him. You yourself did not save yourselves. Rather, God gave you this salvation. You did not earn it by what you did. Therefore no one can boast about what he has done' (pp. 53f.). Sawyer gives Old Testament examples for this Chomskyesque procedure: to take one of the simplest, both 'the Lord saved his anointed' (Psalm 20:7 (6, English versions)) and 'save me' (Jeremiah 17:14) are analysable into the same 'kernels', NP (Noun phrase) 1 + V (Verb) + NP2.[28]

It may be doubted whether such formulaic approaches represent more than a stage towards the appreciation and conveying of the meaning of the original (any more than the *Today's English Version/Good News Bible*, hailed by Nida and Taber, *The Theory and Practice of Translation*, p.47, as the English translation which most closely follows the practice they advocate, can be regarded as the most successful English version). While acknowledging the need for disciplined approaches, there must remain room for flair where literary studies are concerned and for intuition, not least in an area where non-native speakers are working with a limited corpus of texts. Biblical study is likely to continue to employ pragmatically the fruits and insights of both comparative historical and structural linguistics.

## Notes

1  G. Grey, *Polynesian Mythology, and Ancient Traditional History of the New Zealand Race, as Furnished by their Priests and Chiefs* (London: John Murray, 1855), pp. vi–viii.

2  J. de Waard, E. A. Nida, *From One Language to Another: Functional Equivalence in Bible Translating* (Nashville, Camden, New York: Thomas Nelson, 1986), p. 181.

3  J. H. R. Biesenthal and F. Lebrecht (eds.), *Rabbi Davidis Kimchi radicum liber* (Berlin: Bethge, 1847).

4  Oxford: Oxford University Press, first edn. 1907, reprinted with corrections frequently.

5  An English version is in process of publication (M. E. J. Richardson (ed.), *The Hebrew and Aramaic Lexicon of the Old Testament by Ludwig Koehler and Walter Baumgartner* . . . (Leiden, New York, Köln: Brill, 1994–)).

6  I use here and below terms which feature in J. Aitchison's standard manual of general linguistics, *Teach Yourself Linguistics* (London, Sydney, Auckland: Hodder & Stoughton, 1992).

7  I have critically evaluated a case in point in W. Johnstone, 'Yd' II: "be humbled, humiliated"?', *Vetus Testamentum* 41 (1991), pp. 49–62.

8  G. Fohrer, *Hebrew & Aramaic Dictionary of the Old Testament* (London: SCM Press, 1973), Introduction, Section 2.

9  M. J. Dahood, *Psalms*, Anchor Bible, 16, 17, 17A (New York: Doubleday, 1966, 1968, 1970).

10  The third course, which is the basis of the published account (the two earlier courses were in 1906–7, 1908–9); see R. Harris, *F. de Saussure: Course in General Linguistics* (London: Duckworth, 1983).

11  Sheffield: Sheffield Academic Press, 1993–. For the rationale see the Introduction to vol. I, pp. 14–29; also D. J. A. Clines, 'The Dictionary of Classical Hebrew', *Zeitschrift für Althebraistik* 3 (1990), pp. 73–80.

12  Clines, Introduction to vol. I of DCH, 1993, p. 17. But cf. Koehler already in Richardson, 1994, p. lxx.

13  Cf. the discussion of Ariel in the 'Moabite Stone' in J. C. L. Gibson, *Syrian Semitic Inscriptions* (Oxford: Clarendon Press, 1971), vol. I, p. 80.

14 For the second cf. M. J. de Goeje, *Annals of Tabari* (Leiden:Brill, 1951), p. 16, l.9; for the third, P. K. Hitti, *The Origins of the Islamic State being a translation . . . with annotations of the Kitâb Futûḥ al-Buldân of . . . Balâdhuri* (Beirut, Khayat, 1966), p. 223 n.3.

15 For a comparable development in New Testament studies, see P. Louw, E. A. Nida, *Greek-English Lexicon of the New Testament based on Semantic Domains* (New York: United Bible Societies, 1988, 1989); E. A Nida, P. Louw, *Lexical Semantics of the Greek New Testament* (SBL Resources for Biblical Studies 25, Atlanta GA: Scholars Press, 1992).

16 E.g., W. Wright, *Lectures on the Comparative Grammar of the Semitic Languages* (Cambridge: Cambridge University Press, 1890).

17 Cf. J. C. L. Gibson, 'Keeping Up with Recent Studies 18. Hebrew Language and Linguistics', *Expository Times* 104 (1992–93), pp. 105–9; and *Davidson's Introductory Hebrew Grammar – Syntax* (Edinburgh: T. & T. Clark, 1994).

18 Gibson, 'Keeping Up', p. 106; cf. *Davidson's Introductory Hebrew Grammar*, p. 24.

19 Gibson, *Davidson's Introductory Hebrew Grammar*, p. 143.

20 Gibson, 'Keeping Up', p. 107; cf. *Davidson's Introductory Hebrew Grammar*, p. 60.

21 Gibson, 'Keeping Up', p. 107; cf. *Davidson's Introductory Hebrew Grammar*, pp. 83–102.

22 W. Johnstone, 'Reading the Hebrew Bible with Arabic-sensitized eyes' in W. Johnstone (ed.), *William Robertson Smith: Essays in Reassessment*, JSOTS 189 (Sheffield: Sheffield Academic Press, 1995), pp. 390–7.

23 A. J. C. Verheij, *Grammatica Digitalis 1: The Morphological Code in the 'Werkgroep Informatica' Computer Text of the Hebrew Bible*, Applicatio 11 (Amsterdam:Vrije Universitet University Press, 1994).

24 E. Talstra, *Solomon's Prayer: Synchrony and Diachrony in the Composition of 1 Kings 8,14–61*, Contributions to Biblical Exegesis and Theology 3 (Kampen: Kok Pharos, 1993).

25 Stocksfield, MA: Oriel Press, 1976.

26 On whom see Aitchison, *Teach Yourself Linguistics*, pp. 25–7, 163–99. The at times fierce debate surrounding Chomsky's ideas and the revisions in his position are described in colourful language in R. A. Harris, *The Linguistic Wars* (New York and Oxford: Oxford University Press, 1993).

27 E. A. Nida and C. R. Taber, *The Theory and Practice of Translation*, Helps for Translators 8 (Leiden: Brill, 1969), especially pp. 33–55 (p. 39, in particular, for the modified relation to Chomsky's 'transformational grammar'), and Glossary, pp. 198–210.

28 J. F. A. Sawyer, *Semantics in Biblical Research: New Methods of Defining Hebrew Words for Salvation*, Studies in Biblical Theology: Second Series 24 (London: SCM Press, 1972), pp. 62ff.

## Further reading

Aitchison, J., *Teach Yourself Linguistics*, 4th edn, London, Sydney, Auckland: Hodder & Stoughton, 1992.

Barr, J., *The Semantics of Biblical Language*, Oxford: Oxford University Press, 1961.

Cotterell, P., and M. Turner, *Linguistics and Biblical Interpretation*, London: SPCK, 1989.

Dawson, D. A., 'Text-Linguistics and Biblical Hebrew', *Journal for the Study of the Old Testament Supplement Series* 177, Sheffield, Sheffield Academic Press, 1994.

Silva, M., *God, Language and Scripture: Reading the Bible in the Light of General Linguistics*, Foundations of Contemporary Interpretation, 4, Grand Rapids, MI: Zondervan, 1990.

## 10 Aspects of the Jewish contribution to biblical interpretation

STEFAN C. REIF

### INTRODUCTION

As is often the case with such invitations, John Barton's request to me for a contribution to this volume represented a challenge to think seriously about how each of us was viewing the topic, and about how best to tackle it in the present context. In the original letter inviting me to submit a chapter, the editor explained that the volume would attempt to cover the principal approaches to the Bible in the modern 'critical' era. Conscious as he was of the continuation of older methods and approaches, 'whether naive in the sense of simply untouched by criticism, or anti-critical and conscientiously opposed to criticism', he was anxious that Jewish and Christian conservatism, including fundamentalist interpretations, should receive attention. Given that Christian conservatism was likely to be discussed in other chapters, he thought it would be good if the chapter I was being invited to write could be 'preponderantly Jewish in its concerns'. He was hoping for an article that not only covered the field but represented personal opinions, not just 'bland consensus'.

As I indicated to Professor Barton in my reply, there were a number of presuppositions and definitions in his overture that made me feel uneasy and that were in themselves at the heart of the differences between Jewish and Christian approaches to the interpretation of the Bible. If I were to take on the assignment, I should wish to deal with these and to offer some comments that challenged their validity, as well as attempting to say something general about Jewish interpretation of the Bible. I immediately received a kind and encouraging response, accepting my proposal and welcoming the challenges it might offer to the assumptions underlying the volume.[1] What this chapter will therefore try to do is to formulate one Jewish scholar's personal analysis of the kind of biblical studies that currently dominate the field in what, for want of a better term, may be called 'the cultured Western world'; his brief survey of Jewish approaches to the subject in the past and the present; and, throughout the chapter, his assessment of how the one relates to the other.

## CHRISTIAN PRESUPPOSITIONS

What then are the 'presuppositions and definitions' that underlie the creation of this volume and much similar literature being produced in departments of biblical study at many academic institutions, and what is the wider context in which they should be placed and understood? The Bible is of course defined as the Old Testament *and* the New Testament. This specific terminology is retained in all cases and takes it as axiomatic that the former's validity can continue only in the context of its fulfilment in the latter. The two are integral parts of the biblical whole and are to be globally understood and interpreted. Such theological foundations notwithstanding, the study of the Bible in academic contexts is seen as critical and scientific while the traditional interpretations that predate the modern period are regarded as naive and unhistorical. Such interpretations are often fundamentalist in nature and, it is assumed, are similarly represented in both the Christian and Jewish traditions. They are of interest to *bona fide* scholars, not for any serious contribution they make to modern study but as examples of views that were once widely held and that are now representative of a rigidly conservative minority.[2]

Not all of such presuppositions are by any means held by every scholar of Christian background, nor are some restricted to Christian interpreters of the Bible. There is indeed a considerable tension between those who subscribe to them and refuse to take seriously much postmodernist interpretation and those who are aware of the biased nature of the standard approach and seek to disassociate themselves from it.[3] There are also Jewish Bible critics who are content to accept some of the results of the presuppositions, without allying themselves theologically with those who take them for granted.[4] Since, however, the majority of those teaching and researching the Old Testament at the higher educational level in Europe and North America are practising Christians, some comments will be in order about the background to their assumptions concerning scriptural texts.

As is well known, it was the Protestant Reformation that placed the Bible, divorced from ecclesiastical traditions, at the centre of its theology and challenged the individual believers to strengthen their understanding of the faith and their commitment to it by creating a personal as well as an institutional relationship with the words of God. To that end, a knowledge of

Hebrew and Greek became more widely regarded as a prerequisite, and every encouragement was given to the development of related theological studies at the universities. Jewish exegetical traditions and linguistic prowess could be employed in the interpretation of the Old Testament but the overall approach had to remain a predominantly Pauline–Lutheran one. Those parts of the Old Testament that stressed faith, morals, spirituality and universal values (at least in Christian eyes) were of continuous significance, while details of laws, rituals and particularly Israelite concerns could be subsumed under 'works' rather than 'faith'. They therefore had a limited importance, overtaken as they had been by greater theological events and ideas centred on the figure of the messianic Jesus. The early leaders of the Reformation gave expression to their theological ideas very much by way of biblical exegesis and when converted Jews with hebraic insights could be joined to the cause, so much the better. If Jews remained loyal to their own rabbinic traditions, they might still be permitted to function as 'language teachers' in limited contexts but their understanding of the Old Testament was severely flawed, particularly since they rejected an essential tool for its valid interpretation, namely, the New Testament.[5]

## MODERN OLD TESTAMENT VIEWS

Surely, then, such Christian theological notions were a part of the scholastic philosophy only in the premodern period and were widely replaced by critical and scientific propositions when the historical approach became dominant in the nineteenth century? The remarkable fact is that only in a very limited sense can this be said to be true. There are faculties in which biblical civilization is today taught in a truly open and liberal fashion, usually in the context of religious studies, by scholars whose own religious commitments are to a large extent irrelevant to their professional activities. This is, however, a recent phenomenon and the truth is that the rise of modern biblical criticism has, over the past century and a half, failed to have any major impact on the theological presuppositions and religious pre-judices of many of those who teach the Old Testament. Far from seeing the historical approach as a replacement of the theological one, generations of Christian scholars have insisted on achieving a harmonization of the two.

Beginning with Julius Wellhausen, the leading figures have adopted an approach that has permitted them to retain all the Protestant principles of exegesis, while claiming to have absorbed the best of modern literary and historical analysis. As Edward Greenstein has put it, 'so many categories in the study of Biblical literature, and its religion in particular, derive from patently Christian doctrines'.[6] Students of the Old Testament have speculatively reconstructed pristine forms of biblical religion, of Hebrew text and of Israelite identity that may comfortably be associated with the 'true Israel' and have traced the continuation of those authentic forms into Christianity. All those elements of the Old Testament tradition that do not fit in with this reconstruction – the best example is of course legal material – are downgraded and regarded as a corrupted version of the religion. They are not linked with Christianity but with the ideology that made no further spiritual progress but ended in the sterile religion of the rabbis. The rabbinic tradition may generally be ignored, if not debunked, unless it is needed for completing the historical or linguistic picture, while the continuation of the greatest biblical ideas may be traced in the ongoing Christian tradition. The systematic description of these religious ideas is a central part of Old Testament studies and cannot be achieved without the adoption of a coherent integration of the Old and New Testaments. An essential element in academic Hebrew studies is a close acquaintance with, if not a commitment to, such an understanding of the Old Testament. A recent book on the methodology of Old Testament exegesis openly explains that a particular chapter 'would teach the Christian to understand Christ as the holy place . . . as a person . . . as the release of meaning . . . as the guide'.[7]

This has undoubtedly had an impact on the attitudes of modern Christian Bible scholars to Jews as such. Some have welcomed Jewish scholars as colleagues and have even struggled to have them accepted in traditional faculties, not generally as valid interpreters of the Old Testament, which activity remains a Christian prerogative and commitment, but as teachers of Hebrew grammar, post-biblical texts, medieval and modern Hebrew language and literature, Jewish history and the like.[8] There have been those, at the other extreme, who have allied themselves with political and social anti-Semitism and have been party to the exclusion of Jews not only from universities but also from civilized society as a whole.[9] The majority have eschewed any policy of discrimination in the wider context while, often unaware of the consequences of their educational philosophy, have maintained positions that permit them to indulge in various aspects of cultural anti-Judaism, and to call it scientific scholarship. Raphael Loewe has pointed out that for a century before the discovery of the Dead Sea Scrolls forced a rethink, many Christian scholars ignored rabbinics even as a tool for New Testament studies.[10] Overall, it is important to distinguish between those who are aware of the bias in at least part of their Old Testament work and those who make a virtue out of it. This has been clearly expressed by J. D. Levenson: 'Even if we do not subscribe to the naive positivism that claims the historian simply tells what really happened (*wie es eigentlich gewesen ist*), we can still differentiate scholars who strive after a not fully realisable objectivity from those who openly acknowledge their transcendent commitments and approach their work in the vivid hope of deepening and advancing them.'[11] It has to be admitted that the former are thinner on the ground in Europe's traditional centres of learning than they are in the more pluralistic educational institutions of North America.

### JEWISH POSITIONS

It may of course immediately be countered that much Jewish interpretation of the Bible is open to a similar accusation of theological *tendenz*. It arises out of the talmudic and midrashic traditions, takes for granted the existence of an integral link between the written and oral versions of the Torah, and makes central use of the Hebrew Bible, particularly of the Pentateuch, for the validation of halakhic norms. Jewish exegesis also emphasizes the people, the land and the language more than it does any systematic theology and sees the continuity of the covenant between God and Israel in terms of the history of the Jews from ancient to contemporary times. It has repeatedly returned to the Torah, not only as the foundation for its development of the legal and more generally religious ideologies of *halakhah* and *aggadah* but also as a source for the novel ideas of each generation. The Hebrew Bible has also been extensively used in the liturgical and educational activities of both synagogue and academy and the distinction between religious practice and scholarly analysis may consequently be said to have become blurred to such a degree that the Jewish interpretation is no more capable of being disinterested than its Christian counterpart.[12] If, therefore, it is claimed that much of current biblical scholarship is insufficiently unbiased to be regarded as seriously scientific, it must surely be admitted at the same time that two thousand years of Jewish biblical exegesis has little to contribute to current understanding of the Hebrew Bible in a serious academic context.

While the latter admission would indeed be made by some contemporary Jewish scholars, I myself believe that a brief overview of certain parts of what has been achieved by Jewish commentators on the Bible over the centuries will point out to today's students of the Old Testament the need to be more inclusive of older traditions than they might otherwise be, as well as stressing the ways in which the relationship of Jews to the Bible differs in its basic nature from that of Protestant Christians. Before proceeding to such an *Überblick*, another point requires to be made in response to the suggestion that the correct scholarly response must be 'a plague on both your houses'. It is that among Jewish academic institutions it is only in the traditional *yeshivot* (rabbinical academies) that one would find a strong and exclusive ideological commitment to the kind of tendentious interpretations noted above. In most other contexts, there is a greater degree of open-mindedness, even a conviction that 'there are seventy different ways of interpreting the Torah',[13] and certainly no confident assertion that one's own form of exegesis is the only truly scientific one. It is not Christian exegesis to which many Jewish scholars take exception but the apparent inability of many Old Testament scholars to recognize that what to them appears as critical and scientific Hebrew study may be anything but that to those who feel unable to share their theological convictions.

### EARLIEST EXEGESIS

As far as the origin of Jewish exegesis of the Hebrew Bible is concerned, a strong argument could and indeed has been made for locating this in the expansions, variations and alternatives that are found for some earlier texts in their later occurrences in the *Tenakh* itself. There is even specific mention in Nehemiah (8:8) of the public exposition of the 'divine Torah'.[14] One might also look upon the Septuagint as an early commentary on biblical Hebrew texts, as they were understood in the Hellenistic world of Egyptian Jewry. That world produced its own interpretation of the Bible, most commonly known from the work of Philo and Josephus but undoubtedly more variegated and extensive.[15] Certainly the *pesher* method recorded among the Judean scrolls testifies to a Jewish belief in the eternal message of the Bible and a need to find guidance for today in the divine message of yesterday.[16] If we define all such exegetical activity as 'Jewish', we enter into the controversial area of how, and to what degree, that sense of 'Jewish' differs from the later Jewish approach to Scripture and, indeed, from the early Christian understanding of sacred texts. It therefore seems sensible to leave such matters unresolved in this context and to proceed to the earliest forms of the rabbinic exegetical tradition.

The forms that I here have in mind are those to be found in the rabbinic literature of the period between the rise of Christianity and the emergence of Islam. For our purposes, it is essential to note the manner in which such literature looks upon the Hebrew Bible. It is without question the word of God but there is no one dogmatic and systematic function for it in the tradition, nor one true meaning for it in parts or as a whole, which the individual, rather than the Jewish community, has to search out and absorb. Since the central element in rabbinic Judaism is the commitment to Jewish religious law (*halakhah*) and the performance of the 'precepts' (*miṣvot*), the Hebrew Bible, particularly the Pentateuch, is regarded as the authoritative source (the Written Torah), linked to the practice (the Oral Torah) by the interpretation of the relevant verses. The authority is, however, to be found in the *halakhah* and not in the process of interpretation, for which there exist various types.[17]

These types of interpretation may be legal and tied to laws specifically mandated in the Pentateuch or they may be more generally associated with the fields of ethics, behaviour and current problems, known broadly as *aggadah*. Sometimes the exegetical treatment of the text has the aim of offering a running commentary, while in other cases a specific difficulty is addressed, or a homiletical idea is pursued in various verses. Linguistic and literary points may be made, as well as theological and historical ones, with some exegetes indicating a preference for paying attention to minute details of the text while others opt for understanding the particular passage of Scripture as a piece of literature. Literal, expansive and fanciful interpretations are to be found and are even compared but no clearly defined distinction is made in the early rabbinic literature between what later commentators saw as the opposing systems of simple meaning (*peshaṭ*) and applied exegesis (*derash*).[18] There is an obvious tendency to react to understandings of the Hebrew Bible and its message that are based on allegorical, typological and rhetorical treatments favoured by Christians, on the intellectual and mystical approaches of the Gnostics or on the unsympathetic attitudes of pagan thinkers. This leads to changes of stress, particularly with regard to such matters as the identity and reputation of Israel, the nature of deity, the messianic period, the value of ritual and the character and activities of major pentateuchal figures.[19]

The sources of such rabbinic treatments of Scripture are the Babylonian and Palestinian Talmuds, where the exegesis occurs incidentally, and the various early Midrashim, where the coverage is more systematic. It would seem to be the case that interest in commenting on biblical verses was more pronounced in the Holy Land than in Babylon, and that both Origen and Jerome were influenced by such an interest. It is difficult to date the targumic traditions but there can be little doubt that they existed and were developed side by side with the talmudic and midrashic traditions, influencing and being influenced in their turn.[20] How precisely the synagogal, academic and literary contexts for these various works emerged and interrelated is too large a question even to be touched on here, but what may be said with confidence is that the Hebrew Bible had an important place in each. The devotional and liturgical use of the pentateuchal, prophetic and hagiographical books took the form of lectionaries for sabbaths, festivals and fasts; public expositions and homilies; and psalms readings.[21] It must be acknowledged that as the talmudic tradition grew and dominated, so did the tendency in at least some Jewish circles, perhaps particularly in Babylon, where the major talmudic academies flourished, to concentrate on the applied religious senses of the Hebrew Bible, rather than on any more literal meaning.

### THE ISLAMIC WORLD

An approach that remained closer to the Hebrew Bible did not, however, lack its Jewish protagonists in the centuries between the Islamic conquest of the Near East and the end of the Babylonian talmudic hegemony in the eleventh century. Perhaps inspired by earlier Palestinian trends, and by the concerns of the Samaritans, Christians and Muslims to establish what they saw as pure and authentic versions of scriptural text and tradition, the Karaite Jews took up the cudgels on behalf of the Bible and wielded them powerfully in the early period of their existence. Their interpretation of Judaism came to the fore in the eighth century and their Bible scholars made remarkable progress in ensuring the accurate transmission of the text, its literal translation and its didactic clarification. Suspicious as they were of the rabbinic traditions, they produced their own word-for-word translations, alternate renderings and interpretations, amounting to what has been called 'scientific literalism', and were at the forefront of the important Masoretic developments of the period.[22]

The Karaites were not the only group to force rabbinic Judaism to reconsider the degree of attention that it was paying to the *Tenakh*. In vindication of its own qur'anic version of the monotheistic revelation, the Muslims not only argued that the Jews had falsified Scripture but also made every effort to protect and promote their own sacred texts. They entered into polemical discussions with both Christians and Jews about the validity of the accounts and ideas contained in the Hebrew and Greek Bibles.[23] Jews too were among those who repeated and expanded what had already been said in the Classical world about the questionable content of the Jewish Scriptures. A ninth-century Persian Bible critic, Ḥiwi al-Balkhi, raised 200 objections, arguing that there were clear-cut instances of divine injustice, anthropomorphism, contradictions and irrationalities.[24]

Natronai ben Hilai, head (*ga'on*) of the Sura academy in the ninth century, expressed criticism of the relative neglect of the Hebrew Bible in his circles and the trend to correct this alleged imbalance may be traced among his successors.[25] Perhaps the most famous of all the geonic scholars, Saadya ben Joseph (882–942), set out to respond to all the challenges facing rabbinic Judaism on various fronts and some of his most important scholarly activities were concentrated in the biblical field. He produced new, authoritative translations and interpretations of the biblical books, in which his linguistic and rational approach predominated, and his grammatical and lexicographical works made a major contribution to the better understanding of biblical Hebrew. He preferred the literal rendering, except when he regarded it as irrational, unnatural, contradictory or untraditional.[26] Similarly, another *ga'on* of Sura, Samuel ben Ḥofni (d. 1013), wrote a commentary that demonstrated how one could remain faithful to the biblical source, provide rational responses to the problems raised by the texts and offer sound linguistic explanations of difficult words and passages.[27] There can be little doubt that such scholars laid the foundations on which were built the considerable exegetical achievements of the Jewish exegetes of medieval Spain, France and Provence.

## MEDIEVAL EUROPE

Very much underpinning such foundations was the Islamic-Jewish cultural symbiosis and the linguistic interchange between Hebrew, Aramaic and Arabic. This led to the development of a primitive form of comparative Semitic linguistics and the creation of new and extensive dictionaries and grammars, thus considerably influencing and expanding the field of Jewish biblical exegesis.[28] The earliest manifestations of such progress were still very much tied to the Arabic language and Islamic trends but as they moved from Spain, where they first flourished, into Provence and France, they also acquired a Hebrew garb, thus bringing the results of the latest linguistic research deeper into non-Mediterranean Europe. The overall theme of that research is that one can distinguish clearly between literal and applied meanings, some exegetes going further than others in rejecting anything that is not pure *peshaṭ*, or simple sense. Although the period under discussion ranges from the eleventh to the thirteenth century and is replete with names, works and scholarly variety, all that is possible in the present limited context is a brief survey, with a few examples, of each geographical sphere.

Inheriting as he did the finest linguistic scholarship of the Jews in Islamic Spain, and best representing as he does its application to biblical interpretation, Abraham Ibn Ezra (1089–1164) deserves special mention at the outset. His commentaries reflect an itinerant and unsettled life but also one that is open to many influences and ideas. He rarely misses an opportunity of introducing technical matters of grammar, philosophy and the physical sciences and he often challenges traditional rabbinic views, more often by implication than directly. His preference is for the rational and the literal but his cryptic and elliptic style ensures that only the scholar will understand the significance of many of his comments. By the time that Moses ben Naḥman, or Naḥmanides (1194–1270), was active in Bible commentary, there was a move in Spain towards the mystical and the pietistic, and he challenged many of Ibn Ezra's comments, often preferring more traditional rabbinic interpretations. Nevertheless, he still paid attention to linguistic, contextual, medical and chronological points and is not averse to criticizing biblical heroes for what he regards as their moral shortcomings.[29]

It is not yet clear how much of the approach of Solomon ben Isaac, or Rashi (1040–1105), was due to the influence of his teachers and the wider environment but what is without doubt is that he became the leading commentator of Franco-German circles and ultimately the most popular Jewish exegete of all time. He tried to answer the basic questions the reader might ask and produced a remarkable blend of the literal, the linguistic and the fanciful that informed and edified many generations. His attempt to distinguish contextual from applied interpretation and in this way to distinguish between *peshat* and *derash* was taken much further by a number of his pupils, especially by his grandson, Samuel ben Meir, or Rashbam (1080–1160), who reports that he directly and successfully confronted his grandfather with the need for change. He committed himself to pursuing the 'absolutely literal meaning of the text' and concerned himself with words, context and style rather than the rabbinic message, often finding himself seriously at variance with traditional interpretations. There is undoubtedly a mutual influence between his exegesis and that of some of the Christian mendicant orders of his time, apparently the result of personal exchanges.[30]

The Jewish scholarship of twelfth- and thirteenth-century Provence is a remarkable blend of the latest developments with the best of rabbinic learning, the field of biblical exegesis being best represented by the Qimḥi family, the father Joseph and the sons, Moses and David. Though only David's work is extensively preserved, it is clear that they were all devoted to literal interpretation, to careful linguistic analysis, and to the kind of exegesis that could challenge the dominant Christian use of the Hebrew Bible in their day. David (Redaq) produced a sound synthesis of various types of treatment, including science and philosophy as well as concentrating on grammatical and Masoretic matters.[31]

Before concluding the medieval achievements, a word about the late Italian contribution is in order. Don Isaac Abrabanel (1437–1508) was reared in the Iberian peninsula but spent his adult life as a diplomat in Italy and very much reflects the early Renaissance world. He demonstrates knowledge of, and even sometimes sympathy for non-Jewish explanations of Scripture and is able to apply his practical knowledge of politics to the better understanding of such matters as court intrigue. He deals with literary structure and matters of authorship, as well as attempting to explain the intent of the writer. Another link between the medieval and modern worlds is Obadiah Sforno (1470–1550), a broadly educated North Italian doctor who is concerned with conveying the various humanistic and universalistic aspects of the text. He is interested in the literary as well as the literal and is keen to analyse structure and content. As a teacher of Johannes Reuchlin, he, together with many of his Jewish predecessors, contributed in no small degree to the flowering of early modern Christian hebraism, and consequently to the creation of such literary masterpieces as the King James Version.[32]

### THE MODERN WORLD

The attitudes of Jewish scholars in the modern world to the study of the Hebrew Bible are closely bound up with issues of intellectual enlightenment and socio-political emancipation. The process of transition from the more established and traditional sources and outlooks to 'purely' secular or religiously disinterested positions began in Germany with the work of Moses Mendelssohn (1729–86) and his team of collaborators. Their idea was to combine the best of older Jewish scholarship with the latest linguistic expertise and religious thinking and to produce an aesthetic translation of the Bible (*Bi`ur*) that could serve to educate Jews not only in Scripture but also in modernity. Such notions were also attractive to those who developed the scientific study of Judaism (*Wissenschaft des Judentums*) in Germany and the Austro-Hungarian Empire in the nineteenth century but there was still a caution about approaching the biblical text, particularly that of the

Pentateuch, in any sort of iconoclastic fashion and radical criticism was preferably applied to rabbinic texts and ideology.[33]

Further steps in the transition were taken by the Italian scholar, Samuel David Luzzatto (1800–65), who succeeded in widening the *wissenschaftliche* approach to include at least the books of the Prophets and Hagiographa. Although observant and traditional in his life-style, he was capable of sharp and novel analysis and applied this to various aspects of biblical study. He acknowledged the importance of acquainting oneself with Christian scholarship and set out principles of exegesis that included consideration not only of rabbinic and linguistic matters but also of literary, text-critical and chronological interpretation. Arnold Ehrlich (1848–1919) went further along the critical path, basing his work on the conviction that linguistic meaning was as important as language itself, while Benno Jacob (1862–1945) challenged many of the ideas of the Christian Bible critics with a blend of philology and lexicography and with a commitment to internal Jewish interpretation and the Torah's own sense of its message.

Although the traditional rabbinic commentators, particularly of Eastern Europe, were averse to such developments because of their possibly negative influence on traditional philosophy and practice, they were sufficiently moved by their existence to pay greater attention to the study of the Hebrew Bible, even if still part of the combined revelation of Written and Oral Torah. Such leading rabbinic figures as Elijah ben Solomon of Vilna (1720–97), Naphtali Tsevi Yehudah Berlin (1817–93), Meir Leibush ben Yeḥiel Michal (Malbim) (1809–79) and Samson Raphael Hirsch (1808–88) succeeded in winning afresh for the *Tenakh* itself the attention and affection of many observant Jews. What is more, their return to *peshaṭ,* their inclusion of wider cultural material, and their desire to respond to the questions being raised outside their circles, combined to ensure that they produced important insights into the biblical texts.[34]

In the century just coming to an end, Jews have been represented in all manner of modern and traditional approaches to the Hebrew Bible and it becomes more difficult to trace any special tendency. What can, however, be stated is that in addition to the purely secular stance and, at the other end of the spectrum, the strongly traditional angle on exegesis, one must acknowledge the existence of trends that are not wholly consistent with those of the 'Protestant' world of scholarship, earlier described. Particularly in such 'Jewish' institutions as the Israeli universities and the theological seminaries of the United States and Europe, and indeed among many individual specialists elsewhere, there still continues to be less concern with intensive source criticism and the search for a systematic theology, and greater interest in textual criticism, history and archaeology, and the Semitic background to Hebrew language and literature. On the other hand, there continues to be a hesitancy about tackling head-on some of the textual, literary and historical problems highlighted by pentateuchal criticism.[35]

## CONCLUSIONS

A number of brief remarks require to be made in conclusion. At most points in the history of exegesis Christians and Jews have, of course, confidently believed in the rightness of their own positions but have also been aware of each other's treatment of the texts. In response, they have either absorbed the best of the 'devil's tunes' or made a conscious effort to deny any euphony in their sound. They have recognized the value of earlier achievements and have often used these as foundations for their own exegetical structures. The quest for the literal sense is represented in both traditions but has always been particularly strong among the Jews, for whom language rather than theology has dominated. What is needed today is a genuine attempt at unbiased scholarship and a willingness to question one's own position by asking, in all honesty, whether a degree of tendentiousness is so inbuilt as to have become virtually unrecognizable to those whom it surrounds; whether all that is modern is necessarily more scholarly than the learning that precedes it; and whether approaches associated with one religious group need be rejected by another.[36]

# Notes

1 Correspondence between John Barton and Stefan Reif, dated 28 September, 3 October and 8 October 1995.

2 In a series of open lectures given in the spring of 1996 in the Faculty of Divinity at the University of Cambridge, on the theme of the future of biblical theology, all the speakers (Professor R. Clements, Dr G. Davies, Professor M. Hooker and Professor D. Ford) appeared to subscribe to most or all of these presuppositions.

3 An excellent example of the tension may be found in the exchange between I. W. Provan and P. R. Davies in *Journal of Biblical Literature* 114 (1995), pp. 585–606 and 683–705.

4 M. Haran denies the serious critical value of premodern exegesis in his 'Midrashic and Literal Exegesis and the Critical Method in Biblical Research',

in S. Japhet (ed.), *Studies in Bible*, Scripta Hierosolymitana 31 (Jerusalem: Magnes Press, 1986), pp. 19–48, but his case is overstated.

5 S. D. Greenslade (ed.), *The Cambridge History of the Bible. The West from the Reformation to the Present Day* (Cambridge: Cambridge University Press, 1963).

6 On the whole topic, see J. D. Levenson, *The Hebrew Bible, the Old Testament and Historical Criticism* (Louisville, KY: Westminster/John Knox Press, 1993), especially chapters 1, 2 and 4; and E. L. Greenstein, *Essays on Biblical Method and Translation*, Brown Judaica Series 92 (Atlanta, GA: Scholars Press, 1989), pp. 24–6.

7 O. H. Steck, *Old Testament Exegesis. A Guide to the Methodology*, English translation; SBL Sources for Biblical Study 33 (Atlanta, GA: Scholars Press, 1995), p. 207.

8 The situation at Cambridge over the years may serve to illustrate the point; see S. C. Reif, 'Hebrew and Hebraists at Cambridge. An Historical Introduction', in *Hebrew Manuscripts at Cambridge University Library. A Description and Introduction* (Cambridge: Cambridge University Press, 1997), pp. 1–35.

9 One of the best known anti-Semitic semitists was Paul de Lagarde, who was an outstanding student of the ancient versions but also regarded the Jews as 'a repulsive burden with no historical use'; *Encyclopaedia Judaica*, vol. X (Jerusalem: Keter Publishing House, 1971), col. 1356.

10 R. Loewe, 'Christian Hebraists', *Encyclopaedia Judaica*, vol. VIII (Jerusalem: Keter Publishing House, 1971), cols. 9–71, with the relevant comment in col. 19.

11 Levenson, *The Hebrew Bible*, pp. 37–8; see also S. D. Sperling's volume about North America, *Students of the Covenant. A History of Jewish Biblical Scholarship in North America*, Confessional Perspectives Series (Atlanta, GA: Scholars Press, 1992).

12 On the general history of Jewish biblical interpretation, see M. Soloweitschik and S. Rubascheff, *The History of Bible Criticism* (Hebrew; Berlin: Dewir-Mikra, 1925); B. M. Casper, *An Introduction to Jewish Bible Commentary* (New York and London: Thomas Yoseloff, 1960); M. H. Segal, *Parshanut Ha-Miqra* (Jerusalem: Kiryat Sepher, 2nd edn 1952); E. I. J. Rosenthal, *Studia Semitica. 1. Jewish Themes* (Cambridge: Cambridge University Press, 1971), pp. 165–85 and 244–71; L. Jacobs, *Jewish Biblical Exegesis* (New York: Behrman House, 1973); and M. Greenberg (ed.), *Jewish Bible Exegesis. An Introduction* (Hebrew; Jerusalem: Bialik Institute, 1983).

13 Midrash Rabbah Numbers, 15:13.

14 Soloweitschik and Rubascheff, *The History of Bible Criticism*, pp. 9–11; Segal, *Parshanut*, pp. 5–7; and Haran, 'Midrashic and Literal Exegesis', pp. 19–20. See also, in general, M. Fishbane, *Biblical Interpretation in Ancient Israel* (Oxford: Clarendon Press, 1985).

15 M. E. Stone (ed.), *Jewish Writings of the Second Temple Period. Apocrypha, Pseudepigrapha, Qumran, Sectarian Writings, Philo, Josephus*, Compendia

Rerum Judaicarum ad Novum Testamentum 2/2 (Assen: Van Gorcum, 1984), pp. 1–481 for the whole background.

16 *Ibid.*, pp. 503–13.

17 S. Safrai (ed.), *Literature of the Sages*, Compendia Rerum Judaicarum ad Novum Testamentum 2/3a (Assen: Van Gorcum, 1987).

18 G. Stemberger, *Introduction to the Talmud and Midrash*, English translation (Edinburgh: T. & T. Clark, 2nd edn 1996); G. G. Porton, *Understanding Rabbinic Midrash. Texts and Commentary* (Hoboken, NJ: Ktav Publishing House, 1985); and R. Loewe, 'The "Plain" meaning of Scripture in Early Jewish Exegesis', *Papers of the Institute of Jewish Studies London* 1 (1964), pp. 140–85. See also D. Weiss-Halivni, *Peshat and Derash. Plain and Applied Meaning in Rabbinic Exegesis* (New York and Oxford: Oxford University Press, 1991).

19 M. Hirshman, *A Rivalry of Genius. Jewish and Christian Biblical Interpretation in Late Antiquity*, English translation, SUNY Series in Judaica (Albany, NY: State University of New York Press, 1996); and G. Stemberger, 'Exegetical Contacts between Christians and Jews in the Roman Empire', in M. Sæbø (ed.), *Hebrew Bible/Old Testament. The History of its Interpretation* (Göttingen: Vandenhoeck & Ruprecht, 1996), vol. I, part 1, pp. 569–86.

20 Greenberg, *Jewish Bible Exegesis*, pp. 11–13; M. J. Mulder (ed.), *Mikra. Text, Translation, Reading and Interpretation of the Hebrew Bible in Ancient Judaism and Early Christianity*, Compendia Rerum Judaicarum ad Novum Testamentum 2/1 (Assen: Van Gorcum, 1988).

21 S. C. Reif, 'Codicological Aspects of Jewish Liturgical History', *Bulletin of the John Rylands University Library of Manchester* 75 (1993), pp. 119–25; 'The Cairo Genizah and its Treasures, with Special Reference to Biblical Studies', in D. R. G. Beattie and M. J. McNamara (eds.), *The Aramaic Bible. Targums in their Historical Context, Journal for the Study of the Old Testament Supplement Series*, 166 (Sheffield: Sheffield Academic Press, 1994), pp. 30–50.

22 M. Polliack, 'Alternate Renderings and Additions in Yeshu 'ah ben Yehudah's Arabic Translation of the Pentateuch', *Jewish Quarterly Review* 84 (1993–4), pp. 209–25; 'The Medieval Karaite Tradition of Translating the Hebrew Bible into Arabic; its Sources, Characteristics and Historical Background', *Journal of the Royal Asiatic Society* 6 (1996), pp. 189–96.

23 H. Lazarus-Yafeh, *Intertwined Worlds. Medieval Islam and Biblical Criticism* (Princeton: Princeton University Press, 1992).

24 On the latest poetic version to be discovered (in the Cambridge Genizah Collection), see E. Fleischer, 'A Fragment from Ḥiwi al-Balkhi's Criticism of the Bible', *Tarbiz* 51 (1981), pp. 49–57.

25 S. W. Baron, *A Social and Religious History of the Jews* (New York, London and Philadelphia: Columbia University Press and the Jewish Theological Seminary of America, 1958), vol VI, pp. 235–6.

26 A. S. Halkin, (Hebrew) 'Jewish Exegesis in Arabic outside Spain and Early Karaite Exegesis', in Greenberg, *Jewish Bible Exegesis*, pp. 16–19; Rosenthal, *Studia Semitica*, pp. 86–125; M. Zucker, *Rav Saadya's Translation of the Torah*

(New York: Feldheim, 1959) and *Saadya's Commentary on Genesis* (Hebrew; New York: Jewish Theological Seminary of America, 1984).

27 A. Greenbaum (ed.), *The Biblical Commentary of Rav Samuel ben Ḥofni Gaon according to Geniza Manuscripts* (Hebrew; Jerusalem: Rav Kook Institute, 1979).

28 D. Téné, 'Comparative Linguistics and the Knowledge of Hebrew' (Hebrew), in M. Bar-Asher, A. Dotan, G. B. Sarfati and D. Téné (eds.), *Hebrew Language Studies Presented to Professor Zeev Ben-Hayyim* (Jerusalem: Magnes Press, 1983), pp. 237–87.

29 U. Simon, (Hebrew) 'The Spanish Exegetes', and J. S. Licht, (Hebrew) 'Ramban', in Greenberg, *Jewish Bible Exegesis*, pp. 47–68; and S. C. Reif, 'Classical Jewish Commentators on Exodus 2', in M. Bar-Asher (ed.), *Studies in Hebrew and Jewish Languages Presented to Shelomo Morag on the Occasion of his Seventieth Birthday* (Jerusalem: Bialik Institute, 1996), pp. *81–*82.

30 Greenberg, *Jewish Bible Exegesis*, pp. 68–85; and Reif, 'Classical Jewish Commentators', pp. *79–*80.

31 F. Talmage, (Hebrew) 'The Exegetes of Provence in the 12th and Early 13th Centuries', in Greenberg, *Jewish Bible Exegesis*, pp. 86–91; and F. Talmage, *David Kimḥi. The Man and the Commentaries* (Cambridge, MA: Harvard University Press, 1975).

32 S. Z. Leiman, (Hebrew) 'The Last of the Spanish and Provençal Exegetes, and the Italian Exegetes', in Greenberg, *Jewish Bible Exegesis*, pp. 96–100; Rosenthal, *Studia Semitica*, pp. 21–54, 56–85 and 127–64; and Reif, 'Classical Jewish Commentators', pp. *83–*84.

33 Y. Horowitz, (Hebrew) 'Jewish Exegesis in Recent Generations', in Greenberg, *Jewish Bible Exegesis*, pp. 113–22; B. A. Levine, 'The European Background', in Sperling, *Students of the Covenant*, pp. 15–32.

34 Horowitz, 'Jewish Exegesis', in Greenberg, *Jewish Bible Exegesis*, pp. 122–36; Levine, 'The European Background', in Sperling, *Students of the Covenant*, pp. 15–32.

35 Sperling, *Students of the Covenant*. Challenges to Jewish exegetes to deal with the source-critical approach, particularly as it relates to the Pentateuch, are now made from time to time, as at various points in the publications of Haran, ('Midrashic and Literal Exegesis') and Levenson (*The Hebrew Bible*), and in the essay by B. B. Levy, 'On the Periphery. North American Orthodox Judaism and Contemporary Biblical Scholarship', in Sperling, *Students of the Covenant*, pp. 159–204. See also Greenstein's volume *Essays on Biblical Method*.

36 See the wise and balanced remarks of Segal, *Parshanut*, pp. 128–31. This chapter was written while I was a professorial fellow in the Institute for Advanced Studies at the Hebrew University of Jerusalem and I welcome the opportunity of thanking the Institute for its facilities and many kindnesses.

## Further reading

Casper, B. M., *An Introduction to Jewish Bible Commentary*, New York and London: Thomas Yoseloff, 1960.

Fishbane, M., *Biblical Interpretation in Ancient Israel*, Oxford: Clarendon Press, 1985.

Greenstein, E. L., *Essays on Biblical Method and Translation*, Brown Judaica Series 92, Atlanta, GA: Scholars Press, 1989.

Haran, M., 'Midrashic and Literal Exegesis and the Critical Method in Biblical Research', in S. Japhet (ed.), *Studies in Bible*, Scripta Hierosolymitana 31, Jerusalem: Magnes Press, 1986, pp. 19–48.

Hirshman, M., *A Rivalry of Genius. Jewish and Christian Biblical Interpretation in Late Antiquity*, English translation, SUNY Series in Judaica, Albany, NY: State University of New York Press, 1966.

Jacobs, L., *Jewish Biblical Exegesis*, New York: Behrman House, 1973.

Levenson, J. D., *The Hebrew Bible, the Old Testament and Historical Criticism*, Louisville, KY: Westminster/John Knox, 1993.

Mulder, M. J. (ed.), *Mikra. Text, Translation, Reading and Interpretation of the Hebrew Bible in Ancient Judaism and Early Christianity*, Compendia Rerum Judaicarum ad Novum Testamentum 2/1, Assen: Van Gorcum, 1988.

Reif, S. C., 'Classical Jewish Commentators on Exodus 2', in M. Bar-Asher (ed.), *Studies in Hebrew and Jewish Languages Presented to Shelomo Morag on the Occasion of his Seventieth Birthday*, Jerusalem: Bialik Institute, 1996, pp. *73–*112.

Sperling, S. D. (ed.), *Students of the Covenant. A History of Jewish Biblical Scholarship in North America*, Confessional Perspectives Series, Atlanta, GA: Scholars Press, 1992.

# 11 The Bible in literature and art

STEPHEN PRICKETT

Any discussion of the Bible in relation to the arts carries its own not-so-hidden agenda. As the extensive range of biblical stories in Islamic painting reminds us,[1] not all biblical art is Christian, or even Judaeo-Christian. Just as it is impossible to speak of the Bible as a 'neutral' piece of writing free from a particular hermeneutic context, so it is impossible even to begin to speak of its artistic interpretations without realizing that these have always constituted a two-way exchange. What may look at first sight like the Bible casting a wide cultural penumbra was, in fact, a dynamic interpretative relationship through which the perception of the text was itself transformed. If the Bible helped to create a particular aesthetic, what was understood by the Bible was, equally, a creation of that aesthetic – indeed, it is my thesis here that biblical interpretation has historically followed, rather than created, aesthetic interpretation.

## THE BIBLE AND THE MEDIEVAL ARTS

Medieval polysemous typology, for instance, was an essentially literary solution to a hermeneutic problem. The belief of Paul and the other early Church leaders that Jesus was the predicted Jewish Messiah, though it had reinforced the importance of the Hebrew Bible as the major section of the Christian scriptures, meant also that those scriptures had, from the outset, to be radically reinterpreted. Christianity was, in this sense, born of a critical debate about the nature and meaning of texts.

Many of the books of the Hebrew canon prescribed rituals which had little or no relevance to the practices or beliefs of the new Hellenistic Christian communities. Jewish narratives, laws and even ethical teachings often seemed to contradict those of the New Testament. For authorities like Irenaeus and Eusebius, who believed the Hebrew writings to be divinely inspired, and therefore indispensable, some method had to be found to harmonize them with what was now believed to be their fulfilment. What

Austin Farrer has called, in Revelation, a 're-birth of images',[2] was, in effect, a massive metaphorical reinterpretation affecting the entire Bible. Though allegory was not a characteristic form of Jewish writing,[3] rabbinic interpreters had already shown how the Song of Songs could be given a non-literal meaning, and this tradition was reinforced by similar Greek methods of exegesis begun as early as the fifth century BCE by Empedocles and Theagenes.[4] In the first century CE, Philo, a Hellenized Jew, foreshadowed the later Christian synthesis of Hebrew and Greek traditions by claiming that not only were the Hebrew scriptures compatible with Greek philosophy, but that in many cases the Greek writers had been influenced by the Hebrew ones.[5] In so doing he also showed how Greek allegorical methods could be used on Hebrew scriptural texts. The claim that Christianity was the key to understanding the Hebrew scriptures was soon supported by an increasingly elaborate system of figurative and allegorical interpretation – which was even extended to other pagan classical texts. Virgil's fourth *Eclogue*, with its prophecy of a coming ruler, was read as a parallel to Isaiah and a foretelling of Christ, and the *Aeneid* was allegorized as the Christian soul's journey through life. This complex and polysemous system of exegesis, begun by such commentators as Origen and Augustine, was to cover the entire Bible so comprehensively that by the Middle Ages even Paul's letters were given figurative readings.

Different schools differed as to the precise number of figural interpretations possible to a given passage of Scripture. Some Alexandrian authorities detected as many as twelve, but four was by far the most widely accepted number.[6] This could itself be arrived at by typological reasoning. Irenaeus, for example, argued for the canonical primacy of the four Gospels from the fact that God's world was supplied in fours: just as there were 'four zones', and 'four winds', so there were four Gospels, and four levels of interpretation. According to St John Cassian in the fourth century these were a literal, or historical sense, an allegorical, a tropological (or moral) and an anagogical. Tropological related to the Word, or doctrine conveyed by it, and therefore carried a moral sense; the anagogical concerned eternal things. Cassian takes as his example the figure of Jerusalem. Historically, it may be seen as the earthly city; allegorically, it stands for the Church; tropologically, it represents the souls of all faithful Christians; anagogically, it is the heavenly city of God.[7]

Such an allegorization of the canon, moreover, helped to prize stories loose from their original setting and to give them the possibility of universal significance. Erich Auerbach argues convincingly that this new Christian interpretative theory was an essential ingredient in its becoming a world religion.

Figural interpretation changed the Old Testament from a book of laws and a history of the people of Israel into a series of figures of Christ and the Redemption – so Celtic and Germanic peoples, for example, could accept the Old Testament as part of the universal religion of salvation and a necessary component of the equally magnificent and universal vision of history conveyed to them along with this religion . . . Its integral, firmly teleological, view of history and the providential order of the world gave it the power to capture the imagination . . . of the convert nations. Figural interpretation was a fresh beginning and a rebirth of man's creative powers.[8]

It was, in effect, the prime tool not merely of the Christian appropriation of the Hebrew scriptures, but of the evangelization of Europe; and the effect of this, now almost-invisible, tradition upon the subsequent development of European literature can scarcely be overestimated. Until almost the end of the eighteenth century, for instance, the literal meaning of the Bible was seen as only one among many ways of understanding it. Not merely did allegorical, figural and typological modes of reading coexist with the literal one, but, because they were more generalized, they were often in practice given higher status. Moreover, since the Bible, together still with the classics, was the model for all secular literature, such multi-levelled modes of reading naturally also influenced the way in which other books were read. Allegorical levels in Dante's *Divine Comedy*, or the popular medieval love-story, *The Romance of the Rose*, were not optional extras, but a normal and integral part of what was expected from literature.

But if the medieval Bible was itself the construct of an essentially literary method of reading, its appeal was to a largely illiterate people. Until the invention of movable-type printing in the fifteenth century and the gradual growth of literacy through the sixteenth century, popular interpretation of the Bible was primarily visual rather than textual. The cliché that the medieval cathedral was 'the poor man's Bible' is true not merely in the obvious sense that stained glass windows and sculptured friezes portrayed biblical persons and scenes, but also more specifically in that the visual simultaneity of such illustrations reflected the innate simultaneity of polysemous modes of interpretation. The same is true of the illustrations in medieval bibles, prayerbooks and psalters. In the Duc de Berry's *Book of Hours* – a work which, like a cathedral, involved many hands and took over seventy years to complete[9] – the biblical illustrations typically show an entire story. The second of the eight full plates (figure 1) represents no fewer than four stages of the Fall from

1. 'Paradise on Earth', *Les Très Riches Heures du duc de Berry*
   (Musée Condé, Chantilly) reproduced by permission of Giraudon.

left to right. In the first, on the extreme left, Eve is tempted by a semi-human serpent whose face and long golden hair curiously, but deliberately, resemble her own. In the second, she offers the golden fruit to Adam. In the third, a blue-robed and haloed God confronts the guilty pair, and finally, on the extreme right, an angel pushes the reluctant and fig-leaved pair out of the Gothic gateway of Paradise. The garden, with its rich grass and loaded fruit trees, is in stark contrast with the barren landscape hinted at on the outside of the golden wall. The fountain in the midst of the garden is an elaborate Gothic one, an idealized version of the sort sometimes found at the market cross in a wealthy medieval town. Unusually for this Book of Hours, but no less deliberately, there is no frame to the picture and the lumpy terrain of the fallen world runs straight into the white of the parchment and therefore into the world of the viewer.

It is this that links the picture with its audience. There is no attempt at proportion or perspective to position the viewer. The garden is the perfect circle required by theological tradition, not the ellipse it would appear to the eye, and the wall is made very low for us to see over it. The picture presents neither the illusion of space nor time. Everything is flat and simultaneous. Yet the realistic modelling of the figures, Eve, with a fashionable protruding belly, and Adam, whose kneeling posture is based on a Hellenistic statue still to be seen in the Museum of Aix-en-Provence, should remind us that the artist was neither anatomically incompetent nor unaware of the differences between his own style and that of the classical world that had preceded it. The loss of the antique knowledge of perspective with the coming of Christian art is often presented as a technical collapse, resulting in part from the wholesale and deliberate destruction of much of classical Roman art,[10] but it should rather be seen as the logical outcome of exactly the same reinterpretative process that had allegorized both the Hebrew scriptures and the classics.

Typology eliminates both time and space. To read in the story of Cain and Abel the type of the death of Christ, or in that of Jacob and Esau the type of Christians inheriting the blessing intended for the Jews, is to flatten history into a simultaneous panorama. To find in the Bible all things necessary for salvation, with the grand narrative of humanity beginning with the Creation in Genesis and concluding with the Apocalypse in Revelation, is to see all history in a timeless present composed of separable incidents related less to their own immediate context than to their typological place in the whole. In this respect, all the medieval arts show parallel characteristics. In music, the earlier Gregorian plainchant gave way to polyphonic forms, where the same words, phrase or sentence could be sung repetitively (as in a round) or even out of sequence – once again stressing simultaneity rather than linear temporal progression. While mosaic was invented in antiquity, it is no accident that it reached its height in early Christian art and architecture. Lacking any illusion of depth, its often highly decorated surface consisted of thousands of individual fragments relating to one another on a two-dimensional surface. Similarly, in their fragmentation and visual simultaneity, medieval painting and stained glass, like the carvings on the exteriors of churches and cathedrals, were entirely of a piece with the rest of medieval critical theory.

### PERSPECTIVE

It is hardly surprising, therefore, that the first changes in that critical theory should originate not in the interpretation of the biblical text, but in *visual* convention. About a hundred years before the *Très Riches Heures* was completed by the brothers Limbourg, Jean Colombe and at least one other, Giotto had begun to investigate the art of perspective. Its secrets were at first closely guarded, and it was not until 1435 that the first scientific treatise on perspective was published by Alberti. Others followed: Pelerin of Toul (1505) and Albrecht Dürer (1525). But perspective rapidly became far more than a technique for realism in painting – or even of calculating the ballistic trajectories of missiles. It constituted nothing less than a new way of ordering visual experience. Not merely was the relationship of objects in space now defined according to certain invariable constants, but the position of the viewer was also fixed – outside the frame, no longer as a participant in a divine symbol, but an observer of an imaginary world. Position was a condition of viewing. Finally, and perhaps most important of all, perspective also implied a linear view of time. Simultaneity of action was impossible in an art that presented a snapshot, a frozen moment of time. It was no longer possible to show simultaneously all the stages of a story such as the Fall within a single design.

The discovery of perspective was to prove ultimately the death-knell of multi-levelled typology in biblical interpretation – though vestiges were to survive well into the nineteenth century,[11] and, if we include Freudian analysis and symbolic theory, it is still with us. In medieval painting, as in literature, the setting was always a timeless present. Biblical characters (once clothed) always wore contemporary dress and appeared in the local context. In Canterbury cathedral a stained glass panel shows Jesus, in thirteenth-century dress, raising Jairus's daughter in a diagrammatic medieval merchant's house. In the Townley Shepherds' Play, the shepherds are Yorkshire rustics. The life of Albrecht Dürer (1471–1526) was in many ways a watershed where we can actually follow the development from visual perspective to historical realism in his art. His early training in Nuremberg, Colmar and Basel, was in the German Gothic tradition, and it was only when he crossed the Alps for the first time to visit Italy that he began to draw landscapes and study the Italian 'secrets' of perspective.[12] The series of woodcuts entitled *The Life of the Virgin* made mostly between 1502–5, and published in 1511, show all the excitement of the new principles in action. In 'The Meeting of Mary and Elizabeth: the Visitation', two bourgeois ladies in delicately flowing robes embrace each other against a dramatic alpine backdrop of crags and castles. The same delight in perspective appears in 'The Adoration of the Magi' which apparently takes place in the outhouse of a ruined teutonic castle (figure 2). But the schema of the picture betrays an uneasy mixture of the realistic and the symbolic. The Magi are Germans in turbans; they arrive not through the door, but round the end of a wall, the right-hand section of which has been cut away so that we can see what is going on behind it. Despite the liturgical tradition separating the adoration of the shepherds at Christmas from the arrival of the Magi at Epiphany (the symbolic showing of Christ to the Gentiles) on 6 January, the shepherds are still watching in the background. A stylized star shines in the heavens, and three angels of the Nativity sing in the upper right. We know they are singing, not merely because their mouths are open, but because they are holding sheet-music in front of them, and the middle angel has his right hand raised conducting the group. However, there is evidently a breeze up there and the left-hand angel's tunic is billowing outwards, clearly revealing his penis – and giving the lie to those medieval schoolmen who maintained *a priori* that angels were sexless.

In an engraving of the same theme only a few years later, in 1511, there is no such symbolic simultaneity. The same rigid perspective is observed, but shepherds and angels have vanished. Two of the three Magi appear at least generally 'Turkish' in dress, and one attendant seems to have a scimitar. The infant Jesus, instead of extending an arm in stylized welcome, is burrowing with childish excitement into the casket of gold proffered by the first Magus. Another group of small woodcuts, 'The Small Passion', engraved 1509–11, treats the gospel story as a series of 'snapshots' – almost like a modern comic strip – telling the story sequentially as a narrative through a series of linked incidents. It is not difficult to see in such determined realism the signs of a new approach to the Bible. Certainly the deeply pious Dürer was quickly

2. 'The Adoration of the Magi', by Albrecht Dürer, from *The Life of the Virgin*,
1511 (*Albrecht Dürer: The Complete Woodcuts*, Artline Editions, Bristol,
1990, p. 61).

caught up in the Reformation after 1517, when Martin Luther nailed his theses to the church door in Wittenberg. In 1521, when he believed Luther had been arrested by his enemies after the Diet of Worms, Dürer, then in the Netherlands, turned furiously on Erasmus for what he saw as cowardly equivocation with 'the powers of darkness' in Rome.

Though Dürer was to continue to illustrate scenes from the Bible to the end of his life, the later pictures show an increasingly sharp divide between symbolic and realistic schemata. Two heavily symbolic crucifixions of about 1515, and 'Mary, Queen of Angels' (1518), are totally flat designs, with almost no gestures towards realism at all. 'The Last Supper' (1523) (figure 3) on the other hand, is set in a heavily perspective but almost diagrammatic room without view or decoration. On the table there is neither food nor drink: only a single chalice. A basket of bread and a jug of wine are on the floor in the foreground. Though Christ retains a halo, the eleven disciples are positioned almost as for a group photograph. Unlike Leonardo's 'Last Supper' (1495–8), where the disciples seem gathered casually at the far side of the table, those of Dürer's who had their backs to us are now standing crowded awkwardly in at the left in order not to obscure our view.

## THE LIMITS OF REALISM

If the discovery of perspective had heightened the sense of difference between realistic and miraculous elements in biblical narrative, and introduced a quite new sense of time, it was also to transform the stage itself: cosmological space. The difference is very clear in the two great Renaissance religious epics: Dante's *Divine Comedy* (begun c.1300) and John Milton's *Paradise Lost* (1667). That the word 'Renaissance' can be stretched, even thus controversially, to cover 350 years, is a mark of the time it took to reach northern Europe – as well as of the inherent elasticity of the term. Though Dante uses a multitude of biblical allusions, it is typical that his framework of Hell, Purgatory, and Heaven is derived from medieval Catholic theology rather than the Bible. Distinctions between material and spiritual worlds are blurred by the symbolic geography: which is at once local and inaccessible. Hell is located at the centre of the earth, Purgatory on a huge mountain on the far side, diametrically opposite Jerusalem, and Heaven is in the sky, somewhere above the Mount of Purgatory. One of the famous climactic moments of the poem is when Dante, having descended to the nethermost pit of Hell to find Satan sealed for ever in a lake of ice, finds that to continue he must no longer descend, but begin to climb. To enquire to what degree Dante himself

3. 'The Last Supper', by Albrecht Dürer, from *The Life of the Virgin*, 1511 (*Albrecht Dürer: The Complete Woodcuts*, Artline Editions, Bristol, 1990, p.167).

may or may not have believed in this scheme is as irrelevant as to ask whether the painters of the *Très Riches Heures* 'believed' in their representation of Eden; just as reality and symbolic fantasy merge geographically, so fact and fiction merge in the narrative of the poem. Though the action lasts a symbolic twenty-four hours, it takes place effectively outside time or space. Real historical characters coexist with known mythical ones, people still living as well as dead occupy their appropriate niches in the grand judgement of the universe. Virgil, the greatest poet of the pagan world, accompanies Dante through Hell and Purgatory. Beatrice, whom Dante had only glimpsed twice in his life, the last time shortly before she died at the age of twelve, seems to occupy (in spite of disclaimers) a status seemingly only marginally below that of the Virgin herself.

No such ambiguities and liberties were available to Milton 350 years later. The simultaneity of myth had given way to a time-scheme that dominated not only the material universe, but even heaven itself. Since the Son is not co-eternal with the Father, his creation had to take place at some 'later' stage, and it is his presentation to the assembled ranks of heaven that provokes Satan's fall. If the creation of the Son reflects Milton's personal Unitarian theology, in dealing with the fall of Satan *Paradise Lost* is only bringing into the open an ambiguity already present in the trinitarian Catholic tradition that only pre-perspectival assumptions could have concealed. For Satan, once unfallen Lucifer, to have rebelled and been cast out (for whatever form of pride), the dimension of time must *always* have been present.

More dramatic were changes to Milton's material universe. Not merely had the science of perspective transformed artillery and ballistics, it had also led to a series of improvements in navigation culminating in the invention of the sextant in the late sixteenth century. The world had been circumnavigated, and Hell and Purgatory, if not reduced in reality, had been banished to somewhere else. Copernicus had revolutionized cosmology, and Galileo's famous discoveries with his telescope had subsequently confirmed the heliocentric universe. Neither Dante's limited cosmos nor his ambiguity were available to Milton. Satan's journey towards earth and Eden in *Paradise Lost* Book III is more poetic than precise, but two things about it are clear. One is that though this universe remains Ptolemaic, rather than the Copernican one that Milton knew to be correct, it involves traversing huge distances, unimaginable in Dante's tightly parochial cosmology; the other follows from it, in that although heaven and hell are somehow still apparently to be found within the confines of the physical universe, the distances have now become so vast as to make their presence effectively *outside* our space. The arrival of perspective means that when Milton's God 'looks down' on earth, he has to do so in some quite different manner from Dante's. The result is perhaps the opposite of what might have been expected. Milton, because he does not think typologically, is actually more literal in his inter-pretation of the Bible than Dante, but just because he *tries* to take it literally, the resultant narrative is more clearly metaphorical. Heaven and hell cannot any longer belong to our post-Copernican space-time. Milton is the least ironic of writers, but, in the reader's consciousness that (even after Raphael's brave efforts) the narrative cannot tell the whole story, there is a new quality of irony present only just beneath the surface.

Something very similar had already begun to happen in painting. The formal realism of Dürer's biblical illustration had been taken a stage further by Caravaggio (1565?-1610). Rejecting classical and ideal models of beauty, he incurred charges of irreverence and even blasphemy for his literal repre-sentations of biblical scenes. His 'Doubting Thomas' (*c*.1600), for instance, shows the apostle as a bent old man taking quite literally the risen Jesus' invitation to 'Reach hither thy hand and thrust it into my side' (John 20:27). As in literature, the effect of such 'realism' was to emphasize rather than diminish the clash between the mundane and spiritual. The weathered faces and wrinkled brows of the puzzled disciples and Jesus' own concentration as he guides Thomas's hand, contrast with the normal impossibility of the scene portrayed. The clash becomes even more visibly evident in one of Rembrandt's early etchings, *The Angel Appearing to the Shepherds* (1634) (figure 4). Here there is an almost total separation between the 'spiritual' and the 'earthly' spheres. The heavenly host appears with a burst of brilliant light in the top left from a cloud-mass so solid-looking that the announcing angel can stand firmly on it. The effect of this dazzling irruption into the world below is catastrophic. A shepherd stumbles for cover in the foreground, while behind him cattle, sheep, and goats panic and flee in all directions. Three other figures, including that of a woman, are in a cave in the back-ground, but, though they are aroused by the stampeding animals, cannot see the cause. In the centre of the circle of light cast by the angelic arrival, an elderly shepherd, almost overbalancing on one knee, looks directly at the angel, while beside him another, standing with a lamb in his arms, is shielded from the glare by a broad-brimmed hat, and seems to look directly at the viewer. He bears a suspicious resemblance to Rembrandt's self-portraits.

Though this is art as snapshot, people and animals frozen in motion, the details follow closely the account in Luke 2 – this is, perhaps, the only version

4. '*The Angel Appearing to the Shepherds*', Rembrandt (Fitzwilliam Museum, Cambridge).

to take seriously the words 'and they were sore afraid'. But there are some significant additions. Quite legitimately, Rembrandt has interpreted the word 'flock' (Greek *poimnē*) to include cattle and goats as well as sheep. But while the sheep and cows are fleeing, the goats remain unmoved. Is this a reference to the parable of the sheep and the goats (Matthew 25:32)? Are the goats unaware of the angel, or simply unafraid? Even more suggestive is the position of the cave, where the inhabitants, like those of Plato's cave-myth, can see the shadows cast by the light of the great event outside, but not the angels themselves. Are they symbolic of the mass of humanity ? And what of the Rembrandt look-alike apparently challenging the viewer with his direct gaze?

The point about such questions is that, unlike the formal precision of medieval painting, there is, and can be no final answer here. Rembrandt may have been demonstrably faithful to his text, but his iconography is essentially personal not conventional. In the absence of clear conventional structure, we must remain uncertain and in doubt – and that uncertainty from thenceforth must be part of our 'reading' of the picture. What was happening was that the kind of 'narrative' conveyed by both the visual arts and literature was itself again changing. Perspective had not only been a way of seeing the world, but of understanding it. In providing a new visual and temporal realism it had seemed to offer a mathematical certainty in its own way as powerful as the medieval conventions it had replaced. Now that quest for ever greater realism was itself permeated by a new quality of irony, not so much through any arbitrary shift of fashion or convention, but through the discovery that uncertainty and subjectivity were an essential part of any such realism.

## IRONY AND HERMENEUTICS

Biblical studies have always been reactive rather than pro-active in relation to the arts. In so far as this new sense of irony in narrative was largely unconscious, biblical stories themselves could for a while remain immune from the inherent ironies of secular realistic narrative. But about the time that Laurence Sterne was developing the implicit ironies of Lockeian psychology into one of the greatest comic novels of all time, *Tristram Shandy*,[13] he was also exploring the ironies of biblical narrative in his sermons. Number 18, for instance, on the Levite's Concubine (Judges 19), involves reading and rereading the text to produce not a single authoritative meaning, but instead question after question – for so 'much of it depends on the telling'.[14] Though his starting-point is entirely consonant with the new historical criticism pioneered by Robert Lowth's epoch-making Oxford *Lectures on the Sacred Poetry of the Hebrews* in the 1740s, what Sterne discovers in the Bible is not so much evidence of historical context, but of layers of irony and fluidity of meaning.[15] By the end of the eighteenth century, in the wake of the growing popularity of the novel, it was normal to find biblical narrative being read by the same criteria as prose fiction.[16]

We have no evidence whether the German romantics of the late eighteenth century knew of Sterne's sermons, but it was by no means impossible: Friedrich Schleiermacher's earliest published works, for instance, were translations of English sermons.[17] Certainly the so-called *Athenaeum* group centred on Jena in the 1790s, including the Schlegel brothers, Novalis, Fichte, Schelling, and Schleiermacher, were steeped in his novels.[18] It is significant that when Schleiermacher came to write his *Speeches on Religion*, originally intended for his anti-clerical circle of friends, his defence of religion should have rested on the unspoken and inherently inexpressible element in experience that gave an ironic depth to all human utterance. Perhaps more significantly for biblical criticism, with the full (twentieth-century) publication of his *Hermeneutics* we can see how much of his later work was directly addressed to this very problem of the ambiguity of all human utterance and of the necessary subjectivity of interpretation. At one level this can be seen as the philosophical complement to the rules of visual perspective advanced by Alberti five hundred years earlier, and completed by Immanuel Kant's insistence that space and time are themselves constructs of the mind: all texts are created by individuals from within specific cultures with particular ways of thinking; all understanding comes from specific 'points of view'. But there is always an aesthetic dimension to Schleiermacher's thought. The Romantics were fully conscious, as their neo-classical predecessors were not, of the way that any statement contains within it an ironic recognition of other implicit interpretations. The fruition of this line of thought from Sterne runs through Schleiermacher to Sören Kierkegaard's classic reading and rereading of the story of Abraham and Isaac in *Fear and Trembling* – arguably as much a work of 'literature' as 'philosophy'.

Sterne, Schleiermacher and Kierkegaard all prepare the way for what is undoubtedly the greatest biblical novel of the twentieth century, and perhaps the most striking retelling of biblical grand narrative since *Paradise Lost*. Thomas Mann's epic *Joseph and his Brothers* was begun in the 1920s, and published as a tetralogy between 1933 and 1946. Drawing on the long tradition of German historical scholarship, and avoiding both miracles and anachronisms, in one sense Mann's vast novel represents the most extensive and thoroughgoing portrayal of the world of the Patriarchs ever attempted. But it is much more than that. Begun in Germany, and completed in exile in California, it was, not least, an act of political defiance to Hitler and the Nazis. The saga of Jacob and Joseph is seen as one of the emergence of humanity from mythic to historical self-consciousness. Joseph himself becomes the type of the artist, in the tradition of the Old Testament Patriarchs and prophets, endeavouring both to understand his world and to change it by means of his interpretation of it. Mann's narrative begins from the underlying sense of irony that informs all Enlightenment and post-Enlightenment authoritative texts, but in so doing it brings out, as no previous retelling has done, the layers, even convolutions, of irony underlying the Genesis story itself. Lest the connection be missed, Mann admitted to reading and rereading Sterne while at work on *Joseph*.[19] Nevertheless his saga is also inescapably twentieth-century, not just in its hermeneutic interpretation of the past but also in the way his account impinges on the interpretation of his time. This was a point not lost on the Nazi censors who moved swiftly against him when they came to power in 1933, forcing Mann into exile first in Switzerland and then the USA. The greatest biblical epic of the twentieth century was (correctly) read by its enemies as also being the most powerful criticism of contemporary affairs.[20]

Though, as the Contents page of this Cambridge Companion bears witness, current biblical interpretation continues to be heavily influenced by twentieth-century literary and aesthetic theory and practice, there is still little evidence that the historical centrality of that relationship to biblical studies has been fully recognized, or that its implications for the future have been considered. It must form part of the agenda for twenty-first-century biblical studies.

## Notes

1 See, for instance, Na'ama Brosh and Rachel Milstein, *Biblical Stories in Islamic Painting* (Jerusalem: Israel Museum, 1991).

2 Austin Farrer, *A Rebirth of Images* (London: Dacre Press, 1944).

3 Though it does exist: see, for instance, Nathan's denunciation of David (2 Samuel 12:1–15).

4 See John Boardman, Jasper Griffin and Oswyn Murray (eds.), *The Oxford History of the Classical World* (Oxford: Oxford University Press, rpt. 1991), p. 119.

5 See E. R. Goodenough, *Introduction to Philo Judaeus,* 2nd edn (Oxford: Blackwell, 1962); and Henry Chadwick, 'Philo', in A. H. Armstrong (ed.), *Cambridge History of Later Greek and Early Mediaeval Philosophy* (Cambridge: Cambridge University Press, 1967), pp. 137–57.

6 See John Wilkinson, *Interpretation and Community* (London: Macmillan, 1963), esp. pp. 119–57.

7 Marjorie Reeves, 'The Bible and Literary Authorship in the Middle Ages', in S. Prickett (ed.), *Reading the Text: Biblical Criticism and Literary Theory* (Oxford: Blackwell, 1991), p. 16.

8 Erich Auerbach, 'Figura', trans. R. Mannheim, in Auerbach, *Scenes from the Drama of European Literature* (New York: Meridian Books, 1959), p. 28.

9 *Les Très Riches Heures du duc de Berry*, text by Edmond Pognon, trans. David Macrae (Chantilly: Musée Condé, 1969), pp. 10–12.

10 An argument summarized by Leonard Shlain, in *Art and Physics: Parallel Visions in Space, Time, and Light* (New York: Morrow, 1991), pp. 37–43.

11 See, for instance, George P. Landow, *Victorian Types, Victorian Shadows* (London: Routledge, 1980).

12 *Albrecht Dürer: The Complete Woodcuts*, Introduction by André Deguer, trans. Lilian Stephany (Kirchdorf/Inn: Berghaus Verlag, 1990), pp. 6–9.

13 See A. D. Nuttall, *A Common Sky: Philosophy and the Literary Imagination* (London: Chatto, 1974), chs. 1 & 2.

14 *The Works of Lawrence Sterne*, ed. James P. Browne, 2 vols., 1885, vol II, p. 218.

15 See Stephen Prickett, *Origins of Narrative: The Romantic Appropriation of the Bible* (Cambridge: Cambridge University Press, 1996), pp. 119–31.

16 See Hans Frei, *The Eclipse of Biblical Narrative* (New Haven: Yale University Press, 1974), and Prickett, *Origins of Narrative*.

17 Fawcett's *London Sermons* (1798). See Richard Crouter's Introduction to his translation of Schleiermacher's *On Religion: Speeches to its Cultured Despisers* (Cambridge: Cambridge University Press, 1988), p. 5.

18 See, for instance, Friedrich Schlegel, *Dialogue on Poetry and Literary Aphorisms*, trans., introduced and annotated by Ernst Behler and Roman Struc (University Park: Pennsylvania State University Press, 1968), pp. 95–6.

19 Walter E. Berendsohn, *Thomas Mann*, trans. George C. Buck (Tuscaloosa: University of Alabama Press), 1973, p. 90.

20 See Prickett, *Origins of Narrative*, ch. 6.

## Further reading

Atwan, Robert and Laurance Wieder, *Chapters into Verse: Poetry in English Inspired by the Bible*, 2 vols., Oxford: Oxford University Press, 1993.

Auerbach, Erich, 'Figura', trans. R. Mannheim, in Auerbach, *Scenes from the Drama of European Literature*, New York: Meridian Books, 1959.

*Mimesis. The Representation of Reality in Western Literature,* Princeton, NJ: Princeton University Press, 1974.

Berendsohn, Walter E., *Thomas Mann*, trans. George C. Buck, Tuscaloosa: University of Alabama Press, 1973.

Boardman, John, Jasper Griffin and Oswyn Murray, (eds.), *The Oxford History of the Classical World*, Oxford: Oxford University Press, rpt. 1991, p. 119.

Brosh, Na'ama and Rachel Milstein, *Biblical Stories in Islamic Painting*, Jerusalem: Israel Museum, 1991.

Chadwick, Henry, 'Philo', in A. H. Armstrong (ed.), *Cambridge History of Later Greek and Early Mediaeval Philosophy*, Cambridge: Cambridge University Press, 1967.

Crouter, Richard, Introduction to his translation of Schleiermacher's *On Religion: Speeches to its Cultured Despisers*, Cambridge: Cambridge University Press, 1988.

Dürer, Albrecht, *The Complete Woodcuts*, Introduction by André Deguer, trans. Lilian Stephany, Kirchdorf/Inn: Berghaus Verlag, 1990.

Farrer, Austin, *A Rebirth of Images*, London: Dacre Press, 1944.

Frei, Hans, *The Eclipse of Biblical Narrative*, New Haven: Yale University Press, 1974.

Goodenough, E. R., *Introduction to Philo Judaeus*, 2nd edn, Oxford: Blackwell, 1962.

Jasper, David, 'The Old Man Would Not So, but Slew his Son', *Religion and Literature* 25, 2 (1993), pp. 120–9.

'The Bible in Arts and Literature: Source of Inspiration for Poets and Painters: Mary Magdalen', *Concilium* 1 (1995), pp. 47–60.

'Seeing Pictures: Reading Texts', *Readings in the Canon of Scripture*, London: Macmillan, 1995.

Jeffrey, David Lyle (ed.), *A Dictionary of Biblical Tradition in English Literature*, Grand Rapids, MI: Eerdmans, 1992.

Landow, George P., *Victorian Types, Victorian Shadows*, London: Routledge, 1980.

*Les Très Riches Heures du duc de Berry*, text by Edmond Pognon, trans. David Macrae, Chantilly: Musée Condé, 1969.

Norton, David, *A History of the Bible as Literature*, 2 vols., Cambridge: Cambridge University Press, 1993.

Nuttall, A. D., *A Common Sky: Philosophy and the Literary Imagination*, London: Chatto, 1974.

Prickett, Stephen, 'Words and the "Word": Language, Poetics and Biblical Interpretation', Cambridge: Cambridge University Press, 1986.

*Origins of Narrative: the Romantic Appropriation of the Bible*, Cambridge: Cambridge University Press, 1996.

Prickett, Stephen (ed.), *Reading the Text: Biblical Criticism and Literary Theory*, Oxford: Blackwell, 1991.

Schlegel, Friedrich, *Dialogue on Poetry and Literary Aphorisms*, trans., introduced and annotated by Ernst Behler and Roman Struc, University Park: Pennsylvania State University Press, 1968.

Shlain, Leonard, *Art and Physics: Parallel Visions in Space, Time and Light*, New York: Morrow, 1991.

Sterne, Lawrence, *Works*, ed. James P. Browne, 2 vols., 1885.

Wilkinson, John, *Interpretation and Community*, London: Macmillan, 1963.

**Part two**

*Biblical books in modern interpretation*

## 12 The Pentateuch

JOSEPH BLENKINSOPP

### THE SEARCH FOR A NEW PARADIGM

By the last decades of the nineteenth century, a more or less coherent account of the formation of the Pentateuch had emerged and was widely accepted by Hebrew Bible scholars. The main tenet of this newer documentary hypothesis, as it was called, was that the Pentateuch reached its present form incrementally, by way of an accumulation and editing together of sources over a period of about half a millennium, from the first century of the monarchy to around the time of Ezra in the fifth or early fourth century BC.[1] With its emphasis on origins, sources and development, the hypothesis was a typical product of academic research in the late eighteenth and throughout the nineteenth century. A century before the appearance of Julius Wellhausen's *Prolegomena to the History of Israel* in 1883, which laid out the documentary hypothesis in its classic form, Friedrich August Wolf published his *Prolegomena to Homer* which argued along much the same lines for the composite nature of the two epic poems.[2] For both scholars the identification of sources was dictated by the goal of historical reconstruction, in the case of Wellhausen the reconstruction of the religious history of Israel and early Second Temple Judaism. To this end the chronological sequencing of the sources of the Pentateuch (known under the sigla J, E, D, P) was obviously of great importance. The standard approach, therefore, was decidedly referential, diachronic and objectivist, and relatively little attention was paid to the purely literary and aesthetic qualities of the texts in question.

In the form presented by Wellhausen, the documentary hypothesis provided a dominant paradigm within which, or at least with reference to which, practically all research on the Pentateuch has been carried out during this century. It would nevertheless be inaccurate to speak of a consensus. The whole idea of sources, and the historical-critical method in general, were from the beginning totally unacceptable to fundamentalist students of the Bible.[3] Official reaction to the modernist movement in Roman Catholicism included a reaffirmation of Moses' authorship of the Pentateuch in 1906, and had a chilling effect on biblical studies in general.[4]

Wellhausen's well advertised aversion to Judaism as a religious system led prominent Jewish scholars Umberto Cassuto (1883–1951) and Moshe Hirsch Segal (1876–1968) to reject the hypothesis out of hand. Yehezkel Kaufmann (1889–1963), the leading Jewish biblical scholar of this century, used the same historical-critical and exegetical methods as Wellhausen, accepted the existence of sources and documents in principle, but came up with radically different conclusions.[5] One of the linchpins of Wellhausen's system was the conviction that the Priestly source (P), consisting in a highly distinctive narrative and a great deal of cultic and ritual law, dates from and reflects the character of the emergent Judaism of the early Second Temple period (sixth to fourth century BC), a religious system which Wellhausen did not admire. Those Jewish scholars in Israel and North America who have followed Kaufmann's lead, including several who still accept the documentary hypothesis in some form, argue for dating P in the pre-exilic period, and therefore construe the development of Israelite religion quite differently from Wellhausen. We shall return to this issue of the displacement of P at a later point.

The documentary hypothesis also postulated more or less parallel and continuous sources from the early period of the kingdoms, the Yahwist source (J) from Judah and its more fragmentary counterpart the Elohistic source (E), deemed to originate in the Kingdom of Samaria before its incorporation into the Assyrian empire in 722 BC. Not that there was ever anything like agreement on how the narrative was to be divided between the two sources, or how extensive they were, or in what kind of historical and cultural situation they arose. The criteria according to which their respective contributions were decided, especially the incidence of divine names (Yahweh, Elohim), also proved difficult to apply consistently, with the result that the more rigorously the criteria were applied the more the strand in question tended to unravel, resulting in a plurality of subsidiary sources. The threat of fragmentation was therefore always present. More ominously for the hypothesis, an increasing number of scholars over the last three decades have questioned the extent, the early date and even the existence of J and E. One result of these revisionist tendencies is that, while the adherents of the Kaufmann school were moving P back into the pre-exilic period, others have been moving J forward into the exilic or post-exilic period. It is difficult to see how the classical documentary hypothesis can survive these displacements.

It has come to be generally accepted that the formation of Deuteronomy moved along a quite distinct trajectory, that its original connections were with the six books following (the Deuteronomistic History) rather than the four preceding it, and that at some point it was amalgamated with the P source, bringing the Pentateuchal narrative to an end with the death of Moses. Over the last few decades no significant progress has been made in clarifying the origins of Deuteronomy, but we note a tendency to assign a significant narrative role in Genesis and Exodus, and to a lesser extent Numbers, to Deuteronomist authors at the expense of J and E. This is especially evident in certain key texts, e.g. the 'covenant of the pieces' in Genesis 15 and the Sinai-Horeb pericope in Exodus 19–34, and in connective passages which speak of a conditional divine promise to Israel's ancestors.

We also note a sharp loss of interest in this whole business of origins and sources, especially in English language areas, together with a tendency to reject what one literary critic has referred to as the 'excavative techniques' of historical-critical scholarship.[6] For these scholars the paradigm shift is away from the identification and dating of sources to the text as it is, from authorial intentions to 'readerly' points of view, and from the text as a historical and cultural artefact to the text – almost invariably a narrative text – as a closed system, unencumbered by the baggage of its prehistory, waiting and eager to render a meaning consistent with the hermeneutic and ideology (deconstructionist, postmodernist, feminist, liberationist, etc.) of its interpreter. The theological counterpart of these synchronic and 'holistic' approaches is what has come to be known as 'canonical criticism', to which we shall return.

Though well represented, none of these newer interpretative options is in secure possession of the field, and only time will tell which will outlive the cultural climate which generated them.

## THE FINAL STAGES IN THE FORMATION OF THE PENTATEUCH
### DIFFERENT APPROACHES

The pioneers of Pentateuchal criticism – conspicuously Oratorian priest Richard Simon (1678), Lutheran pastor Henning Bernhard Witter (1711), and court physician Jean Astruc (1753) – concentrated primarily on the earliest stages of the literary history of the Pentateuch and on the book of Genesis. One assumes they were motivated by a prudent concern to relate these early stages in some way to the person of Moses. But even long afterwards, in the work of leading scholars of the mid twentieth century such as Albrecht Alt,

Gerhard von Rad and Martin Noth, the emphasis remained on the earliest phase, the pre-state period and the early monarchy, as decisive for the formation of the literary tradition eventuating in the Pentateuch. Von Rad postulated a Hexateuch and Noth a Tetrateuch, but neither explained how we get from either to a Pentateuch. In the last two or three decades the movement has been more frequently in the opposite direction, starting out from the post-exilic period as the formative phase. This chronological shift owes a great deal to the high level of interest in the hitherto neglected Persian period (sixth to fourth century BC), beginning in the 1970s. But it was also a response to the perceived weakness of the arguments for the high antiquity of the basic narrative sources (J and E), conjoined with reaction to the naive historicism of much conservative scholarship with its predilection for high dates. The matter of high or low dates is still, at this writing, one of the most contentious issues in Pentateuchal studies.

Some conclusions may, nevertheless, be proposed. Few doubt that the Pentateuch in its completed form is a product of the Persian period, though Wellhausen's precise date for its promulgation (444 BC) is rather too optimistic.[7] That it emanated from the elite of Babylonian origin who controlled the temple community in the province of Judah at that time is supported by the few sources at our disposal, especially Chronicles and Ezra–Nehemiah, as well as by evidence internal to the Pentateuch itself. What we know of Achaemenid policy also suggests that the compilations of laws in the Pentateuch, including ritual laws, represent the imperially approved, perhaps imperially mandated, law and constitution of the Jewish ethnos in the province of Judah and beyond. If, moreover, the laws had to represent a compromise among different interest groups, as we know to have been the case in contemporary Egypt, we would have an explanation of the discrepancies and different perspectives within the legal material in the Pentateuch.[8] The narrative from creation to the death of Moses, in which the laws are embedded, responded to the need for a national and ethnic founding myth urgently felt after the hiatus of the Babylonian conquest and subsequent deportations. Older narrative material in both written and oral form which survived the disasters of the late sixth century BC would presumably have been incorporated into this story of founding events.

The preceding account would, I imagine, be widely accepted, but there is a more radical perspective on the Pentateuchal story, and the exodus in particular, namely, that it is an example of an *invented* tradition. It would therefore be comparable to the Roman myth of Trojan origins in the form created by Virgil at a similar point of transition and new beginnings, the passage from republic to principate.[9] Both traditions report the non-autochthonous origins of the respective peoples, and perhaps for similar reasons, but arguments *e silentio* are always risky, and it would be rash to conclude from the relative or even absolute absence of inscribed or artefactual evidence that either tradition was a pure invention. And in fact the name Aeneas appears on a fourth century B C inscription from Tor Tignosa, it was known among the Etruscans and contacts between Asia Minor and Italy are well attested for the Late Bronze Age. It is true that we have no archaeological evidence for the exodus from Egypt or Palestine, but we can at least be certain that the tradition was in place long before the Persian period.[10]

The recent high level of interest in the Persian period has therefore provided scholars with the pretext for reversing the direction of research into the formation of the Pentateuch, that is, beginning at the end and working backwards. Even those who regard the documentary hypothesis as being in terminal disarray agree that the Priestly source (P) has proved to be remarkably durable. All agree that both the P narrative and the cultic and ritual prescriptions have been put together serially, out of several distinct components, e.g., a book of generations (*toledot*) and various manuals of ritual law (Leviticus 1–7, 11–15, and 17–26, the so-called 'Holiness Code').[11] Still in question is the extent of the P narrative, some rounding it off at the death of Moses (Deuteronomy 34:9–12), others with the setting up of the wilderness sanctuary at Shiloh and the distribution of land to the tribes (Joshua 18–19). Another issue under discussion is whether P was composed as an independent narrative or simply as a reworking and expansion of existing narrative material. Attempts continue to be made to determine the historical and social situations likely to have precipitated the successive stages of composition. The preferred time span is still from the Neo-Babylonian to the early Achaemenid period, with a special predilection for the time when temple worship was restored towards the end of the sixth century B C.[12] In this connection the obscure history of the priesthood, and in particular the obscurity surrounding the rise of the Aaronite branch to power, presents a formidable obstacle to further progress.

Adherents of the Kaufmann school in Israel and the United States have left no stone unturned in their effort to establish a pre-exilic date for P and thus blunt Wellhausen's prejudicial assessment of early Judaism referred to earlier. Lexicographical and linguistic arguments have been marshalled, P has been aligned with Early Biblical Hebrew and ritual practices in P have been compared with similar practices in ancient Near-Eastern societies. The degree of commitment to this goal is impressive, but the endeavour is vitiated by failure to distinguish clearly between the date of individual rituals and the compilation of P as a whole, the frequent massaging of the data to produce the desired result and the tendency to draw conclusions on the basis of one section only of P, generally dealing with legal material. It seems preferable at this stage to concentrate in the first place on a theological re-evaluation of P in its many positive aspects, which would have the advantage of creating a less contentious climate for further discussion of the chronological issue.[13]

No significant progress has been made in recent years on the issue of the authorship and origins of the book of Deuteronomy; and one suspects that in the absence of new information little progress can be expected. It is agreed that there existed a Deuteronomic school, however constituted, which was active over several generations and whose literary productions are recognizable by their rhetorical style and ideological content. These productions include the Deuteronomic law, more properly described as a programme or blueprint of a somewhat utopian nature attributed to Moses on the last day of his life; a history of the people of Israel from the death of Moses to some years into the Babylonian exile (known in the Hebrew Bible as the Former Prophets); expansions of narratives referring to key events prior to the death of Moses; and a compilation of prophetic material covering a span from Moses represented as protoprophet to Jeremiah. While there is uncertainty as to which books were included in this collection, and to what extent they underwent Deuteronomic redaction, it is agreed that Jeremiah (to whom also forty years of activity are assigned) has been heavily edited to align him with the Deuteronomic doctrine on prophecy.[14] Whenever it was that the school emerged and achieved social visibility, the bulk of this literary activity must have taken place after the fall of Jerusalem and subsequent deportations.

The final stage of redaction from which the Pentateuch emerged as we know it is still quite obscure. We might guess that, at some point in time under Achaemenid rule, scribes attached to the Jerusalem temple inserted Deuteronomy into the more inclusive P narrative by adding a date in the Priestly fashion at the beginning of the book (Deuteronomy 1:3) and a revised version of the commissioning of Joshua, followed by the death of Moses, at the end (Deuteronomy 32:48–52; 34:1–9).[15] The exclusion of the conquest and occupation of the land was no doubt dictated by a prudent regard for imperial Persian sensitivities, but there was more to it than that. Rounding off the story at the death of Moses, and backdating all laws, whenever promulgated, to his lifetime, made a firm statement about law as basic to the survival and identity of the emerging Jewish commonwealth of that time.

## J AND E: FACING AN UNCERTAIN FUTURE

Quite apart from hypotheses about sources and their combination, it is obvious that the Pentateuch is composed of blocks of narrative material each with its own distinctive character. The history of early humanity in Genesis 1–11 is an Israelite version of an origins tradition current in the Near East and Levant over many centuries, from the *Atraḥasis* epic to the *Babyloniaca* of Berossus.[16] This opening segment is linked with a quite different form of narrative, the prehistory of the people of Israel traced through four generations of ancestors the last of which, featuring Joseph, leads into the birth of the nation in Egypt. Different again is this next section centred on the life and work of Moses and ending with the giving of a new law and covenant on the eve of entry into the promised land. Summarizing a long history of research, Wellhausen postulated parallel sources of early date (*c.*850–750 BC) covering all three segments, though he prudently refrained from distinguishing in detail between J and E. In due course the Yahwist emerged as a distinct author, even as a literary genius, probably male, less probably female.[17] Some thought of this author as 'the Bible's first theologian', a distinguished representative of what von Rad called 'the Solomonic renaissance' or its afterglow some time in the tenth or early ninth century.[18]

It would be difficult to find any critical scholar who holds views identical with these today. Beginning in the late 1960s, we note an increasing tendency to make a vertical rather than horizontal cut, therefore to take the literary history of each narrative block separately and independently of any thesis of continuous early sources.[19] Another tendency, already noted, is to shift the burden of proof on to the exponents of early dating, partly on account of scepticism about the historical value of the traditions narrated in J E, but even more due to the perceived weakness of the arguments advanced for early dating. The thesis of continuous early sources has also been undermined for those who reassign parts of the J E narrative to D or simply redescribe J as Deuteronomic or proto-Deuteronomic.[20]

The task remaining for those who relocate the compilation of the non-P narrative content of Genesis–Exodus–Numbers in the exilic period or later is to provide a plausible alternative account of literary developments during the period of the kingdoms. Comparativist studies in oral tradition have shown that the idea, popular not so long ago, of Israelite oral traditions transmitted intact over centuries has a very low percentage of probability.[21] But there are indications that at least in the last two centuries of the monarchy traditions about origins were in circulation, and a considerable amount of literary activity was going on, and it is unlikely that none of it survived the disasters of the early sixth century B.C.[22] On this issue, then, much work remains to be done.

## LAW AND THE ETHICAL CONTENT OF THE PENTATEUCH

One of the most underdeveloped areas of biblical studies in general, and Pentateuchal studies in particular, is that of law and ethics. Few biblical scholars are acquainted with the procedures and terminology used by philosophical and theological ethicists, and fewer still have either the time or the inclination to master the relevant literature. But quite apart from this obvious problem, the study of legal material remains on a very minor scale compared with the massive concentration on narrative.[23] There is also perhaps a residual sense that the study of biblical law belongs with the study of Mishnah and Talmud, and is therefore the province of Jewish scholars. And in fact Jewish scholars continue to make significant contributions to our understanding of biblical law.[24] Law, finally, does not lend itself to treatment according to certain high profile literary theories currently in vogue.

While the form-critical study of law still tends to take off from the foundational essay of Albrecht Alt, not unexpectedly much has changed since its publication in 1934.[25] Archaeological research into early Israelite settlement patterns has not supported Alt's clean distinction between Canaanite and Israelite culture; his theory of an early Israelite amphictyony has passed from the scene, and with it the *Sitz im Leben* of the apodictic legal formulations which Alt took to be unique to Israel. The same fate has overtaken the once highly favoured analogy between the covenant formulation and Hittite suzerainty treaties of the Late Bronze Age. Many of the biblical texts dealing with covenant have been shown to be more probably of later, Deuteronomic origin, and Assyrian vassal treaties of roughly the same period (seventh century B C) seem to many to offer a closer analogy to the covenant features of Deuteronomy, especially the curses which formed an essential component of covenant making.[26]

If the study of Pentateuchal law has lagged at the literary level, the current spate of sociological writing on ancient Israel has clarified several aspects of the institutional and cultural context of the laws. Since the appearance of Roland de Vaux's *Institutions de l'Ancien Israël* in 1957 much progress has been made on such issues as kinship systems, family and marriage customs, the legal status of women, funerary rites and land tenure.[27] The considerable overlap between the aphoristic and didactic literature (e.g.

in the longer collections in the book of Proverbs) and legal formulations has led a number of scholars, beginning with Erhard Gerstenberger in 1965, to identify the traditional ethos of the household and the kinship network as an important source of Israelite law. Comparative legal studies have also revealed further connections with Near-Eastern laws (Sumerian, Hittite, Babylonian and Assyrian), but the complete lack of documentation on Canaanite and Phoenician law makes it difficult to locate early Israelite law more precisely in this international context.[28]

### CHANGING PERSPECTIVES

Some time in the late 1960s, and especially in the English-speaking world, a sense of disillusionment with the standard academic methods of reading biblical texts seems to have set in. At the same time, biblical scholars were beginning belatedly to follow the trend in literary criticism set in motion almost half a century earlier by the New Criticism. The change can be conveniently if very roughly dated to the presidential address to the Society of Biblical Literature delivered by James Muilenburg in 1968 and published the following year.[29] Muilenburg argued that form criticism had run its course and urged a different approach to which he gave the name rhetorical criticism. What he wished to recommend was close attention to the aesthetic features of the text, its structural patterns and literary devices, without regard to its origin or the quite hypothetical intention of its putative author. The last three decades have seen a spate of close readings of biblical texts by literary critics of the calibre of Northrop Frye, Amos Wilder and Robert Alter, together with numerous others. A cross-section of their writing is available in *The Literary Guide to the Bible* edited by Robert Alter and Frank Kermode, though the decision to present essays on the biblical books as a whole arranged in sequence imposed severe limitations on what could be included.[30]

Since readings of this kind are restricted almost without exception to narrative and poetry, it is not surprising that, in the Pentateuch, Genesis and Exodus continue to receive the lion's share of attention. The passages to which critics keep returning include the Garden of Eden narrative (Genesis 2–3), the Tower of Babel (Genesis 11:1–9), the Binding of Isaac (Genesis 22:1–19) – subject of a justly celebrated essay by Erich Auerbach,[31] the Jacob cycle (Genesis 25–35), and the Joseph *Novella* (Genesis 37–50).[32] Containing as it does a wealth of folktale material and an impressive sequence of type scenes (e.g. the hero saved from death in infancy, Exodus 2:1–10), the exodus story (Exodus 1–15) has also attracted a great deal of attention, apart from serving a talismanic function for liberation theology emanating from different 'interpretive communities'.³³

In the years since Muilenberg issued his call for a new departure in reading biblical texts, literary critical theory has, so to speak, lost its innocence and become vastly more complex. In its application to writing, structuralist analysis had its point of departure in Lévi-Strauss's essay on 'The Structuralist Study of Myth'.³⁴ Lévi-Strauss himself discouraged the application of structural analysis to biblical and classical material, though he could not resist analysing the Oedipus myth. He explained his reticence by the circumstance that biblical texts are for the most part heavily edited and come to us without their ethnographic context. And, as a matter of fact, the impact of structuralism on the Pentateuch has been minimal. Roland Barthes produced a strikingly original analysis of Jacob's struggle at the Jabbok ford (Genesis 32:22–32) which has become part of the commentary tradition, while Edmund Leach's idiosyncratic essay on the Garden of Eden narrative has been widely ignored by biblical scholars. Other structuralist essays appear from time to time, but one has the impression that this is not the wave of the future.³⁵

An unfortunate aspect of the present, transitional situation in the reading and study of biblical texts, including the Pentateuch, is the tendency of each new approach to stake out its territory at the expense of alternatives, in the process excommunicating its predecessors. It is easily forgotten that the method adopted in reading and interpreting texts depends on the purpose one has in mind. The purpose of the historical-critical method was not aesthetic but historical, namely, wherever possible to open a window on the past through the text. Depending on the purpose one has in mind, both synchronic and diachronic approaches are legitimate and necessary, and there is no reason why they should not peacefully coexist.

Characteristic of most of the newer literary methods in use today is insistence on the text as a complex unity, on interpreting the parts in function of the whole. The length and complexity of the Pentateuch obviously complicates the task of 'holistic' interpretation, though D. J. A. Clines has attempted such an interpretation with respect to theme (the promise) and R. N. Whybray with respect to genre (historiography comparable with Herodotus).³⁶

A theological version of this holistic approach to the interpreter's task, and one equally leery of sources and documents, goes under the designation of canonical criticism. This method first came into view in the seventies and has since been the object of much critical attention, not all by any means favourable. Since we cannot give it the space it deserves, we may summarize by saying that its proponents, among whom Brevard S. Childs of Yale University is *facile princeps*, maintain that only the final form of a biblical text, read within a believing and interpreting community, is the appropriate object of theological reflection. With respect to the Pentateuch, Childs holds that its canonical shaping is distinct from the history of its formation and is therefore, as he puts it, post-critical; it also derives from a community of faith, and is not what he calls a post-Old Testament rabbinic development.[37] It will be obvious that at several points this argument calls for clarification. The systematic separation between the history of the formation of a biblical text and its canonical shaping would seem to be quite arbitrary, and the theological implications of an exclusive concentration on the canon of the Christian Church are not clearly worked out. In his recent writing on the subject of the canon, Rolf Rendtorff has avoided some of these difficulties by discussing the canonical shaping of the literature without reference to dogmatic traditions and with a much fuller and more informed appreciation for the Jewish exegetical tradition. His rejection of the documentarian approach is, notwithstanding, even more decisive and vehement than that of Childs.[38]

In the course of the last two or three decades feminist interpretations of the Pentateuch and of biblical texts in general have been much in evidence. Since feminist biblical hermeneutics are discussed elsewhere in the volume, we need mention here only two specific aspects relevant to the Pentateuch. At the most basic level, feminist criticism has concentrated on biblical women whose characters and roles are considered to have been underinterpreted or misinterpreted throughout the history of exegesis. We therefore have a large and growing number of retellings of the stories of women narrated in the Pentateuch – Eve, of course, but also Hagar, Dinah, Tamar, Miriam and several others.[39] More significant in the long run, perhaps, is the recent proliferation of sociological and anthropological studies, many by female biblical scholars, on the situation of women in Israelite society – their position in the household and the larger kinship network, their legal status in the different roles which they occupied, their place in the round of ritual and cultic activity, and so on.[40] One contribution which these studies are making to the feminist cause in general is that they translate the generalized and somewhat vague category of patriarchalism into the more precise language of patriliny and those associated social structures which perpetuated the subordination of women in ancient Israel and elsewhere.

## Notes

1 The most recent surveys in J. Blenkinsopp, *The Pentateuch. An Introduction to the First Five Books of the Bible* (New York and London: Doubleday, 1992), pp. 1–30; C. Houtman, *Der Pentateuch. Die Geschichte seiner Erforschung neben einer Auswertung* (Kampen: Kok Pharos, 1994), pp. 98–342.

2 Wolf was, however, influenced by J. G. Eichhorn's methods of investigation in his *Einleitung ins Alte Testament* which began to appear in 1780.

3 J. Barr, *Fundamentalism*, 2nd edn (London: SCM Press, 1981), pp. 40–89.

4 R. E. Brown and T. A. Collins, 'Historical Background for Recent Pronouncements', in R. E. Brown, J. A. Fitzmyer, R. E. Murphy, *The New Jerome Biblical Commentary* (Englewood Cliffs, NJ: Prentice Hall, 1990), pp. 1166–74.

5 Y. Kaufmann, *The Religion of Israel from its Beginnings to the Babylonian Exile* (New York: Schocken Books, 1960): T. Krapf, *Die Priesterschrift und die vorexilische Zeit* (Göttingen: Vandenhoeck & Ruprecht, 1992).

6 R. Alter, *The Art of Biblical Narrative* (New York: Basic Books, 1981), pp. 13–14.

7 J. Wellhausen, *Prolegomena to the History of Israel* (Atlanta, GA: Scholars Press, 1994), pp. 404–10.

8 E. Blum, *Studien zur Komposition des Pentateuch* (Berlin: de Gruyter, 1990), pp. 333–60; Blenkinsopp, *The Pentateuch*, pp. 239–43.

9 P. R. Davies, *In Search of 'Ancient Israel'* (Sheffield: Sheffield Academic Press, 1992), pp. 116–20.

10 E.g. Hosea's appellation 'Yahweh your God from the land of Egypt' (12:9; 13:4) and other pre-exilic prophetic allusions.

11 The existence of the Holiness Code (*Heiligkeitsgesetz*), identified as a distinct document by August Klostermann towards the end of the nineteenth century, is sometimes questioned. I. Knohl ('The Priestly Torah versus the Holiness School: Sabbath and the Festivals', *Hebrew Union College Annual* 58 (1987)) argued that it was not an earlier compilation incorporated into P but a later and more ethically explicit corrective to the P *Weltanschauung*.

12 J. Blenkinsopp, 'The Structure of P', *Catholic Biblical Quarterly* 38 (1976).

13 On Kaufmann's view of P see Krapf, *Die Priesterschrift*. Among the many lexicographical studies of A. Hurvitz see especially A. Hurvitz, 'The Evidence of Language in Dating the Priestly Code', *Revue Biblique* 81 (1974), and *A Linguistic Study of the Relationship between the Priestly Source and the Book of Ezekiel* (Paris: *Cahiers de la Revue Biblique*, 1982).

14 W. McKane, *Jeremiah I* (Edinburgh: T. & T. Clark, 1986), pp. xli–lxxxviii; R. P. Carroll, *Jeremiah. A Commentary* (Philadelphia: Westminster Press, 1986), pp. 38–50.

15 Blenkinsopp, *The Pentateuch*, pp. 229–32.

16 See most recently J. Van Seters, *Prologue to History. The Yahwist as Historian in Genesis* (Louisville, KY: Westminster/John Knox Press, 1992).

17 For the view that J was composed by a noble lady in early middle age at the

court of Rehoboam, successor of Solomon, see D. Rosenberg and H. Bloom, *The Book of J* (New York: Grove Weidenfeld, 1990).

18 G. von Rad, *Old Testament Theology I* (Edinburgh and London: Oliver & Boyd, 1962), pp. 36–56.

19 N. E. Wagner, 'Pentateuchal Criticism: No Clear Future', *Canadian Journal of Theology* 13 (1967); R. Rendtorff, *Das überlieferungsgeschichtliche Problem des Pentateuch* (Berlin: de Gruyter, 1977).

20 H. H. Schmid, *Der sogenannte Jahwist* (Zurich: Theologischer Verlag, 1976); H. Rose, *Deuteronomist und Jahwist* (Zurich: Theologischer Verlag, 1981).

21 J. Vansina, *Oral Tradition. A Study in Historical Methodology* (Chicago: Aldine Press, 1965); R. C. Culley, *Studies in the Structure of Hebrew Narrative* (Philadelphia: Fortress Press, 1976).

22 On archaeological indications suggesting a high level of literary activity from Hezekiah to Josiah see D. W. Jamieson-Drake, *Scribes and Schools in Monarchic Judah* (Sheffield: Almond Press, 1991).

23 Summary of recent work and bibliography in S. Greengus, 'Biblical and Ancient Near Eastern Law' and R. Sonsino, 'Forms of Biblical Law', *The Anchor Bible Dictionary*, ed. D. N. Freeman (New York: Doubleday, 1992), vol. IV, pp. 252–4.

24 Leaving aside ritual law, see e.g. Z. W. Falk, *Hebrew Law in Biblical Times* (Jerusalem: Wahrmann Books, 1964); D. Daube, *Studies in Biblical Law* (New York: Ktav Publishing House, 1969); B. S. Jackson, *Theft in Early Jewish Law* (Oxford: Oxford University Press, 1972); J. J. Finkelstein, *The Ox that Gored* (Philadelphia: The American Philosophical Society, 1981); M. Fishbane, *Biblical Interpretation in Ancient Israel* (Oxford: Clarendon Press, 1985).

25 A. Alt, *Essays on Old Testament History and Religion* (Oxford: Blackwell, 1966), pp. 79–132.

26 D. R. Hillers, *Treaty-Curses and the Old Testament Prophets* (Rome: Pontifical Biblical Institute Press, 1964) and *Covenant. The History of a Biblical Idea* (Baltimore: Johns Hopkins University Press, 1969); R. Frankena, 'The Vassal Treaties of Esarhaddon and the Dating of Deuteronomy', Oudtestamentische Studiën 14 (1965); M. Weinfeld, 'Traces of Assyrian Treaty Formulae in Deuteronomy', *Biblica* 46 (1965); L. Perlitt, *Bundestheologie im Alten Testament* (Neukirchen-Vluyn: Neukirchener Verlag, 1969); D. J. McCarthy, *Old Testament Covenant. A Survey of Current Opinions* (Oxford: Blackwell, 1972); S. Parpola and K. Watanabe, *Neo-Assyrian Treaties and Loyalty Oaths* (Helsinki: Helsinki University Press, 1988).

27 C. H. J. de Geus, *The Tribes of Israel*, Studia Semitica Neerlandica 18 (Assen: van Gorcum, 1976); N. P. Lemche, *Early Israel. Anthropological and Historical Studies on the Israelite Society before the Monarchy* (Leiden: Brill, 1985); T. J. Lewis, *Cults of the Dead in Ancient Israel and Ugarit* (Atlanta, GA: Scholars Press, 1989); C. J. H. Wright, *God's People in God's Land* (Exeter: Paternoster Press, 1990); R. Westbrook, *Property and the Family in Biblical Law* (Sheffield: JSOT Press, 1991); V. H. Matthews and D. C. Benjamin, *Social World of Ancient Israel 1250–587 BCE* (Peabody, MA: Hendrickson Publishers, 1993);

N. Steinberg, *Kinship and Marriage in Genesis: A Household Economics Perspective* (Minneapolis: Fortress Press, 1993); B. B. Schmidt, *Israel's Beneficent Dead* (Tübingen: J. C. B. Mohr, 1994).

28 D. Patrick, *Old Testament Law* (Atlanta, GA: John Knox Press, 1984).

29 J. Muilenburg, 'Form Criticism and Beyond', *Journal of Biblical Literature* 88 (1969).

30 R. Alter and F. Kermode, *The Literary Guide to the Bible* (Cambridge, MA: Belknap/Harvard University Press, 1987).

31 E. Auerbach, *Mimesis* (Berne: Franke, 1946), pp. 1–20; Eng. trans. *Mimesis* (Princeton: Princeton University Press, 1974).

32 Since the quantity of writing on these passages defies documentation, the reader is referred to the bibliographical references in Alter and Kermode, *The Literary Guide to the Bible*, P. R. House, *Beyond Form Criticism. Essays in Old Testament Literary Criticism* (Winona Lake, IN: Eisenbrauns, 1992); and D. M. Gunn and D. N. Fewell, *Narrative in the Hebrew Bible* (Oxford: Oxford University Press, 1993).

33 Michael Walzer, *Exodus and Revolution* (New York: Basic Books, 1985).

34 C. Lévi-Strauss, *Structural Anthropology* (New York: Basic Books, 1967), pp. 206–31.

35 E. Leach, *Genesis as Myth and other Essays* (London: Jonathan Cape, 1969); R. Barthes, 'La lutte avec l'ange: analyse textuelle de Genèse 32.23–33', in F. Bovon (ed.), *Analyse structurale et exégèse biblique* (Neuchâtel: Delachaux et Niestlé, 1971).

36 D. J. A. Clines, *The Theme of the Pentateuch* (Sheffield: JSOT Press, 1978); R. N. Whybray, *The Making of the Pentateuch* (Sheffield: JSOT Press, 1987).

37 B. S. Childs, *Introduction to the Old Testament as Scripture* (Philadelphia: Fortress Press, 1979), pp. 127–35.

38 R. Rendtorff, *Canon and Theology* (Minneapolis: Fortress Press, 1993).

39 See especially the contributions of Susan Niditch, Drorah O'Donnell Setel, Judith Romney Wegner, Katherine Doob Sakenfeld and Tikva Frymer-Kensky in C. A. Newsom and S. H. Ringe, *The Women's Bible Commentary* (London: SPCK, 1992).

40 P. Bird, 'The Place of Women in the Israelite Cultus', in P. D. Miller et al. (eds.), *Ancient Israelite Religion* (Philadelphia: Fortress Press, 1987), pp. 397–419; C. Meyers, *Discovering Eve: Ancient Israelite Women in Context* (New York: Oxford University Press, 1988); N. Steinberg, 'The Deuteronomic Law Code and the Politics of State Centralization', in D. Jobling et al. (eds.), *The Bible and the Politics of Exegesis* (Cleveland, OH: The Pilgrim Press, 1991), pp. 161–70; N. Jay, *Throughout Your Generations Forever* (Chicago: Chicago University Press, 1991).

## Further reading

Alt, A., *Essays on Old Testament History and Religion*, Oxford: Blackwell, 1966.

Alter, R., *The Art of Biblical Narrative*, New York: Basic Books, 1981.

Alter, R. and F. Kermode, *The Literary Guide to the Bible*, Cambridge, MA: Belknap/Harvard University Press, 1987.

Auerbach, E., *Mimesis. The Representation of Reality in Western Literature*, Princeton, NJ: Princeton University Press, 1974.

Barr, J., *Fundamentalism*, 2nd edn, London: SCM Press, 1981.

Bird, P., 'The Place of Women in the Israelite Cultus', in P. D. Miller et al. (eds.), *Ancient Israelite Religion*, Philadelphia: Fortress Press, 1987.

Blenkinsopp, J., 'The Structure of P', *Catholic Biblical Quarterly* 38 (1976). *The Pentateuch. An Introduction to the First Five Books of the Bible*, New York and London: Doubleday, 1992.

Blum, E., *Studien zur Komposition des Pentateuch*, Berlin: de Gruyter, 1990.

Bovon, F., *Analyse structurale et exégèse biblique*, Neuchâtel: Delachaux et Niestlé, 1971.

Brown, R. E. et al. (eds.), *The New Jerome Biblical Commentary*, Englewood Cliffs, NJ: Prentice-Hall, 1990.

Carroll, R. P., *Jeremiah. A Commentary*, Philadelphia: Westminster Press, 1986.

Childs, B. S., *Introduction to the Old Testament as Scripture*, Philadelphia: Fortress Press, 1979.

Clines, D. J. A., *The Theme of the Pentateuch*, Sheffield: JSOT Press, 1978.

Culley, R. C., *Studies in the Structure of Hebrew Narrative*, Philadelphia: Fortress Press, 1976.

Daube, D., *Studies in Biblical Law*, New York: Ktav Publishing House, 1969.

Davies, P. R., *In Search of 'Ancient Israel'*, Sheffield: Sheffield Academic Press, 1992.

Falk, Z. W., *Hebrew Law in Biblical Times. An Introduction*, Jerusalem: Wahrmann Books, 1964.

Finkelstein, J. J., *The Ox that Gored*, Philadelphia: The American Philosophical Society, 1981.

Fishbane, M., *Biblical Interpretation in Ancient Israel*, Oxford: Clarendon Press, 1985.

Frankena, R., 'The Vassal Treaties of Esarhaddon and the Dating of Deuteronomy', *Oudtestamentische Studiën* 14 (1965).

de Geus, C. H. J., *The Tribes of Israel*, Studia Semitica Neerlandica 18, Assen: Van Gorcum, 1976.

Gottwald, N. K., *The Bible and Liberation. Political and Social Hermeneutics*, Maryknoll, NY: Orbis, 1983.

Greengus, S., 'Biblical and Ancient Near Eastern Law', in *The Anchor Bible Dictionary*, ed. D. N. Freedman, New York: Doubleday, 1992, vol. IV, pp. 242–52.

Gunn, D. M. and D. N. Fewell, *Narrative in the Hebrew Bible*, Oxford: Oxford University Press, 1993.

Hillers, D. R., *Treaty-Curses and the Old Testament Prophets*, Rome: Pontifical Biblical Institute Press, 1964.

*Covenant. The History of a Biblical Idea*, Baltimore: Johns Hopkins University Press, 1969.

House, P. R., *Beyond Form Criticism. Essays in Old Testament Literary Criticism*, Winona Lake, MN: Eisenbrauns, 1992.

Houtman, C., *Der Pentateuch. Die Geschichte seiner Erforschung neben einer Auswertung*, Kampen: Kok Pharos, 1994.

Hurvitz, A., 'The Evidence of Language in Dating the Priestly Code. A Linguistic Study in Technical Idioms and Terminology', *Revue Biblique* 81 (1974).

*A Linguistic Study of the Relationship between the Priestly Source and the Book of Ezekiel. A New Approach to an Old Problem*, Paris: Cahiers de la Revue Biblique, 1982.

Jackson, B. S., *Theft in Early Jewish Law*, Oxford: Oxford University Press, 1972.

Jamieson-Drake, D. W., *Scribes and Schools in Monarchic Judah*, Sheffield: Almond Press, 1991.

Jay, N., *Throughout Your Generations Forever. Sacrifice, Religion and Paternity*, Chicago: Chicago University Press, 1991.

Kaufmann, Y., *The Religion of Israel from its Beginnings to the Babylonian Exile*, trans. and abridged by M. Greenberg, New York: Schocken Books, 1960.

Knohl, I., 'The Priestly Torah versus the Holiness School: Sabbath and the Festivals', *Hebrew Union College Annual* 58 (1987).

Krapf, T., *Die Priesterschrift und die vorexilische Zeit. Yehezkel Kaufmanns vernachlässigter Beitrag zur Geschichte der biblischen Religion*, Göttingen: Vandenhoeck & Ruprecht, 1992.

Leach, E., *Genesis as Myth and Other Essays*, London: Jonathan Cape, 1969.

Lemche, N.-P., *Early Israel. Anthropological and Historical Studies on the Israelite Society before the Monarchy*, Leiden: E. J. Brill, 1985.

Lévi-Strauss, C., *Structural Anthropology*, New York: Basic Books, 1967.

Lewis, T. J., *Cults of the Dead in Ancient Israel and Ugarit*, Atlanta, GA: Scholars Press, 1989.

Matthews, V. H. and D. C. Benjamin, *Social World of Ancient Israel 1250–587 BCE*, Peabody, MA: Hendrickson Publishers, 1993.

McCarthy, D. J., *Old Testament Covenant. A Survey of Current Opinions*, Oxford: Blackwell, 1972.

McKane, W., *Jeremiah I*, Edinburgh: T. & T. Clark, 1986.

Meyers, C., *Discovering Eve: Ancient Israelite Women in Context*, New York: Oxford University Press, 1988.

Muilenburg, J., 'Form Criticism and Beyond', *Journal of Biblical Literature* 88 (1969).

Newsom, C. A. and S. H. Ringe, *The Women's Bible Commentary*, London: SPCK, 1992.

Parpola, S. and K. Watanabe, *Neo-Assyrian Treaties and Loyalty Oaths*, Helsinki: Helsinki University Press, 1988.

Patrick, D., *Old Testament Law*, Atlanta, GA: John Knox Press, 1985.

Perlitt, L., *Bundestheologie im Alten Testament*, Neukirchen-Vluyn: Neukirchener Verlag, 1969.

von Rad, G., *Old Testament Theology I*, Edinburgh and London: Oliver & Boyd, 1962.

Rendtorff, R., *Das überlieferungsgeschichtliche Problem des Pentateuch*, Berlin: de Gruyter, 1977 ( = *The Problem of the Process of Transmission in the Pentateuch*, trans. J. J. Scullion, Sheffield: JSOT Press, 1990).

*Canon and Theology*, Minneapolis: Fortress Press, 1993.

Rose, M., *Deuteronomist und Jahwist: Untersuchungen zu den Berührungspunkten beider Literaturwerke*, Zurich: Theologischer Verlag, 1981.

Rosenberg, D. and H. Bloom, *The Book of J*, New York: Grove Weidenfeld, 1990.

Schmid, H. H., *Der sogenannte Jahwist*, Zurich: Theologischer Verlag, 1976.

Schmidt, B. B., *Israel's Beneficent Dead*, Tübingen: J. C. B. Mohr, 1994.

Sonsino, R., 'Forms of Biblical Law', in *The Anchor Bible Dictionary*, ed. D. N. Freeman, New York: Doubleday, 1992, vol. IV, pp. 252–4.

Steinberg, N., 'The Deuteronomic Law Code and the Politics of State Centralization', in D. Jobling et al. (eds.), *The Bible and the Politics of Exegesis*, Cleveland, OH: The Pilgrim Press, 1991.

*Kinship and Marriage in Genesis: A Household Economics Perspective*, Minneapolis: Fortress Press, 1993.

Van Seters, J., *Prologue to History. The Yahwist as Historian in Genesis*, Louisville, KY: Westminster/John Knox Press, 1992.

Vansina, J., *Oral Tradition. A Study in Historical Methodology*, Chicago: Aldine Press, 1965.

Wagner, N. E., 'Pentateuchal Criticism: No Clear Future', *Canadian Journal of Theology* 13 (1967).

Weinfeld, M., 'Traces of Assyrian Treaty Formulae in Deuteronomy', *Biblica* 46 (1965).

Wellhausen, J., *Prolegomena to the History of Israel*, Atlanta, GA: Scholars Press, 1994.

Westbrook, R., *Property and the Family in Biblical Law*, Sheffield: JSOT Press, 1991.

Whybray, R. N., *The Making of the Pentateuch. A Methodological Study*, Sheffield: JSOT Press, 1987.

Wolf, F. A., *Prolegomena to Homer*, Princeton: Princeton, University Press, 1985.

Wright, C. J. H., *God's People in God's Land. Family, Land, and Property in the Old Testament*, Exeter: The Paternoster Press, 1990.

# 13 The historical books of the Old Testament

IAIN PROVAN

The biblical books to be considered in this chapter are Joshua, Judges and Ruth; 1–2 Samuel, 1–2 Kings and 1–2 Chronicles; Ezra, Nehemiah and Esther. Together they tell the story of Israel from the point at which the people entered Canaan down to the Persian period, when some Jews had returned to their homeland and others still remained in foreign lands. The state of current research on these books may perhaps best be summarized in the following way. There is a lively debate among interpreters as to whether they are indeed best considered as 'historical books' at all, and in which sense they might be best considered so. There is a further debate about the proper or primary task of interpreters in relation to these books. In what follows we shall join these two debates and reflect upon the various issues that arise from them. In this way we shall form a rounded, if somewhat generalized, view of the ways in which our literature is currently being approached.

## HISTORY OR STORY?

The phrase 'historical books' is a modern term as attached to the books in question, and one which already implies that an interpretative decision has been made about their nature. It might be argued that the phrase 'narrative books' would be a better term with which to begin. This is just as clearly a modern label, which in no way corresponds to the nomenclature of earlier times. In the Massoretic Hebrew canon, for example, Joshua, Judges, 1–2 Samuel and 1–2 Kings make up 'The Former Prophets', while all the remaining books mentioned above form part of 'The Writings'. If a modern label is sought, however, 'narrative' is perhaps a good first choice. It certainly has the merit of enabling us to avoid in the first instance the question of reference – do the books in question 'refer' to the real world of the past or not?

In spite of the fact that the phrase 'historical books' has been so commonly used in the modern period, the phrase 'narrative books' corresponds at least in a general sense much more closely to how many modern interpreters have in practice thought of this literature. At least in the period during which the historical-critical method has dominated biblical interpretation in the scholarly world, history has not been regarded as something which can straightforwardly be read off the surface of these texts. On the contrary, the task of extracting history from them has been regarded as a more or less arduous quarrying operation. The text in itself has not commonly been regarded as historical. It has been viewed simply as the narrative mine out of which the skilled interpreter may dig nuggets of history. The extent to which individual books in our group have in fact been regarded as allowing a window on to the past has naturally varied widely, depending on various factors – differing preconceptions as to what history looks like, differing assessments of the worth or implications of extra-biblical evidence and so on. On the whole, however, it would be fair to say that in this period and up until fairly recently the books of the Former Prophets along with Ezra and Nehemiah would have been fairly highly rated in terms of their ability to divulge historical information (Samuel–Kings especially so), while Ruth and Esther would not have scored so well and 1–2 Chronicles would have received mixed reviews.

It is one of the interesting ironies of this period of historical-critical domination that although interpreters were thus aware that they were dealing with books which were not simply historical, and indeed sometimes (in many minds) not historical at all, yet the vast majority of the effort in interpretation went into the task, not of interpreting the narratives as narratives, but in extracting from them such data of a historical kind as was thought possible. Thus in the case of 1–2 Kings, for example, it is not difficult to find interpreters in this period hypothesizing about the original source material used by the editors of Kings or the various levels of editing which might exist in the text, or writing about the historical and cultural background against which various parts of Kings might be read.[1] It is somewhat more difficult in the period before the 1980s to find readings of the book as it stands *as narrative.*

The explanation of this fact lies not simply in an obsession with history which rendered scholarship virtually blind to other aspects of the texts which were the object of their study. It lies also in a deep-seated and in large measure unexamined assumption that the historical books, although in a very general sense narrative rather than history, were not truly narrative literature. That is, when historical critics looked at the historical books, they did not generally see works of impressive narrative art. They saw relatively incoherent and self-contradictory collections of material, put into some kind of narrative order by their editors, but not in a very convincing manner. These were books which suggested to scholars that their creators were not free agents, but rather were to a greater or lesser extent constrained by the material available to them and unable or unwilling to impose complete consistency upon it. In a real sense, the only coherence to be found in these books was the coherence provided by the historical time-line. There was nothing else there to interpret but the historical process to which the texts bore witness.

Such an unexamined assumption could not long stand critical scrutiny once a sufficient number of interpreters had taken time to step back from their subject-matter and look at it afresh. Thus it is that the pendulum has in the past two decades swung away from historical-critical approaches to the historical books, and towards literary approaches – interpretation which takes its starting-point from the narrative shape of the texts, and may not even move beyond this to ask historical questions at all. As momentum has moved behind the pendulum, in fact, historical-critical methodology has been pushed on to the defensive. Historical critics are no longer able to make the sorts of assumptions they once made about texts like Joshua or Kings, safe in the knowledge that because such assumptions were widely shared they would in all probability remain unchallenged. On the contrary, challenge is all around, and debate is fierce. If in the older paradigm it was generally accepted, for example, that repetition in a text was an indication of composite sources or redaction, now it is asked whether repetition cannot itself be an aspect of literary artistry (e.g. in 2 Kings 17:1–6; 18:9–12). If variation in style and language was likewise widely regarded as a sign that more than one hand had been at work on a text, now it is asked whether such variation cannot have many explanations other than difference in authorship (e.g. in the construction of the various 'regnal formulae' of the books of Kings). And if it was often claimed that texts were replete with 'inconsistencies' which must perforce indicate the presence of more than one mind active in their construction, now it is asked whether 'inconsistent' has not been a word often used in historical-critical scholarship where terms such as 'theologically complex' or 'ironic' would do just as well[2] (e.g. in discussion of the interesting 2 Kings 17:24–41).[3]

In such a manner, then, has the focus of scholarly interest in interpretation of the historical books of the Old Testament shifted markedly in the past two decades.[4] If we have now arrived at a time in which their nature as narrative is much better understood, however, we find ourselves at the same time and for obvious reasons in an interpretative era in which their nature as historical books is even more widely questioned than previously. For if the history in the historical books was previously found underneath the narrative, as it were, in those remnants of texts which could be salvaged from the narrative through historical-critical means; and if we are now told that in fact there is no access of this kind to the depths of the text, such that salvage is possible; what then of history? If an artistically constructed narrative is what we have, and we may no longer exploit incoherence in pursuit of the earlier layers of text which offer up the buried treasure that is historical fact, in what sense may we consider the historical books 'historical' at all? Thus it is that the narrative studies of the recent decades of biblical interpretation have played their part in producing a much greater degree of scepticism about the historicality of these biblical narratives, and an increasing reluctance among biblical exegetes to move beyond the story to anything recognizable in the modern context as history. We may observe the trend at its most marked in a scholar like Philip Davies, who is quite ready to oppose biblical story and history, claiming that 'the reason why many things are told in the biblical literature, and the way they are told, has virtually everything to do with literary artistry and virtually nothing to do with anything that might have happened'.[5] Narrative studies are judged from this perspective as having serious implications in terms of the use of narrative texts as a window on the ancient past.

Such a point of view has gathered numerous adherents in recent work on both the biblical texts and the history of Israel, in the latter of which there is a noticeable tendency to regard the historical books as much more problematic for historians than hitherto. It is not just Ruth, Esther and Chronicles which are treated with a high degree of scepticism now, when scholars ask historical questions about Israel. Already in 1986 J. M. Miller and J. H. Hayes[6] displayed a marked reluctance to offer historical reconstructions of the pre-monarchic period because of perceived difficulties in using Joshua and Judges for this purpose, and even in the case of the Samuel traditions they were somewhat tentative. This book is commonly perceived as something of a watershed among scholars currently interested in the history of Israel, some of whom have even more doubts about biblical tradition than Miller and Hayes.[7] It is of course not only narrative studies which have brought about the current state of affairs. The perspective of archaeology on ancient Palestine has also been important, and broader philosophical and cultural currents have played their part. In particular, it is unsurprising that in a postmodern context in which biblical scholarship shows signs of becoming as obsessed with ideology as it was previously obsessed with history we should find that even where the biblical texts are regarded as offering testimony to a real past, that testimony is widely perceived, because of its ideological nature, as offering little help to modern scholars in reconstructing that real past. Yet it cannot be doubted that of all the factors which have combined to create the interpretative context in which our historical books are now read and in which the term 'historical' as attached to these books has become ever more problematic, it is the new interest in the narrative character of these texts which has been the most important.

In which direction discussion of this matter of history and story will proceed remains to be seen. Certainly there are manifest indications of intellectual incoherence at the very heart of much of the current interpretative endeavour in this area which might suggest that it cannot long continue on the path it has chosen without collapsing with exhaustion brought on by internal contradiction. Much of what has been written in the area of the ideology of the biblical texts in particular is difficult to take with much seriousness, since it apparently asks its readers to believe that biblical narratives alone are to be disqualified from consideration as referents to a real past on the grounds of ideology, other narratives (including those of modern scholars) remaining untouched by difficulty. For those who share some residual vestige of concern for truth and rationality, this kind of argumentation is unlikely to hold out much long-term attraction. Yet one of the difficulties about the interpretation of the historical books of the Old Testament in the present climate is precisely that truth and rationality are not necessarily any longer held by interpreters as self-evident goods. These things too can be portrayed as simply the tools of the ideologue,[8] and indeed ideology can be claimed as being virtually all that in any case exists. One cannot be sure, therefore, that intellectual incoherence will indeed in the end be eschewed and rationality embraced. For those who do wish to embrace it and to move ahead some interesting questions remain. Is it really the case that artistically constructed narratives cannot also and at the same time refer to a real past? What precisely is the difference between narrative and historiography in any case? Is not modern historiography itself both ideologically loaded and also (if well-written) artistically shaped narrative? Does archaeology, in particular, not require a narrative in which its mute data can be located and thus interpreted? Whence should come that narrative – from the imaginations of modern scholars, perhaps informed by (inevitably ideologically loaded) extra-biblical texts? Why should such a narrative not be informed by the only comprehensive account of the history of Israel that we possess, namely by the biblical account? These are some of the broader questions which interpreters of the historical books of the Old Testament are now discussing and debating. It is on the answers given to such questions that the continued viability of the label 'historical' for the books we are considering will depend.

### TEXTS OR READERS?

Mention of ideology brings us now to our second main area of debate concerning the historical books: the matter of interpretative responsibilities. It would fairly characterize the historical-critical school of interpretation if we were to say that proponents of that school see their primary task as to understand and to expatiate upon Old Testament historical texts in their own terms and within their own context. They mean by this, of course, the original context, historically speaking – or perhaps we should rather say original *contexts*, to allow for the idea of successive redaction. Thus if 1 Samuel 8, for example, characterizes Israelite kingship as something which arose out of the initiative of the people of Israel and represented a rejection of Israel's God, then the primary and important thing is not what this means in the context of the Old Testament or perhaps the Christian Bible as a whole, nor what significance this has for the reader. The important thing is what the passage tells us about the institution of the monarchy in Israel, its development and the attitude of various ancient Israelite parties thereto. If 1 Kings 14:21–4 is found criticizing the religion of Judah in the time of king Rehoboam, then the important thing is likewise to locate the passage within the development of Israelite religion, drawing conclusions about what religion actually looked like 'on the ground' during the pre-exilic period, how far the 'Deuteronomistic' perspective which now dominates a book like Kings represents an early or a later perspective, and so on. History is again the key to the whole interpretative process. The primary task of the interpreter is to use that key to open doors on meaning.

A question has lately been addressed to interpreters adopting such a stance, however. Why should our interpretation of the text be confined by the alleged communicative intentions of its author(s) or editor(s) in writing it or editing it in their historical contexts? It is a question asked from two very different points of view, but by scholars who nevertheless have in common that they do not agree with historical critics in their view of primary interpretative responsibility.

### The freedom of the reader

On the one side are those who wish to know why the primary interpretative task should be defined in terms of clarifying the perspectives of those Israelites who were, after all, only a very few of those capable of offering a perspective on life in Israel during the periods described by our historical books. What we have in these books are ideologically loaded pictures of the past produced by an intellectual elite (since it is always such people who produce literature), all of them Israelites and all of them (probably) men. It is the perspective of those who had the power to transmit their vision of society, and in the process to suppress or contextualize other, perhaps different visions. What of the perspectives of the marginalized? How might Israelite women, or indeed Philistine or Moabite men, have told the story? How might Israelites holding religious convictions quite different from those of the orthodox Yahwists whose vision the Bible now passes on? The stories of such people are surely just as valid and just as important, if not more so, as the story told by the biblical authors. Thus it is that much of the newer work on the historical books has not taken as its task the elucidation of the texts-as-intended-by-their-authors. The goal has rather been to reach behind authorial meanings and intentions and to give expression to alternative visions. The text becomes simply a springboard for interpretation, rather than its foundation. Sometimes, indeed, the text provides little more than the starting point for hostile criticism of the biblical tradition, which may then be left behind as the interpreter moves on to higher things.

Let us take as an example the question of the nature of Israelite religion in the pre-exilic period. The idea that the 'Deuteronomists' (the authors of Joshua–Kings) have distorted reality with regard to Israelite religion in this period is not new, and is already found in traditional historical criticism. The basis for the historical-critical analysis, however, is the perceived presence of differing perspectives on certain matters in the historical books themselves (as well as elsewhere). Certain texts appear to speak in terms different from the book of Deuteronomy and other passages influenced by Deuteronomy on matters such as the centralization of the Israelite cult. In more recent writing on Israelite religion, on the other hand, interpretation is not necessarily constrained by what texts actually have to say. These texts, after all, even if they differ somewhat from one another on specifics still represent only a very limited number of perspectives on the past. The interpretative horses come, as it were, from a similar ideological stable. Recent interpretation feels itself free, therefore, to move beyond and behind texts in pursuit of alternative points of view. The case of the goddess Asherah well illustrates the difference between the older and newer approaches. Previous scholarship was generally content to accept on the basis of widespread biblical testimony that whatever else might be true about Israelite religion, it was certainly true that basic distinctions existed even in the earlier periods between 'Israelite' and 'Canaanite' religion, not least in attitudes to female deities. It is now argued, however, that worship of Asherah, who is referred to or alluded to frequently in the historical books along with cultic objects apparently associated with her, was far from incompatible with authentic worship of Yahweh. Where the Deuteronomists criticize the Asherah-inclusive religion of Rehoboam's time because it was conducted according to the abominations of all the peoples which Yahweh had dispossessed before the Israelites, for example, it is now maintained rather that it was 'in harmony with its time, no more and no less'.[9] Worship of Asherah was far from being an alien element in Israelite religion, the corruption of an original purity. She was worshipped by the Israelites from the earliest times, and even had a place in the Jerusalem temple.[10] Particularly on the basis of extra-biblical inscriptions we may now say that Asherah was the female consort of Yahweh in Israelite religion in much the same way that the goddess Athirat/Ashratu is found in special relationship to the chief deity of whichever other ancient Near Eastern culture she appears in.

The important thing to notice about this position is just how little it is grounded in anything that might be considered in the conventional way as evidence. Archaeologists may or may not have uncovered data suggesting that some Israelites in certain places and at certain times regarded Asherah as Yahweh's consort.[11] Even if they have, this would not prove that the religion of Israel was syncretistic in origin and in essence. There is, in fact, no hard evidence which establishes that the worship of Asherah was an indigenous and original feature of Israelite religion. Nor is there any evidence which demonstrates that Asherah found a place in the Jerusalem temple before the time of Manasseh, and even then the evidence is only that of the biblical text itself (2 Kings 21:7), which forthrightly condemns what is seen as an innovation. It is not then *evidence*, textual or otherwise, which is driving this vision of the Israelite past. The fuel which powers this scholarly construction may be suspected to lie, in fact, much more clearly in the present – in the desire of scholarly interpreters influenced by the religious or secular Western culture in which most of them live and work to find a past which is congenial to their present. An ancient world of religious pluralism, and in particular an ancient world in which it turns out after all that Israel has a female goddess, represents such a congenial world, whether to those who think monotheism dangerous or the Judaeo-Christian God a little too resolutely male.

It is always an aspect of the interpretation of texts, of course, that interpreters bring their world with them to the text. That is inevitably so. In the historical-critical past, however, there was at least a theoretical acceptance that interpreters should not simply absorb the biblical narrative texts (or any others) into their world, reading their own dreams and visions into it. The text had its own integrity, and that integrity had to be respected in the interpretative process, with due attention to what the text itself was saying. What is problematic in much recent interpretation of biblical texts, including biblical narrative texts, is that with the general move away from the notion that the communicative intentions of author(s) or editor(s) are centrally important to the interpretative task – that what the text itself is saying is centrally important – we have arrived in an interpretative era in which the distinction between text and interpreter has become blurred. For those who care not in the end whether the voices of the 'marginalized' which they claim to hear behind the biblical texts represent simply the externalized figment of their own imagination – whether the past which they claim to find behind the texts is simply a reflection of and validation for what is important to them in the present – this is not a problem. It is at least a question, however, whether those who adopt such a stance are engaged in an activity which may reasonably be called *biblical* interpretation at all, rather than something else. It is certainly sometimes the impression of the reader of such interpreters that he or she is finding out considerably more about the interpreter than about the Old Testament.

### The constraints of the canon

In contrast to this kind of recent response to historical-critical methodology we may consider now the response of an interpreter like Brevard Childs. Childs certainly does not wish to argue for readerly freedom in relation to textual meanings. He is, on the other hand, no happier than those who so argue with the idea that the primary task of the biblical interpreter is to offer interpretation of texts in their original historical context(s). That is not the way in which to arrive at the true communicative intention of biblical texts, narrative or otherwise. It is the canonical context of a text, rather than its historical context, which should be regarded as decisive in its interpretation.

Childs's central contention is that the concept of canon, pushed to one side in the Enlightenment in the name of academic and religious freedom, must be brought back to the centre of the agenda in Old Testament studies.

Canon does not represent, as many have claimed, an arbitrary and late imposition on the Old Testament texts by religious authorities, alien to and distorting of the essence of the Old Testament and without hermeneutical significance. Canon is rather a complex historical process within ancient Israel which entailed the collecting, selecting and ordering of texts to serve a normative function as Scripture within the continuing religious community. It is intrinsically bound up with the Old Testament texts as we have them, and should be taken seriously by those who study them. It is indeed these Old Testament texts *as we have them* that should be the focus of readerly concern. It is precisely the disregarding of canonical shaping by historical-critical interpretation that has in large measure led to the modern hermeneutical impasse. The text is transported into the hypothetical past by destroying the very elements which constitute its canonical shape, the vehicle which has enabled its journey to the present. It is little wonder that having destroyed this essential vehicle, historical critics are then unable to devise a way of relocating the text in any modern religious context. Childs's approach, on the other hand, while not wishing to bypass two hundred years of critical research, nevertheless demands that historical-critical tools be used to illuminate the canonical text as we have it, rather than for some other purpose. He does not deny the theological significance of a depth dimension of the tradition; but features within the tradition which have been subordinated, modified or placed in the distant background of the text cannot be interpreted apart from the role assigned them in the final form.

Here, then, is an approach which clearly insists on the primacy of the text rather than the reader. To that extent Childs lines up with traditional historical criticism. Where Childs parts ways with such criticism, however, is in his understanding of the primary context in which texts are to be read. The primary context is itself textual, rather than historical. We may illustrate the difference in terms of the approach taken to the historical books by returning to the example of 1 Samuel 7–12.

Historical criticism understood its primary task in relation to such a section of text as involving such things as elucidating the origin and development of monarchy in Israel and the attitude of various ancient Israelite parties thereto. It was this kind of matter that the biblical interpreter had above all a duty to investigate and explain. Much has therefore been written, for example, on whether chapter 8 is later than chapter 9, where a noticeably warmer welcome to kingship is perceived. If so, perhaps chapter 8 represents an Israelite perspective on monarchy from a later (exilic or post-exilic) time when monarchy had been found wanting, and chapter 9 represents an earlier, more optimistic view. In opposition to this view some have argued that there was already in the beginning a difference in perspective over monarchy in Israel, some Israelites thinking it a necessary and right development and others believing it to be in tension with some fundamental Israelite principles. Our two chapters simply preserve side by side the two viewpoints in the debate.

Childs does not object in principle to this kind of historical reading of 1 Samuel 7–12. On the contrary, it is this kind of reading which provides us with the depth dimension of the tradition. Whatever various Israelite authors might have meant to say about the monarchy when they first wrote their pieces of text about it, however, these meanings are not determinative when it comes to modern biblical interpretation of 1 Samuel. Childs sees his task as an interpreter as lying rather in presenting a theological reflection on the Old Testament king which does justice to the peculiar canonical shaping of the biblical literature.[12] The canonical process has given the anti-monarchical source pre-eminence, bracketing the earlier pro-monarchical source at both beginning and end. We must recognize, therefore, that the dominant note sounded by our text is that of prophetic warning. Yet the message of the pro-monarchical source in its new context must still also be heard – that the establishment of the kingdom, although arising out of unbelief, is not to be regarded as a purely secular act. Israel cannot move from judge to king in the manner described in 1 Samuel 7–12; yet kingship becomes part of God's plan for Israel in David, whose career (canonically speaking) adumbrates Israel's messianic hope.

Thus does Childs's interpretation of 1 Samuel 7–12 and indeed the historical books overall differ markedly from that both of historical critics and of those interpreters who stress the freedom of the reader. The interpreter is not free from constraint. The constraint is not ultimately that of authorial meanings in historical contexts, however, but that of canonical shaping. It is in the elucidation of texts in their canonical context that the primary responsibility of the biblical interpreter consists.

How far Childs's stance on interpretation will be widely adopted remains to be seen. Doubts have been expressed about the coherence of his notion of canon, both in terms of the depth of 'canonical consciousness' within the Old Testament texts and in terms of the concept of canon itself. It has further been asked whether texts can really have communicative intentions that are not wholly related to the intentions of the human authors or editors who produced them, and why these intentions (if they exist) rather than others must form the basis of the interpretative task.[13] My own view is that Childs can be adequately defended in all these areas. Whether one considers that the programme which he outlines is entirely satisfactory as it stands, however, will depend not simply on convincing responses being given in these areas of concern, but also on one's convictions about the long-term viability or otherwise of the historical-critical method. For what is striking about Childs is the way in which he characteristically takes historical-critical reality as a fairly obvious and self-evident starting point for his interpretative work. He pays far from sufficient attention to the massive amount of work carried out in the last two decades which has gone some way towards undermining the very historical-critical approach which he presupposes. Narrative studies have affected scholarly approaches to 1 Samuel 7–12, for example, just as much as other sections of the historical books, and whether there is any need to see the kind of tension between the chapters that historical critics have exploited whose work Childs builds upon must now be considered open to question.[14] If the foundations are questioned, however, then so of course must the superstructure. It may be, then, that those who are otherwise attracted by a canonical approach to the historical books of the Old Testament will wish to begin the interpretative process at a more fundamental level than Childs has done – with the texts themselves, rather than with historical-critical theories concerning them.

## Notes

This chapter was written during a period of sabbatical leave in Tübingen, Germany, during which I wish gratefully to acknowledge that I was the beneficiary of a grant from the Alexander von Humboldt-Stiftung.

1 Those interested in an overview of such scholarship might consult, e.g., S. L. McKenzie, *The Trouble with Kings: The Composition of the Book of Kings in the Deuteronomistic History*, Vetus Testamentum Supplement 42 (Leiden: Brill, 1991), pp. 1–19.

2 I note the following among the many books which have raised questions like these and in the process contributed to a change in climate within biblical studies where narrative is concerned: J. Licht, *Storytelling in the Bible* (Jerusalem: Magnes, 1978); R. Alter, *The Art of Biblical Narrative* (London: Allen & Unwin, 1981); and M. Sternberg, *The Poetics of Biblical Narrative: Ideological Literature and the Drama of Reading* (Bloomington: Indiana University Press, 1985). For detailed examples from Kings in which passages are read from both an historical-critical and a narrative-critical point of view, see I. W. Provan, *1 and 2 Kings* (OT Guides, Sheffield: Sheffield Academic Press, 1996).

3 See further on these points I. W. Provan, *1 and 2 Kings*, chapter 2.

4 This is well illustrated in Kings if one simply compares with their historical-critical predecessors such recent commentaries as take narrative issues much more seriously: T. R. Hobbs, *2 Kings* (Waco, TX: Word Books, 1985); R. D. Nelson, *First and Second Kings* (Louisville, KY: John Knox, 1987); B. O. Long, *1 Kings*, and *2 Kings* (Grand Rapids, MI: Eerdmans, 1991); I. W. Provan, *1 and 2 Kings* (Peabody, MA: Hendrickson, 1995).

5 P. R. Davies, *In Search of 'Ancient Israel'* (Sheffield: Sheffield Academic Press, 1992), p. 29.

6 J. M. Miller and J. Hayes, *A History of Ancient Israel and Judah* (London: SCM Press, 1986).

7 K. W. Whitelam, *The Invention of Ancient Israel: The Silencing of Palestinian History* (London: Routledge, 1996), for example, argues that it is not simply the information provided by the biblical texts *about* ancient Israel which is problematic, but the very *idea* of ancient Israel itself, which all these texts (and not just Joshua–Samuel) have put in the scholarly as well as the popular mind. In thus inventing ancient Israel, Western scholarship has contributed to the silencing of Palestinian history.

8 *Ibid.*, for example on p. 207: 'The appeal to what is reasonable is part of the rhetoric of objectivity in order to support the dominant construction of Israel's past within the discourse of biblical studies.' See further I. W. Provan, 'The End of (Israel's) History? A Review Article on K. W. Whitelam's *The Invention of Ancient Israel*', *Journal of Semitic Studies* (forthcoming).

9 G. W. Ahlström, *The History of Ancient Palestine from the Palaeolithic Period to Alexander's Conquest*, ed. D. V. Edelman (Sheffield: JSOT Press, 1993), p. 561.

10 *Ibid.*, p. 477.

11 S. A. Wiggins, *A Reassessment of Asherah: A Study According to the Textual Sources of the First Two Millennia BCE* (Neukirchen-Vluyn: Neukirchener Verlag, 1993), pp. 163–81.

12 B. S. Childs, *Old Testament Theology in a Canonical Context* (Philadelphia: Fortress Press, 1985), pp. 115–21.

13 Among Childs's several critics see, for example, J. Barr, *Holy Scripture: Canon, Authority, Criticism* (Oxford: Clarendon Press, 1983).

14 See, e.g., V. P. Long, *The Reign and Rejection of King Saul: A Case for Literary and Theological Coherence* (Atlanta, GA: Scholars Press, 1989).

## Further reading

Childs, B. S., *Biblical Theology of the Old and New Testaments: Theological Reflection on the Hebrew Bible* (Minneapolis: Fortress Press, 1993). See esp. pp. 53–94.

Gunn, D. M. and D. N. Fewell, *Narrative in the Hebrew Bible* (Oxford: Oxford University, 1993).

Long, B. O., *1 Kings, with an Introduction to Historical Literature* (Grand Rapids, MI: Eerdmans, 1984), pp. 14–21.

Noble, P. R., *The Canonical Approach: A Critical Reconstruction of the Hermeneutics of Brevard S. Childs*, Biblical Interpretation Series 16 (Leiden: Brill, 1995).

Provan, I. W., 'Ideologies, Literary and Critical: Reflections on Recent Writing on the History of Israel', *Journal of Biblical Literature* 114 (1995), pp. 585–606.

'Canons to the Left of Him: Brevard Childs, His Critics, and the Future of Old Testament Theology', *Scottish Journal of Theology* 50 (1997), pp. 1–38.

# 14 The prophetic books

ROBERT R. WILSON

Throughout the history of biblical interpretation, readers have understood the prophetic books in a variety of different ways and have employed a variety of different tools to interpret them. This plurality of understandings and interpretations has been due largely to the fact that the books themselves are highly diverse and complex. Although all of them except Jonah are primarily collections of prophetic oracles interspersed with a few narratives about their prophetic authors, each book has a distinctive literary style and history and reflects its own particular set of concerns. This diversity has historically provided readers with support for a wide range of interpretative options and has caused many contemporary biblical scholars to exhibit extreme reluctance to generalize about how the prophetic books are to be understood. Even when such generalizations are made, there is little scholarly agreement about the nature and interests of the prophetic books or about the proper way to interpret them. Contemporary scholarship on this literature provides examples of most of the approaches traditionally taken by general readers and then augments these approaches with a number of others that have not yet reached the non-specialist.

At first glance, then, the current scholarly study of the prophetic books seems to be in disarray. There is no commonly accepted understanding of the nature of the books themselves and no agreement about the methods that should be used to interpret them. In addition, there is a strong suspicion that each book must be considered individually and that generalizations of any sort should be avoided. However, even when the unique character of each book is recognized, it is still possible to chart several general trends in the history of interpretation.

## PROPHETS AND THE PROPHETIC BOOKS

In order to understand the shifting currents in the interpretation of the prophetic books, it is useful to recognize that until quite recently most readers accepted in some form the biblical claim that these books were written by the prophets whose names are attached to them. The interpretation of the books themselves, then, has usually been bound tightly to the interpreter's ideas about the nature and character of the ancient Israelite prophet. Some of these ideas have been derived from the text itself while others have not, but in either case interpreters have brought a particular picture of the prophet to the task of reading. This picture has always included the notion that the prophet was an intermediary through whom God spoke directly to Israel, but beyond this basic affirmation there have often been more specific claims about the prophet's traditional role. Elements of a given picture have sometimes involved the prophet's historical setting and personality as these could be gleaned from the text, and even in antiquity there was a recognition that there were different aspects to the prophetic persona. As a result, readers of the prophetic books have tended to see a variety of things in them according to the pictures of the prophet that lie behind the reading. These pictures are not always mutually exclusive. They sometimes overlap or supplement each other, and they are not easily arranged in historical sequence. However, for analytical purposes they can provide some insight into why the interpretation of these books has developed in the way that it has.

## TRADITIONAL VIEWS OF PROPHETS AND THE PROPHETIC BOOKS

### Prophets as predictors of the future

The idea that the biblical prophets were primarily concerned with predicting future events is deeply imbedded in the history of the interpretation of the prophetic books. General readers even today usually associate prophets with foretelling the future, and scholarly interpreters have held similar views since antiquity. Within the biblical text itself, there is ample evidence to suggest that ancient writers too believed the prophets to have had privileged divine foreknowledge of things to come. In Deuteronomy 18:9–22, for example, God forbids the Israelites to consult various sorts of spirit mediums in order to determine the divine will but instead promises to send Israel a series of prophets 'like Moses', who will be the true channels of God's word. So that the people will be able to distinguish the prophet whom God has actually sent from the prophet who only claims to have a divine word, God further explains that the prophet whom God did not send will speak words which will not take place or prove true (verse 22). Lying behind this explanation is the assumption that when a genuine prophet predicts the future the prediction will always come to pass. Although the writer of the

Book of Jonah did not think that the matter was so simple, the writers of 1 and 2 Kings accepted this test for genuine prophecy and point out to the reader particular historical events which are to be interpreted as fulfilling an earlier prophetic prediction (1 Kings 14:1–16/15:27–30; 16:1–4/16:11–14; 21:20–4/22:37–8, 2 Kings 9:36–7/10:17; 2 Kings 1:2–4/1:17–18; cf. 1 Kings 13:1–10/2 Kings 23:15–18).

Such explicit references to the fulfilment of earlier prophecies are rare within the prophetic books themselves, but there can be no doubt that the authors of this material believed that genuine prophets could accurately foretell future events. The clearest evidence on this point comes from passages which discuss the problem of false prophecy, particularly in the predictions of prophets considered genuine by the Israelite community (for example, Jeremiah 27–8).

This concern to vindicate the predictions of the authors of the prophetic books can also be seen in a few passages where the prophets or their followers have reinterpreted prophecies to explain their apparent non-fulfilment. A clear case of such reinterpretation is Ezekiel's prediction in 587 BC that the Babylonian king Nebuchadrezzar would lay siege to the Phoenician city of Tyre and would eventually destroy it completely (Ezekiel 26:7–14). In fact, the Babylonians were unsuccessful in capturing Tyre and ended their siege against it sometime around 573 BC. This unsuccessful outcome caused Ezekiel or his followers to revise the earlier prophecy, and in the latest dated oracle in the book (571 BC) it is explained that God has substituted Egypt for Tyre as a reward for the Babylonians' hard work during the siege (29:17–20). In a similar vein, Isaiah's oracles against Moab (Isaiah 15–16) conclude with an acknowledgement that most of the predictions have not come to pass (16:13) and that God is now issuing a new word calling for the destruction of Moab within three years (16:14).

Although these explicit revisions of earlier predictions indicate the great concern which the biblical writers had to explain the apparent non-fulfilment of prophecy, it would be misleading to suggest, as some modern scholars have, that this issue was the primary one stimulating biblical interpretation. In reality the situation seems to have been more complex, for the prophetic books also contain examples of the reinterpretation of predictions that were in fact fulfilled. In addition, there are cases of interpreting non-predictive oracles as predictions. Both of these phenomena suggest that in the eyes of the biblical writers the prophetic word was a word about the future whether it was in the form of a prediction or not and that the meaning of oracles was not exhausted by a single fulfilment.[1]

Although the biblical writers were concerned about the fulfilment of judgement oracles against Israel, they were even more worried about prophetic promises of salvation and restoration. As Jeremiah had already noted (Jeremiah 28:8–9), prophets who spoke of future well-being for Israel had a heavy burden of proof, and this problem intensified when Israel's situation did not improve substantially after the exile. The writers of the prophetic books therefore began to look for the fulfilment of promise oracles in an increasingly distant future and often moved in the direction of apocalypticism, looking for Israel's salvation and the punishment of Israel's enemies as the result of a direct intervention by God that would lead to an inversion of the present oppressive world order. For this reason apocalyptic passages were added to many of the prophetic books in order to set existing oracles into a new temporal framework (Ezekiel 38–39; Isaiah 24–27; Zechariah 9–14; Malachi 4).

Interpretative trends which began within the prophetic books themselves have been continued throughout the history of interpretation. In early Jewish tradition the most graphic example of reading the prophets as predictors of the future comes from the scrolls found at Qumran, where certain types of biblical commentaries interpret virtually every line of books such as Habakkuk as pointing to the recent history and future of the Qumran community. On a more restricted scale, Jews and Christians both interpreted Isaiah's references to the servant of God (especially Isaiah 52:13–53:12) as prophecies of the messiah, the future anointed king. For Christians, of course, the messiah had already come in Jesus, and the New Testament is full of references to Old Testament prophecies that are taken to refer to Jesus' life and times. This line of interpretation has continued in Christian circles down to the present day, where it remains alive in many Christian groups even though it has largely been rejected by biblical scholars.[2]

### Prophets as ethicists and theologians

A prominent feature of the prophetic books is that they speak of the present as well as the future. Indeed, the prophets often tie the two together, suggesting that Israel's future is the result of its present activities and that future disaster can be avoided if the people will change their present behaviour. The prophets thus advocate a particular way of living and can be seen as advocates for a particular ethical position, even though that position varies somewhat from prophet to prophet and from situation to situation.

Examples of ethical concern abound in the prophetic books. The Book of Amos opens with a condemnation of Israel's neighbours for violating their mutual treaty obligations that they incurred by being vassals within the Davidic empire (Amos 1:3–2:3), while Judah and Israel are similarly chastised for violating God's law, particularly with respect to their treatment of the poor and needy (2:4–8; 8:4–6). Similar concerns are raised by Isaiah, who urges the people to be obedient and to trust in God's ability to protect the land from its enemies (Isaiah 1:1–23; 7–9). The early oracles of Jeremiah often urge Israel to repent in order to avoid otherwise certain destruction (Jeremiah 3:12–14, 22–3; 4:1), and even Ezekiel, who proclaimed that Jerusalem's future doom could not be avoided under any conditions, urged the Israelites already suffering the judgement of exile to keep themselves righteous (Ezekiel 18).

Given the prophetic stress on right behaviour, it is not surprising that the ethical and theological dimensions of the prophetic books have been a part of the history of interpretation from the beginning. This has been particularly true in Jewish communities, where the rubric 'prophetic books' also includes the books of the Former Prophets (Joshua, Judges, Samuel and Kings). In rabbinic sources these books are all often linked with the Torah (the Christian Pentateuch), although the exact nature of this relationship is not always clear. In general early Judaism seems to have seen a connection between the prophet Moses, the writer of the Torah, and the later prophets (Deuteronomy 18:15), although the tradition also affirmed the superiority of Moses (Deuteronomy 34:10). In any case, the later prophets were thought by the rabbis to be transmitters of the Oral Torah, and it was also possible to understand the prophetic books as teaching Torah in some way. All of this added up to a strong stress on the prophetic interest in personal and communal behaviour.

On the Christian side the use of the prophetic books for ethical instruction may already appear in late New Testament writings, but this particular line of interpretation does not seem to have been as important for early Christians as it was for their Jewish contemporaries.[3] That situation began to change dramatically with the rise of critical biblical scholarship in the nineteenth century. At that time scholars such as Bernhard Duhm and W. Robertson Smith wrote on the theology of the prophets and argued that ethical idealism was the chief characteristic of their work. Seen from this point of view, the prophetic books represented the highest development of Israelite moral thought, while later Jewish priestly writings signalled a decline in the religion's ethical insights.[4] Such an evolutionary view of Israelite religion, of course, overlooked much in the prophetic books themselves and was eventually rejected by biblical scholars, although stress on the ethical and theological dimensions of the prophets remains a prominent feature of contemporary scholarship, particularly among Jewish interpreters such as Martin Buber, Abraham Heschel and Yehezkel Kaufmann.[5]

### Prophets as poets and mystics

In the middle of the nineteenth century biblical scholarship was strongly influenced by two intellectual streams that had a profound and lasting impact on the interpretation of the prophetic books. The first of these streams was German romanticism, which, among other things, stressed the spiritual, almost mystical character of artistic creativity. At roughly the same time, biblical scholars became newly aware of the distinctive character of Hebrew poetry. Jewish interpreters in the middle ages had already noted the way in which poetic lines in Hebrew tended to occur in pairs, with each of the paired lines related to the other in meaning, and this insight was later rediscovered by the Englishman Robert Lowth.[6] Lowth provided biblical scholars with a set of precise tools for recognizing and analysing Hebrew poetry, and when these tools were combined with the romantic notion that poetic and prophetic inspiration were closely related to each other, there emerged the picture of the prophet as inspired poet.

The importance of this idea for the interpretation of the prophetic books began to be clear around the end of the nineteenth century. Scholars had long noted that the prophetic books contain a number of poetic oracles, but they also contain a good bit of narrative and exhortatory prose, as well as material that seems to fit neither of these categories. If the prophets were in fact inspired poets, then it followed that the non-poetic portions of the prophetic writings could not be from the prophets, or at least could not have the same degree of inspiration as the poetic portions. This conclusion established an interpretative principle that began to be employed in commentaries with Bernhard Duhm's work on Isaiah and that has continued in some circles down to the present day.[7] Following this principle, the interest of the commentator is in using poetic analysis to uncover the genuine words of the prophet in order to isolate the true divine revelation. The additional material in the book is either ignored or thought to have lesser religious value.

While some modern commentators are still interested in this sort of approach to the prophetic books, the general tendency of contemporary scholars is to recognize the importance of the non-poetic material and to challenge the notion that the prophets only wrote (or spoke) poetry. However, Duhm and his followers did raise for subsequent interpreters a series of problems that still have found no generally accepted solution in the scholarly guild. By calling attention to the various types of material in the prophetic books and then by attributing only some of this material to the prophets, Duhm raised in sharp relief the question of how the prophetic books came to be in their present form. The implied answer to this question is that later writers or editors, perhaps disciples of the prophets, were responsible for collecting and elaborating the original poetic oracles, but in spite of numerous scholarly attempts to study this process, it remains mysterious. To be sure, many modern critics adhere to a commonly accepted account of how each prophetic book came to be in its present form, but there is still much argument, and some would claim that no theory on this question can carry any degree of conviction.[8]

The problem of how the prophetic books grew from prophetic utterances to finished literary works is even more complicated if the phenomenon of ecstasy is thought to be part of the prophetic experience. Since the German scholar Gustav Hölscher in 1914 advanced the hypothesis of the ecstatic roots of prophecy, scholars have struggled with the problem of how the basically uncontrolled and perhaps unconscious revelatory experience of the prophet could have yielded intelligible and more or less well organized prophetic literature. Modern studies of prophetic trance behaviour shed some light on this question by highlighting the often stereotypical and controlled nature of the trance state, but precisely how the process worked in the biblical period remains a mystery.[9]

### Prophets as oracle givers

Although scholars had long recognized that the Israelite prophets delivered their oracles orally, this observation became the basis of an approach to prophetic literature in the work of Hermann Gunkel (1862–1932). In a series of programmatic works, Gunkel set out to explore the origins and history of Israelite literature in general. Strongly influenced by contemporary German folklore studies, he concluded that all biblical literature was originally oral and relatively brief. At the oral stage there was a heavy use of stereotypical or formulaic speech patterns, which were derived from and used in specific settings in the life of the Israelite people. When Gunkel applied these conclusions to the prophetic literature, he suggested that prophetic oracles were originally short threats of impending doom, to which the prophets often joined an explanation for the coming disaster. At a later stage in the prophetic tradition, the prophets devised additional oracle forms, some of which were borrowed from other spheres of Israelite life, although the literary patterns of these forms were not so firmly fixed as the threat of impending doom. Later on, the short oral oracles were written down by the prophets or their disciples, and in written form were expanded by subsequent generations of editors.

Although later scholars have refined Gunkel's theories about the history of prophetic literature, his fundamental observations have remained the basis of much contemporary analysis of the prophetic books. Thus many modern scholars would accept the claim that prophetic oracles were originally oral and would also agree with a modified version of Gunkel's formal literary analysis. Even though there is not always agreement on genre labels, many moderns would accept the premise that prophetic oracles commonly began with an explanation or indictment ('because you have done this'), followed by a logical connector ('therefore'), a 'messenger formula' introducing a direct quotation from God ('thus says the Lord'), and then the threat of impending doom or announcement of judgement, perhaps concluded by another authentication formula ('says the Lord; oracle of the Lord'). In addition to this common oracle pattern, scholars have also suggested others, such as the prophecy of salvation, the proof saying or self-disclosure oracle, the disputation or trial speech, the woe oracle, the exhortation and the prophetic instruction, although there is often much disagreement concerning the precise original shape of these literary forms.[10]

The approach which Gunkel pioneered has remained influential in modern scholarly circles because it provides a convenient way of bringing order out of the often confusing collections of materials in the prophetic books. By using formulas and standard oracle patterns to determine where literary units begin and end, the reader is in a better position to spot atypical material and to understand the way in which the books are organized. At the same time, it is important to note that Gunkel's approach involves a number of problematic features which in many ways are the sources of much of the current ferment in the scholarly study of the prophetic books.

In the first place, the standard literary patterns which Gunkel and his successors isolated rarely appear in a pure or unmodified form, and there is a good bit of literary variation in prophetic oracles. This fact has led some scholars to question whether Gunkel laid too much stress on what was typical in prophetic literature and ignored the distinctive characteristics of individual prophets and books.

Second, Gunkel and his followers assumed an orderly development of the prophetic literature from short oral oracle to complex written document. However, recent studies of oral literature have brought into question this basic assumption. Oral literary units can in fact be quite long and complex, although they often do make some use of stereotypical building blocks. Furthermore, in any given culture there is rarely a simple progression between the stage where all of the culture's literature is oral and the stage where writing is the primary means of communication. In all societies, both ancient and modern, oral and written literatures interact in more complex ways and often coexist, so it cannot automatically be assumed that all Israelite prophecy was originally in oral form.[11]

Third, Gunkel was never able to bring much clarity to the social settings in which the prophets did their work, and in this respect an important part of his programme was never realized. Early on it was suggested that much prophetic activity took place within the context of Israel's cult, and it is certainly true that several of the prophets are said to have been priests or to have had cultic connections. Nevertheless, other settings, such as the royal court, were also involved. Beyond the question of the location of prophetic activity, Gunkel also left unanswered the question of the location of the production of the prophetic literature itself. Although recent archaeological discoveries at Mari and Emar in Syria have provided examples of prophet-like figures from the second millennium BC and thus supplied some clear examples of social context, this information is still lacking for Israel. Modern sociological approaches to the prophetic literature have allowed the formation of some suggestive hypotheses, but the absence of hard data has encouraged a wide range of alternative proposals, none of which can be definitively adjudicated.[12]

Finally, Gunkel's proposal was rather vague about the processes by which oral oracles became written books, and this vagueness often led scholars to ignore this aspect of the prophetic literature entirely. However, some important work was done on this question because of Gunkel's influence. An early effort is represented in Sigmund Mowinckel's study of Jeremiah, which in many ways is still the starting-point for work on this book. After a careful study of the literary forms in Jeremiah, Mowinckel was able to distinguish four genres: poetic oracles of judgement, exhortatory prose passages, biographical narratives about Jeremiah and poetic promise oracles. The first of these Mowinckel assigned to the prophet, but the exhortatory material he traced to the work of the Deuteronomists and the biographical narrative to the scribe Baruch. The promises, along with some miscellaneous passages, Mowinckel took to be late editorial additions.[13]

The same sort of approach has been applied to other prophetic books, although with considerably less success. In Amos and Hosea, for example, there is still little scholarly agreement on which oracles are primary and which are secondary. The same is true in the case of Isaiah. Outside of a general scholarly consensus that Isaiah 40–55 (and perhaps 34–5) are an exilic addition to the book while Isaiah 56–66 were added even later, scholars do not agree on how the compositional process worked. The literary history of Ezekiel has been studied exhaustively by Walther Zimmerli, who sees each of the book's complex oracles to be composed of a core from the prophet plus later additions. However, alternatives to this analysis have been suggested in recent years.[14]

Although the editorial history of the prophetic books remains far from clear, it has been used as the basis for a more sophisticated approach to prophetic theology. Particularly noteworthy in this respect is the work of Gerhard von Rad, who has analysed the compositional layers in the prophetic books and then used this literary history to trace the ways in which Israel's earliest religious traditions were preserved and modified by the prophets.[15] A somewhat similar approach has been taken by Brevard Childs, who attends to the literary and tradition history displayed in prophetic literature but who in the end pays much more attention to the theology reflected in the final shape of the text.[16]

## CONTEMPORARY VIEWS OF PROPHETS AND THE PROPHETIC BOOKS

Although most of the traditional views of prophets and their literature continue to be influential in the current scholarly discussion, the difficulties associated with earlier approaches have caused some interpreters to strike out in new directions. It is still too early to determine whether these new perspectives will replace their ancestors or will simply become one more approach among others, but it is at least possible to chart these current approaches.

### Prophets as authors and editors

In keeping with trends elsewhere in the field of biblical studies, scholars have increasingly been focusing their attention on the final form of the prophetic books and treating the prophets as authors of literary works or as editors of earlier prophetic writings. The people who have adopted this position have done so for a number of reasons. On the one hand, some have claimed that certain of the late prophetic books were never in fact in oral form but were first created in writing by their prophetic authors, whose work should therefore be treated as coherent literary units. Among the studies taking this approach, Moshe Greenberg's commentary on Ezekiel provides the most important example. Rejecting completely the literary and tradition-historical analysis of Zimmerli, Greenberg considers Ezekiel to be the work of the prophet himself and normally rejects the hypothesis of a great deal of later editing.[17] Each of the book's long oracles and visions is treated as a unit having multiple parts within an overall coherent structure. A similar approach has been taken to Joel, Malachi, Zephaniah and Isaiah 40–55 (Second Isaiah), among others, but at least in the last of these the overall structure of the work remains somewhat undefined.

At a slightly higher level of abstraction, scholars have become more interested in the structure of whole books, although this interest is not usually accompanied by the claim that the structure is the work of the prophet. In recent years much attention has been given to the shape of the Book of Isaiah, and there is growing agreement that its structure is intentional and not simply the result of random growth over a long period of time. However there is to date no agreement either on the significance of the final shape or on the process that led to it.[18] Similar uncertainty accompanies recent efforts to understand how the books of the twelve minor prophets came to be organized into a single literary unit ('The Book of the Twelve').[19]

On the other hand, some scholars have rejected entirely the traditional claim that prophets were in some way responsible for the prophetic books and have suggested that the biblical pictures of the prophets, as well as the literature attributed to them, were relatively late creations from the post-exilic period. In this case the prophetic books should be seen as literary works, perhaps even poetic works, and should be analysed as such without any attention being given to their hypothetical literary histories.[20] In a curious way this approach is a return to the older claim that the prophets were primarily poets, even though it dispenses with the prophets themselves.

### Prophets as interpreters of Scripture

Approaching the prophetic books in a much more traditional way, some scholars have recently suggested that the writers responsible for editing and elaborating the prophets' original oracles were neither prophets themselves nor creative authors but were attempting through their work to interpret the words of the prophets for a new day. The driving force behind this interpretative effort was not the old problem of unfulfilled prophecy but rather the conviction that the prophetic word was a boundless source of meaning and was capable of multiple fulfilments.

Although this approach to the prophetic books is still in its infancy, it has provided some intriguing perspectives on difficult passages. In Isaiah 7–11, for example, there is a collection of oracles that are clearly dated to the time of the Syro-ephraimite war (735–2 BC). Yet mixed in with Isaiah's words from this period are oracles that seem to stem from the Assyrian invasion of 701 BC (8:5–10; 10:5–19; 11:1–9) and even from the destruction of Jerusalem in 587 and the eventual return of Israel from exile in Babylon (11:10–16). These later oracles may not simply be new material but later attempts to interpret Isaiah's words from 735–2, words which had already been fulfilled.[21] In a similar way, some scholars have tried to see the occasional exhortatory prose units in the Book of Jeremiah (for example 3: 6–11) as interpretative commentaries on the earlier poetic oracles that surround them, although it appears to be difficult to carry out this approach consistently throughout the entire book.[22]

Both this approach to the prophetic books and the one discussed above suggest that the general direction of contemporary scholarship is towards close literary readings of some type, although there is still much disagreement about the concept of prophecy and about the literary history lying behind the present text. No matter how these arguments are eventually resolved, it is likely that older approaches will continue to coexist with the ones in vogue at the moment. In the end the very nature of the prophetic books seems to be to resist systematic approaches and to encourage if not to demand continual reinterpretation. If this is so, then this particular portion of Scripture is sure to demonstrate a great variety of interpretations in the future just as it has since its creation.

## Notes

1  Michael Fishbane, *Biblical Interpretation in Ancient Israel* (Oxford: Clarendon Press, 1985), pp. 443–524; Robert P. Carroll, *When Prophecy Failed: Reactions and Responses to Failure in the Old Testament Prophetic Traditions* (New York: Seabury Press, 1979).

2  John Barton, *Oracles of God* (London: Darton, Longman and Todd, 1986), pp. 179–234; Emil G. Kraeling, *The Old Testament Since the Reformation* (New York: Harper & Brothers, 1955); Paul Boyer, *When Time Shall Be No More: Prophecy Belief in Modern American Culture* (Cambridge: Harvard University Press, 1992).

3  Barton, *Oracles*, pp. 154–78.

4  Bernhard Duhm, *Die Theologie der Propheten* (Bonn: Adolph Marcus, 1875); W. Robertson Smith, *The Prophets of Israel*, 2nd edn (London: Adam and

Charles Black, 1902); Ronald E. Clements, *One Hundred Years of Old Testament Interpretation* (Philadelphia: Westminster Press, 1976), pp. 51–4.

5 Martin Buber, *The Prophetic Faith* (New York: Harper & Brothers, 1960); Abraham J. Heschel, *The Prophets* (New York: Harper & Row, 1962); Yehezkel Kaufmann, *The Religion of Israel* (London: George Allen & Unwin, 1961), pp. 343–446.

6 Robert Lowth, *De Sacra Poesi Hebraeorum*, ed. E. F. C. Rosenmüller (Leipzig: A. G. Weigel, 1815; 1st edn 1753).

7 Bernhard Duhm, *Das Buch Jesaia* (Göttingen: Vandenhoeck & Ruprecht, 1892).

8 Terence Collins, *The Mantle of Elijah: The Redaction Criticism of the Prophetical Books* (Sheffield: JSOT Press, 1993).

9 Gustav Hölscher, *Die Propheten* (Leipzig: J. C. Hinrichs, 1914); Robert R. Wilson, 'Prophecy and Ecstasy: A Reexamination', *Journal of Biblical Literature* 98 (1979), pp. 321–37; Joseph Blenkinsopp, *A History of Prophecy in Israel* (rev. edn Louisville, KY: Westminster/John Knox Press, 1996), pp. 35–9.

10 Claus Westermann, *Basic Forms of Prophetic Speech* (Philadelphia: Westminster Press, 1967); rpt. edn with a foreword by Gene M. Tucker (Louisville, KY: Westminster/John Knox Press, 1991); Marvin A. Sweeney, *Isaiah 1–39 with an Introduction to Prophetic Literature* (Grand Rapids, MI: Eerdmans, 1996), pp. 1–30.

11 Susan Niditch, *Oral World and Written Word* (Louisville, KY: Westminster/John Knox Press, 1996).

12 Sweeney, *Isaiah*, pp. 14–15; Blenkinsopp, *History*, pp. 30–9; Robert R. Wilson, *Prophecy and Society in Ancient Israel* (Philadelphia: Fortress Press, 1980); R. P. Carroll, 'Prophecy and Society', in R. E. Clements (ed.), *The World of Ancient Israel* (Cambridge: Cambridge University Press, 1989), pp. 203–25.

13 Sigmund Mowinckel, *Zur Komposition des Buches Jeremia* (Kristiania: Jacob Dybwad, 1914).

14 Walther Zimmerli, *Ezekiel*, 2 vols. (Philadelphia: Fortress Press, 1979, 1983); Collins, *Mantle*, pp. 88–103.

15 Gerhard von Rad, *Old Testament Theology vol. II: The Theology of Israel's Prophetic Traditions* (New York: Harper & Row, 1965).

16 Brevard S. Childs, *Introduction to the Old Testament as Scripture* (Philadelphia: Fortress Press, 1979), pp. 305–498.

17 Moshe Greenberg, *Ezekiel, 1–20* (Garden City, NY: Doubleday, 1983).

18 H. G. M. Williamson, *The Book Called Isaiah: Deutero-Isaiah's Role in Composition and Redaction* (Oxford: Clarendon Press, 1994); Christopher R. Seitz, *Zion's Final Destiny: The Development of the Book of Isaiah* (Minneapolis: Fortress Press, 1991).

19 James Nogalski, *Redactional Processes in the Book of the Twelve* (Berlin: de Gruyter, 1993); Paul R. House, *The Unity of the Twelve* (Sheffield: Almond Press, 1990).

20 A. Graeme Auld, 'Prophets through the Looking Glass: Between Writings and Moses', *Journal for the Study of the Old Testament* 27 (1983), pp. 3–23; Robert P.

Carroll, 'Poets Not Prophets', *Journal for the Study of the Old Testament* 27 (1983), pp. 25–31.
21 Williamson, *Isaiah*, pp. 116–55.
22 W. McKane, 'Relations Between Poetry and Prose in the Book of Jeremiah with Special Reference to Jeremiah iii 6–11 and xii 14–17', in Supplements to *Vetus Testamentum* 32: *Congress Volume Vienna 1980*, ed. J. A. Emerton (Leiden: Brill, 1981), pp. 220–37.

## Further reading

Barton, John, *Oracles of God*, London: Darton, Longman and Todd, 1986.

Blenkinsopp, Joseph, *A History of Prophecy in Israel*, Louisville, KY: Westminster/ John Knox Press, 1996.

Clements, Ronald E., *One Hundred Years of Old Testament Interpretation*, Philadelphia: Westminster Press, 1976.

Collins, Terence, *The Mantle of Elijah: The Redaction Criticism of the Prophetical Books*, Sheffield: JSOT Press, 1993.

Sweeney, Marvin A., *Isaiah 1–39 with an Introduction to Prophetic Literature*, Grand Rapids, MI: Eerdmans, 1996.

Westermann, Claus, *Basic Forms of Prophetic Speech*, Louisville, KY: Westminster/ John Knox Press, 1991.

Wilson, Robert R., *Prophecy and Society in Ancient Israel*, Philadelphia: Fortress Press, 1980.

# 15 The poetic and wisdom books

ROBERT ALTER

Any critical interpretation of the poetic books of the Hebrew Bible is dependent, or certainly should be dependent, on an understanding of the distinctive character of biblical poetry. On this question there has been less of a consensus than one might have expected at this late date in modern biblical studies. Broadly speaking, I would say that the investigation of biblical poetry since the beginning of the 1980s has made some real if uneven advances, against an unfortunately persistent background of confusions, misperceptions and aridly academic overcomplications.

The notion that biblical poetry is organized on a parallelism of meaning and structures between the two – sometimes three – parts of a line was first systematically articulated by Robert Lowth in his *Lectures on the Sacred Poetry of the Hebrews*, originally published in Latin in 1753. Though the first two of his three categories of parallelism – synonymous and antithetical – are demonstrably operative in thousands of lines of biblical verse, his third category, 'synthetic parallelism', would come to seem in the eyes of many critics no parallelism at all, leading to some uneasiness with the theory as a whole. In the course of time, scholars would propose the most intricate varieties of sub-categories of parallelism in order to save the system, and, in the opposite direction, especially beginning in the 1970s, counter-systems would be put forth that relegated parallelism to a purely secondary role. Thus, syllable-count, sentence-types, syntax, musical quantity, thought-unit were each in turn promoted by various scholars as being the real organizing principle of biblical poetry. None of these theories has won general acceptance, and each, I believe, can be shown to be compromised by either internal contradictions or some basic misunderstanding of how poetry works.

At the beginning of the 1980s, James Kugel's *The Idea of Biblical Poetry*[1] made a bold step forward, together with a giant step backward, in understanding the nature of biblical poetry. He shrewdly saw that synonymity was an imprecise, even misleading, concept for defining biblical parallelism, that some kind of *development* of meaning typically transpired between the first

226

and second half of the line, a development that he formulated (perhaps a little too schematically) as 'A, what's more, B'. Kugel's focus is on the single line, so he does not have much to say about development along the larger text continuum or on the relation between poetic form and meaning. A still graver limitation is his stubborn resistance to the notion that there is such a thing as biblical poetry. Sensing that the very rubric of poetry is an alien Greco-Roman implant on sacred soil, he argues that we should rather think of a stylistic continuity between the more tightly parallelistic structures perceptible in what we call verse and the somewhat looser parallelisms of what we conventionally designate as biblical prose. This strikes me as a peculiar blurring of a valid distinction because in most literatures there are elements of continuity between poetry and prose (the fondness for symmetrical antitheses in Pope's heroic couplets and Fielding's prose, the iambic cadences in Dickens and Melville, and so forth). The biblical authors themselves were clearly aware of the distinction between the two kinds of writing, for they often used formal introductions that marked the transition from prose to poetry, as when Balaam's poetic prophecy is introduced with the words, 'and he took up his theme [*mashal*] and he said'. Adele Berlin, in a useful linguistically oriented study of biblical parallelism, incisively refutes Kugel's argument against the existence of biblical poetry: 'Poetry uses parallelism as its constitutive or constructive device, while nonpoetry, though it contains parallelism, does not structure its message on a systematic use of parallelism.'[2]

In order to see precisely how parallelism is constitutive of biblical poetry, it is necessary to understand both that it is an organizing principle the biblical poets used *flexibly* and that parallelism involves the interaction of several different aspects of language and is not limited to semantics. Both these features of parallelism have come to be more firmly grasped over the last decade. In fact, an elegantly concise definition of the phenomenon was offered as early as 1971 by the literary theorist Benjamin Hrushovski (now Harshav) in his *Encyclopaedia Judaica* article on Hebrew prosody – he proposed that biblical poetry was based on a 'semantic-syntactic-accentual rhythm' in which there could be parallelism between one or two or all three of these elements. His proposal, however, has been ignored by biblical scholarship, perhaps because of its lapidary formulation as well as the place where it appeared. Adele Berlin's excellent study, following the observations on parallelism of Roman Jakobson and other linguists, speaks, in terms entirely compatible with Harshav's, of the constant presence of 'equivalence' in biblical parallelism – in lexical items, phonetics, morphology, syntax and so forth – and equivalence means similarity, not identity, and therefore also contrast. Luis Alonso-Schökel, one of the pioneers in the contemporary study of biblical poetry, similarly argues in his perceptive handbook on the subject that parallelism is 'a flexible technique, with a variety of formulations and arrangements according to the different situations', or, as he says elsewhere, in words conceptually akin to both Berlin and Harshav, parallelism is a means of dividing and rebuilding data as a new unity from the continuum of experience through 'articulation of sound, syntactic articulation, articulation of semantic fields, of rhythm'.[3]

Old ways of thinking, however, die slowly, and biblical studies are still not wholly free of the predisposition to conceive ancient Hebrew poetry, and parallelism in particular, as a mechanical system, or perhaps more typically, as a mechanically combinational system. The consequence of this view is a proliferation of taxonomies as well as frequent misperceptions of the relation between form and meaning in biblical poetry. A striking symptom of this persistent tendency is Wilfred G. E. Watson's *Classical Hebrew Poetry*,[4] a far more relentlessly taxonomic handbook than Alonso-Schökel's (and one, indeed, about which Alonso-Schökel complains). I want to focus briefly on just one repeated contention made by Watson, which has behind it a long tradition of biblical scholarship, because an understanding of his misconception will position us better to see some of the distinctive directions of the poetic books of the Bible. Though Watson has read Kugel, he continues to assume a kind of automatism or inertness in parallelistic poetry. 'Quite often', he claims, with italic emphasis, '*only one element of a word-pair is intended* by the author, its companion being merely used for the sake of parallelism', and he goes on to assert that in Proverbs 4:3 (which I shall quote, as with all subsequent biblical texts, in my own translation) '*only the first element* is intended'.[5] The line in Proverbs reads as follows: 'for a son was I to my father, / tender and an only child to my mother'. It is a little mystifying that a critic should presume to know what the author intended, but the language itself suggests that the second of these two versets is by no means a throwaway. Even if it is the father (as Watson goes on to say) who is the mentor in the lines that follow, the speaker here is expressing through the parallelism a double sense, not a single one, of the filial relationship – the basic link of son to father, and then the emotional and vulnerable bond between tender only child (mistranslated by Watson as 'lonely') and mother. The second verset in this way amounts to an intensification of the declaration of filial status, and that, as I have argued elsewhere,[6] is a characteristic pattern in biblical poetry.

Watson makes a related observation in perpetuating the idea of the so-called ballast variant, a notion that by this point in time should be thoroughly discredited: 'It is now clear that a ballast variant is simply a *filler*, its function being to fill out a line of poetry that would otherwise be too short.'[7] One may wonder whether there was ever a poet beyond the level of doggerel-writer who was in the habit of producing lines in this fashion merely to pad out the metre, to introduce the requisite balance of accents and words in the second verset. Watson's illustration, from the Song of Deborah (Judges 5:28) vividly exemplifies just the opposite of what he claims: 'Why does his battle-car tarry in coming? / Why is the pounding of his chariots so late?' The speaker is the mother of the Canaanite commander Sisera, anxiously waiting at the window for the return of her son from the battle-field, while he in fact lies dead in Jael's tent. In the first verset, she wonders in general about his delayed return, using the short form for the term that designates 'chariot' (*rikhbo*). It is true that in the second verset, because 'in coming' is not repeated, there is rhythmic space to employ the longer form of this same term (*markebotaw*), which also follows a general pattern of using a standard word in the first verset and a fancier form or exotic synonym in the second verset. But it is also true that the second verset is more immediate, more concrete, and further along on the temporal continuum of the imagined return, than the first verset. Now we have not just the idea of the delayed chariot, but the vivid sensory datum of the chariot's clatter – or perhaps preferably, the pounding (the usual meaning of *pe'amim*) of the hoofbeats of the chariot-horses. The move from 'chariot' in the singular to the plural may also be more than elegant variation, suggesting not just a Sisera solo in his war-car but Sisera the commander leading an army of victorious charioteers. There is scarcely anything in this second verset that deserves to be called either ballast or variant. The dynamism of this single line, moreover, is a microscopic intimation of what happens in the broad spectrum of biblical poetry in different genres: events are represented; the events that develop out of them are represented in a close overlap that is the favoured vehicle of narrativity in biblical verse, rather like the closely sequenced images on a strip of film; general ideas introduced in the first part of the line are focused, intensified, given the heft of concreteness, in the second part of the line. Here is a neat four-step illustration of the paradigm, two lines of verse from Isaiah (10:17) that will confirm the pattern and suggest how consistent it is in its recurrence. Each successive step is a narrative development of what precedes it:

For evil has flamed like a fire,
> thorn and thistle consumed,
And kindled the forest's thickets –
> they billow in pillars of smoke.

What difference might be made by such an understanding of the compli-cation of meaning of parallelistic poetry in our reading of the poetic books of the Bible? Clearly, no single generalization can cover the whole spectrum of biblical poetry because the poetic vehicle is bound to differ appreciably as it variously serves the purposes of devotion and public worship, of didactic dis-course, philosophic enquiry or the celebration of love. There are neverthe-less some continuities among the several genres of biblical poetry, and I shall try to delineate them in brief compass in the remainder of this chapter.

Psalms is obviously the most public form of poetry in the Bible. Many of the psalms bear indications of having been sung in the temple cult to the accompaniment of instruments, and the preponderance of the poems in the collection proves to be texts that could be used by individual worshippers either in acts of supplication or in conjunction with thanksgiving offerings. In fact, the dominant emphasis in the scholarly investigation of Psalms for much of the twentieth century has been on the conjectured cultic uses of the poems, often with elaborate reconstructions of their *Sitz im Leben*, or 'life-setting'. Perhaps the most influential synthesis of this trend has been Sigmund Mowinckel's *The Psalms in Israel's Worship*[8] (originally published in Norwegian in 1951). Of late, notes of scepticism have been sounded about the conjectural reconstruction of specific cultic settings, with the concomi-tant predisposition to identify psalmodic genre with those settings. As Walter Brueggemann aptly puts it in a recent essay, 'In much of the scholarship, the notion of genre has been reified so that the specific psalm must submit to the proposed genre.'[9] The volume in which Brueggemann's article appears reflects a new interest by many scholars, perhaps indirectly influenced by canon criticism of the Bible, in the architectonic design of the edited collec-tion of Psalms that has come down to us,[10] and in lines of intertextuality between Psalms and other elements of the biblical corpus.

What many recent students of Psalms tend to question is the positivist assumption of determinant historical context underlying much of the older scholarship. But if it now seems doubtful that every psalm, in all the details of its imagery and rhetoric, can be referred to a concrete ritual or liturgic occasion, the generally public character of most of the psalms can scarcely be denied. There is not much room for surprises in a collection of poems framed for such an institutional setting, and in a purely descriptive sense, Psalms is the most conventional poetry in the Bible: with only occasional exceptions, the imagery is stock-imagery, and both structurally and thematically, the individual poems generally follow the set patterns of their psalmodic sub-genres with such regularity that a particular psalm may often seem no more than a variation on a dozen or more others. But as modern readers, we need to remind ourselves that literary conventionality – that is, poetry that works by finely inflecting or reconfiguring the materials of a familiar tradition – can be a vehicle of subtle and profound expression. Many of the psalms reflect personal or collective crises, and the dynamic of intensification within the line that I have indicated is typically projected forward from line to line, creating a compelling sense of urgency. The celebratory psalms register a complementary movement of joyous intensification – as, for example, the poems praising God's kingship which evoke sky and earth and sea, field and forest, all singing out as, climactically, He comes down to rule the world. Let me cite one brief instance of the poetry of crisis in Psalms, which most often occurs, as in this case, in the supplication. My translation of Psalm 70 (I shall begin after the superscription in verse 1) is deliberately literal in order to make clearer the purposeful pattern of development in a text where the older criticism of biblical poetry would chiefly see formulaic repetition.

2. God, to save me,
    O LORD, to my aid hasten!
3. Shamed and thwarted be they who seek my life,
    let them fall back, be disgraced, those who wish my harm.
4. Let them retrace their own shameful footsteps,
    who say, 'Aha! Aha!'
5. Rejoicing and gladdened in You
    be all who seek You.
  Let them always say, 'God is great!'
    they who love Your deliverance.
6. And I am poor and needy,
    God, hasten to me!
  My aid and my rescuer You are,
    O LORD, do not delay.

It is remarkable how much power is generated through the simplest means (in this instance, there is not even any use of figurative language). The first line employs, quite unusually, a double-duty verb ('hasten') in the second verset instead of the first. This effectively makes the whole line a periodic sentence, its full meaning revealed only by 'hasten' at the end, and the urgency of that imperative verb drives the whole poem, with the verb itself resurfacing at the end in a strong envelope structure. The interlinear parallelism of the last two lines ('God, hasten to me . . . O LORD, do not delay') has the effect of underscoring the key verb, as if to say, 'Hurry, don't wait another moment', and thus nicely illustrates how parallelism is not simply an echoing but an intensification. The implicit narrativity and the impulse to concretize of parallelistic verse are also manifest in this poem. Verse 3, which introduces the enemies seeking to destroy the supplicant, explains why he has so urgently implored God to rescue him and so opens up a narrative situation. The paired verbs of frustration and shame in the first half of this line are neatly matched by the paired verbs of the second half of the line. The very next verset then concretizes the fate of defeat that the speaker wishes for his enemies by picking up the root 'shame' and imagining the foes 'retrac[ing] their own shameful footsteps' (very literally, 'going back on the heel of their shame'). The little snatch of dialogue assigned to these malicious people – 'who say, "Aha! Aha!"' – actually dramatizes their nastiness and thus reinforces the focusing effect of the poem's dynamic. The two lines that comprise verse 5 are a pivotal moment in the supplication as they introduce an antithetical group of people, those who are happy in the Lord. The point of antithesis is made formally by the paired verbs of rejoicing at the beginning of verse 5 that counterbalance the paired verbs of frustration at the beginning of verse 3, and 'they who seek my life' is now replaced by 'all who seek You'. In the narrative logic of the poem, the speaker cannot yet confidently place himself in the ranks of all who rejoice because he is, after all, compassed about by murderous foes. And so at the end he declares that he is poor and needy, and, as at the beginning, invokes God as his aid ('ezrah, 'ezer), reminding Him that the desperately needed deliverance must come quickly. In all this use of cumulative repetition, there is little that would qualify as poetic fancy footwork, but in the very spareness and traditionalism of its poetic means, the psalm takes eloquent advantage of the focusing and intensifying impulse of parallelistic verse.

When we move from Psalms to Proverbs, the aim of the poetry is not expressive but didactic, hortatory, perhaps sometimes even mnemonic. Proverbs is, of course, the biblical repository of mainline wisdom literature (as against the radical or sceptical wisdom literature of Ecclesiastes and Job), and the purpose of the poetic vehicle is largely to impress received wisdom of a generally pragmatic sort in vivid formulations on the minds of the audience. This function sets the wisdom books apart from the rest of biblical literature and, as scholarship has long recognized, makes them the most international in character in the whole biblical corpus. The usual scriptural focus on the distinctiveness of Israel and its covenantal relationship with God is entirely absent; revelation and, arguably, theological perspectives are not much in evidence. Sources and parallels for the wisdom books in Egyptian and Mesopotamian literature have been abundantly documented, and it seems likely that this activity of 'cultivating experiential knowledge'[11] in memorable aphoristic utterance was common – perhaps, it has been conjectured, in actual schools – throughout the ancient Near East.[12]

Against this background, the poetic vehicle is utilized in Proverbs in a way that is quite different from the deployment of poetry in all other biblical books, with the partial exception of Ecclesiastes. Although there are a few continuous poems with narrative elements in the early chapters (the most remarkable is probably the tale of the gullible young man and the seductress that comprises all of chapter 7), the characteristic form of Proverbs is the one-line aphorism. Neat balance and antithesis are the hallmarks of the poetic parallelism in these single lines of verse, schematically exemplified in the scores of lines in which the just man (*tsadiq*) appears in the first verset, enjoying a happy fate, and the wicked man (*rashaʿ*) stares across at him from the second verset, confounded by the disaster his wickedness has brought on him. Nevertheless, much of Proverbs is of considerable interest as a poetry of wit, as the recent study of biblical poetry should encourage us to see. If, for the reasons just mentioned, there is a high degree of predictability in its use of parallelistic verse, this feature is balanced by certain elements of surprise (what Adele Berlin describes as the intertwining of similarity and difference). Some lines in Proverbs are actually cast as riddles: the materials of a simile are put forth in the first verset, and their referent is then identified in the second verset. Thus, 'Like vinegar to the teeth and smoke to the eyes, / so is the sluggard to those who send him' (10:26). The case of such riddle-proverbs is instructive because it suggests that the ancient audience, in looking for the parallelistic fit between the first verset and the second, might well have expected a little revelation rather than mere repetition. There are, admittedly, a good many pat proverbs in the canonical collection, but many others, not just the riddling ones, unveil a small surprise through some mode of intensification in the second verset. Two examples will suffice to suggest this underlying dynamic of the Bible's didactic poetry of wit. 'A worthy wife is her husband's crown, / and like rot in his bones, she who shames' (12:4). The antithesis of the second verset generates an element of verbal violence one would have scarcely anticipated from the note of placid celebration in the first verset. The good wife is a splendid ornament (*'atarah*) to her husband – and that, after all, is something external, an enhancement of his prestige or standing in the eyes of the world. But, startlingly, a shameful wife is like rot in the bone, a blight that gets inside you, eats you from within like a cancer. Another way of raising the rhetorical ante through parallelism is evident in 15:11: 'Sheol and perdition are in the LORD's view, / how much more so the hearts of men.' In this instance the parallelism moves from large to small, from the cosmic Pit to the human heart, compelling us to a disquieting awareness of God's knowledge of our innermost being: we may think the heart is a hidden place, and perhaps a murky one like Sheol, but if the underworld itself is perfectly exposed to God's all-seeing eye, what secrets can be held by the puny abyss of the heart? Even in the didactic poetry of Proverbs, the semantic alignment of verset with verset is quite often not just a way of saying something twice but a challenging juxtaposition of similarities and differences, of pointedly imperfect analogies and sometimes shocking antitheses.

From a poetic viewpoint, then, what a radical wisdom text such as Ecclesiastes does with Proverbs is not so much to turn it on its head as to push some of its characteristic rhetorical strategies in subversive directions.[13] 'Better a name than goodly oil, / and the day of death from the day he was born' (Ecclesiastes 7:1). The first verset could easily have been the beginning of a line in the canonical Proverbs, unexceptionably expressing the idea that a good reputation is to be more prized than luxurious possessions. The second verset follows the pattern we have observed in Proverbs in the way it introduces a surprise, and a new element of semantic vehemence, but the perception it exposes is a darker one than would ever be encountered in Proverbs, and there is a disorienting swerve away from the concordance of meanings that would be expected in poetic parallelism: there is no coherent correspondence between the day of death and a good name or the day of birth and goodly oil, and we are left with only the residual parallelism that in each half of the line one thing is better than another. If the general procedure of biblical poetry is to exploit both the second verset and the line-to-line continuum in order to sharpen themes and images and insinuate new ideas in seeming repetition, what Ecclesiastes often does is to reverse expectations unsettlingly in the sequence of versets, as in this triadic line: 'Wisdom is better than valour / and the wisdom of the poor man is scorned, / and his words are not heard' (9:16). The first verset again sounds like an orthodox wisdom pronouncement. But as the term 'wisdom' (*hokhmah*) is repeated in the second verset, it turns out that the all-powerful efficacy of wisdom vanishes if you happen to be out of pocket – your insight into things, however genuine, is held in contempt, and should you presume to offer advice (third verset), no-one will listen. Elsewhere in biblical poetry, triadic lines often exhibit semantic parallelism between the first two versets and then some sort of turn or tension of meaning in the third verset. Here, the second and third versets are semantically parallel, while through the *faux raccord* of the word 'wisdom' they actually subvert the meaning of the initial verset.

The most radical wisdom text in the Bible is the Book of Job, and it is also one of the most awesomely powerful poetic achievements in all of ancient literature. Although Job has been the subject of countless philosophical, theological and historical discussions, surprisingly little attention has been paid to the relation between its poetic originality and its profundity in questioning received notions about the divine order of justice. This is clearly too complex a topic to treat adequately in a few paragraphs,[14] but I shall try to indicate the general thrust of the poetry of Job, with particular consideration to the effects of parallelistic verse that have been our overall concern. Nowhere in biblical poetry is the vector of intensification more palpable, or more crucially pertinent to meaning. Broadly speaking, Job in his anguish uses the poetic vehicle to push the acute articulation of his existential pain from one peak to another: the poet's uncanny ability to make the line of poetry and the continuum of the poem constantly go beyond themselves in intensity becomes a means of insistently exposing the human creature's pathetic vulnerability, the poignant brevity of the human lifespan, the outrage of undeserved suffering. After all this, the Job poet audaciously gambles in a way that only a great artist confident of his mastery would dare to do, by creating for God's Voice from the Whirlwind an order of poetry, a scale of intensification, which transcends that of the poetic voice of Job: instead of a poetry driving constantly inward to the speaker's tortured core of pain, the poetry spoken by God sweeps outward in great surging waves (with an implicitly narrative movement) from cosmogony to meteorology to the animal kingdom, imaginatively realizing an unfathomable and even cruel beauty in the vast panorama of creation that does not 'answer' the question of Job's suffering but in effect dwarfs it.

All this, both the poetry of Job's debate and that of the Voice from the Whirlwind, is accomplished in the Hebrew with the most stunning technical virtuosity and inventiveness. In sharp contrast to the stock-imagery of Psalms, the figurative language here abounds in fresh and surprising comparisons and unexpected terms (Job utilizes the richest vocabulary of any biblical poet). And within the tight compass of the parallelistic line, remarkable complications of meaning are repeatedly produced. Thus, in his great confession of innocence, Job swears, 'If my heart was beguiled by a woman, / and I lurked at my neighbour's door' – note the characteristic relation of narrativity and causality between the two halves of the line – and then goes on to say: 'May my wife grind for another, / upon her may others kneel' (31:9–10). The second half of this line shockingly steps up the assertion of the first half. Instead of the usual decorous biblical locutions for sexual intercourse (to know, to come into, to lie with), we have a physical image of males mounting Job's wife – and not just one lover, as in the first verset, but a plurality of them. The sexual image is not only an intensification of the 'grinding' in the first verset but compels us to reread it as coarse metaphor instead of literal utterance: at first the line seems to present a progression from an image of domesticity (the wife's performance of the conjugal duty of grinding flour, but for another man) to one of sexual subjugation, but then the second verset invites a double-take of the first, the grinding now seen as a figure for the woman's strenuous physical participation in the sexual act.

Let me offer just one further example, in which Job articulates a sense of the endlessly protracted frustration of his life, which is coupled with the complementary awareness of life's desperate brevity. These are the first verses of chapter 7:

1.  Does not man have a term upon earth
    and like the days of a hireling his days?
2.  Like a slave who pants for the shade
    and like a hireling who waits for his wage,
3.  So I'm apportioned futile months
    and nights of misery allotted to me.
4.  When I lie down, I think, 'When shall I rise?'
    I'm sated with tossings till the gleam of dawn.[15]

The general image in the opening line of human life as a hired worker's set term of service becomes more concrete in the second line, which visualizes the labourer in the hot sun panting for shade and awaiting his payment. But if the parching day is a trial to the worker, for Job the nights as well are torment. Man has 'days' upon earth, but in effect Job has only insomniac nights (the Hebrew for 'months' is literally 'moons', in antithesis to the implied sun of verse 2, and so makes the reader think of night). The word for misery, *'amal*, usually means just that in Job, but in another late biblical book, Ecclesiastes, it means 'labour', and so we get an ironic double sense that Job's

work is tossing in sleeplessness, awaiting the first crepuscular light of day –
*neshef* can refer to morning or evening twilight – as the slave waits for the
evening shadows. Job goes on in the next line after this excerpt to a sudden
imagining of his body decomposing in the grave, and then to an assertion of
his life's sheer transience that concludes with a stunning pun: 'My days are
swifter than a shuttle, / they end without hope', for the word for 'hope' is a
homonym for 'thread', and in the dynamics of parallelism, the declaration of
despair doubles back to the metaphor of the weaver's shuttle, showing us
simultaneously a life that is hopeless and pointless, a shuttle without a
thread.

The Song of Songs, another late poetic book, has received a good deal of
scholarly attention in recent years, with a particular stress on its ancient
setting and on possible analogues and influences from love-poetry elsewhere in the ancient Near East.[16] There has been rather less emphasis on the
distinctive features of the poetry of the Song, though Chana Bloch's introductory essay to her and Ariel Bloch's fine translation[17] is admirably sensible
and subtly perceptive about the poetry. Chana Bloch makes a series of apt
observations on the wonderfully poised balance of delicacy of expression
and frank, exuberant sensuality in the distinctive poetic idiom of the Song. It
would be tempting to follow the exquisite play of these qualities through
examples, but, keeping to the line we have been following, we have space
only for some brief remarks on the role of poetic parallelism in the Song.

Much of the parallelism in these poems is a relatively straightforward
matching of terms, syntax and rhythmic units, as in 'skipping over the
mountains, / leaping over the hills' (2:8b), where 'mountains' and 'hills', in
that order, are a set word-pair in the biblical poetic tradition, and the poet has
only to produce the synonymous participles 'skipping' and 'leaping' in order
to make a neatly symmetrical parallelism. The pattern of intensification of
biblical poetry, which attains a grand climax in Job, is much less evident in
the playful lyric world of the Song. Instead of a principle of progressive
heightening, development in the line and from line to line very often occurs
through a principle of contiguity. In the vertical descriptions of the lovers,
this contiguity is spatial: the enraptured eye of the speaker begins with the
head and moves by stages down the desired body, except for the description
of the dancing Shulamite in chapter 7, in which, because she is dancing, the
lover begins with the feet and works his way upward. The other mode of
development through contiguity in these poems is temporal. That is, the
strong impulse of microtextual narrativity manifested in biblical poetic
parallelism – and not sufficiently perceived, I think, by critics – predominates

in much of the Song. This is hardly surprising because the Song has such striking narrative elements: the sundry retreats of the lovers to various bucolic trysting-places, the nocturnal episode in which the young woman rushes through the streets of the town in search of her vanished lover and is pursued by the watchmen, and so forth. Let me cite one sequence, from the end of chapter 7:

12.  Come my lover, let us go out to the field,
         let us spend the night in the henna,
13.                 let us rise early to the vineyards.
    Let us see if the vine has flowered,
        if the blossoms have opened,
            if the pomegranate is in bud.
    There will I give
        my love to you.
14.  The mandrakes give off scent.
        and at our doorsteps are all the rare fruits,
  old and new, too,
        my love, I have stored up for you.

These lines, of course, exhibit a certain degree of what Bishop Lowth would have called synonymous parallelism: field and vineyard; flowering vine, opening blossom and budding pomegranate. What is more salient, however, is the enticing narrative trajectory the young woman traces in her invitation to her lover. The verbs of the initial, triadic line adumbrate the story: 'let us go out', 'let us spend the night' (*nalina*), 'let us rise early' (*nashkima*). As elsewhere in the Song, every detail of landscape and scene becomes an analogue or correlative for the story of the lovers. After they look at the new flowers of the open field (which themselves correspond to the blossoming of love), the young woman promises – a climactic narrative development in the strict sense – to give herself in love. The words 'give my love' then become a pivot turning back to the floral world as the poet uses the same verb, to give, with 'mandrakes', *duda'im*, instead of 'love', *dodim*. The heaps of rare fruits on the threshold stored up by the young woman for her lover are another extension of the love-plot, for even if we read them literally as choice gifts she has set aside for her lover's delight, there is a persistent metaphoric equivalence in the Song between fruit and the pleasures of love-making. In any case, this whole narrative line from the expedition to the countryside and the night among flowers to the morning of love's fulfilment unfolds through the parallelisms with such sinuously fluid grace that one is not always sure, and perhaps that is the poet's intention, where one line stops and another begins.

We have not witnessed, I think, any radical new perception in recent scholarship of what the poetic books of the Hebrew Bible are all about. Incrementally, however, we are coming to a keener, more precise appreciation of the distinctive character of biblical poetry, and so we are in a somewhat better position to see the paramount role that poetry plays in these books. What urgently needs to be kept in mind when we read biblical poetry, as I hope the examples I have surveyed will suggest, is that the play of supposed synonyms and antonyms in biblical parallelism is by no means inert repetition, that something is always going on, moving forward, as the phrases and clauses appear to build on the echoes of meanings and sounds just uttered. The last two poetic books we have touched on are two different instances of the extreme that exposes a basic mechanism of the typical: in Job, the pattern of intensification of parallelistic verse presses towards an unbearable climax, and then to a shattering revelation; in the Song, the implicit narrativity of parallelism becomes the vehicle for the story of lovers longing, divided, inviting, fulfilled.

## Notes

1 James Kugel, *The Idea of Biblical Poetry* (New Haven, 1981).

2 Adele Berlin, *The Dynamics of Biblical Parallelism* (Bloomington, 1985).

3 Luis Alonso-Schökel, *A Manual of Hebrew Poetics* (Rome, 1988), pp. 57, 51.

4 W. G. E. Watson, *Classical Hebrew Poetry* (Sheffield, 1984).

5 *Ibid.*, p. 139.

6 Robert Alter, *The Art of Biblical Poetry* (New York, 1985). See especially chapter 3.

7 Watson, *Classical Hebrew Poetry*, p. 344.

8 Sigmund Mowinckel, *The Psalms in Israel's Worship*, English translation (Oxford, 1962).

9 Walter Brueggemann, 'Response to James L. Mays', in J. Clinton McCann (ed.), *The Shape and Shaping of the Psalter* (Sheffield, 1993).

10 An important recent study in this regard is G. H. Wilson's *The Editing of the Hebrew Psalter* (Chico, CA, 1985).

11 The phrase is Gerhard von Rad's in his classic introduction to this topic, *Wisdom in Israel* (Nashville and New York, 1972).

12 An apt recent overview of biblical wisdom is Roland E. Murphy's *The Tree of Life* (New York, 1990). The multiple historical contexts of wisdom in the

ancient Near East are extensively explored in John G. Gammie and Leo G. Perdue (eds.), *The Sage in Israel and in the Ancient Near East* (Winona Lake, MN, 1990). T. A. Perry's *Wisdom Literature and the Structure of Proverbs* (University Park, PA, 1993) proposes a structuralist-literary approach that links biblical wisdom with didactic-pragmatic literature written later and elsewhere.

13  The presence of 'anti-proverbs' in Ecclesiastes was observed long ago by Robert Gordis in *Koheleth: The Man and His World* (New York, 1968).

14  I discuss the question in some detail in *The Art of Biblical Poetry*, pp. 85–110.

15  In the last line, I have omitted two problematic Hebrew words from the Masoretic Text, *midad ʿereb*, because they look suspiciously like a scribal error and also break the poetic rhythm.

16  Marvin Pope's massive commentary (Garden City, 1977) is the most ambitious of these undertakings. Michael V. Fox's *The Song of Songs and the Ancient Egyptian Love Songs* (Madison, 1985) is particularly noteworthy.

17  *The Song of Songs: A New Translation* (New York, 1995).

## Further reading

*Biblical poetry*
Alonso-Schökel, Luis, *A Manual of Biblical Poetics*, Rome, 1988.
Alter, Robert, *The Art of Biblical Poetry*, New York, 1985.
Kugel, James, *The Idea of Biblical Poetry*, New Haven, 1981.
Watson, W. G. E., *Classical Hebrew Poetry: A Guide to its Techniques*, Sheffield, 1984.

*Wisdom*
Crenshaw, James G., *Old Testament Wisdom*, Atlanta, 1981.
Murphy, Roland E., *The Tree of Life*, New York, 1990.
Perry, T. A., *Wisdom Literature and the Structure of Proverbs*, University Park, PA, 1993.
von Rad, Gerhard, *Wisdom in Israel*, Nashville and New York, 1972.
Williams, James G., *Those Who Ponder Proverbs: Aphoristic Thinking and Biblical Literature*, Sheffield, 1981.

*Psalms*
McCann, J. Clinton, *The Shape and Shaping of the Psalter*, Sheffield, 1993.
Mowinckel, Sigmund, *The Psalms in Israel's Worship*, Oxford, 1962.
Westermann, Claus, *The Praise of God in Psalms*, Atlanta, 1965.
Wilson, G. H., *The Editing of the Hebrew Psalter*, Chico, CA, 1985.

# 16 The Synoptic Gospels and Acts of the Apostles Telling the Christian Story

PHEME PERKINS

## SOURCES OF THE GOSPELS

Critical study of the Gospels has sought the human Jesus behind the mythic and theological symbols of Christianity. Analysis of material common to Matthew, Mark and Luke and of sayings common to Matthew and Luke (designated 'Q', German *Quelle*, 'source') has provided an explanation of the sources of the synoptics (Fitzmyer, *The Gospel According to Luke (I–IX)*, pp. 63–106). Mark was the earliest narrative account of Jesus. References to war in Judea (Mark 13:5–8, 14–19) as well as to persecution (8:34–8; 13:9–13) suggested that it was written during Nero's persecution of Christians in Rome or the Jewish revolt in Judea (*c.* 66–70 CE; see Donahue, 'Windows and Mirrors'). Independently of each other, Matthew and Luke expanded Mark. Their sayings material (Q) came to each evangelist in different forms (cf. Matthew 5:3–10 and Luke 6:20–6; see Betz, *The Sermon on the Mount*, pp. 22–44, 105–10). Matthew and Luke sometimes substituted the Q version of an episode for Mark's (cf. Mark 1:12–13; Matthew 4:1–11 and Luke 4:1–13). In other cases, oral tradition underlies the agreements of Matthew and Luke against Mark (e.g. Mark 14:65; Matthew 26:68; Luke 22:64).

Isolation of other sources used by individual Gospel writers is more controverted. Efforts to reconstruct a pre-Markan passion narrative have not led to consensus (see M. Soards, Appendix IX: 'The Question of the Premarcan Passion Narrative', in Brown (ed.), *The Death of the Messiah*, pp. 1492–524). Mark knows collections of parables (4:1–34) and miracles (see the cycles, 4:35–5:43; 6:30–56; 7:31–8:10). Some Markan sayings are similar to Q (4:21 and Matthew 5:15//Luke 11:33; Mark 4:25 and Matthew 25:29//Luke 19:26).

Discovery (1945) of a Coptic collection of Jesus' sayings in gnostic texts (copied in the fourth century CE), the *Gospel of Thomas* provided evidence for independent collections of Jesus' sayings. Scholars have used the Q traditions and variants from the *Gospel of Thomas* to construct pre-Gospel texts for Q. Some propose to isolate stages in the collected sayings that separate earlier versions in which Jesus is a spokesperson for wisdom, from later depiction of Jesus as a prophet of the coming judgement (see Catchpole, *The Quest for Q*). These results seek evidence for Jesus' teaching from the earliest decades of Christianity.

The claim to uncover a Jesus wisdom figure who promised experience of God's saving presence and did not speak of God's impending judgement has been sharply criticized. It would remove Jesus from the Jewish religious sentiments associated with John the Baptist. The Gospels insist that Jesus' message that the reign of God is breaking into human experience constituted his response to the Baptist (Mark 1:2–15; Matthew 3:1–17, 4:12–17; Luke 3:1–22; and John 3:22–30; 4:1–3). Other scholars retain the apocalyptic expectation found in the Matthew//Luke stratum of Q. The Jesus represented by Q and the synoptic depictions of Jesus' teaching present him as healer and eschatological prophet/teacher (see Meier, *A Marginal Jew*).

### GENRE OF THE GOSPELS

How the Synoptic Gospels describe Jesus' teaching and death is not merely a question of reconstructing sources. It also asks what literary models shaped their composition (Aune, *The New Testament*; Burridge, *What Are the Gospels?*). Use of the word 'gospel' in Mark 1:1 parallels the Pauline epistles: 'gospel' designates the apostolic preaching of salvation in the crucified and risen Son of God (Romans 1:1; 1 Corinthians 9:14; Galatians 2:2; Philippians 1:7). Matthew and Luke have each replaced Mark's introduction with literary designations. Matthew 1:1 opens with 'book of the genealogy of Jesus Christ'. *'Biblos geneseōs'* probably refers just to the account of Jesus' descent, birth and how he came to be from Nazareth (Matthew 1–2). It reminds readers of the genealogical lists which established the identity of the people of God (Moloney, 'Beginning the Gospel of Matthew').

Luke's prologue reflects the conventions of Greco-Roman author. An ordered account, *diēgēsis*, of events will provide a literary patron with reliable information (Luke 1:1–4). Like other Hellenistic authors, Luke indicates that he has consulted and revised those who came before him (Nolland, *Luke 1–9:20*, pp. 4–11).

Scholars debate whether or not the Gospels are examples of the Greco-Roman 'life'. Mark's narrative recounts only the ministry of Jesus that leads up to his death. The passion narrative focuses on a death seen as dishonourable by ancient standards. Divine exaltation of Jesus in resurrection does not appear in Mark. Both Luke and Matthew expand Mark in ways more typical of a Greco-Roman biography. The 'infancy narratives' (Matthew 1:18–2:23; Luke 1:5–2:52) draw on independent traditions to describe the birth and childhood of the hero. Matthew and Luke both conclude with resurrection as divine vindication, which establishes the universal validity of Jesus' teaching. By incorporating sayings material into Mark, Matthew and Luke establish Jesus' superiority as a teacher. Matthew provides discourses which summarize Jesus' message (Matthew 5–7, 10, 13, 18, 24–5). The Sermon on the Mount (Matthew 5–7) adapts a well-known Greco-Roman form, the 'epitome' or compendium of a philosopher's teaching (Betz, *The Sermon on the Mount*). These additions indicate that Matthew and Luke understood the gospel genre as a 'life' of its central figure. Jewish story patterns also play an important part in the Gospel accounts. For example, the stories of Elijah and Elisha (1 Kings 17–19, 21; 2 Kings 1–2) include healing, multiplication of loaves, and raising the dead. The *Lives of the Prophets* (first century CE) extends the violence found in the life of Jeremiah to the other prophets. This pattern provides a context for ending the Gospel with Jesus' rejection and death *(Lives of the Prophets* 23,1, on the death of Zechariah; see Luke 11:51//Matthew 23:35).

### COMMUNAL SETTING AND GOSPEL NARRATIVE

Do the Gospel narratives provide clues to a communal setting for which each evangelist wrote? The turmoil found in the apocalyptic discourse (Mark 13:14, 23, 37) leads some scholars to treat Mark as a example of sectarian apocalyptic which aims to shore up the faith of a minority (lest they deny Jesus like Peter, Mark 14:29–31, 66–72). Since Mark explains Jewish customs (7:3,4,11,19), currency (12:42) and Aramaic words (5:41; 7:34; 15:22,34), the audience would appear to be unfamiliar with Palestinian Jews. Other interpreters highlight the passion of Jesus. Halfway through Mark, Peter's identification of Jesus as messiah leads to the first passion prediction (8:27–38). The disciples' incomprehension (8:32; 9:32; 10:32) mirrors cultural reactions to crucifixion, the ignominious punishment for slaves and criminals (cf. Philippians 2:8; 1 Corinthians 1:22–4). Therefore one might conclude that though the primary audience is believers, Mark addresses an apologetic to sympathetic outsiders (see the summary in Guelich, *Mark 1–8:26*, pp. xxxvii–xliii).

Other approaches focus on ideological tensions between source materials and the Gospel as a whole. Mark's readers first encounter a Jesus whose words and miraculous deeds impress others with his authority (1:21–8). But these impressive deeds fail to produce a reliable faith in disciples, who are often frightened and uncomprehending (e.g. 4:13, 40). Some interpreters think that this tension was directed against the ideology of a miracle-working Jesus and his charismatic imitators (see Matthew 7:22–3, for such charismatics). Other interpreters treat the suppression of charismatic prophecy as evidence of the tension between the world of oral preaching with its emphasis on immediate experiences of Jesus' power and that of a textualized tradition which sets its founding figure and deeds in the past (see Bryan, *A Preface to Mark*).

Attempts to move from the text of a Gospel to statements about the author's community have been challenged by insights from modern literary criticism (Donahue, 'Windows and Mirrors'). Analysis should attend to the narrative whole. The reader's interaction with a text creates a picture of the narrator and the audience. In the Gospels, the narrator is a reliable, third-person voice with access to the innermost thoughts of Jesus (e.g. Mark 14:32–42). Readers identify with that voice rather than the misunderstandings attributed to Jesus' disciples. Since the narrator provides interpretations of what transpires, the failings of Jesus' followers should not be considered evidence for either the actual relationship between Jesus and his disciples or for conflict between the evangelist and others claiming the authority of the Twelve (Best, *Mark. The Gospel as Story*; 'Mark's Narrative Technique').

## DISCIPLES AND OTHER CHARACTERS

The disciples and other groups within a Gospel are figures whose relationship to Jesus changes during the narrative. Mark presents four groups: opponents, relatives of Jesus, crowds and the Twelve. The opposition is predominantly Jewish religious leaders. Readers are told that Jesus' authority is greater than theirs (1:22); that he is preaching in *their* synagogues (1:45), challenging their understanding of the Law (2:1–3:6; 7:1–23). The hostility Jesus provokes will prove deadly (3:6). Jesus' exorcisms lead to charges of practising magic, as well as isolation from relatives who think that he is demented (3:20–34). The ensuing exchange reveals that scribe-opponents are committing the deadly sin of calling the work of God's Spirit Satan's (3:29–30).

Jesus calls for a new definition of 'family'. Biological relationships do not count. Jesus' family consists of those who do the will of God (3:34; see Smith, '"Inside" and "Outside"'). Where Mark's account leaves some uncertainty over the attitude of his relatives (heightened in 6:1–6a), Matthew and Luke indicate that Jesus' family are among the faithful. For Luke, Jesus' family are among the pious of Israel who await God's salvation. Mary is an exemplary disciple (1:38; 2:19, 35, 51; 8:21). Matthew describes Joseph as a 'righteous man' (1:19). 'Righteousness' is the key term in Matthew's understanding of Christian discipleship. To be 'righteous' means doing the will of God (7:21; 12:50; 21:31). God reveals the identity of Jesus to Joseph in a dream (Matthew 1:21): 'he will save his people from their sins'. This salvation is realized when Jesus sheds his blood on the cross (Matthew 26:28). By developing the picture of Jesus' family as part of Jesus' ministry, Matthew and Luke both bring their narratives closer to the *bios* genre where the hero's origins indicate his future destiny.

Matthew and Luke also provide different perspectives on the opposition to Jesus. Just as Luke's Jesus was born among a pious, expectant people (Luke 1:44–5; 2:22–38), so the people continue to hang on Jesus' words. Their leaders are responsible for the execution of this popular teacher (Luke 19:47–8; 20:1–6, 19, 26, 45; 22:2; 23:5, 35; 24:19–20). They are repeating the ancestral pattern. Jerusalem continues to murder prophets (Luke 13:33–5) instead of becoming the city of peace (19:41–4). The Jewish historian Josephus attributed the destruction of the city to extremist leaders, who overwhelmed the moderates urging peace (Josephus, *War XVI*, 4–5).

Like Josephus, Luke presumes that the Herodians interpreted Jewish affairs for the Romans. Consequently, his passion narrative has Pilate send Jesus to Herod for a hearing (23:6–12; also Agrippa and Bernice in Paul's trial, Acts 25:13–26:32). Hostile parties manage to manipulate the situation. Luke retains the opposition of scribes and Pharisees from his sources, but moderates its vehemence (6:11; contrast Mark 3:6). Luke also introduces a new motive in describing the Pharisees. Their failure to respond to Jesus stems from greed (Luke 16:14) and lack of compassion (7:36–50). However, their opposition is not presented as uniform. Some show hospitality (7:36; 14:1) or concern for Jesus (13:31).

Matthew treats the Pharisees as the primary enemy (see Saldarini, 'Boundaries and Polemics'). They are castigated for outward forms of religion that gain them honour and respect while disregarding justice and mercy (Matthew 6:2–6; 15:1–9; 23:1–36). Jesus' denunciation of their hypocrisy (23:37–9) makes them responsible for Jerusalem's fate. Tensions between Matthew's audience and other Jews appear in references to 'their' synagogues (4:23; 9:35; 10:17, responsible for persecuting Jesus' followers; 12:9; 13:54), scribes (7:29; contrast 'scribe trained for the Kingdom', 13:52) and 'the Jews to this day' (28:15). Yet affirmation of Jesus' mission to the lost sheep of Israel (10:5–6), the continued validity of the Law (5:17–19) and even of some Jewish teaching (23:2) as well as solidarity with fellow Jews in paying the Temple tax (17:24–7) suggest an ongoing relationship between Matthean Christians and the larger Jewish community. Is the mission to the lost sheep of Israel over (see Luz, *The Theology of the Gospel of Matthew*)? Or does Matthew still anticipate bringing together Jew and Gentile under the messiahship of Jesus (so Saldarini, 'Boundaries and Polemics')?

Matthew contains warnings about persecution. In the Sermon on the Mount, those who seek to follow Jesus' path of a 'higher righteousness' can anticipate suffering (5:10) and forms of verbal slander (5:11–12). Disciples must love and pray for their persecutors (5:44; cf. Romans 12:14). What was an apocalyptic sign of the evil endtime in Mark 13:9–13 has become part of the routine preparation of the disciple missionary in Matthew 10:16–23. Though Matthew depicts this mission as limited to the lost sheep of Israel (10:5, 23), disciplinary actions are not confined to synagogues, but include testimony before leaders, kings and the gentiles (verses 16–17). A prophetic woe oracle against scribes and Pharisees depicts them as filling up the sins of their ancestors by crucifying, beating in their synagogues and persecuting the prophets, wise men and scribes whom God sends (Matthew 23:34). Since this oracle is followed by the lament over a destroyed Jerusalem (23:37–9), Matthew shows that Jesus' prophetic word came true. Matthew's ending demonstrates that Jesus' disciples are now to go beyond the towns of Israel to the nations (28:16–20).

### JESUS' DISCIPLES AS GOSPEL CHARACTERS

The question of historical fact over against literary portrayal emerges as soon as one attends to Mark's description of the disciples. The crowds are leaderless sheep (6:34) who follow Jesus because of his impressive miracles and teaching (1:27; 3:7–8; 6:53–6; 11:18) but do not have real understanding (4:12 citing Isaiah 6:9). Their reaction to miracles contrasts with the individuals who demonstrate their faith (Marshall, *Faith as a Theme*). Such persons are outsiders who have to overcome some social boundary in order to experience healing (paralytic, 2:1–12; Jairus, 5:21–4, 35–43; woman with a haemorrhage, 5:25–34; Syrophoenician woman, 7:24–30; blind Bartimaeus, 10:46–52). Matthew and Luke generally follow Mark's description of the crowd and the unusual examples of faith that emerge from the margins of society.

Mark's paradoxical description of Jesus' disciples will be considerably modified by the other evangelists. Apart from Jesus, the disciples are the key figures in the story. Mark's portrayal is not intended to be historical description. It engages readers in a process of re-evaluating Jesus' mission. (On Mark's use of narrative surprises, see Best, 'Mark's Narrative Technique'.) Insofar as the disciples fail to grasp Jesus' teaching at key points, the reader's attention to those points is sharpened. Mark follows the summary of Jesus' preaching (1:15) with the call of the first four disciples (1:16–20). Three of the four, Peter and the sons of Zebedee, have special experiences of Jesus' ministry (healing of Jairus' daughter, 5:37; Transfiguration, 9:2; in Gethsemane, 14:33). But this special relationship does not enable them to understand Jesus' messiahship. The Transfiguration leaves them confused and silent. In Gethsemane, they fail to watch with the Lord. Though Peter recognizes Jesus as God's anointed, he rejects the suffering Son of Man (8:31–3). James and John think that the 'kingdom' means Jesus will be handing out positions of authority (10:35–45). Their request recapitulates an episode in which the disciples were arguing over greatness (9:33–7). Thus Mark's readers are reminded that disciples follow the model of the suffering messiah (8:34–8; 9:35–7; 10:38–9, 42–5). The Gospel prepares for these misunderstandings by showing that the disciples had difficulty with Jesus' parables (4:13). Jesus' invitation to discipleship is refused by the rich man (10:17–22). That episode reminds readers that Jesus' disciples were willing to leave all things (10:29).

Elsewhere fear overwhelms the disciples. Despite evidence of Jesus' divine power, they lack faith (4:35–41). Even the disciples can have hardened hearts (6:45–52). Consequently, the reader is not surprised by the fearful disciples during the events of the passion. The fleeing disciples are joined by a mysterious young man, who runs away naked (14:50, 51–2). Peter's attempt to follow Jesus is thwarted by his denial (14:66–72). Both the flight and Peter's denial are predicted by Jesus (14:27–31). Thus, whatever their failures, the bond which unites Jesus with his disciples is not broken (Brown, *The Death of the Messiah*).

The other evangelists moderate the problematic elements in Mark. Where Jesus charged the disciples with 'no faith' (Mark 4:40), Matthew has 'little faith' (8:26) and Luke simply has Jesus ask where their faith is (8:25). Luke omits Peter's protest against Jesus' prediction of suffering. Matthew separates that episode from Peter's confession of Jesus as messiah by sayings about God as the source of Peter's insight, Peter's name, 'rock' and the indestructibility of the church built on this apostolic foundation (16:17–23). Luke assures readers that although Peter will deny Jesus, Jesus' prayer on his behalf guarantees his repentance and the future strengthening of the others (22:31–4). Luke transposes the dispute over greatness to the Supper narrative (22:24–6) and follows it with Jesus' self-description as 'one who serves' (22:27) and the promise that the disciples will share the messianic banquet (22:28–30). Matthew shifts the burden of requesting authority in the Kingdom from the sons of Zebedee to their mother (20:20–1). He follows Mark's version of the sleeping disciples in Gethsemane, but Luke moderates that incident in two ways. He reduces the triadic repetition to a single event framed with injunctions to pray not to enter into temptation (22:40–6) and explains the sleeping as evidence of sorrow (verse 45).

### RESOLVING AMBIGUITY

These modifications resolve semantic ambiguity in the inherited story and depart from Mark's tactic of forcing the reader to decipher its meaning. Mark's conclusion pushes the strategy of surprising the reader by withholding anticipated meaning to the extreme (Hester, 'Dramatic Inconclusion'). Jesus cries out as the abandoned sufferer of Psalm 22 (15:34–7). This cry might appear to confirm the mocking charge (referred to as 'blasphemy' in verse 29) that Jesus had been able to save others but could not rescue himself (15:30–2). Has Jesus been taken in by the hostility of his enemies? Suddenly, the 'destroyed' temple prophecy is proleptically fulfilled in the torn Temple veil (verse 38). Jesus' power to 'save' is demonstrated by the centurion's confession, 'truly this man was Son of God' (verse 39). However, the evangelist does not let the story rest there. An angelophany at the empty tomb (16:6–7) confirms Jesus' earlier prediction that he would be raised (14:28) only to have the Gospel conclude with the women fleeing in silence (verse 8a). Readers must resolve this new tension from experiences of Christian faith.

Mark 15:39 is the last of three scenes in which the phrase 'Son of God' reveals Jesus' mission: at his baptism, the divine voice speaks to Jesus (Mark 1:11); at the Transfiguration, to three uncomprehending disciples (9:7). Otherwise, only the demons whom Jesus exorcizes and silences refer to him as 'Son of God' (5:7) until the interrogation of Jesus by the High Priest links the claim to be anointed by God with a claim to be 'son of the Blessed One' (14:61). Modern interpretations of Mark recognize the dramatic significance of a human voice acclaiming Jesus 'Son of God' at the moment of death on the cross. But the implausibility of a centurion voicing the central christological affirmation of the Gospel (1:1) has generated conflicting explanations. The simplest presumes that Mark has adapted an inherited tradition to set the faith of his Gentile church in a positive light. What the Jewish high priest called blasphemy, Christians recognize as the saving message of the gospel (cf. Romans 3:21–6; 1 Cor 1:18–25; 2:6–9). Viewed from a dramatic perspective, having the confession of faith voiced by an outsider leaves room for the mysterious ambiguity and tragedy of the Gospel's conclusion (on Mark as tragedy, see Smith, 'Divine Tragedy').

Matthew and Luke take different approaches to resolving the ambiguity of the centurion's confession in Mark 15:39 (see Brown, *The Death of the Messiah*). Matthew does not assume that the centurion represented later believers. He adds apocalyptic signs, which terrify the Roman guards into recognizing that a great man has died (27:51–4). Just as astronomical signs accompanied Jesus' birth (2:1–2), so cosmic disruption occurs at the moment of death. Luke's Jesus is an exemplary martyr. Some New Testament manuscripts include a prayer for the forgiveness of his enemies (23:34). A dialogue with the criminals demonstrates that heavenly life with Jesus will come to those who repent (23:39–43). Jesus dies calmly. The centurion glorifies God by proclaiming Jesus righteous, and the crowds, who remained sympathetic to Jesus, lament (23:44–7). Thus, Jesus does not die alone, abandoned and mocked by all. For Matthew, God responds at the moment of death with signs of judgment. For Luke, Jesus' piety and goodness shine through.

## MATTHEW REVISES MARK

The dynamic activity of constructing the story from paradoxical narrative clues, an ironic posture towards the heroic and scepticism about the realist claims that God raised Jesus bodily also makes modern literary critics appreciate Mark's narrative style. Discipleship that comes from the margins and follows Jesus in unseating the centres of power, whether demonic, deriving from illness or sin, religious or socio-economic, makes the suffering Son of Man in Mark a model for effective action, not social conformity. Believers are reassured that 'all things are possible to those who believe' (9:23, 28–9; 11:24–5).

Unlike modern readers, Matthew and Luke read Mark within the conventions of the ancient 'life' that highlight the exemplary character and teaching of the hero (*pace* Luz, 'Fiktivität', who treats Matthew as realistic historical fiction in which the post-Easter situation of the Church is mirrored in the Jesus story). Matthew's catechetical interests are most evident in the five discourses which form the core of the account of Jesus' ministry. The Sermon on the Mount (chapters 5–7) summarizes Jesus' teaching. The Beatitudes (5:3–12) describe those who will experience God's salvation. As the 'poor in spirit', the pious who wait for God's salvation, their single-hearted devotion to God puts them among the lowly and the persecuted of this world. However, they are not passive victims. They exhibit the active characteristics of mercy, striving to make peace and willingness to suffer in order to testify to Jesus. Their witness fulfils the ancient prophetic promise of bringing God's light to the nations (5:13–16). The Lord's Prayer (6:9–13) and sayings about being anxious (6:25–34) assure disciples that God will provide for their needs. Evidence that Jesus' teaching brings the Law to its intended perfection (5:17–20) is given in a series of antithetical sayings and illustrative examples (5:21–48). Though these sayings are often treated as an 'impossible ideal', ancient Jewish and pagan moralists commonly agreed that the truly wise person has control of the passions which dominate most human lives.

The brief catechesis on piety (6:1–13) addresses another topic which ancient moralists considered essential to the good life. It has been organized around the three elements of Jewish piety: fasting, almsgiving and prayer. Like the antitheses, this piety does not depend upon the social support or public praise that lead others to engage in these activities. In the style of Old Testament prophets (e.g. Isaiah 1:12–17), Matthew reminds readers that piety cannot be separated from the justice and mercy that are at the heart of the Law (cf. Matthew 23:23). Disciples must extend the forgiveness for which they pray to others (6:14–15) and refrain from passing judgement (7:1–5). The golden rule concludes the Sermon's ethical teaching (7:12). Warnings about distorted teaching within the community follow (7:13–27). The Sermon's conclusion describes the disciples' response, recognition that Jesus' authority is greater than that of the scribal interpreters of the Law (7:28–9).

As an epitome of Jesus' teaching, the Sermon on the Mount speaks of moral conduct in general. However, Matthew has incorporated warnings for the Christian community. False teachers might undermine Jesus' teaching. Throughout his Gospel, Matthew insists that belief in Jesus together with following his teaching does not exempt believers from God's judgement (7:21–3). He attaches a judgement parable about the guest who lacks the wedding garment to the parable of the elect gathered from the margins into God's banquet (22:11–14). Two discourses speak directly to communal concerns: missionary activity (10:1–11:1) and relationships within the community (18:1–35). The parables discourse (3:1–52) has taken the idea that parables are concealed speech from Mark. Jesus' followers recognize the 'secrets of the kingdom'. Outsiders whose hearts remain closed to God's word fulfil the prophecy of Isaiah 6:9–10 (13:10–17; Mark 4:10–12). Matthew modifies the Markan hint that Jesus' disciples might share the hardness of heart found among outsiders (cf. Mark 8:17–18).

Matthew 13:34–5 also corrects the suggestion in Mark 4:33 that parabolic speech was an accommodation, not a hindrance, to the understanding of the crowds. Jesus speaks in parables to fulfil the words of the prophet (citing Psalm 78:2). Matthew clarifies Jesus' words for the audience. Explanations are for the disciples (as in Mark 4:34; Matthew 13:10, 17, 36, 51–2a). The parables of the sower (13:1–9), weeds among the wheat, mustard seed and leaven (verses 24–33) are directed at the crowds.

The Gospel's final discourse contains judgement sayings and parables (24:1–25:46). The opening section, a revision of the apocalyptic discourse in Mark 13:1–37, follows the demands of the genre for private instruction of Jesus' disciples. Parables warn readers to remain vigilant, since the day of judgement will come without warning. Three concluding parables underline the need to observe the teaching of Jesus. The allegory of prudent and foolish serving girls warns that those who lack 'oil' cannot make up for it at the last minute (25:1–13); servants who fail to increase an absent master's wealth will be cast out (verses 14–30); and the separation between the 'sheep' and 'goats' depends upon how they have responded to the 'little ones', the poor, the prisoner, the stranger (verses 31–46).

Though the servant parables suggest addressees who are attached to a particular 'lord', the parable of the sheep and the goats has neither group recognize Jesus' identity. The expressions 'my brothers' (verse 40) and 'little ones' (verse 45; identified as referring to Christians in 18:10, 14) used for those with whom the master identifies implies that Christians are the objects of the activities represented. Consequently, the final scenario shifts from judging disciples to humanity in general. Non-Christians, who have no explicit relationship to Jesus, will be held accountable for how they have responded to the suffering 'little ones' in their midst. The weighty matters of the Law, which Matthew thinks can never be overridden, 'justice, mercy, and faith', are not peculiar to Christians. Nor should Matthew's emphasis on judgement obscure the equally strong conviction that God offers forgiveness to those who are willing to show mercy. Other interpreters point out that the 'little ones' in this passage are like the Christian missionaries of Matthew 10, radically dependent upon the hospitality of those among whom they work

(10:9–14, 40–2). They argue that this passage only speaks of persons who would have heard of Jesus through Christian preaching – even if they did not respond by joining the church. According to this reading, Matthew is not proposing a theological answer to the question of anonymous Christianity among the pagans. Instead, the evangelist has a more limited agenda. Humans will be judged by their response to those who come bearing God's word (see Hagner, *Matthew 14–28*). This passage looks forward to the mission among the nations with which the Gospel concludes (28:16–20).

## LUKE CONTINUES THE STORY

Matthew has embedded a vision of the church's future as 'light of the world' in the story of Jesus. Though such hints can also be detected in Luke (e.g. Luke 21:7–24), his Gospel ends with a striking new turn (24:47–53). A second volume (Acts) describes the emergence of the church. Both are embraced by the designation at the beginning of the Gospel, *diēgēsis*, an exposition of events that happened – or could have happened (Tannehill, *The Narrative Unity of Luke–Acts*). The ascension of Jesus (Acts 1:6–11) highlights the difference between the time of Jesus and the time of the Church's mission which is to continue until Jesus returns (verse 11). Stories about the apostles parallel similar accounts in the Gospels. In some cases details from an Acts story are not found in Luke's Gospel, but might have been taken from Luke's source. The healing of Tabitha/Dorcas in Acts 9:36–41 repeats the raising of the dead in a manner similar to the daughter of Jairus (Mark 5:35–43; Luke 8:49–55). Unlike the version in his Gospel, in Acts Luke retains the Aramaic flavour of Jesus' words found in the Markan story. The Aramaic form of Dorcas' name, 'Tabitha', combined with the command to arise (verse 40) is close to Mark's version of the miracle. Other details reflect Luke's familiarity with the Septuagint. Peter prays alone in the presence of the dead body as Elisha had done (2 Kings 4:33). Tabitha opens her eyes as in the Elisha story (2 Kings 4:35). This story also has ties with Jesus healing the widow's son at Nain (Luke 7:11–17). At the healer's word of command, both sit up. Knowledge of the miracle spreads around the region and leads people to faith in the Lord.

This example indicates that detecting sources within the text of Acts is complicated by the author's ability to draw multiple allusions into a single episode. Some manuscripts of Acts contain an additional phrase attached to Peter's command in 9:40, 'in the name of our Lord Jesus Christ'. While it is easy to see this phrase as an expansion of a theme attached to healings by the apostles in Acts, which are done by the power of Jesus' name (Acts 3:6, for example), the variant appears in manuscripts which are classified as belonging to the Western text type. It diverges sharply from the Alexandrian text type generally considered closest to the original text and the basis for modern editions of the Greek text. Primary witnesses to the Western text type include the bilingual (Greek/Latin) Codex Bezae (*c.* fifth century CE), the Syriac Peshitta and the citations of Acts found in Irenaeus (*c.* 180 CE). The Western text type serves as a reminder that the stable text which modern readers take for granted in literary analyses did not exist in the world of hand copied manuscripts (see Barrett, *The Acts of the Apostles*, pp. 20–9; on books in early Christianity, see Gamble, *Books and Readers*).

Luke's narrative employs variations as the same episode is retold. See the accounts of Paul's conversion (Acts 9:1–31; 22:6–21; 26:9–23). They contradict Paul's own assertion that he remained unknown to Christians in Judea after his conversion (Galatians 1:17–24). The geographical formalism of Luke's account requires that Paul, like the other apostles, begin his activity in Jerusalem. Through Paul the risen Lord's directions will be accomplished. The Gospel will be taken from Jerusalem to Rome. The second and third accounts of Paul's conversion belong to speeches made during the trial process that will send him to Rome. Paul highlights his obedience to divine commands. He did not remain in Jerusalem because of hostility against him. God's providence preserved the apostle by sending him among the Gentiles (22:17–21). In the second speech, Paul has sealed his destiny by appealing to the right of a Roman citizen to appear before Caesar in Rome (25:21–7; on citizen rights, see Rapske, *The Book of Acts*, pp. 71–112). The speech is framed as a finding of evidence. Paul describes his anti-Christian persecutions as evidence that he once belonged among the authorities who now accuse him. He emphasizes the divine origins of his preaching, its continuity with ancestral tradition and its moral rectitude. Preaching Christ to the Gentiles is a call to convert from doing evil to doing good (26:16–23). Paul succeeds in persuading his audience. Had he not appealed to Caesar, they would have freed him (verses 24–32).

These examples indicate that Luke follows the practice of ancient writers and provides speeches suitable to the narrative circumstances in which characters find themselves (Soards, 'The Speeches in Acts'). Peter's sermon on Pentecost (2:14–36) initiates a series of speeches in which the appeal to conversion outlines the Christian message: (1) Jesus' life, death and resurrection proves that the age of salvation has dawned; (2) Jesus is exalted at the right hand of God; (3) the Holy Spirit operating through the apostles demonstrates the power and glory of the exalted Christ; (4) Christ will return at the end of the age; (5) summons to conversion. In the earliest speeches, Peter calls those responsible for the death of Jesus to repent (3:19–21). Large numbers of the people respond positively. The community they form lives in exemplary piety, peace and solidarity (Acts 2:43–7; 4:23–37).

The apostles are steadfast in their testimony to the gospel despite imprisonment (4:1–23; 5:17–42). Luke brings this period to its climax with the martyrdom of Stephen. His sharp condemnation of the Temple cult and Jewish unbelief strikes a jarring note (7:1–53). This speech follows the common pattern in which martyrs about to die challenge impious tyrants who attack the righteous (see 2 Maccabees 7:1–42). Stephen's death marks a major transition in the story. Persecution forces many Christians out of Jerusalem so that the message begins to spread among the nations. Determination to eradicate the growing sect also sets Paul on the Damascus road where he is converted by a vision of the Lord (9:1–30). Other visions orchestrate Peter's journey to baptize the pious centurion, Cornelius (10:1–11:18). Ancient readers cannot but recognize the hand of God at work in directing the growth of the Christian movement. Divine judgement is at work when Herod meets a gruesome death (12:1–23).

At this point, Luke introduces another development. The incidental episodes of Gentile conversion give way to the systematic missionary journeys undertaken by Paul. The first is sponsored by the church at Antioch (13:1–14:28). Since Paul worked in Antioch prior to undertaking the independent missionary efforts reflected in his letters (Galatians 2:1–14), some scholars think that Luke may have employed sources from Antioch. Paul and Barnabas follow the established pattern. They preach in synagogues until hostility forces them to turn to the Gentiles (13:44–52).

Paul's missionary activities also involve dramatic encounters with representatives of pagan religion (14:8–18; 16:16–19; 19:23–41). These tales illustrate the religious and moral superiority of Christianity. Preaching the gospel challenges magicians, false prophets and advocates of other cults who enrich themselves by exploiting superstition. However, Luke does not depict the apostles as entirely successful. Hostility undermines their effectiveness and leads to imprisonment or expulsion (14:2, 19–20; 16:19–40; 19:28–20:1). These episodes have been carefully crafted to show the reader that accusations against the apostles are groundless.

Charges are brought by persons of inferior status, who show no concern for civic order. At Lystra, Jews from other cities stir up the crowds to stone Paul (14:19–20). In Ephesus officials rescue Paul. The town clerk warns the populace against civic disturbances (19:35–41). Historical details of the legal proceedings in Philippi (16:19–40) continue to draw considerable attention (see White, 'Visualizing the "Real" World of Acts'). Paul's appeal to his citizenship (16:36–40) only after the indignities of beating and being chained in prison has led some to doubt his citizenship. However, historical examples in which individuals found their rights ignored by provincial governors can be adduced. Luke's use of the Roman citizenship motif plays an important role in establishing Paul's status relative to his accusers wherever it occurs. Paul can compel the magistrates to make a public apology and politely conduct his party out of the city. Later Paul's inherited citizenship makes him superior to the Roman tribune, Lysias, who was about to examine Paul under torture (22:22–9). When plots in Jerusalem endanger Paul's life, the tribune sends him to the Roman governor in Caesarea with an extensive escort (23:23–30). God's plan for Paul to witness in Rome (23:11) is fulfilled because Paul appeals to his citizen rights (25:9–12; 26:30–2). Throughout the concluding imprisonments, Paul is treated as a prominent person, held under relaxed confinement and permitted to speak before officials and visiting dignitaries, and to receive visitors.

The social dynamics of these scenes illustrate the class-consciousness and xenophobia of Greco-Roman cities. The town clerk in Ephesus asserts that Paul has not threatened the goddess Artemis or her temple. Instead Demetrius and the artisans who rile the crowd are endangering their city by acting outside proper legal channels (19:38–40). Paul is a person of social prominence whose life is threatened by those of inferior education and status. This narrative positioning of the apostle is illustrated by the converts who provide him hospitality as well. Heads of household, first a Greek woman from Asia (16:15) and then a Roman man (16:33–4) host Paul and his entourage at banquets. They represent the social status of those who are converted by the apostle's preaching. Why emphasize the social status of Paul's converts? The Christian mission has powerful patrons whose hospitality establishes the social context for the new movement within their respective cities (17:5–9). The concluding scene has Paul repeat this pattern in Rome, itself. Permitted 'house arrest' characteristic of a prominent citizen, Paul can assemble local Jewish leaders for one final appeal (28:17–28). When they reject God's messenger, the apostle turns to the Gentiles for the final time. Though prophecies have indicated that Paul will be martyred (20:22–4, 38; 21:10–14), Luke leaves his readers with a different picture. The apostle has sufficient resources to set up a school for instruction in his own domicile (28:30–1). Combined with the testimony of the unbelieving Jewish leaders that no one had sent formal charges against Paul from Jerusalem (28:21), readers can only conclude that there is no case against the apostle.

### CONCLUSION

This analysis of Acts might serve to describe the Synoptic Gospels as well. They seek to make the case for faith in Jesus of Nazareth as Son of God, the agent of God's saving power for all people. Readers interested in tracking down the many details of the first-century social, political and religious world that can be detected in the Gospel narratives should refer to commentaries. Whatever the narrative conventions employed by the evangelists, the Gospels remain rooted in their own time and place. They are not romantic fiction or myths of a founding age. To treat them as such negates the fundamental claim that God has once again come into the world of humanity to call forth a people from among the nations. Further, this gathering of the elect represents the decisive coming of God. It cannot be revoked. God's next manifestation marks the end of the world.

Insights from contemporary narrative criticism have opened the way to appreciate the distinctive features of each evangelist. This chapter has highlighted features of such interpretation that are accessible to readers of an English version of the Bible. The evangelists are authors, not record-keepers. This awareness needs to be set against a tendency of readers new to the Gospels to treat the Gospels as though they were accounts from a local paper about what happened. Preachers often move from text to sermon in a way that reinforces that viewpoint, taking every Gospel reading as an account of 'what Jesus did'. Little attention is paid to the evangelist in question, the place of the particular story in the Gospel or its difference from other versions. If the gospels were merely records or reports, that would be normal. We always build up our understanding of a news event by piecing together interviews from different sources. But even there, the point of view of the person speaking matters. Consequently, reading the Gospels and Acts as narrative should lead one to appreciate their individuality. It should not erase their confessional perspective, since the claims they support are religious in character, not merely literary.

# Further reading

Allison, Dale C., *The New Moses*, Minneapolis, 1993.

Aune, David E., *The New Testament in its Literary Environment*, Philadelphia, 1987.

Barrett, C. K., *The Acts of the Apostles. Volume I: I–XIV*, Edinburgh, 1994.

Best, Ernest, *Mark. The Gospel as Story*, Edinburgh, 1983.
  'Mark's Narrative Technique', *Journal for the Study of the New Testament* 37
    (1989), pp. 43–58.

Betz, Hans Dieter, *The Sermon on the Mount,* Minneapolis, 1995.

Brown, Raymond E., *The Death of the Messiah,* New York, 1994.

Bryan, Christopher, *A Preface to Mark,* New York, 1993.

Burridge, Richard A., *What Are the Gospels?*, Cambridge, 1992.

Catchpole, David, *The Quest for Q*, Edinburgh, 1993.

Davies, W. D. and Dale C. Allison, *The Gospel According to Matthew. Volume I: I–VII.*
    Edinburgh, 1988; *Volume II: VIII–XVIII*, Edinburgh, 1991.

Donahue, John R., 'Windows and Mirrors: The Setting of Mark's Gospel', *Catholic
    Biblical Quarterly* 57 (1995), pp. 1–26.

Fitzmyer, Joseph A., *The Gospel According to Luke (I–IX)*, Garden City, NY, 1981;
    *The Gospel According to Luke (X–XXIV)*, Garden City, NY, 1985.

Gamble, Harry Y., *Books and Readers in the Early Church,* New Haven, 1995.

Gill, David W. J. and Conrad Gempf (eds.), *The Book of Acts in Its First Century
    Setting. Volume II,* Grand Rapids, MI, 1994.

Green, Joel B., *The Theology of the Gospel of Luke*, Cambridge, 1995.

Guelich, Robert A., *Mark 1–8:26*, Dallas, 1989.

Hagner, Donald A., *Matthew 1–13*, Dallas, 1993.
  *Matthew 14–28*, Dallas, 1995.

Hester, J. David, 'Dramatic Inconclusion: Irony and the Narrative Rhetoric of the
    Ending of Mark', *Journal for the Study of the New Testament* 57 (1995), 61–86.

Johnson, Luke Timothy, *The Acts of the Apostles*, Collegeville, MN, 1992.

Lentz, John Clayton, *Luke's Portrait of Paul*, Cambridge, 1993.

Lindemann, Andreas, 'Literatur zu den Synoptischen Evangelien 1984–1991',
    *Theologische Rundschau,* 59 (1994), 113–85; 252–84.

Luz, Ulrich, 'Fiktivität und Traditionstreue im Matthäusevangelium im Lichte
    griechischer Literatur', *Zeitschrift für die neutestamentliche Wissenschaft* 85
    (1994), pp. 153–77.
  *The Theology of the Gospel of Matthew*, Cambridge, 1995.

Marshall, Christopher D., *Faith as a Theme in Mark's Narrative*, Cambridge, 1989.

Meier, John P., *A Marginal Jew. Rethinking the Historical Jesus. Volume Two,* New
    York, 1994.

Moloney, Francis J., 'Beginning the Gospel of Matthew. Reading Matthew 1:1–2:23',
    *Salesianum* 54 (1992), pp. 341–59.

Nolland, John, *Luke 1–9:20*, Dallas, 1989; *Luke 9:21–18:34*, Dallas, 1993; *Luke
    18:35–24:53*, Dallas, 1993.

Rapske, Brian, *The Book of Acts in Its First Century Setting. Volume III :* Grand Rapids, MI, 1994.

Saldarini, Anthony J., 'Boundaries and Polemics in the Gospel of Matthew', *Biblical Interpretation* 3 (1995), pp. 239–65.

Smith, Stephen H., 'A Divine Tragedy: Some Observations on the Dramatic Structure of Mark's Gospel', *Novum Testamentum* 37 (1995), pp. 209–31.

' "Inside" and "Outside" in Mark's Gospel', *The Expository Times* 102 (1991), pp. 363–7.

Soards, Marion L., 'The Speeches in Acts in Relation to Other Pertinent Ancient Literature', *Ephemerides Theologicae Lovanienses* 70 (1994), pp. 65–90.

Tannehill, Robert C., *The Narrative Unity of Luke–Acts. Volume II,* Minneapolis, 1990.

White, L. Michael. 'Visualizing the "Real" World of Acts 16', in Michael White and O. Larry Yarbrough (eds.), *The Social World of the First Christians,* Minneapolis, 1995, pp. 234–61.

# 17 John and the Johannine literature
## The woman at the well

JOHN ASHTON

### INTRODUCTION

Of all the writings of the Bible none is more obviously an integrated whole than the Gospel of John. The first-time reader lionized by reader-response critics is sure to find it, as David Friedrich Strauss famously did, a 'seamless garment'. Its themes (judgement, mission, revelation, truth) and symbols (light, water, bread, healing, life) are skilfully interwoven into the familiar gospel story of Jesus' brief career as a teacher and wonder-worker, with its dramatic ending of death and resurrection. In this, the fourth version of the story, the parts are more than usually representative of the whole. Besides the sustained self-allusiveness consequential upon the evangelist's interpenetrative technique, the reason for this is that once under way the story is dominated throughout by the powerful presence of Jesus, who keeps introducing fresh variations on the single theme of life-giving revelation. This is what justifies the synecdochic approach of the present chapter. In John 4 the Samaritan woman, passing from incredulity to belief, invites a similar response from the readers of the Gospel. Those acquainted with the whole Gospel know that the same invitation is issued on almost every page: any episode of comparable length could be used, as this one is here, to illustrate models of interpretation.[1]

All the writers whose work is assessed here are responding to the same text. Almost all have decided upon its meaning after reading it carefully over and over again. Most have made careful appraisals of their predecessors' opinions. Many have pondered the same evidence and the same arguments. Yet each has his or her own point of view: a point of view implies an angle; an angle implies a slant. In one or two cases, not more, the slant might reasonably be ascribed to blinkered vision; but if this is true of only a few how are we to account for the remarkable divergences of the rest?

Part of the reason is the sheer complexity of the text itself, the rich ambiguities that make the very idea of a definitive exegesis palpably absurd. But if we are to get beyond a helpless shrug of the shoulders we must begin by out-lining a number of interpretative options that no student of the Gospel can entirely evade. Some of these permeate the whole of biblical criticism; others are especially relevant to John. Even the most particular (a tiny example is the meaning of the verb συγχράομαι in verse 9)[2] indicate the *kind* of choice that faces us wherever we look.

### Rough versus smooth

The most significant of all the issues on which Johannine scholarship continues to be split involves what has come to be known, after the great lin-guistician Ferdinand de Saussure, as the distinction between synchronic and diachronic approaches to the Gospel. Those who adopt a synchronic or 'smooth' approach insist upon reading the text as it has been transmitted, without delving into its prehistory. A diachronic or 'rough' approach, on the other hand, demands both a recognition of the presence of successive layers in the text (usually attributed to source, author and redactor) and some attempt to prise these apart. These two approaches are rarely combined, though why this should be so is something of a mystery, since the possibili-ties of dialectic enrichment are, one would have thought, fairly obvious. Commentators occasionally make some grudging acknowledgement of the justification of source and redaction theories, but the vast majority, when they get down to business, prefer the smooth approach. As for articles and monographs, I know of only two 'rough' studies of John 4:1–42, the first by Luise Schottroff,[3] a pupil of Bultmann, the second, much more recent, a doc-toral thesis by Andrea Link.[4] A first-time reader of the other books, articles and extracts discussed below would certainly conclude that there is nothing at all to be said for a diachronic analysis of the text.

### History versus exegesis

Are we to approach this passage as exegetes, simply asking what it means, or as historians, more interested in what it can tell us about the origins and growth of the community for which it was composed? Here too, although in theory the alternatives are not mutually exclusive, they are rarely combined in practice. Yet we should at least remain alert to the possibility that a purely historical insight might open a window on to a fresh interpretation.

### Background

Introducing his commentary on John (subtitled 'how he speaks, thinks, and believes') Adolf Schlatter observes that he has been variously regarded:

'as a Greek, a Paulinist, a philosopher of religion, a poet, a mystic, and a gnostic'.[5] His own work is suffused with his perception of John as a Palestinian. An abyss yawns between him and Rudolf Bultmann,[6] for whom the evangelist is a converted Gnostic with a redeeming message for all mankind; and an even deeper chasm separates him from C. H. Dodd,[7] convinced that John is a Greek whose work was intended in the first place for the perusal of well-educated Hellenistic pagans. Our views on this matter cannot but affect our own understanding of the Gospel text. These days, thanks largely to the pioneering efforts of Raymond Brown[8] (for Schlatter's work had little impact) the Jewish provenance of John is mostly taken for granted; but we should not forget that this too is an interpretative choice.

### Readership

John's intended readership may have changed more than once during the composition of the Gospel, and in any case its nature is hard to determine with any precision. This is nevertheless the kind of problem that historical critics take in their stride: it causes them no discomfort. On the other hand they are likely to bristle at the sound of the term 'ideal reader' as this comes ringing down from the citadel of narrative criticism. Whatever our point of view, whether it be old-fashioned and traditional, modern or postmodern, we are living at a time when the notion of the reader has become no less problematic than that of the author. In the present context the question is further complicated by the fact that individual interpreters may themselves have different readerships in mind – expert or lay, critical or uncritical, committed or uncommitted. All of which prompts a warning: *caveat lector*.

### Genre

One of the drawbacks of selective exegesis, the isolation of a single passage for close scrutiny, is that it may cause the reader to forget the relevance for interpretation of the genre of the whole work. John's Gospel is a proclamation of faith in narrative form, paradoxically recounting Jesus' earthly career in order to persuade its readers to accept him as their Risen Lord. This means that it has to be read on two levels, first the story level and secondly the level of spiritual understanding.[9] The riddles of the Gospel, its symbols and its ironies are all aimed at reinforcing this purposeful ambivalence. That is why the most helpful studies are generally those that highlight one or more of these features, those for instance of G. R. O'Day,[10] emphasizing the irony of the gospel, or D. A. Lee[11] focusing on its symbolism.

### Context

A second possible disadvantage of selective exegesis in the sense in which I am using this term is the risk of neglecting the many links, both structural and thematic, that tie the various episodes of the Gospel together. A small example is Jesus' assertion, in verse 34, that his 'food' is 'to accomplish the work' of the one who sent him. The singular 'work' is also used in this strong sense in 17:4, where Jesus speaks of 'having accomplished' the work that he had been given to do (see too 6:29). A very teasing question of a different kind is posed by the statement, in verse 22, that 'salvation comes from the Jews'. How could the fourth evangelist, elsewhere so hostile to those he portrays as Jesus' adversaries, have written that? It is all too easy to miss internal allusions and contextual difficulties if you are preoccupied with the interpretation of a single chapter.

Of more immediate significance (and indeed noticed by many interpreters) are all the binary oppositions that set this passage off against the Nicodemus episode in chapter 3 – Pharisee/Samaritan, named/unnamed, man/woman, night/day, secret/open, indoors/outdoors; but the resemblances are important too, especially John's use in both chapters of his favourite device of the riddle. In each case the riddle is contained in a single expression, ἄνωθεν in chapter 3, ὕδωρ ζῶν in chapter 4. English has no word that does justice to the double meaning of ἄνωθεν (from above/a second time), so the ambiguity is always in evidence. Yet when it comes to chapter 4 all translations without exception render ὕδωρ ζῶν, even where it first occurs, as 'living water', thus missing the deliberate ambiguity of the Greek (where the first meaning of the term is simply fresh or running water) and making it impossible for the Greekless reader to sympathize with the woman's initial confusion.

### Weighting

We now come to yet another choice that confronts anyone seriously attempting to understand a text from which he or she is separated by a temporal or cultural gap (which is what makes interpretation necessary in the first place). This is what may be called the problem of weighting, felt here most acutely in the problem of how to deal with Jacob's well. That the location of the encounter between Jesus and the woman has some bearing on the meaning cannot be doubted. But when we ask *how* it should be brought into the interpretation opinions differ widely; and there is no way of arbitrating between them that would satisfy all the contestants. Yet we must suppose that the allusion would have been picked up quickly, almost instinctively, by

John's first readers. Nineteen centuries later it is impossible, surely, to state with any confidence just what significance they may have attached to it.

This kind of apparently trivial problem crops up everywhere. It is as if, planning a journey to a distant country, we were to depend on a compass reading that we could only glimpse with blurred vision from a long way off. The slightest mistake will lead us far astray; and the same is true for any other traveller. Tiny differences in perception may have great consequences.

### Literal versus symbolic

Here is another sort of problem on which it is impossible to reach any agreement. 'You have had five husbands', Jesus tells the woman (verse 18), and there is nothing else in the Gospel to advise us whether we should take this information literally or symbolically. All are agreed that the preceding dialogue concerning living water must be interpreted symbolically. What then are we to make of the five husbands? Some favour an allegorical reading: the five gods of the Samaritans, the five books of the Pentateuch, even the five senses – though in that case, as A. Loisy drily enquires, how are we to identify the woman's present partner (a sixth sense, perhaps?).[12] Feeling that none of these suggestions fits in very easily with the preceding dialogue, we may opt instead for a literal reading. But in that case how do we explain the abrupt shift from the symbolic to the literal mode? We shall see that there are various ways of tackling this problem.

Many other questions may come into our minds as we dig deeper into the story, but these are the ones best capable, in my judgement, of dividing 'soul from spirit, joints from marrow'.

### Method

There are probably as many methods of biblical criticism as there are kinds of music, and as many new methods as there are kinds of pop music. The champions of the new methods are likely to dismiss the censures of old-fashioned historical critics just as abruptly as admirers of, say, heavy metal are likely to brush aside the remonstrances of those who prefer the classical tradition. The result is a *dialogue de sourds*, with each side convinced of the deafness of the other. How in such circumstances can an unreconstructed and (so far) undeconstructed historical critic hope to give a reasonably impartial account of modern approaches?

ANALYSIS

The interpreter's task is threefold: analysis, application and explanation. Though distinguishable, the three tasks are not always distinct. Usually, though not always, analysis is absorbed into explanation, and very often application is too. Even where a writer is chiefly interested in analysis on the one hand or application on the other some explanation is always felt to be indispensable.

To analyse a text is to spell out one's understanding of its structure and meaning. Analysis used to be carried out without tools: all one needed was a good eye and a sensitive nose. The modern form of analysis, text-linguistics, is a much more complex affair, but its aims are the same. Here too analysis does its utmost to rely exclusively upon information provided by the text itself. Hendrikus Boers states quite frankly: 'If the analysis were to suggest something which cannot be recognised by a sensitive reader *without* the analysis ... I would consider the analysis to have introduced alien material into the text.'[13] After this candid admission he justifies and explains the elaborate procedures of the first part of his book (backed up by nearly eighty diagrams, some of a truly daunting complexity) by comparing them to the laborious business of reading a foreign language with the aid of a grammar. First he offers a quite simple preliminary analysis. Thereafter, appealing to the semiotics of A. J. Greimas and J. Courtés, he discusses what he calls the textual syntax of the episode, clarifying it on the three levels of its surface narrative, syntactic deep structure and discursive syntax. A comprehensive analysis of the deep structure leads him to the conclusion that 'contrary to an analysis of only the surface by traditional means, John 4 is a syntactically tightly cohesive text' (*Neither on this Mountain*, p. 77). He then tackles the semantic component of the chapter, starting with 'the concrete figures' and moving on to 'the more abstract level of the values expressed by these figures' (p. 79), the values of sustenance, life, obedience, human solidarity and salvation. He explains in great detail how these are interrelated within the story. The second part of the book (pp. 144–200) attempts to flesh out the preceding analyses in a full interpretation, and the concluding pages summarize the meaning of the passage as 'the process of revelation of Jesus as the savior of the world'.

Employing rather different procedures, but equally dependent upon a synchronic reading and equally committed to the use of text-oriented techniques, Birger Olsson[14] and J. Eugene Botha[15] have arrived at rather different results. Although each of the three is offering an 'objective' analysis of the same text, they all find it impossible in the long run to detach analysis cleanly from explanation.

## APPLICATION

All texts carry meaning; many, including the Bible, also carry a meaning for their readers. Meaning for, significance in the strong sense, is traditionally covered by the Latin term *applicatio*. In pre-critical days the application was generally caught up in the interpretation. Historical critics are for the most part anxious to exclude it. Raymond Brown for instance prefaces his remarkable two-volume commentary by confessing a 'stubborn refusal to make a biblical text say more than its author meant to say'. He can do this because of his sense of 'the clear difference between the thoughts of the various biblical authors (which are the concern of the biblical scholar) and the subsequent use and development of those thoughts in divergent theologies (which are the concern of the theologian)' (*The Gospel According to John*, p. vi). Since then, however, the legitimacy of separating explanation and application has increasingly come under question.[16] Whoever is right on this contentious issue, all agree on what application means in a hermeneutical context: it is the appropriation of a biblical text in such a way that it speaks to its readers directly in their own situation and demands from them an active response.

We may distinguish two main kinds of application in the interpretation of John 4:1–42, the psychologizing and the feminist.

### Psychology

The first of the psychologizing explanations, that of François Roustang,[17] now nearly half a century old, draws its inspiration more from Hegel than from Freud or Jung. It uses the 'woman at the well' episode as a model of the transition from indifference to faith, and its tone is in some respects less psychological than philosophical or theological. Yet Roustang's brilliant analysis of the woman's progress from appearance to reality and from falsehood to truth depends, like many of Hegel's ostensibly 'logical' moves, upon enduringly valid psychological insights into the difficulties human beings encounter when trying to confront and acknowledge the truth. This is a bold study, elaborating upon John's text much as a skilful composer develops the potential of a single melodic line; and it may well, as Roustang fears, offend the purists: 'professional exegetes are unlikely to follow us here' ('Les Moments de l'acte de foi', p. 344). Yet it does less violence to the text than many other interpretations, and merits respect for its religious sensitivity.

Unlike Roustang, who directs a polite nod towards those he calls 'les exégètes de métier' before boarding his own train, Eugen Drewermann[18] has no time for traditional biblical scholarship. Towards the beginning of his huge two-volume work, *Tiefenpsychologie und Exegese*, he launches a fierce attack on the historical-critical method as generally practised. Viewed hermeneutically, he says, it is extremely limited; viewed theologically it is downright wrong (*geradezu falsch*). He goes on to accuse professional exegetes of hiding behind the so-called objectivity of their theoretical reconstructions (vol. I, pp. 23–5).

In Roustang's interpretation the conclusion of the story (verses 35–8) provides an effective counterpart to the preceding section by outlining the conditions of the possibility of an act of faith. Drewermann breaks off before this conclusion, but like Roustang he follows what he calls a *Zerdehnungsregel*: this allows him to stretch out and slow down the very rapid movement of the text itself and to read from it the story of a gradual coming-to-faith in the Messiah that he sees as equivalent to the step-by-step process of Jungian individuation (which is what, for him, genuine religion is all about). The term 'spirit' in the phrase 'spirit and truth' (verse 23) he takes to mean personal conviction (as opposed to tradition) and 'truth' to mean personal integrity. Jesus acts as a kind of Jungian analyst, enabling the woman to find her true self (*Tiefenpsychologie*, vol. II, pp. 686–97). Drewermann ends by asserting that theological exegesis cannot get by ('nicht auskommen kann') without the help of depth psychology.

Where Roustang turns for help to Hegel (though without naming him) and Drewermann to Jung, Stephen Moore[19] appeals to Lacan and Derrida. In his Lacanian reading of the episode he goes beyond all other interpreters by placing the emphasis not on the woman's thirst but on that of Jesus himself. The interchange between the two is driven, Moore insists, by *Jesus'* longing to instil in the woman a desire for the living water he has come to bring: 'Only thus can his own deeper thirst be assuaged, his own lack be filled' ('Are There Impurities', p. 208). With Lacan's assistance Moore is able to plunge much deeper into the well, theologically speaking, than the rest of us, still clinging to the ropes of traditional exegetical methods, can possibly manage. He then calls upon Derrida's deconstructions to help him highlight the change of register in the crucifixion scene. Two levels of meaning of the water symbol (physical and spiritual) that had been quite properly held apart in the dialogue suddenly collapse into one (p. 222). The newly discovered meaning, however, cannot hold, and the result is the deconstruction of the text and the disorientation of the reader.

### Feminism

Certain readers (who may, as we have seen, be psychologists but are more often theologians) approach the Bible brandishing an axe. When applied to the passage which concerns us here this is generally a feminist axe, and it is wielded in three ways. First, by a proceeding analogous to what is generously called positive discrimination, it is possible to hew a meaning out of the text in the service of a higher cause. A second tactic is to point out the underlying androcentrism of the biblical authors themselves, a characteristic that men, in the nature of the case, are less likely to notice than women. Sometimes the claim is made that the reading now being proposed is the right one and that only the prejudices of earlier scholars blinded by phallocentrism or misogyny have prevented them from seeing it.

The little interchange between Jesus and the woman beginning 'Go and call your husband' (verse 16) is an excellent example. Some scholars attach a symbolic significance to the five husbands; even so it is arguable that the text itself exhibits a misogynistic bias. Others, mostly male, opt for a literal reading: the woman's marital life is in total disarray. This exposes them to the charge that their unconscious bias has led them to shift the interpretation from the symbolic to the literal without first trying to give a coherent reading of the whole episode by remaining on the symbolic level appropriate, as all agree, to the dialogue concerning living water. Stephen Moore, feminist as well as deconstructionist, has some fun citing a series of commentators thundering moral disapproval of the woman's behaviour ('profligacy and unbridled passions', 'a tramp', 'an illicit affair', 'bawdy past', 'immoral life', etc.).[20] He then points out that the commentators in question, only too ready to underline the woman's failure to grasp the symbolic import of 'living water', 'effectively trade places with her by opting to take Jesus' statement in 4:18 at face-value' ('Are There Impurities', p. 212).

Sandra Schneiders,[21] equally dismissive of literal readings of the five husbands, writes of the episode as 'a textbook case of the trivialization, marginalization, and even sexual demonization of biblical women' ('A Case Study', p. 188). But whereas Moore signally fails to follow up his own criticisms of literal readings with a symbolic interpretation of his own, Schneiders is braver. 'The entire dialogue between Jesus and the woman', she urges, 'is the "wooing" of Samaria to full covenant fidelity in the New Israel by Jesus, the New Bridegroom' (p. 191). Like many other interpreters she stresses the symbolic significance of the meeting by the well (we shall return to this theme), but goes further than some by asserting that 'Jesus has already been identified at Cana as the true Bridegroom who supplied the good wine for the wedding feast (John 2:9–11) and by John the Baptist as the true Bridegroom to whom God has given the New Israel as Bride (John 3:27–30)' (p. 187). (A much cruder reading, drawing on some of the same evidence, is Lyle Eslinger's suggestion that the woman was employing a series of *double entendres* whilst making 'sexual advances' to the attractive stranger in an attempt to seduce him.)[22]

In her seminal work *In Memory of Her* Elisabeth Schüssler-Fiorenza[23] makes a brief but important contribution to the debate. 'The dramatic dialogue', she observes, 'is probably based on a missionary tradition that ascribed a primary role to a woman in the conversion of the Samaritans' (p. 327) – an exceptionally interesting comment because the Samaritan woman now takes on historical significance as the leader of an early Christian mission to the Samaritans (who took their name from the capital city of ancient Israel). The evangelist, reluctant to leave her in the centre of the stage for too long, is quick to add that true faith consists in listening to Jesus himself (verse 42); but in underlining the plain statement that many of her fellow-citizens 'believed on the strength of her word' (verse 39), Fiorenza performs the service of reminding us that the Gospel is available to the historian as well as to the exegete.

### EXPLANATION

The business of exegetes is to use all the information at their disposal to explain the text in question. To illustrate the explanation of the 'woman at the well' episode I have chosen three works published within the last decade: a doctoral thesis by a Nigerian sister, an extract from a grandly conceived 'reading' of the whole Gospel by the veteran French scholar, Xavier Léon-Dufour and a thesis from within the German tradition by Andrea Link.

Teresa Okure,[24] alone among present-day exegetes, regards the evangelist as an eye-witness of the events he records (*The Johannine Approach*, pp. 272–3). Having selected an episode in Jesus' own life that corresponds to the situation of the audience he is addressing, he goes on to portray him in the exercise of the mission given him by God (p. 292). The readers John has in mind may be insiders, but they too, Okure insists, fall within the sphere of the evangelist's own missionary endeavour, standing as they do 'in special need of being reminded of Jesus' uniqueness as God's eschatological agent of salvation ... and of the resulting need for their total dependence on him' (p. 287). As her title suggests, she concentrates entirely on the theme of mission. By the end of her book this theme, which started as a leitmotif of the gospel (p. 2), has become *the* leitmotif (p. 291).

Léon-Dufour,[25] a past master in the French art of *haute vulgarisation*, offers a discursive (and synchronic) reading of the Gospel that manages to integrate a wide range of reference, especially to the Old Testament, into a searching exegesis. He explains this episode, which he sees as 'a symbolic narrative', with the aid of his own theory of two levels of understanding, of Jesus and of the Church. On the first level the living water symbolizes the revelation that Jesus has come to bring, on the second level the spirit, that has to wait upon his going. He refuses to choose between a literal and a symbolic reading of the five husbands: certainly the woman is the symbolic representative of her people as they move from idolatry to the service of the true God; but at the same time she has her own importance as an individual standing in urgent need of the life and salvation brought by Jesus. Major biblical references are inserted into the discussion rather than being crammed into footnotes: here is unobtrusive scholarship directed to an uncomplicated reading of the text.

Andrea Link is the only commentator in recent times to take a diachronic approach. In the first half of her book *'Was redest du mit ihr?'*,[26] she summarizes and criticizes earlier views. Then, after a long verse-by-verse study of the redactional history of the episode (pp. 178–324) she devotes a shorter, concluding section to what she calls *Theologiegeschichte* (pp. 325–71). This focuses on the theological differences between the three levels of redaction: first the source or *Grundschrift*, and then the work, successively, of evangelist and redactor. The source is a missionary document in which 'the woman from Sychar' figures as a dialogue partner of Jesus, a disciple of Moses and an active missionary eager to promote faith in Jesus (p. 352). It also portrays Jesus as a prophet closely resembling Elijah (verse 19) and as Messiah (verse 25). The evangelist goes beyond the source in seeing Jesus as revealer (verses 10–15) and saviour of the world (verse 42). Although Link's redactor has some affinities with Bultmann's ecclesiastical redactor (he is interested in sacramentalism (verse 2) and futuristic eschatology (verse 14)), his most important obsession, anti-docetism, was first ascribed to him by Georg Richter.[27] Link also detects his interfering hand in the transformation of the woman into a Samaritan (verses 7, 9) and above all in the assertion that 'salvation is from the Jews' (verse 22). Ultimately, however, she agrees with Okure about the missionary thrust of the story, as it insists that the goal of all missionary endeavour is 'to lead humans to the direct experience of God in Jesus Christ' (p. 365).

## CONCLUSION

Of all the methodological options that dominate present-day exegesis of the gospels the most deplorable, it seems to me, is the almost unanimous rejection by English-speaking scholars of a diachronic approach to the text. Leaving aside all the other 'aporias' that keep rearing up from beneath John's deceptively smooth surface text, the startlingly abrupt transition in 4:16 should be enough to arouse the suspicions of any alert reader that some cutting and pasting has been going on. 'Go and fetch your husband' is a decidedly odd response to a request for water. Many commentators ignore the difficulty. Some have idiosyncratic explanations of their own. C. M. Carmichael,[28] for instance, judges that 'the switch in conversation would be inexplicable if it were not for the underlying marital theme', a suggestion that fits in with an unusually lavish treatment of that particular motif. Dorothy Lee, after acknowledging the apparent abruptness, takes the opposite view that 'the image of the second scene is dependent on the primary image of water/the well in the first scene' (*Symbolic Narratives*, pp. 74–5). M.-J. Lagrange[29] engagingly proposes that the woman's incredulity must have shown in her face and prompted Jesus to change tack ('prendre un autre ton'). J. E. Botha[30] credits Jesus with a particularly subtle strategy: having failed thus far to coax the woman on to his own wavelength, he determines to flout three key maxims generally observed in two-way conversations, those of relevancy, manner and sequencing: 'this "break" created by the flouting of maxims indicates to the other character that the current line of discussion should be terminated, and it gives Jesus the opportunity of continuing the conversation and introducing a new programme or topic' ('John 4.16a', pp. 188–9). Thus Botha cleverly justifies the apparent dislocation in terms of his speech-act theory, paradoxically underlining the extent of the difficulty as he does so. Boers disagrees: only a naive reader would be bothered by the apparent inconsequence: 'at the deeper level Jesus' command prepares for the revelation of his miraculous ability which the woman mockingly denied him by challenging him with Jacob's miracle' (*Neither on this Mountain*, p. 170). This may indeed be the right solution *on the level of the final redaction*, but not, I think, otherwise. Jürgen Becker[31] proposes that in the source what is now verse 16 followed verse 9; so too Link. This suggestion has much to be said for it, as long as we see that in the text as we have it the dialogue on living water (verses 10–15) helps to account for the woman's amazed admiration: 'I perceive that you are a prophet' (verse 19).

To adopt this solution is also to dodge Stephen Moore's strictures on those who, on reaching the five husbands, slide unreflectingly from the symbolic to the literal mode. Yet none of the suggested symbolisms is very impressive. By far the most popular of them, the false gods of the Samaritans, is open to the objection that according to 2 Kings 17 the Samaritans had seven false gods, not five, and not all male. Where arguments are inconclusive exegetes will continue to wrangle. I myself am inclined to accept Andrea Link's suggestion that the number five (which she speaks of as 'ein Annäherungswort' – an approximation) simply serves to reinforce the reader's sense of the urgency of the woman's need for the salvation proffered by Jesus (*'Was redest du mit ihr?'*, p. 269). This conversion story provided John with a framework for his own symbolic dialogue concerning living water.

The weakness of Link's work lies not in her approach or her method but in her failure to invest her redactor with the slightest verisimilitude: how could any whole-hearted anti-docetist have made such a botched job of the Gospel as a whole? The conclusion of verse 9 ('Jews have no truck with Samaritans') may, it is true, be the work of a glossator, but the remainder of the narrative is much better explained as the combination by the evangelist of two stories, one his own, one taken from a source. The best account of the problem posed by verse 22, I persist in thinking, is that of Klaus Haacker[32] (known seemingly to only a few later commentators). Haacker argues that it reflects the kind of controversy between Jews and Samaritans that is seen in Ecclesiasticus 50:25–6 and *Testament of Levi* 7. But this need not have prevented it from figuring in a document used by missionaries who were carrying the gospel from Judaea, already recognized as Jesus' native-land, into Samaria.

What then of Jacob's well? The most informative discussion of this topic, with abundant references to Jewish sources, is Jerome Neyrey's 'Jacob Traditions'. Neyrey (1979)[33] is one of the first among an increasing number of modern scholars (Bligh, 'Jesus in Samaria',[34] Carmichael, 'Marriage and the Samaritan Woman', Eslinger, 'The Wooing of the Woman', Schneiders, 'A Case Study') to take the view that the story in John is a variant of the classical Jewish betrothal scene, as found in Genesis and Exodus. But although this suggestion cannot be ruled out, a simpler explanation is ready to hand. Jacob is mentioned because he is the father of both Judah, from whom the Jews took their name, and Joseph (cf. verse 5), the greatly revered ancestor (through

Ephraim and Manasseh) of the Samaritans. Jacob's dying blessing embraced both Judah and Joseph (describing the latter as 'a fruitful bough by a spring' (Genesis 49:9–10, 22; cf. Deuteronomy 33:13–17). No doubt this view reduces the significance of the well by making it serve simply as a natural backdrop for a dialogue about water; but, as Haacker saw, it also furnishes a plausible setting for the opposition between the two sacred mountains, Gerizim and Zion.

### A NOTE ON COMMENTARIES

Boers artlessly informs his readers that from the vast array of commentaries at his disposal he limited himself to '35 of the most promising'. Time, he adds resignedly, 'can be better spent' (*Neither on this Mountain*, p. 144, n. 1). Truly much perusal of commentaries is a weariness of the flesh.

Publishers approve of commentaries, especially those that belong to a series. It is easy to see why. They sell well, especially to libraries. Occupying as they do so much space on the shelves, no interpreter of interpretations can afford to neglect them entirely.

Writing nearly a century ago, in 1904, the great Hermann Gunkel[35] made some trenchant remarks about biblical commentaries of his own day. He was struck by the vast array of information that they provide, in an almost limitless profusion ('eine fast unübersehbare Fülle') that can only bewilder beginners and is hardly likely to satisfy more experienced readers. He gloomily concluded that despite the extraordinary variety of the fare on offer one thing is in danger of being left behind, and that is the text!

Gunkel was writing primarily of the exegesis of the Old Testament, but said himself that most of his comments apply equally well to the New. In the case of John's Gospel there is only one commentary that escapes the pitfalls he so ruthlessly reveals, and that is Rudolf Bultmann's magisterial *Das Evangelium des Johannes*,[36] which did not appear in English until three decades after its publication in Germany during the war (1941). Despite the many criticisms that can be made of this work, Bultmann penetrates to the heart of John's message with extraordinary insight, focusing unerringly on the evangelist's special interest in revelation, not least in the passage under discussion. Convinced as he is of the abiding relevance of Jesus' life-giving message, he conveys it to his own readers, if they allow themselves to be led by him, with great urgency and power. This is probably the greatest commentary on any New Testament writing in the second millennium, and leaves one wondering what may be expected from the third.

## Notes

1 The same cannot be said, unfortunately, of the Johannine Epistles, whose precise relationship with the Gospel is still disputed by scholars. Judith Lieu discusses this question with fairness and lucidity in *The Theology of the Johannine Epistles* (Cambridge: Cambridge University Press, 1991).

2 David Daube has suggested an alternative meaning to the usual 'have dealings with', that is 'use the same utensils as': 'Jesus and the Samaritan Woman: The Meaning of συγχράομαι', *Journal of Biblical Literature* 69 (1950), pp. 137–47. In my view this would not significantly affect the interpretation of the episode as a whole.

3 L. Schottroff, 'Johannes 4; 5–15 und die Konsequenzen des johanneischen Dualismus', *Zeitschrift für die neutestamentliche Wissenschaft* 60 (1969), pp. 199–214.

4 A. Link, *'Was redest du mit ihr?' Eine Studie zur Exegese-, Redaktions- und Theologiegeschichte von Joh 4, 1–42* (Regensburg: Friedrich Pustet, 1992).

5 A. Schlatter, *Der Evangelist Johannes: Wie er spricht, denkt und glaubt. Ein Kommentar zum vierten Evangelium*⁴ (Stuttgart: Calwer, 1975), p. vii.

6 R. Bultmann, *The Gospel of John* (Oxford: Blackwell, 1971) (= *Das Evangelium des Johannes* (Göttingen: Vandenhoeck & Ruprecht, 1941), with the Supplement of 1966).

7 C. H. Dodd, *The Interpretation of the Fourth Gospel* (Cambridge: Cambridge University Press, 1953).

8 R. E. Brown, *The Gospel According to John*, 2 vols., Anchor Bible 29 and 29A (New York: Doubleday, 1966/70).

9 For a full defence of this view of the Gospel see ch. 11 ('The Gospel Genre') of J. Ashton, *Understanding the Fourth Gospel* (Oxford: Clarendon Press, 1991), pp. 407–42.

10 G. R. O'Day, *Revelation in the Fourth Gospel* (Philadelphia: Fortress Press, 1986), pp. 49–92.

11 D. A. Lee, *The Symbolic Narratives of the Fourth Gospel. The Interplay of Form and Meaning*, JSNT Supplement Series 95 (Sheffield: JSOT Press, 1994), pp. 64–97.

12 A. Loisy, *Le Quatrième Évangile* (Paris: Picard et fils, 1903), p. 354, n. 1.

13 H. Boers, *Neither on this Mountain nor in Jerusalem. A Study of John 4*, SBL Monograph Series no. 35 (Atlanta, GA: Scholars Press, 1988), p. 148.

14 B. Olsson, *Structure and Meaning in the Fourth Gospel: A Text-Linguistic Analysis of John 2: 1–11 and 4: 1–42* (Lund: CWK Gleerup, 1974).

15 J. E. Botha, *Jesus and the Samaritan Woman. A Speech Act Reading of John 4. 1–42*, Supplements to *Novum Testamentum* 65 (Leiden: Brill, 1991).

16 Notably by Christopher Rowland in his inaugural lecture as Dean Ireland Professor of the Exegesis of Holy Scripture, University of Oxford: '"Open thy Mouth for the Dumb". A Task for the Exegete of Holy Scripture', *Biblical Interpretation* 1 (1993), pp. 228–45.

17 F. Roustang, 'Les Moments de l'acte de foi et ses conditions de possibilité. Essai d'interprétation du dialogue avec la Samaritaine', *Recherches de science religieuse* 46 (1958), pp. 344–78.

18 E. Drewermann, *Tiefenpsychologie und Exegese*, 2 vols. (2nd edn, Olten/Freiburg im Breisgau: Walter, 1991).

19 S. D. Moore, 'Are There Impurities in the Living Water that the Johannine Jesus Dispenses? Deconstruction, Feminism, and the Samaritan Woman', *Biblical Interpretation* 1 (1993), pp. 207–27.

20 Raymond Brown is less censorious, finding the woman 'mincing and coy, with a certain light grace' (*The Gospel According to John*, p. 175).

21 S. M. Schneiders, 'A Case Study: A Feminist Interpretation of John 4: 1–42', in *The Revelatory Text: Interpreting the New Testament as Sacred Scripture* (San Francisco: HarperCollins, 1991), pp. 180–99.

22 L. Eslinger, 'The Wooing of the Woman at the Well: Jesus, the Reader and Reader-response Criticism', *Literature and Theology* 1 (1987), pp. 167–83.

23 E. Schüssler-Fiorenza, *In Memory of Her. A Feminist Theological Reconstruction of Christian Origins* (New York: Crossroads, 1983).

24 T. Okure, *The Johannine Approach to Mission: A Contextual Study of John 4: 1–42* (Tübingen: J. C. B. Mohr (Paul Siebeck), 1988).

25 X. Léon-Dufour, *Lecture de L'Évangile selon saint Jean*, vol. 1 (Paris: Seuil, 1988), pp. 339–95. For other examples of 'discursive readings' see O'Day, *Revelation in the Fourth Gospel*; Lee, *The Symbolic Narratives*.

26 '*Was redest du mit ihr?*'

27 G. Richter, *Studien zum Johannesevangelium*, Biblische Untersuchungen 13, ed. J. Hainz (Regensburg: Friedrich Pustet, 1977).

28 C. M. Carmichael, 'Marriage and the Samaritan Woman', *New Testament Studies* 26 (1980), pp. 332–46.

29 M.-J. Lagrange, *Évangile selon Saint Jean* (7th edn, Paris: J. Gabalda, 1948), p. 109.

30 J. E. Botha, 'John 4.16a: A Difficult Text Speech Act Theoretically Revisited', in M. W. G. Stibbe (ed.), *The Gospel of John as Literature: An Anthology of Twentieth-Century Perspectives* (Leiden: Brill, 1993), pp. 183–92.

31 J. Becker, *Das Evangelium des Johannes*, 2 vols., Ökumenischer Taschenbuch-Kommentar zum Neuen Testament 4/1–2 (Gütersloh: Gerd Mohn, 1979/81), p. 165.

32 K. Haacker, 'Gottesdienst ohne Gotteserkenntnis. Joh 4, 22 vor dem Hintergrund der jüdisch-samaritanischen Auseinandersetzung', *Wort und Wortlichkeit: Fs. E. Rapp*, ed. B. Benzing et al., vol. 1 (Meisenheim am Glan: Hain, 1976), pp. 110–26. For a full discussion of the significance of the phrase in the context of the whole gospel see J. Ashton, *Studying John: Approaches to the Fourth Gospel* (Oxford: Clarendon Press, 1994), pp. 44–9.

33 J. H. Neyrey, 'Jacob Traditions and the Interpretation of John 4: 10–26', *Catholic Biblical Quarterly* 41 (1979), pp. 419–37. The fullest information on the various ideas associated with water is to be found in H. Odeberg, *The Fourth Gospel*

*Interpreted in its Relation to Contemporaneous Religious Currents in Palestine and the Hellenistic-Oriental World* (Uppsala: Almquist & Wilksell, 1929), pp. 149–70.

34 J. Bligh, 'Jesus in Samaria', *Heythrop Journal* 3 (1962), pp. 329–46.

35 H. Gunkel, 'Ziele und Methoden der Erklärung des Alten Testamentes', *Reden und Aufsätze* (Göttingen: Vandenhoeck & Ruprecht, 1913), pp. 11–29.

36 *The Gospel of John*. For a critical appreciation of Bultmann's work on John, see ch. 2 of Ashton, *Understanding the Fourth Gospel*, pp. 44–66.

## Further reading

*Commentaries*

Barrett, C. K., *The Gospel According to John*, 2nd edn, London: SPCK, 1978.

Becker, J., *Das Evangelium des Johannes*, 2 vols., Gütersloh: Gerd Mohn, 1979/81.

Brown, R. E., *The Gospel According to John*, 2 vols., New York: Doubleday, 1966/70.

Bultmann, R., *The Gospel of John: A Commentary*, Oxford: Blackwell, 1971.

Lindars, B., *The Gospel of John*, London: Oliphants, 1972.

Schnackenburg, R., *The Gospel According to St John*, 3 vols., London: Burns & Oates, 1968/80/82.

*Other books*

Ashton, J., *Understanding the Fourth Gospel*, Oxford: Clarendon Press, 1991.
*Studying John: Approaches to the Fourth Gospel*, Oxford: Clarendon Press, 1994.

Brown, R. E., *The Community of the Beloved Disciple: The Life, Loves and Hates of an Individual Church in New Testament Times*, London: Geoffrey Chapman, 1979.

Dodd, C. H., *The Interpretation of the Fourth Gospel*, Cambridge, Cambridge University Press, 1953.

Käsemann, E., *The Testament of Jesus: A Study of the Gospel of John in the Light of Chapter 17*, London: SCM Press, 1968.

Martyn, J. L., *History and Theology in the Fourth Gospel*, 2nd edn, Nashville: Abingdon Press, 1979.

Rensberger, D., *Overcoming the World: Politics and Community in the Gospel of John*, London: SPCK, 1989 (published in the USA as *Johannine Faith and Liberating Community*, Philadelphia: Westminster Press, 1988).

Smith, D. M., *The Theology of the Gospel of John*, Cambridge: Cambridge University Press, 1995.

# 18 The Pauline Letters

JAMES DUNN

Paul is undoubtedly the most important Christian thinker of all time. His letters are the only Christian writings we can confidently date to the first generation of Christianity; they define the first distinctives of Christian faith as do no other New Testament documents. They reflect and document the most crucial period in Christian history – the expansion of a Jewish messianic sect into the non-Jewish world, the emergence of Christianity as a (soon to be) predominantly Gentile religion. And their theology has been a primary formative influence in most of the great theological confessions and statements of the Christian churches to the present day. Their interpretation has therefore always been at the heart of attempts to understand Christian beginnings and to reformulate Christian faith and life.

## THE EXTENT OF THE PAULINE CORPUS

The initial task in the study of the Pauline Letters has traditionally been the introductory issues of authenticity, date and circumstances, and these remain basic to sound interpretation. Fortunately the areas of disagreement have been relatively few. The letters were written in the course of Paul's work as a Christian missionary. That work extended from the mid-30s AD (soon after his conversion) to the early 60s, when he was executed, according to popular tradition, in Rome. The period of the letter-writing was much briefer, covering only the last ten to fifteen years of his life. This means, among other things, that the letters come from Paul's most mature period; none of them is the work of a young Christian or inexperienced missionary; they all reflect considerable experience and developed reflection on the Christian gospel. We may not deduce from this that there is no development in Paul's thought from letter to letter; but we should be cautious about assuming that such development was inevitable.

In fact, the most important of the letters come from a single seven or so year period of missionary work in the region of the Aegean (starting about

50 AD), when Paul used first Corinth (in Greece) and then Ephesus (in Asia Minor) as his base of operations. From these headquarters he probably wrote 1 and 2 Thessalonians, Galatians, 1 and 2 Corinthians, Romans, and possibly Philippians, Colossians and Philemon. This period was also the flood tide of Paul's success (cf. Romans 15:17–20), so that these letters reflect the vibrancy of the most provocative and successful of the first Christian missionaries. The last three letters just named, however, the so-called 'prison epistles', may well have been written during Paul's imprisonment in Rome, some four to six years later.

Not all the letters which name Paul as their author are usually attributed to him by modern scholars. Those already named above do not include Ephesians and the Pastoral epistles (1 and 2 Timothy and Titus), which most scholars regard as post-Pauline (written by a disciple after Paul's death), and pseudepigraphic (written in Paul's name). These four letters extend the period covered by the Pauline letters probably for another twenty or thirty years. 2 Thessalonians and Colossians are also regarded by many scholars as post-Pauline, but such a conclusion regarding the former probably depends on a too rigid concept of Paul's thought and pastoral advice, and in the latter case, as we shall see, it is more likely that the letter was actually composed by a close collaborator on Paul's behalf.

The debate on the acceptability of pseudepigraphic writings in the New Testament canon remains unresolved. However, despite assertions to the contrary, the practice of pseudepigraphy need not have involved any intention to deceive or success in so doing. The tradition of the biblical writings, as represented by documents like the Pentateuch, Isaiah and the Gospels, was of a living tradition which could be elaborated and extended for some time after the death of its authoritative originator, with the elaboration and extension still regarded as formulated in the name of the originator. In other words, Ephesians and the Pastoral epistles can be regarded as properly 'Pauline', at least in the sense that they show the continuing influence of Paul's personality and thought in the years and changing situations following his death. Somewhat like the tail of a comet, they tell us something about the comet itself. As the first heirs of Paul's legacy, and recognized by the churches as such (that is, as the proprietors of Paul's name), the Pauline school continued to be a major factor in the growth of Christianity in the Aegean region and in the further shaping of Christian thought.

It should also be noted that not all Paul's letters were preserved for posterity. We know of one or two more letters to the Corinthian church (particularly 1 Corinthians 5:9) and of a letter to the church in Laodicea (Colossians

4:16) which have been lost. And we can hardly exclude the possibility that Paul wrote others which have likewise perished. This reminds us that all Paul's letters were occasional, not intended to become foundation documents for the whole of Christianity. Some presumably were not welcomed or appreciated and may even have been deliberately destroyed. Others may have become lost or destroyed by accident. The more important point for us, however, is the contrary fact that others were preserved and treasured, presumably because their authoritative voice was welcomed. Moreover, as they were passed around other churches (cf. again Colossians 4:16) and read again and again and more widely, their relevance beyond the situations of the particular churches for which they were written was no doubt increasingly recognized. In this way, we may presume, their authoritative status steadily grew, so that in due course, their presence within the earliest Christian (New Testament) canon was a matter of wide and unquestioned acceptance from the first.

## CURRENT ISSUES IN INTERPRETATION

Alongside the traditional evaluation of Paul's letters as the first exposition of Christian theology, three other features have come to particular prominence in the last two decades.

The first is the analysis of the letters as literature. Recent study has noted afresh that all the letters display Paul's familiarity with the epistolary and standard rhetorical conventions of the day. He begins each with the conventional 'from' and 'to' address and greeting, and in most cases he expresses his thanks and prayers on behalf of the recipients before embarking on his main theme. Likewise at the end he regularly indicates his travel plans, appends a sequence of greetings and closes with a personal note and final benediction – patterns familiar to us from the literary and personal letters known to us from antiquity. At the same time, Paul regularly elaborates these conventional rituals, by expanding his own claims for a hearing from his readers, by his characteristic transformation of the greeting ('grace and peace' instead of the normal Jewish 'peace' and the normal Greek 'greeting'), by his extension of the prayer and thanksgiving sequence and by inclusion of particular charges and messages in the conclusion. Even in the most conventional sections of his letters Paul showed himself to be no slave to convention, but one who felt free to adapt his chosen form to the demands of his message.

The same is even more true of the main body of his letters, which transforms them into a unique form for their day – neither a letter proper, as would be generally recognized, nor a treatise as such, but somewhere in between. Nor can they be readily classified in the standard terms and distinctions of classical rhetoric, since the content and sequence seem always to be structured according to the logic of Paul's thought and the circumstances addressed. Paul knew well enough the forms of effective communication, but he demonstrates his literary genius in the way he adapted them to his own purposes.

The other current foci of interest are the use of sociological perspectives and models to shed fresh light on the situations addressed and on the internal dynamic of the letters, and Paul's particular concerns in reformulating the gospel of a Jewish Messiah for Gentile faith. The former has been particularly fruitful in the case of 1 Corinthians, and the latter comes to particular prominence in Galatians and Romans.

### THE LETTERS THEMSELVES

Within the New Testament itself the tradition has been long established that the letters of Paul are ordered in a sequence of diminishing length – starting with Romans, the longest, and ending with Philemon, the shortest. They are best reviewed, however, in the most probable sequence of composition, which should allow us to note any relevant indication of development in Paul's thought. The sequence is far from certain, as we shall see; and the hypothesis of development has always to be qualified by the likelihood that the particular emphases of particular letters were determined in large part by the particular circumstances addressed.

1 and 2 Thessalonians. One or both were certainly written from Corinth in the period described in Acts 18.11. That they are the first of Paul's letters to be preserved is made likely by three features.

One is the fact that in the Thessalonian correspondence Paul does not emphasize his status as apostle, as he does thereafter in almost all his letters. The reason may be given by the (probably) next letter, Galatians, which is Paul's reaction on learning that his apostleship was under question from his opponents. It was presumably this shock which caused him thereafter to emphasize his apostleship more or less as a matter of routine in the opening greetings of his letters.

The second is the related fact that from Galatians onwards we gain a clear and repeatedly confirmed impression that Paul's gospel focused on God's justification (acceptance) of all who believe (Gentile as well as Jew).

The inference is probably fair that it was the same challenge from events in Galatia which caused Paul to highlight this feature of his teaching, what was proving to be his distinctive emphasis among the various Christian missionaries active in Asia Minor and in the Aegean region. In contrast, there is no hint of Paul's distinctive gospel in the Thessalonian letters.

The third is the distinctive character of the teaching of 1 and 2 Thessalonians themselves. The first letter was evidently written some time after Paul's departure from Thessalonica (1 Thessalonians 2:17–18). It was a general pastoral letter of encouragement, but evidently occasioned particularly by anxiety arising from the eschatological teaching which Paul had left with them. Paul had evidently made much of the future (imminent) return of Jesus from heaven (1 Thessalonians 1:9–10; 2:12, 19; 3:13). And this had caused confusion among the Thessalonian believers when some of their number had unexpectedly died. Hence the central teaching of the letter (4:13–5:11), which reassures them that those who have died will not be disadvantaged alongside those still alive at Jesus' coming (4:13–18), but which does little to slacken the eschatological anticipation (5:2–6, 23).

2 Thessalonians seems to be a further response to a situation in which the eschatological excitement had got out of hand. There was teaching, purporting to be from Paul, to the effect that the day of the Lord had already come (2 Thessalonians 2:2) and some of the believers had given up their work, presumably on the assumption that the end of all things was at hand (3:6–13). Paul's response is to maintain the eschatological emphasis (1:5–12), but to explain that, in the tradition of Jewish apocalyptic writings (e.g. Daniel 12:1) and of Jesus' own teaching (Mark 13:5–27), a period of great suffering and deception must first intervene (2 Thessalonians 2:3–12).

Galatians is one of the fiercest and most polemical writings within the Bible. The parallels with Romans are so close that many conclude the two letters were written within a few months of each other. But at most about six years separated them, so that similarity of theme and emphasis is explicable on either dating. It is more likely that the news from Galatia which provoked the letter came during Paul's sojourn in Corinth in the early 50s, causing Paul to emphasize the fact of his apostleship (Galatians 1:1, 11–17) and the distinctive character of his gospel (1:6–9; 2:5–9, 15–21) in his response and thereafter.

The crisis had been caused by other missionaries (1:6–7), Christian Jews (as all agree), trying to convince Paul's Gentile converts in Galatia that in order to share in the inheritance of Abraham's blessing and offspring they had to be circumcised, that is, to become proselytes, converts to Judaism (5:2–12; 6:12). Paul's response was to remind them that the Jerusalem apostles had agreed that no such requirement was necessary for Gentile believers (2:1–10). And though in the incident at Antioch (2:11–14), a focus for much recent debate, the Jewish believers had acted on the assumption that it was necessary for them as Jews to continue to observe the food laws which normally prevented Jews from eating with Gentiles, Paul was in no doubt that such a continuing practice undermined the gospel of God's acceptance only through faith in Christ (2:15–21).

The main body of the letter is a passionate exposition of this gospel: that the (Gentile) Galatians themselves had experienced God's acceptance (the Spirit) solely through their believing what Paul had preached (3:1–5); that Abraham, the father of Israel, was justified (accepted) by God on the basis of his trust in God; and that the blessing of the nations promised to Abraham must therefore be on the basis of the same trust (3:6–14). The law, on which the other missionaries based their teaching, Paul argues had only a temporary role in relation to Israel (during which the requirement of circumcision was appropriate). But now that Christ had come, the extension of Abraham's faith and blessing to non-Jews could be unrestricted (3:15–4:7). Whereas, to require circumcision of Gentiles was in effect to force them back into the period before the blessing and Spirit of God could be so freely and widely enjoyed (4:8–11; 5:3–6; 6:13–15). Fundamental here, then, is Paul's conception of Christianity as an extension of Israel, in fulfilment of the promise to Abraham.

1 Corinthians was written after Paul had left Corinth and was on one of his travels through the Aegean region (or in Ephesus?), in the early to mid 50s. It was dictated in response to several requests, by letter and by delegation, for advice on a number of difficult pastoral issues (1 Corinthians 1:11; 7:1; 16:17). It is arguably the most interesting of Paul's letters, for it 'takes the lid' off one of the earliest Christian churches and shows us the reality of what a (presumably not untypical) church was in the beginning. It is well worth viewing the letter from this perspective.

As recent sociological study has reminded us, the Corinthian church consisted in one or more small groups, meeting in members' houses; 'the whole church' in Corinth could meet in the home of one, presumably well-to-do member (Romans 16:23); that is, the whole Corinthian church may only have been about forty strong. Despite a tendency to factionalism, the members were bonded by their initial reception of the message about Jesus, by the baptism through which they had expressed that belief and commitment to Christ, and by their common experience of acceptance through the Spirit (1 Corinthians 1:10–16; 6:11; 12:13). They were of mixed social status (1:26–30), and social tensions were a major factor in the problems posed to Paul (6:1–6; 11:18–22). They (or different individuals among them) were considerably influenced by the cultural presuppositions of the time: in the high esteem they gave to rhetoric (2:1–5), in the ethical standards from which some found it hard to free themselves (5–6), in the social practices which those of high social status took for granted as part of their life-style (8; 10:14–11:1), in the degree to which they were impressed by experiences of ecstatic inspiration (12:2; 14:12), and in questioning or ridiculing the idea that the body could be raised from the dead (15:12, 35).

In his response Paul provides several unforgettable passages: warning against factionalism within a church (1:10–16), contrasting divine wisdom with wisdom as commonly perceived (1:17–2:5), instructing in believers' responsibility to build wisely and well on the foundation of Christ (3:10–17), rebuking a triumphalism which takes no account of human suffering (4:8–13), steering a careful path between isolation from the world and uncritical conformity to the world's standards (6–7, 8–10), emphasizing the supreme importance of love above even that of the charism of prophecy (13), and sketching out the Christian hope of a future resurrection of the body patterned on that of Christ (15:20–50).

Not least of importance in the letter are its specific references to Jesus' own teaching (exceptional in the Pauline Letters) (7:10; 9:14), particularly the recollection of the institution of the Lord's Supper (11:23–6), and the earliest record of the gospel (passed on to Paul at his conversion within about two years of Jesus' crucifixion) (15:3–7). Most confusing for twentieth-century Christians is the tension in Paul's teaching on marriage (7; but 7:1b is probably a quotation from the Corinthians) and on the role of women in worship (11:2–16; 14:34–6). In each case he was probably trying to steer a middle course between the liberty and demands of the Christian gospel and the social mores of tradition and contemporary society.

2 Corinthians is the most difficult of Paul's letters to grasp as a whole. This is because it seems to be something of a composite. That is to say, its present form may well be the result of different letters of Paul being put together either when his letters were circulated or when they began to be collected into a single corpus. The features which many think point to this conclusion are (1) the abruptness of the transition and change of mood at the beginning

of chapter 10 – so that 10–13 might possibly be identified with the angry letter referred to in 2:3–4; (2) the fact that chapters 8 and 9 seem to be almost self-standing as one or two letters on the theme of the collection Paul was making for the poor Christians in Jerusalem; and (3) the awkwardness of 6:14–7:1, which looks as though it could be an insertion into an otherwise fluent sequence. However, whether one letter or several letters, 2 Corinthians was certainly part of the communication Paul had with the Corinthian church during his Aegean mission in the mid 50s.

The two most striking themes in the letter(s) are on ministry and suffering. The two are connected. Paul writes first to defend his understanding of ministry. It would appear that, rather as in Galatians, Paul's authority was coming under attack from (probably) other Christian Jewish missionaries (11:4, 13). They were basing their claim to authority on the letters of recommendation with which they came (from Jerusalem?) (3:1; 10:9), on the rhetorical skills which they displayed (10:10–12; 11:5), and on the miracles which they performed (12:11–12). They had also been able to make capital from Paul's seeming vacillation in his travel plans (1:15–2:4), from his previous angry letter (2:3–13) and from Paul's insistence on supporting himself (11:7–12). In response Paul spells out his own concept of apostolic ministry, as marked and attested by the Spirit in contrast to the letter of the law (3), and as focusing openly on Christ, as a ministry of reconciliation (4:1–6; 5:11–21). And he registers a clear protest against those who trespass in his field of mission (10:13–16; possibly referring to the division of labour agreed in Galatians 2:7–9).

The most striking mark of his ministry, however, is its suffering – and precisely as a sharing in Christ's suffering (1:3–7), as the manifestation of Christ's life in the midst of a dying humanity (4:7–5:5). This was a lesson Paul had earlier learned: that the power of Christ came to expression characteristically not in experiences of exultation and ecstatic transport, but in and through his own all too human weakness (12:1–10; 13:3–4). 2 Corinthians thus provides the basis for a potentially powerful Christian theology of suffering, and a warning against any assumption that Christian discipleship will necessarily be marked by experiences of glory and self-transcendence; the way to glory is through the cross and not otherwise.

Romans is the most important of Paul's letters so far as his teaching and theology are concerned. It was written almost certainly from Corinth at the close of this phase of Paul's missionary work (15:18–23), when he hoped to take the collection he had gathered from among his Gentile churches to

Jerusalem (1 Corinthians 16:1–3; 2 Corinthians 8:1–4) – but he was nervous about its being accepted (Romans 15:31) – and then to visit the church in Rome on his way to a new missionary venture in Spain (15:24–8). In view of this larger context, and in view of the fact that he had never previously visited Rome (the church was not of his founding – cf. 2 Corinthians 10:16 and Romans 15:20), Paul thought it appropriate to set out his gospel (Romans 1:16–17, the thematic statement of the letter) with care, in orderly fashion and in some detail. This is not to say that Romans is simply a theological treatise, unrelated to the situation of the church in Rome itself. That is an old view, not much entertained today. On the contrary, the treatment in the later chapters, particularly 13:1–7 and 14:1–15:6, shows a lively awareness on Paul's part of the social and political circumstances within which the congregations in Rome had to live out their common life.

The main theological exposition (1:16–11:36) provides the first and classic pattern of a systematically structured Christian theology. It begins with a statement of God's righteousness, the obligation God has taken upon himself to save humankind from its own folly, a salvation which comes to effect through faith (1:16–17). It then contrasts the predicament of humankind, seemingly secure in its delusion of independence from God, but in reality caught in a baser dependence of self-gratification (1:18–32). With chapter 2 the principal counterpoint theme is introduced – Israel's assumption that it stands in a favoured relation with God, which will secure its standing before God in the final judgement. Paul seeks to burst that bubble of presumption: all are in need of God's acceptance (2:1–3:20). The means by which that acceptance is secured is outlined briefly (evidently it was noncontroversial in Christian circles) in 3:21–6, and then Paul presses home his argument that all, Jew and Gentile alike, are accepted by God only through faith (3:27–4:25).

Chapter 5 sets this conclusion within the span of human history, from Adam to Christ. The next three chapters clarify how the conclusion fares in the face of the continuing realities of death, sin and flesh (human nature), clarifying in each case the tension between a process of salvation begun but not yet completed, and the role of the Jewish law within that process, and presenting the Spirit as the power from God which enables the believer to live through that tension in confidence that God's purpose in Christ will be finally fulfilled.

This confidence in God's faithfulness simply raises afresh the troubling question of that same faithfulness to God's chosen people Israel, to which Paul devotes the climax of his theological exposition (9–11). In it Paul defends God's faithfulness in two ways. First, he defines Israel in terms of God's call/choice, and not in terms of physical descent or religious practice (9:6–14). That call of God comes to fulfilment through faith (now faith in God's Christ), and so Gentiles can experience it as much as Jews (9:24–10:17). Second, the reverse side of God's call is his rejection of those not called (9:14–23). But this seemingly harsh predestinarian doctrine is qualified by the overarching theme of God's mercy (9:15–16, 18, 23), by the slow unveiling of Paul's belief that the subjects of God's hardening are not now Gentiles (as opposed to Jews) but the bulk of the Jews as opposed to the influx of Gentiles (11:7–10, 25) and by the final revelation that this is a temporary phase in God's purpose whose climax will be God showing mercy to all (11:11–12, 15, 26–32). The vision is noble, and aims to prick the bubble of Gentile arrogance (11:13–25a) as much as that of Jewish presumption.

This vision then becomes the basis for an exhortation to the Roman Christians to live in harmony together, drawing on the insights and experience of traditional Jewish wisdom (12–13) and with traditionalist and more liberal fully accepting each other (14:1–15:7), before concluding with a final flurry of scriptures which confirm the divine intention for Jew and Gentile to worship together (15:7–13). Contemporary scholarship, however, remains divided on whether Paul's vision is a despairing attempt to solve the fundamental problem of Jewish rejection of Messiah Jesus or the basis of a fundamental identification of Jew and Christian as together constituting the Israel of God's purpose.

Philippians is the first of the four letters which were written from prison. A strongly persisting tradition in New Testament scholarship is convinced that Paul was imprisoned for a time in Ephesus, during his Aegean mission, and that Philippians, Colossians and Philemon were written during that imprisonment. Since Colossae, where also Philemon lived, was only a hundred or so miles from Ephesus, and Philippi within a few days journey by sea, the hypothesis continues to prove attractive. In which case, in a chronological sequence, these letters would have to be placed earlier than Romans. However, we have no independent record of such an imprisonment in Ephesus, and the better attested and (initially) liberal imprisonment in Rome itself (Acts 28:30) is probably, on a fine balance, the more likely place of origin for these letters.

Philippians is often regarded as the most delightful of all Paul's preserved letters. This is because its primary concern is not to rebuke or warn, so much as to thank the Philippians for their very active concern on his behalf

(4:10–19). As has often been noted, the language of 'joy/rejoice' occurs in Philippians more intensively than in Paul's other letters. Paul writes as one delighted that, despite some rivalry among Christians in his place of imprisonment, the gospel is being preached (1:12–18), conscious that his death may be near (1:19–26) and keen that his converts should stand firm in the faith (1:27–30). The appeal for genuine mutual concern (2:1–5) is rooted in the portrayal of Christ's humility in a passage usually taken to be an early Christian hymn (2:6–11). An unexpected interruption (3:2) recalls the fierce warnings of Galatians 5 and 2 Corinthians 10–11, and provides the occasion for a powerful restatement of Paul's gospel and of his understanding of the already/not yet tension of the process of salvation which is the Christian life (3:3–16).

Philemon and Colossians are best taken together, since they were almost certainly written to the same place (Colossae) and at about the same time (cf. Colossians 4:10–14 with Philemon 23–4). As with Philippians, the date and place of writing depend on whether the hypothesis of an Ephesian imprisonment is acceptable. Perhaps decisive in favour of a later date is the fact that Colossians was composed by (not just dictated to) someone other than Paul, as the closest analysis of the style and literary technique of the letter has demonstrated, and the impression which the letter gives that its thought has developed some way from that found in the earlier Pauline letters (cf. particularly Colossians 1:15–20 with 1 Corinthians 8:6, and 2:19 with 1 Corinthians 12:21). At the same time, the details of the final instructions (4:7–17) and the character of the final autograph (4:18) suggest that Paul had been able to approve the letter composed in the joint names of himself and Timothy (probably therefore by Timothy) before adding his own signature. In which case Colossians provides a kind of bridge between the undisputed Pauline letters and the post-Pauline letters, and demonstrates the extent to which the former merged into the latter.

Philemon is the only genuinely personal letter in the Pauline corpus, even though it is clear enough that Paul expected the letter to be read out in the church meeting (2, and the plurals of 22 and 25). In this way Paul was able to put gentle pressure on Philemon, while reminding him that the church could be expected to provide support in a difficult personal decision. The delicacy of the situation is that Onesimus, Philemon's slave, had sought out Paul to intercede for him on a point where Philemon thought Onesimus was in the wrong; this hypothesis fits the facts and the laws governing slaves better than the usual hypothesis that Onesimus was a thief and a runaway.

Paul pleads with a sense of the anomalies of their comparative status (Philemon, the well-to-do householder, converted by Paul, now in prison). The letter gives one of the clearest insights into the realities of slavery in the ancient world.

Colossians is the only other letter in the Pauline corpus (apart from Romans) explicitly written to a church not founded by Paul himself. It had in fact been founded by Epaphras, probably on a mission from Paul's base in Ephesus to the cities of the Lycus valley where he (Epaphras) had been brought up. It is usually likened to Galatians, as being a fervent plea for the Colossian believers not to be swayed by false teaching. The debate about the character of the teaching has been long and complex, but it is usually understood to be a form of syncretistic teaching, with elements from Judaism and early gnostic speculation mixed in.

The letter itself, however, is remarkably relaxed about the threat: it only begins to emerge in 2:4 (contrast Galatians 1:6), and is not at all so fierce as is the polemic of Galatians. At the same time, the sensitive points of conflict do seem similar to those in Galatians – circumcision (2:11–13; 3:11), festivals and food laws (2:16, 21), that is, the characteristic and distinctive marks of traditional Judaism – with beliefs regarding 'elemental forces' (2:8, 20; cf. Galatians 4:3, 9) and mystical worship with angels (2:18; as at Qumran) added in for good measure. Moreover, the assumption is that the Gentile believers addressed have entered fully into Israel's inheritance (1:2 – 'saints'; 1:12; 3:12). And the problem seems to be that such claims are being disqualified by the practitioners of these rituals and mystical worship (2:16, 18). The more likely identification of the Colossian trouble, therefore, is that one or more of the Colossian synagogues, long established in the city, were being dismissive of the new little sect's claims.

The letter is written, therefore, to bolster their convictions about the truly cosmic significance of Christ and of what he had accomplished on the cross (particularly 1:15–20, another early Christ-hymn?, and 2:9–15), with some more conventional ethical exhortations added on (3:5–4:6) to encourage a life-style which would impress their neighbours and secure them against suspicions of fomenting unrest (particularly the household rules in 3:18–4:1).

Ephesians is one of the greater puzzles in the Pauline corpus. Almost certainly the 'in Ephesus' of 1:1 is a later insertion, and, unlike the typical Pauline letter, reference to particular issues and people is markedly lacking. Its style is unlike anything else in the Pauline corpus, marked by very long sentences, repetitions and redundancies; it also has a notably liturgical ring (1:15–3:21 has the character of a long prayer), and seems to draw on the language of Colossians at many points (cf. e.g. Ephesians 6:5–9 with Colossians 3:22–4:1; Ephesians 6:2–11 with Colossians 4:7–8). Its perspective seems to be second generation (particularly 2:20), and the theological themes seem to have been developed beyond even those of Colossians (cf. Ephesians 1:22–3 with Colossians 1:17–19), with 'the church' now understood as universal (not the local churches of the earlier letters), and the eschatology more 'realized' in character (particularly 2:2–6, 8). It looks very much, therefore, as though the letter was written by a disciple of Paul some time after Paul's death, very likely as a way of summing up and celebrating Paul's faith and apostolic achievement, and probably using Colossians as a kind of template.

The most notable feature is 2:11–22, which provides one of the clearest statements of Paul's vision of Jew and Gentile integrated within eschatological Israel, the old alienations and barriers broken down through Christ. Equally striking is the elaboration of Paul's older 'mystery' language (Romans 11:25) in a way which enhances the role of Paul himself (Ephesians 3:1–13). The traditional Jewish confession of God as one has been set as the climax of a fuller Christian confession (4:4–6). And the vision of the church is much more ambitious (not only 4:11–16, but also 1:22–3, 2:21–2 and 5:25–32). Despite its pseudonymous origin, the description of Ephesians as 'the quintessence of Paulinism' is not unjustified.

The Pastorals are usually dated in the last two decades of the first century, though opposing minority opinions argue on the one hand for Pauline authorship during a later imprisonment in Rome, and on the other for a date in the third quarter of the second century. Most likely they represent Paulinism at a stage when the memory of the great apostle was still fresh, and an attempt to draw on his legacy to meet the challenges, including some early form of Gnosticism (particularly 1 Timothy 6:20), confronting a movement well into its second generation of existence. Prominent in the response is a firmer fixing of 'the faith', 'the (sound/good) teaching', 'the faithful sayings', and a more structured form of ministry and church organization (overseers, deacons, elders). See further chapter 19 in this volume: 'The non-Pauline Letters', by Frances Young.

## Further reading

Barrett, C. K., *Paul: An Introduction to his Thought*, London: Chapman, 1994.

Doty, W. G., *Letters in Primitive Christianity*, Philadelphia: Fortress Press, 1973.

Dunn, J. D. G., *The Theology of Paul the Apostle*, Grand Rapids: Eerdmans; Edinburgh: T. & T. Clark, 1997.

Keck, L. E., *Paul and His Letters*, Philadelphia: Fortress Press, 1979.

Meade, David, *Pseudonymity and Canon*, Tübingen: Mohr, 1986.

Murphy-O'Connor, J., *Paul the Letter-Writer: His World, His Options, His Skills*, Collegeville, MN: Liturgica/Glazier, 1995.

Roetzel, C. J., *The Letters of Paul: Conversations in Context*, London: SCM Press, 1983.

Trobisch, D., *Paul's Letter Collection: Tracing the Origins*, Minneapolis: Fortress Press, 1994.

Ziesler, J., *Pauline Christianity*, Oxford: Oxford University Press, 1983, 2nd edn 1990.

There are also two series of which individual volumes are available, but which will be complete over the next few years:

(1) Dunn, J. D. G. (ed.), New Testament Theology, Cambridge University Press, including the following:

J. Murphy-O'Connor, *2 Corinthians* (1991)

J. D. G. Dunn, *Galatians* (1993)

K. P. Donfried and I. H. Marshall, *The Shorter Pauline Letters* (Thessalonians, Philippians, and Philemon) (1993)

A. T. Lincoln and A. J. M. Wedderburn, *The Later Pauline Letters* (Colossians and Ephesians) (1993)

F. Young, *The Pastoral Epistles* (1994)

(2) Lincoln, A. T. (ed.), New Testament Guides, Sheffield Academic Press, including the following:

R. Morgan, *Romans* (1995)

J. D. G. Dunn, *1 Corinthians* (1995)

L. Kreitzer, *2 Corinthians* (1996)

E. Best, *Ephesians* (1993)

J. M. G. Barclay, *Colossians and Philemon* (1997)

M. Davies, *The Pastoral Epistles* (1996)

# 19 The non-Pauline Letters

FRANCES YOUNG

The non-Pauline Letters – what do we mean by that description? The negative suggests that we are dealing with somewhat marginalized texts compared with Paul. Many of our texts[1] have indeed become cinderellas, though one comes from a theologian worthy to rank alongside Paul and 'John', and the rest are increasingly seen as intriguing, for they enable access to the development of diverse traditions within early Christianity. Comparing and contrasting these makes study of these apparent 'oddments' rewarding. For this reason we shall keep them all in play alongside one another. But first to identify them.

Associated with the Pauline tradition, but definitely to be distinguished from Paul's work, is the Epistle to the Hebrews.[2] Even if ascribed to Paul in the process of canonization, this work does not bear his name, and the Church of the third century CE knew not whence it came: one suggested Barnabas (Tertullian), one supposed Paul had written it in Hebrew and Luke translated it (Clement of Alexandria), one knew that Clement of Rome had been suggested but concluded that only God knows the author of the Epistle to the Hebrews (Origen). Modern scholarship has canvassed these ancient suggestions and others. The most plausible case can be made for Apollos, a person associated with the Pauline mission, though possibly in tension with it (1 Corinthians 1:12; 3.4ff.; 16:12). Acts 18:24ff. informs us that Apollos came from Alexandria, was a Jew with skill in interpreting the scriptures, and that he was 'eloquent', which probably means that he had a Greek rhetorical education: such features fit the implied author of this text. But why should the name be missing? Was it because the author was a woman, say Priscilla? We are in the realm of guesswork, and Origen's view must surely prevail.

It would be helpful to be clearer about the date of Hebrews – is it contemporary with Paul? or does it belong to the next generation? There is substantial consensus among scholars that the so-called Pastoral Epistles (1 and 2 Timothy and Titus)[3] represent the Pauline tradition beyond Paul.

Controversy has surrounded the question where authentic Paul ends and pseudonymous writing begins. Increasingly, however, attention is claimed by the implications of that debate: can we trace the development of the Pauline tradition through his followers to a subsequent generation? It is assumed here that the Pastorals are intended to make the absent Paul present in a crisis later and different from those which beset Paul in his own lifetime.

The Epistle of James[4] is a text which seems to emerge from a group that had difficulty with Paul. Again the question of authorship and date remains unsettled. Is this the most primitive Christian writing, barely different from Judaism, perhaps coming from James, the brother of the Lord and leader of the Jerusalem Church? Or is it from a generation after Paul, reacting against Gentile Christianity, reflecting the traditions of Palestinian Christianity and using the name of James to give it authority? The canonical status of this text remained doubtful in the fourth century CE, and here we assume that the work is pseudonymous, though that does not lessen its importance. For we take it to represent a form of Jewish Christianity which had a character unlike that of the Pauline tradition.

Jude[5] is another letter claiming to be associated with a member of the family of Jesus; its authenticity has recently been argued very powerfully.[6] This is not necessarily threatened by its intriguing overlaps with 2 Peter, a letter which has every appearance of being pseudonymous, since the latter probably borrowed from the former. The authenticity of 1 Peter[7] has also been plausibly defended. Once again we are faced with enormous uncertainties about date and origin. Are these three letters a group representing an identifiable tradition within the early Christian movement? Or do they have disparate origins? The tradition(s) represented in these letters perhaps challenge the recent tendency to differentiate between different forms of early Christianity, since there are links with the Pauline stream as well as others. But the basic position of this study is that the non-Pauline letters reveal not a clear mainstream but several parallel and interconnecting rivulets.

In some ways the discussion we are embarking upon is impoverished by not including the Johannine epistles, a group of letters which represent a distinctive tradition which is usefully compared and contrasted with those that concern us. Some of the same issues appear: questions about uniting and ordering the church community, about resisting distortions of the tradition, about where authority lies, about Christian life-style. The suggestion here is that they belong alongside the non-Pauline Epistles being discussed in this chapter, as witnesses to the pressures being exerted on the several diverse traditions of the churches in, say, the late first century.

Assuming that kind of context for all these documents clearly implies their pseudonymity.

The non-Pauline Letters – why are these texts in the form of epistles? This question is not posed simply because it is fashionable to ask literary questions. The issue concerns the extent to which the letter form is artificially adopted as the appropriate genre.[8] Everyone agrees that the letters of Paul were real letters, written in real situations. It is questionable how far the texts that concern us here are really letters in that sense.

Hebrews bears no name because it does not open with an epistolary address. The only reason for supposing that this text is a letter is that it ends like one. After an elaborate blessing which sounds as if it comes from a liturgical context, we suddenly find personal references and greetings. These mention Timothy, 'our brother', and 'those from Italy', providing the only clues as to the source or destination of this text. But being tacked on, as it were, these sentences stimulate other questions: was this text originally a sermon? How did it come to have a letter-ending but no opening greetings?

By contrast, the Pastorals introduce themselves as letters sent by Paul to Timothy and Titus. Intriguingly the Twelve Tribes of the Dispersion are the designated recipients of the greetings sent by a James so well known that he apparently needs no introduction beyond his claim to be 'a servant of God and of the Lord Jesus Christ'. Jude and Peter address recipients in a manner very similar to Paul. There is no doubt that these texts claim to be letters. Yet are they?

The very similarity to Paul's greetings makes one suspicious. Letters in every culture follow conventions. In Greek letters, the opening form was 'X to Y greeting (*chairein*)'; in Jewish letters, 'peace' (*shalom*) replaced 'greeting'. Paul seems to have forged his own, very significant, adaptation of both these forms: 'grace' (*charis*) and 'peace'.[9] The combination of 'grace and peace', with the occasional addition of 'mercy', is subsequently found in most Christian letters, including 1 and 2 Peter, Jude and 2 John. James, with the normal Greek *chairein,* is the exception that proves the rule. Two possibilities, not necessarily mutually exclusive, are suggested by this: that Paul initiated a tradition that rapidly spread for all Christian communications by letter; or that Paul's letters came to provide models for Christian literature, and validated the adoption of the letter genre for the expression of Christian teaching in writing. Like these works, the so-called *Apostolic Fathers*[10] are mostly in the form of letters.

Suspicion is also aroused by the addressees in James, the Twelve Tribes of the Diaspora (Dispersion). The endless scholarly speculation[11] about this is hardly necessary. There had not been twelve tribes since 721 BCE; the Diaspora of the Jews was only of the two tribes that had made up the kingdom of Judah. So in James the 'twelve' must be an eschatological symbol, presumably referring to Christian communities scattered all over the then known world, which, analogously to Diaspora Jews, adopted the identity of aliens and exiles from the kingdom (of heaven) to which they truly belonged. (This may be confirmed by comparing 1 Peter, which addresses Christians as 'the exiles of the Diaspora' in various provinces of Asia Minor.) James is situationless – unless it is the very first encyclical! So are Jude and 2 Peter: they address 'those called', or 'those who have received a faith', with totally unspecific further descriptions. 1 Peter alone of these letters seems to envisage particular recipients and a specific situation. So are most of these texts artificial letters? One suspects that may well be the case, and that would confirm their pseudonymity.

But to accept that is not to dismiss them as 'forgeries'. Rather it confirms their importance as community documents. The genuine Pauline Letters usually associate others with Paul in their writing and reveal their role in the creation and maintenance of community networks. Such networks continued to flourish as these 'aliens' in the Greco-Roman world faced new situations – of persecution, of divergence which they interpreted as betrayal. The communities needed to confirm the authority of their leaders as heirs of the apostles, authenticate the traditions they had received, identify and exclude the troublemakers. This is the context within which most of these non-Pauline letters probably emerged.

Modern scholarship has been preoccupied with how this non-Pauline material relates to Paul. In the case of James the problem was set by Luther who regarded James as a 'right strawy epistle', scarcely different from Judaism. Assuming that 'justification by faith' was the core of Paulinism, and taking it that James challenged that with 'justification by works', the conclusion was obvious. Those who respected its canonical status were exercised by the task of reconciling James with Paul.

James is clearly concerned with 'practical Christianity'. Pure religion is caring for orphans and widows, and keeping oneself unstained by the world (1.26); faith is demonstrated by action (2:14–17). Abraham was justified by works when he offered his son Isaac on the altar (2:21). James takes this as the proper exposition of Paul's prooftext, 'Abraham believed God, and it was reckoned to him as righteousness' (Genesis 15:6, cf. Romans 4:3), namely that works demonstrate faith (2:23–4). It looks like contradiction (compare in particular Romans 3:28 and James 2:24), and yet closer inspection suggests a dialogue of the deaf. For James, faith is mere assent: 'even the demons believe and they shudder!' (2:19). For Paul, however, faith includes behaviour – love and good works (Romans 12), putting on Christ (e.g. Romans 12:14), sinlessness (Romans 6). So how is this discussion related to Paul's? Most have concluded that James had not read Paul but was reacting to hearsay, perhaps even to post-Pauline antinomians a generation later. Some have pleaded for the pre-Pauline dating of James, either Paul being the respondent, or each discussing different issues independently.

What difference might be made to this discussion by the emerging new understanding of Paul?[12] Paul, it is now suggested, rejected not 'good works' but the imposition on Gentile converts of 'works of the Law', or the ethnic marks of a Jew such as circumcision, dietary laws, sabbath-keeping. In other words, the issue for Paul concerned the terms on which Gentiles were to be accepted into an essentially Jewish community, not the question how an introspective individual is to make up for a guilty conscience, as first Augustine and then Luther imagined.[13]

Now if that is so, it is quite evident that James is oblivious of the problem. Relations between rich and poor, rather than Jew and Gentile, are his concern, and the Law, for James, is the Law of liberty (1:25; 2:12), which is not to be an object of criticism (4:11–12), but is the criterion of divine judgement (2:10,13; 4:12, etc.). James's readers are to keep the 'royal' (*basilikon*) Law, which 'according to the scripture' is 'Love your neighbour as yourself' (2:8): does James mean the summing up of the whole Law in Leviticus (19:18)? Or could it be the 'Messianic' Law or the Law of the Kingdom he is thinking of? Whatever the answer, there are deep correspondences between James and the Gospel of Matthew (see especially Matthew 5:17–48). 'Matthew' accepts Gentiles, but speaks with the voice of a Jewish Messianic sect, shaped by a prophetic interiorizing of the demands for obedience and purity which radicalizes rather than rejects all the provisions for Law-keeping. Maybe this tradition is given voice in James too. Maybe there is the same slightly nervous edge to James's discussion of a false faith that fails to issue in charity as we find in 'Matthew's' assertion that not a jot or tittle of the Law will pass away. The controversies that beset Paul are beyond their horizon, let alone addressed. For them, Christian faith simply fulfils rather than challenges the Jewish tradition.

The shift in Pauline scholarship should also transform the perception of how the Pastorals relate to the rest of the Pauline material. The apparent emphasis on works rather than faith was one factor contributing to the conclusion that these texts were not authentically Pauline. That argument now seems misplaced. Yet their post-Pauline character remains evident in the loss of concern with the major issues that Paul faced. Here we seem to hear the voice of the Gentile Christian community: Law is irrelevant, except for keeping criminals in check (1 Timothy 1:8ff.). But Christian life-style is a matter of central importance.

The pattern of Christian life-style is spelt out in the Pastorals by developing the 'household codes' found in Colossians (3:18–4:1) and Ephesians (5:22–6:9). The church is understood as God's household (1 Timothy 3:15), so that the traditional pattern of exhortation to husbands and wives, children and parents, masters and slaves, is reshaped. Discussion of the deportment of men and women at prayer (1 Timothy 2) is followed by character sketches (3:1–13) of the proper overseer (*episkopos*) and servant (*diakonos*); later (4:6, 4:12, 5:1–2) 'Timothy' is told how to be a good *diakonos* for the 'brothers', despite his youth, and instructed to address senior men in the community as if they were his father, younger men as brothers, older women as mothers, younger women as sisters. Instructions follow about widows (5:3–16) and senior men (*presbyteroi*) (5:17–20), and about slaves (6:1–2). (My summary is deliberately phrased to show the ambiguities between the household terminology and later Christian titles for ministerial office.) Clearly the household code is developing into an ecclesiastical canon, but there are tensions both between the language of familial relationships and that implying a hierarchy of domestic attendants, and between advice to 'literal' slaves and instructions to the 'servants' of God. Clearly development is taking place within the Pauline churches, and this is motivated by the desire to preserve the Pauline tradition in the face of false interpretations of it.

2 Timothy, seemingly Paul's last testament before giving his life, appears as the centrepiece of a tripartite work which invests the leaders of the next generation with Paul's authority. Paul has become the model convert and the model martyr. Christians are to be loyal to Christ Jesus, the one who has come to provide cleansing from worldly passions and new birth, and who will return as king to vindicate them and reward their endurance. These epistles seem to imply a certain parody of the Caesar-cult – certainly the theological and christological language is rather different from that of the genuine Paulines. Yet for all the differences, these letters would become the lens through which Paul would be read at least until the time of Augustine.

Hebrews has a different relationship again with the Pauline material. The letter develops certain generative ideas in Pauline theology, particularly the notion that Jeremiah's prophecy of a new covenant has been fulfilled in Christ. Yet, as we shall see, it has its own hermeneutic which, for all the connections, is often quite unlike that of Paul.

Most intriguing is the question how 1 Peter relates to the Pauline tradition. Not only is the Pauline greeting adopted, but phrases of a Pauline character are embedded in a text which has never had a Pauline attribution nor any overt connection with Paul – indeed is attributed to the apostle with whom, according to Galatians, Paul fell out! In particular, this epistle has a 'household code' very like those found in Colossians, Ephesians and the Pastorals. A form-critical approach to 1 Peter reveals patterns of catechetical teaching and liturgical formulae.[14] Thus the similarities with Paul are probably to be attributed to Christian 'in-language'. This kind of analysis suggests that this epistle, like the others considered here, probably belongs to the second generation's concern to transmit the tradition of the apostles.

It seems, then, that with these non-Pauline epistles a new stage has been reached: firstly, in many cases the problem the churches now face is how to distinguish false teaching from true. For some warnings suffice, for others the answer is to do with authority structures, the authorized transmission of tradition from the apostles to the next troubled generation. The clues to the identity of these rival teachers seem to point to what scholars have labelled 'gnosticism',[15] and it is perhaps significant that gnostic teachers would later claim an apostolic origin for their esoteric teachings – a battle of traditions is emerging. Secondly, many of these documents reflect a situation in which Christians, subject to persecution and suspicion, respond by taking on an identity which is neither Jewish nor Gentile – the jibe that they are a 'Third Race' and the claim to supersede Judaism have their seeds here. Internal and external pressures issue in a concern with 'life-style', how Christians were to live in the world.

The Pastorals demonstrate well how this new stage is continuous with what has gone before. Already in Paul's day there were internal controversies, and incipient gnosticism has been suspected in Paul's Corinth.[16] Connections with earlier Pauline material lend plausibility to continued pleas for the authenticity of the Pastorals. However, the opening of 1 Timothy immediately sets a tone different from before: 'Timothy' has been told to stay in Ephesus to ensure that certain people do not 'teach differently' (*heterodidaskalein* is a neologism), or promulgate myths and endless genealogies. Here there is no sustained argument against the ideas rejected, so reconstruction is difficult. But further hints suggest that extreme asceticism, implying the devaluing of creation and a radical challenge to social norms, is allied with speculation about the cosmos and its origins akin to the kind of thing found in apocryphal and apocalyptic texts; such may well have have contributed to the formation of second-century gnostic systems. The response in the Pastorals is to reaffirm the slogans of the Pauline tradition, and endeavour to order the Church institutionally so that its life and its ethics are grounded in conventional order and morality – hence their 'patriarchal' appearance.

Similar problems appear in Jude, whose only concern is to warn the readers against people who are described as having wormed their way in though really the enemies of religion, denying Christ by perverting free grace into a justification of moral licence. Again it is difficult to reconstruct precisely what is at stake, but it seems that the flouting of social convention is described as immorality and treated as fulfilling eschatological prophecies of the terrible things that will happen before the End. The warnings of judgement reappear in 2 Peter's rehash of Jude. Here, as in the Pastorals, the Christian message is contrasted with 'myths' (1:16), the opponents appear not to understand that creation is God's (3:5ff.) and the false teachers are depicted as in it for the money (2:3; cf. 2 Timothy 3:1ff.). It is possible that 2 Peter reuses Jude against a different foe, anti-heretical polemic tarring various opponents with the same brush. But overall the impression is of similar issues being approached in different ways, as the Pastorals use institutional authority to confirm a conservative view of tradition and the Jude/Peter material confronts the problem with scriptural exegesis and eschatological warning.

'Antinomianism' is a term used to describe the concern of many of these texts, including James. Whatever the date and provenance of James and Jude, a perceived breakdown in accepted behaviour, a willingness to denigrate 'bodies' and earthly relationships, a failure of community spirit, love and charity, has justified this characterization. James would seem to attribute the breakdown to Paul's own teaching, whereas the Pastorals present Paul as its opponent – after all, he had himself confronted those who argued 'all things are lawful' (1 Corinthians) and 'the more sin, the more grace' (Romans). It seems most likely that we are dealing with post-Pauline struggles.

For some of these texts, however, the main concern is persecution – even false teaching may be chiefly problematic because it draws the wrong sort of attention to the Christian movement: 2 Timothy, exhorting its readers not to be ashamed of those who suffer for the gospel, is set at the heart of a work which endeavours to order Christian groups in such a way as to gain a good reputation with outsiders. For a long time, critics have passed on the accepted notion that in the Pastorals Christians are becoming 'bourgeois' and settling down in the world, but the texts gainsay this view. Rather they appear to be reacting against radical forms of Christianity which challenged social norms and so endangered adherents to the faith of Christ.

1 Peter most obviously confronts the issue of persecution. Readiness to stand firm and suffer for the gospel is commended as a way of being refined through trials and as imitation of Christ. A baptismal rite has been suggested by the liturgical rhythms of the language, one scholar even suggesting that here is an early Paschal liturgy dressed up as a letter.[17] That seems anachronistic; but still dying and rising with Christ is a clear focus. Suffering is to be endured 'for the name', but Christians must not incur criminal charges before authorities established by God to maintain law and order. Household codes spell out a conventional, ethical life-style, as in the Pastorals; and as in the Pastorals also, life is lived in a waiting period, under the eyes of God, expecting divine judgement.

Hebrews, too, seems to be encouraging Christians to stand firm in the face of potential crisis. The readers have not yet suffered to the extent of shedding blood; they should expect God to discipline those he loves. Significantly, both Hebrews and 1 Peter appropriate for the Christian community the identity of the chosen people of God, offering encouragement and hope through reference to the Jewish scriptures. For Hebrews, Christians are the people of the new covenant, while for 1 Peter, those who once were 'not my people' have become the 'chosen race, royal priesthood, holy nation' of Exodus 19:6. Taken together with the language of aliens, exiles and Diaspora noted earlier, we can see the fateful delineation of Christian identity over against the Jewish people, with all its potential for canonizing later Christian anti-semitism. A new stage has been reached.

The texts under consideration have their own 'hermeneutic'. Our approach to writings which have themselves become canonical has tended to treat them as merely historical documents. Could Christian readers of our own time learn from them about how to handle Scripture? Until recently such a question would have been unthinkable. It was assumed that modern understanding of the Bible had been dramatically enhanced through the development of the historical-critical method, and that ancient readings were misguided by allegory. Now that we are more self-conscious about different reader responses and the 'infinity' of linguistic meaning, maybe we should cease to be so superior.

But first, what can we discern about the 'intertextuality'[18] of these texts themselves? Most use the scriptures as prophetic and exemplary, making them their own, reading themselves into the texts, though surprisingly not the Pastorals. Notoriously they contain the first clear statement (2 Timothy 3:16) about the importance of Scripture in the life of the Church: 'All inspired scripture is also useful for instruction, rebuke, reformation, and training in righteousness.'[19] Along with other directions that 'Timothy' devote himself to the public reading of Scripture (1 Timothy 4:13), the strong impression is created that these texts rely for teaching on a body of literature respected as the Word of God. Yet there is remarkably little reference, quotation or allusion to the scriptures themselves, the only quote being one that could have been lifted from Paul's writings (1 Timothy 5:18, cf. 1 Corinthians 9:9). The author does not know the scriptures as Paul did.

The intertextuality of others of these texts is much more profound. Jude's warnings are accompanied with reminders of the Exodus, Sodom and Gomorrah, Cain, Balaam and Korah, and in speaking of the Archangel Michael in dispute with the devil over Moses' body, or of Enoch prophesying, clearly reflect post-biblical developments found in apocalyptic and apocryphal writings. 2 Peter introduces Noah and the Flood, and spells out some of Jude's allusions more explicitly. For these texts, past accounts of false prophets and of God's judgement become vivid 'types' of what is at stake in the present.

The most sustained biblical reflection is found in the Epistle to the Hebrews – in fact this could be described as largely a christological exegesis of the scriptures, explaining how the sacred texts point beyond the covenant with the Jews to a new dispensation in Christ. The centrepiece is the full quotation of Jeremiah's prediction of a new covenant (Jeremiah 31:31ff.; Hebrews 8). The earthly temple and the ritual provisions of the old covenant are understood to be a shadowy symbol of the true temple in the heavens. As the high priest entered the Holy of Holies once a year on the Day of Atonement with the blood of sacrificial victims, so Christ has entered heaven once for all with his own sacrificial blood, and his blood sealed this new covenant as blood had sealed the covenant with Moses. Around this core idea are woven many detailed correlations and associations with other scriptural texts. Typical allegorical ploys feed an argument which is usually described as 'typological', but the thrust of which is to encourage the readers to persevere, because they have a 'better covenant' and a 'better high priest'.

The scriptures also provide catalogues of examples of faith and perseverance, and proverbial sayings about God testing those who are 'his sons'. The readers are encouraged to think they are on a new exodus journey, that a sabbath rest awaits them, that they are to come not to the terrors of Mount Sinai but to Mount Zion, the heavenly Jerusalem, if only they are not disobedient as their Israelite predecessors were in the desert.

By comparison, 1 Peter appears a less coherent reflection, more dependent on 'prooftexts' brought together in collages, often based on the association of catch-words. But that may be to underestimate the extent to which Hebrews uses similar techniques and 1 Peter has an underlying perspective which is less explicit. For both, the church communities take up the identity and the story of Israel; this is the basis on which warnings, encouragement, 'types' and prophecies can be abstracted and woven into narrative patterns and exhortations that give meaning to the situations in which readers find themselves.

The Epistle of James highlights the fact that for the Christians of this period there was no 'New Testament' as a canonized text: most explicit examples are drawn from the Jewish scriptures. Yet to conclude that it is a Jewish document barely does justice to the parallels with Gospel sayings, especially the many apparent allusions to Matthew's Gospel. It is unlikely that this constitutes 'intertextuality'; rather we observe the interplay of oral traditions about the teaching of a barely mentioned Jesus with the established canon of sacred writings. The only case of intertextual reference to writings which became the New Testament is 2 Peter's reference to Paul's writings. Paul is described as 'our dear friend and brother' and what he wrote to the readers 'with the wisdom God gave him' is endorsed, but what follows is a warning: '[his letters] contain some obscure passages, which the ignorant and unstable misinterpret to their own ruin' (3:15–16). Paul is a contested inheritance and Christian writings, though respected, have not yet reached the status of Scripture (the apparently clear reference to 'the rest of the scriptures' in 3:16 is the product of translation: the Greek is ambiguous, normally meaning 'writings', though acquiring specialized overtones in Jewish and Christian usage).

Thus a variety of ways of relating to 'Scripture' can be discerned in these texts, but what they have in common is a rereading of Scripture in the light of Christ, an 'application' of Scripture to their own situation, and an expectation that Scripture both teaches the way of life and makes sense of their current struggles. There is an awareness that Scripture's meaning shifts in the light of Christ, and that contention surrounds the interpretation of Scripture, indeed of the Christian traditions they have inherited. It is this which may enable us to address the question of how we appropriate these non-Pauline epistles. What they represent to us is a stage in the life of the

Church in which there were both internal and external struggles to establish Christian identity and the right mode of being in the world.

Their social and cultural situation was very different from our own and any present appropriation will have to take account of such differences – hence the attention here to their 'writing-context'. But in a sense, as canon, they authorize Christians of subsequent generations and different 'worlds' to continue the search for a proper expression of Christian identity and life style in ever-changing conditions, and provide certain pointers. Fundamental would seem to be the affirmation of this world as God's created order in which obedience to God's moral standards, as adumbrated in Israel's story and the teaching of Jesus Christ, is the special responsibility of those called and chosen to be God's people. Such a stance has implications which cannot be realized simply by taking over the solutions offered in these texts in an unquestioning way. Hierarchical structures, patriarchal assumptions and other culture-bound elements frame their answers; we shall have to struggle to find ours in a post-Christian world.

## Notes

1 For further reading, together with initial bibliographical guidance, see the relevant volumes in the Cambridge series on New Testament Theology edited by J. D. G. Dunn: Barnabas Lindars SSF, *The Theology of the Letter to the Hebrews* (Cambridge: Cambridge University Press, 1991); Andrew Chester and Ralph P. Martin, *The Theology of the Letters of James, Peter and Jude* (Cambridge: Cambridge University Press, 1994); Frances Young, *The Theology of the Pastoral Letters* (Cambridge: Cambridge University Press, 1994).

2 For serious further study, the commentary by H. W. Attridge (*Commentary on Hebrews*) in the Hermeneia series (Philadelphia: Fortress Press, 1989) is recommended.

3 For serious further study, the commentary by Martin Dibelius (*Commentary on the Pastoral Epistles*), rev. Hans Conzelmann, English translation in Hermeneia series (Philadelphia: Fortress Press, 1972) remains the most comprehensive. Recent sociological studies have made a difference to the discussion, however, and the bibliography in Young, *The Theology of the Pastoral Letters* should be consulted.

4 For further study, see Sophie Laws's commentary in the Black series (London: A. & C. Black, 1980).

5 For further study of Jude and 2 Peter, see the Commentary by Richard

Bauckham (*Commentary on Jude and 2 Peter*), The Word Biblical Commentary (Waco, TX: Word, 1983).

6 Richard Bauckham, *Jude and the Relatives of Jesus* (Edinburgh: T. & T. Clark, 1990); cf. his previously published commentary cited in previous note. Bauckham examines the evidence for the continuing influence of the Holy Family in Palestinian Christianity, and shows how the epistle's exegesis parallels that found in Jewish apocryphal literature. The case mounted has considerable force. If accepted, we must suppose that 2 Peter used Jude at a later date to challenge different opponents, and the position adopted in this chapter would need modification.

7 For further study, J. N. D. Kelly's commentary (*Commentary on 1 Peter*) in the Black series (London: A. & C. Black, 1969) remains the fullest available in English.

8 On the literary genre, see Stanley K. Stowers, *Letter Writing in Greco-Roman Antiquity* (Philadelphia: Westminster Press, 1986).

9 Judith Lieu, '"Grace to you and Peace": The Apostolic Greeting', *Bulletin of the John Rylands Library of Manchester* 68 (1985), pp. 161–75.

10 The texts usually designated by this term are 1 and 2 Clement; the seven letters of Ignatius to the Ephesians, Magnesians, Trallians, Romans, Philadelphians, Smyrnaeans and Polycarp; the letter of Polycarp to the Philippians; The Didache or Teaching of the twelve Apostles; and the Epistle of Barnabas. They are readily available in English translation in the Penguin Classics, *Early Christian Writings*, ed. and trans. Maxwell Staniforth and Andrew Louth (London: Penguin Classics, 1987).

11 It has become a standard issue discussed in commentaries and studies, to which the reader is referred if further discussion is sought.

12 Cf. Dunn's chapter on the Pauline Letters in this volume, pp. 276–89. Reassessment of Paul's theology began with the work of E. P. Sanders, *Paul and Palestinian Judaism* (London: SCM Press, 1977). A good discussion of the issues will be found in J. D. G. Dunn, *The Parting of the Ways between Christianity and Judaism and their Significance for the Character of Christianity* (London: SCM Press, 1991).

13 The classic article is K. Stendahl, 'The Introspective Conscience of the West', *Harvard Theological Review* 56 (1963), pp. 199–215; republished in *Paul Among Jews and Gentiles* (London: SCM Press, 1977).

14 Form criticism was interestingly used by E. G. Selwyn in his commentary (*Commentary on 1 Peter*) (London: Macmillan, 1946)); curiously he combined this with a defence of Petrine authorship.

15 New Testament scholarship has been dominated by questions concerning the origins and influence of gnosticism for most of this century. Contrasting views may be faced by consulting Kurt Rudolph, *Gnosis* (English translation Edinburgh: T. & T. Clark 1983), and Simone Petrement, *A Separate God: the Christian Origins of Gnosticism* (English translation London: Darton, Longman and Todd, 1991). Christopher Rowland, *The Open Heaven* (London: SCM Press, 1982) provides another perspective which indicates the possibility of a link

between apocalyptic literature and gnosticism, a view which I have favoured since reading R. M. Grant, *Gnosticism and Early Christianity* (New York: Columbia and Oxford University Press, 1966); cf. my discussion in *The Theology of the Pastoral Letters*, cited earlier.

16 The classic study is Walter Schmithals, *Gnosticism in Corinth* (Nashville: Abingdon Press, 1971).

17 F. C. Cross, *1 Peter. A Paschal Liturgy* (London: Mowbray, 1954). Cf. the Commentary by F. W. Beare (*Commentary on 1 Peter*) (Oxford: Blackwell, 1947) which adopts this theory and identifies the context of 1 Peter with persecution under Trajan.

18 This term has become standard in recent literary theory since its introduction by Roland Barthes. Most texts depend in some sense on previous texts, if not quoting them then taking them over more subtly, presuming them, whether alluding openly or darkly, or subverting them. This is especially the case when previous texts have a 'canonical' status. In biblical studies important works influenced by this observation are Michael Fishbane, *Biblical Interpretation in Ancient Israel* (Oxford: Clarendon Press, 1985) and Richard B.Hays, *Echoes of Scripture in the Letters of Paul* (New Haven and London: Yale University Press, 1989).

19 There is some dispute as to whether *theopneustos* (inspired) is an attributive or predicative adjective (i.e. whether we should read 'all inspired scripture is useful' or 'all scripture is inspired and useful'). It seems most likely to be the former according to usual Greek conventions, but the insertion of *kai* ('and' or 'also') between the two adjectives (*theopneustos* and *ophelimos* = useful) makes the matter hard to settle. Many English versions take the opposite view to that adopted in the translation here.

## Further reading

Attridge, H. W., *Commentary on Hebrews*, Hermeneia series, Philadelphia: Fortress Press, 1989.

Bauckham, Richard, *Commentary on Jude and 2 Peter*, The Word Biblical Commentary, Waco, TX: Word, 1983.

*Jude and the Relatives of Jesus*, Edinburgh: T. & T. Clark, 1990.

Beare, F. W., *Commentary on 1 Peter*, Oxford: Blackwell, 1947.

Chester, Andrew and Ralph P. Martin, *The Theology of the Letters of James, Peter and Jude*, New Testament Theology Series, ed. James Dunn, Cambridge: Cambridge University Press, 1994.

Cross, F. C., *1 Peter. A Paschal Liturgy*, London: Mowbray, 1954.

Dibelius, Martin, rev. Hans Conzelmann, *Commentary on the Pastoral Epistles*, English translation in Hermeneia series, Philadelphia: Fortress Press, 1972.

Dunn, J. D. G., *The Parting of the Ways between Christianity and Judaism and their Significance for the Character of Christianity*, London: SCM Press, 1991.

Grant, R. M., *Gnosticism and Early Christianity*, New York: Columbia and Oxford University Press, 1966.

Kelly, J. N. D., *Commentary on 1 Peter*, Black series, London: A. & C. Black, 1969.

Laws, Sophie, *Commentary on James*, Black series, London: A. & C. Black, 1980.

Lieu, Judith, '"Grace to you and Peace": The Apostolic Greeting', *Bulletin of the John Rylands Library of Manchester* 68 (1985), pp. 161–75.

Lindars, Barnabas, SSF, *The Theology of the Letter to the Hebrews*, New Testament Theology series, ed. James Dunn, Cambridge: Cambridge University Press, 1991.

Petrement, Simone, *A Separate God: the Christian Origins of Gnosticism*, English translation London: Darton, Longman and Todd, 1991.

Rowland, Christopher, *The Open Heaven*, London: SCM Press, 1982.

Rudolph, Kurt, *Gnosis*, English translation Edinburgh: T. & T. Clark, 1983.

Sanders, E. P., *Paul and Palestinian Judaism*, London: SCM Press, 1977.

Schmithals, Walter, *Gnosticism in Corinth*, English translation Nashville: Abingdon Press, 1971.

Selwyn, E. G., *Commentary on 1 Peter*, London: Macmillan, 1946.

Staniforth, Maxwell and Andrew Louth (eds. and trans.), *Early Christian Writings*, Penguin Classics, London, 1987.

Stendahl, K., 'The Introspective Conscience of the West', *Harvard Theological Review* 56 (1963), pp. 199–215; republished in *Paul Among Jews and Gentiles*, London: SCM Press, 1977.

Stowers, Stanley K., *Letter Writing in Greco-Roman Antiquity*, Philadelphia: Westminster Press, 1986.

Young, Frances, *The Theology of the Pastoral Letters*, New Testament Theology Series, ed. James Dunn, Cambridge: Cambridge University Press, 1994.

# 20 Apocalyptic literature

JAMES C. VANDERKAM

The Bible contains two books that are usually called apocalypses: Daniel (especially chapters 2, 7–12) and Revelation. There are also several sections of books that some scholars label apocalypses; examples are Isaiah 24–7, the visions in Zechariah 1–8, and the Synoptic Apocalypse (Mark 13 with parallels in Matthew 24 and Luke 21). The nature of these literary units as divine disclosures of what is destined to take place sets them off from other scriptural books and has gained for them a certain popular and scholarly fascination. Their concern with the future has led more literal readers to mine the texts for clues to when the end will be and what signs will mark its approach; modern apocalyptic groups have joined a series of predecessors in this effort. The potential dangers of a literal reading have caused some uneasiness, especially about the book of Revelation in Christian history. So much has this been the case that its place in the New Testament was denied by some already in antiquity. In recent times scholars have devoted large amounts of time to clarifying obscure points in Daniel and Revelation and to studying them in connection with other, extra-biblical works that appear to belong to the same literary category. Today the numerous commentators on Daniel or Revelation are expected to be conversant with the non-canonical apocalyptic texts and to examine the similarities and differences that the canonical apocalypses exhibit in relation to them. It will be useful to review the high points of scholarship on the apocalyptic literature in the last several decades in order to see what has been accomplished and what remains to be done.

## TERMS AND TEXTS

From a logical point of view, the first issue is definition, and in fact defining key terms has been a major, if debated, accomplishment of the last quarter century. A problem had been that the word 'apocalyptic' was employed as a cover term for a body of literature, the content of that literature and for whatever social movement(s) lay behind the texts. Such imprecision gave rise to attempts at establishing a more differentiated set of terms. A pioneer in the effort has been K. Koch. In his 1970 book *Ratlos vor der Apokalyptik*, which was translated into English under the bland title *The Rediscovery of Apocalyptic*, he proposed the following distinctions. First, 'apocalypse' denotes a literary form which includes several characteristic features. There is a dialogue in which a heavenly representative reveals, often in a vision, previously secret information about human destiny to a seer whose tormented reactions to the experience are recorded. The seer conveys the message to his audience in discourses through which he exhorts the faithful to endurance in the present time of distress because the end of the tribulations and beginning of the new age will soon arrive. The author usually resorts to the pseudonym of an ancient hero and couches his message in mythical, symbolic images. The resulting literary works, that is, the apocalypses, are composite, the results of lengthy processes of literary development.[1] Second, 'apocalyptic' should be reserved for what Koch terms a historical 'movement of the mind' or 'a group of typical moods and ideas'[2] that are found in the apocalypses. He listed eight such 'moods and ideas': (1) an urgent expectation that present earthly conditions would be overthrown in the immediate future; (2) the end will come about through a cosmic catastrophe; (3) world history consists of predetermined segments of time, with the end closely tied to the history that precedes it; (4) writers resort to hosts of angels and demons in order to explain the course of history and the events that will take place at the end; (5) after the final catastrophe there will be salvation, not understood in purely nationalistic terms but with a tendency towards universalism. That is, within Israel itself not all will experience deliverance; only the righteous will do so, and they will be joined by the virtuous from other peoples; (6) an act of God will effect the transition from disaster to redemption; the kingdom of God will then become visible on earth, although it had been present in a hidden way before this; (7) a mediator with royal functions often brings about the final redemption; and (8) 'glory' characterizes the final state and sets it apart from what has existed before.[3] Koch noted that 'apocalyptic' was one of several trends in Israel's literature and that similar ideas could be found outside Israel in genres such as the Hellenistic oracle literature.

P. Hanson has built upon Koch's terminological proposals but has maintained that three related entities should be distinguished. He agrees that 'apocalypse' should be employed for a literary genre, but, rather than distinguishing it from 'apocalyptic' alone, he suggests that there are two separable phenomena: 'apocalyptic eschatology' and 'apocalypticism'. By the former he means to distinguish apocalyptic thinking from the patterns found in prophetic literature: it is 'a religious perspective which focuses on the disclosure (usually esoteric in nature) to the elect of the cosmic vision of Yahweh's sovereignty – especially as it relates to his acting to deliver his faithful – which disclosure the visionaries have largely ceased to translate into the terms of plain history, real politics, and human instrumentality due to a pessimistic view of reality growing out of the bleak post-exilic conditions within which those associated with the visionaries found themselves'.[4] Hanson reserves the word 'apocalypticism' to designate a social phenomenon; he calls it a 'symbolic universe' of those groups for whom apocalyptic eschatology has become an ideology.

While we may agree that Hanson's three entities should be distinguished, it is worth noting that 'apocalyptic eschatology' ought not to be considered the only content of apocalypses. As we will see below, these texts do, of course, have eschatological concerns but there are others as well. Furthermore, 'apocalyptic eschatology' may be found in texts that formally would not be regarded as apocalypses in any strict sense of the term. Also, it is worth asking whether this eschatology is actually distinct from all prophetic eschatology or whether it also characterizes some of what Israel's pre- and post-exilic prophets preached. Hanson isolates pessimism as a mood that gives rise to apocalyptic thinking and locates it in 'the bleak post-exilic conditions'. Again we may ask whether we know this or whether his characterization of these conditions reflects a bias about the nature of pre- and post-exilic conditions. Even if we could document such a view in an ancient text, we would not know whether this was one person's perception or whether it corresponded with the nature of reality as many read it. Regarding 'apocalypticism', we have some indications of groups who embraced 'apocalyptic eschatology' as a dominant and controlling ideology, but the evidence in this area is more sparse than we would like.

The most widely cited definition of any of these terms has been J. Collins's definition of 'apocalypse', first formulated in an issue of *Semeia* devoted to the subject of apocalypses in different literatures. '"Apocalypse" is a genre of revelatory literature with a narrative framework, in which a revelation is mediated by an otherworldly being to a human recipient, disclosing a transcendent reality which is both temporal, insofar as it envisages eschatological salvation, and spatial insofar as it involves another, supernatural world.'[5]

One of the strong points of Collins's definition is that it recognizes diversity in the principal contents of the apocalypses. The tendency in scholarship has been to focus on the eschatological side of their teachings[6] and less on the other material found in them. M. Stone has drawn attention to what he calls 'lists of revealed things' that appear at central points in the revelations to seers and that are clearly not eschatological in nature but may derive from sources in wisdom books (e.g. Job 38).[7] C. Rowland has emphasized this point in his important book *The Open Heaven*. He maintains that it does not fit the evidence from the apocalypses to say that eschatology dominates their contents; rather the books present varied material. He finds the warning statement of m. Hagigah 2:1 to be a more apt summary of what one finds in the examples of the genre: 'Whosoever gives his mind to four things it were better for him if he had not come into the world – what is above? what is beneath? what was before time? and what will be hereafter?'[8] That is, the apocalypses contain revelations of both cosmological/heavenly and eschatological secrets.[9] While this point is well worth making, it is fair to say that secrets about non-eschatological subjects (e.g., about the heavens) are often if not always connected in some way with eschatological matters and seem intended to reassure the reader about God's ultimate sovereignty over the universe and thus of his ability to rectify what is now wrong with the world. Collins's judicious words 'disclosing a transcendent reality which is both temporal ... and spatial' catch the facts of the matter with precision. It should be added that apocalyptic modes of thought are not confined to works that qualify formally as apocalypses but may be found in other genres such as testaments and oracles.

Collins and the group of scholars with whom he was working distinguished two major types within the genre apocalypse: apocalypses with or without an otherworldly journey by the recipient of the revelation. Within each of these two types they find three subdivisions: '(a) the "historical" type which includes a review of history, eschatological crisis and cosmic and/or political eschatology; (b) apocalypses which have no historical review but envisage cosmic and/or political eschatology ... and (c) apocalypses which have neither historical review nor cosmic transformation but only personal eschatology'.[10]

If we define the genre apocalypse as Collins does, the result is a fairly short list of texts and parts of texts that fit within its limits. Confining ourselves to the Judaeo-Christian tradition and extending the time limit somewhat beyond the New Testament period we may, with the writers in Semeia 14, list the following works as being within the apocalyptic fold. They are classified according to the schema developed by the same scholars.

*Jewish*

1. *no journey*

  *1a. review of history*

  Daniel 7–12

  Animal Apocalypse
    (1 Enoch 85–90)

  Apocalypse of Weeks
    (1 Enoch 93, 91)

  Jubilees 23

  4 Ezra

  2 Baruch

  *1b. cosmic and/or political*
     *eschatology*

  *1c. only personal eschatology*

2. *journey*

  *2a. review of history*

  Apocalypse of Abraham

  *2b. cosmic and/or political*
     *eschatology*

  1 Enoch 1–36

  1 Enoch 72–82

  The Similitudes of Enoch

  2 Enoch

  Testament of Levi 2–5

*Christian*

1. *no journey*

  *1a. review of history*

  Jacob's Ladder

  *1b. cosmic and/or political*
     *eschatology*

  Revelation

  Apocalypse of St John the
    Theologian

  Apocalypse of Peter

  Shepherd of Hermas

  Testament of the Lord 1:1–14

  Book of Elchasai (?)

  *1c. only personal eschatology*

  5 Ezra 2:42–8

  Testament of Isaac 2–3a

  Testament of Jacob 1–3a

  Questions of Bartholomew

  Book of the Resurrection of Jesus
    Christ by Bartholomew the
    Apostle 8b–14a

2. *journey*

  *2a. review of history*

  *2b. cosmic and/or political*
     *eschatology*

  Apocalypse of Paul

  Ascension of Isaiah

  Apocalypse of Esdras

  Apocalypse/Vision of the Virgin
    Mary

| *2c. only personal eschatology* | *2c. only personal eschatology* |
|---|---|
| 3 Baruch | Testament of Isaac 5–6 |
| Testament of Abraham | Testament of Jacob 5 |
| The Apocalypse of Zephaniah | Zosimus |
| | The Apocalypse of the Holy Mother of God concerning the Punishments |
| | Apocalypse of James, the Brother of the Lord |
| | Mysteries of St John the Apostle and the Holy Virgin |
| | Resurrection of Bartholomew 17b–19b |
| | Apocalypse of Sedrach |

The nearly complete absence from the Christian ledger of apocalypses with historical reviews and their plentiful presence on the Jewish side should be noted. Conversely, types 1b. and 1c. are represented only in the Christian column. Collins's definition entails that some works which are considered apocalypses by some scholars (e.g., most of Jubilees, most of the Testaments of the Twelve Patriarchs, the War Scroll from Qumran) are excluded from the list.

There is room for debate about whether some texts belong in the list, and many of the Christian apocalypses may in fact date from centuries after the biblical period. It is questionable whether 1 Enoch 72–82 should be called an apocalypse. Only a few lines in it deal with eschatological matters; most of the treatise concerns itself with disclosure of calendrical and geographical details, not of a transcendent world, but of this world. It is doubtful, too, whether sizable portions of 1 Enoch 1–36 fit Collins's definition; as he recognizes, the journeys of Enoch in chapters 17–36 are more aptly characterized as an apocalypse, less so the earlier chapters.

Before leaving this definition of 'apocalypse', we should note two other items. First, Collins chose to omit the feature of pseudonymity from his formulation. A glance at the lists above shows that it is found in all the Jewish texts and in almost all of the Christian ones, the most prominent exception being the Revelation of John.

Second, in the scholarly discussion of Collins's definition, one of the criticisms was that it included no statement about function. Collins eventually accepted an extension of his definition that supplied the perceived

deficiency: an apocalypse is 'intended to interpret present, earthly circumstances in the light of the supernatural world and of the future, and to influence both the understanding and the behaviour of the audience by means of
divine authority'.[11] One wonders whether the new line expresses the matter
adequately. Of course, we have little basis for making statements about
actual function other than what may be inferred from the texts, but does a
desire to influence understanding and behaviour on the basis of divine
authority sufficiently articulate the urgent appeals that figure in a number of
the apocalypses? Perhaps a stronger verb such as 'exhort' or 'encourage'
should appear in the definition. Moreover, the rather general definition of
function would not distinguish apocalypses from prophetic books or
Pauline letters, both of which also consider the supernatural world and the
future. If the statement of function is to be retained, it would serve to highlight the considerable amount of overlap that exists in this and other areas
between apocalypses and a variety of other genres. That is, the function of
apocalypses would not be unique to works of this literary form.

## ORIGINS

If the list of Jewish apocalypses presented above is exhaustive, we may
infer that none was written before the Hellenistic period began. This would
imply that those who consider passages such as Isaiah 24–7 or Zechariah 1–8
to be apocalypses or at least proto-apocalypses would be operating with
different definitions. F. M. Cross, who holds that 'the origins of apocalyptic
must be searched for as early as the sixth century BC',[12] has noticed 'reformu-
lations of the prophetic tradition and of the royal ideology' in some later
prophetic texts in the Hebrew Bible; these contain some 'rudimentary traits
and motives of apocalypticism'. He lists three: 'democratizing and eschatolo-
gizing of classical prophetic themes and forms'; the doctrine of two ages and
'the resurgent influence of myths of creation used to frame history and to
lend history transcendent significance, significance not apparent in the
ordinary events of biblical history'.[13] O. Plöger and P. Hanson have also
sought apocalyptic origins in earlier periods of post-exilic history and have
attempted to isolate the non-theocratic, eschatologically minded groups
responsible for the rise of apocalyptic thinking.[14] While there can be no
doubt that the authors of the apocalypses drew upon earlier biblical material
and to a certain extent imitated biblical forms, no-one composed an apocalypse in Collins's sense of the term until the third century BC.

Scholars have searched diligently for the literary and doctrinal sources or influences that gave birth to the apocalypses and apocalyptic thought. While no biblical book written before Daniel (*c.* 165 BC) takes the literary form of an apocalypse, there are older scriptural passages that are similar to aspects of its form. One that is often mentioned is the prophetic throne vision (e.g., 1 Kings 22; Isaiah 6) which resembles the setting of Daniel 7, 1 Enoch 14 and John's vision of the heavens in the book of Revelation. Other scriptural models are the visions of Ezekiel (especially chapters 40–8) and of Zechariah 1–8, in both of which an angel explains the meaning of what the prophet is seeing. An other-worldly interpreter is, as we have seen, a defining characteristic of the apocalypses.

The facts that several of the best formal antecedents of apocalypses may be found in prophetic vision reports, that apocalyptic thought is strongly concerned with the future and that the apocalypses make frequent reference to the prophetic books (e.g., Daniel 9 offers an interpretation of the seventy years prophesied by Jeremiah (25:11; 29:10)) encourage one to look to prophetic literature and prophecy as the forerunners and models for apocalypses and apocalyptic thought. And in fact this has been the dominant position. D. S. Russell, author of the widely used *The Method and Message of Jewish Apocalyptic*, formulated the matter thus: 'Its roots were widespread and drew nourishment from many sources, prophetic and mythological, native and foreign, esoteric and exotic, but there can be no doubt that the tap root, as it were, went deep down into Israelite prophecy, and in particular the writings of the post-exilic prophets whose thought and language provided the soil from which later apocalyptic works were to grow.'[15] As an example he referred to the prophetic theme of the day of the Lord, which for the prophets meant a historical intervention by God but which was transformed into the last judgement by the seers.

Since the evidence for prophetic influence is transparent, one may be surprised to discover that not all agree with the position sketched above. No less an authority than G. von Rad, in fact, denied that prophecy was the antecedent of apocalyptic thought because he considered the views of history found in prophetic and apocalyptic literature to be incompatible: 'The prophetic message is specifically rooted in definite election traditions. But there is no way which leads from this to the apocalyptic view of history, no more than there is any way which leads to the idea that the last things were determined in a far-off past.'[16] Rather than finding apocalyptic origins in prophecy, von Rad discerned them in the wisdom tradition. Among the parallels he noted was the assumption of God's predetermination of times.[17] His understanding of the matter evolved over the years, with the result that he narrowed his conception of which aspects of the wisdom tradition had influenced the apocalyptists, limiting them primarily to the areas of dream interpretation and the science of signs, and oracles.[18] Others have further developed von Rad's insight by noting that one widespread and ancient type of wisdom, namely mantic wisdom, does indeed provide impressive parallels to what the apocalyptists assumed and did.[19] Just as diviners read encoded messages about the future from the divine world and announced the results of their interpretation to a specific audience, so the apocalyptists deciphered the symbolic messages mediated to them by a heavenly figure and conveyed them to their circles. Both systems presuppose that the future has already been determined. In this regard it is instructive to note that the oldest Jewish apocalypses are attached to the names of individuals with strong mantic associations: Enoch, who is a Jewish reflection of Enmeduranki, the antediluvian Mesopotamian founder of the *baru* diviners, who interprets the signs of the luminaries and of dreams, and who is described in language drawn from descriptions of the diviner Balaam in Numbers 22–4;[20] and Daniel who interprets dreams and reads obscure writings.[21] These two mantic wise men become the earliest Jewish apocalyptic seers.

If one presses this line of investigation another step, it soon becomes apparent why scholars have found both prophetic and sapiential influences on the rise of Jewish and later Christian apocalyptic literature and thought. The evidence strongly suggests that we are not faced with an either/or but with a both/and situation and that modern categories mislead us into making distinctions where ancient writers would not have made a sharp separation. A number of early texts offer evidence that what we would call prophets/prophecy and seers/apocalypses were believed to belong to the same general category. First, in the sources several individuals who appear to us to be seers of apocalypses are designated prophets or are said to have prophesied. For example, the well known quotation from 1 Enoch 1:9 in Jude 14–15 is introduced by these words: 'It was about these that Enoch, in the seventh generation from Adam, prophesied, saying ...' (verse 14). Or, the Florilegium text from Qumran (4Q174) refers to 'the book of Daniel the prophet' (1–3 ii 3). In this connection it should be noted that although in the Hebrew Bible the book of Daniel appears in the Writings, the third category after the Torah and the Prophets, in the Greek translation (and subsequently in Christian Bibles) and in a work called *The Lives of the Prophets* Daniel is included among the prophetic books. 4 Ezra, one of the Jewish apocalypses, introduces its hero Ezra as a prophet (12:42). The Book of Revelation in the

New Testament, while it uses the word 'apocalypse' or 'revelation' for itself (1:1), also designates itself a 'prophecy' at the beginning of the book ('Blessed is the one who reads aloud the words of the prophecy' (1:3) and at its end ('I warn everyone who hears the words of the prophecy of this book: if anyone adds to them ... if anyone takes away from the words of the book of this prophecy ...' (22:18–19)).[22] What these examples show is that for at least some writers the terms 'prophet' and 'prophecy' had a broader scope than we tend to give them today and that apocalyptists and their writings would fit within these categories.[23] To evidence of this kind we may add that already in some biblical prophetic texts the words 'divining' and 'prophesying' are used of the same individuals. That is, diviners prophesy and prophets divine (Micah 3:5–6, 11; Jeremiah 14:14; 27:9–10; 29:8–9; Ezekiel 13:1–9, 17–23; 22:28). Such overlapping in usage of terms from the realms of prophecy, apocalypticism and mantic wisdom shows that these were perceived to be similar or related areas, not sharply differentiated ones.[24] Claims about these associations, however, should be tempered by a recognition that there are indeed noteworthy differences. One obvious example may be cited: while diviners read messages encoded in media such as sheep's livers or dreams and did so on the basis of their own training in these learned fields, the apocalyptists, who also interpreted dreams, required the assistance of heavenly agents to clarify the message being conveyed.

The proper inference from these data is that prophecy and mantic wisdom, which appear to be the most effective forces acting on the apocalyptic writers, are phenomena that have close relations with each other and share the feature of divine revelation of secrets regarding the future to a human recipient for promulgation to a particular audience.

A WIDER WORLD

Another trend in the recent study of apocalyptic phenomena has been to place the Jewish and Christian apocalypses within the wider context of Near Eastern and Greco-Roman apocalypticism. That is, scholars have recognized that the Jewish and Christian apocalypses of late antiquity find counterparts written by authors from various nationalities. The team of scholars who collaborated on Semeia 14 surveyed not only Jewish and early Christian apocalypses but also Gnostic, Greek and Latin, Rabbinic and Persian apocalyptic texts and material. The volume of papers from the International Colloquium on Apocalypticism held in 1979 bears the title *Apocalypticism in the Mediterranean World and the Near East*[25] and includes essays on: 'The

Phenomenon of Apocalypticism' (in Zoroastrian, Egyptian, Old Testament, Jewish, Qumran, Greek, Roman, Hellenistic, early Christian and gnostic literature); 'The Literary Genre of Apocalypses' (in a similar range of literatures, including the so-called Akkadian Apocalypses); and 'The Sociology of Apocalypticism' (in Jewish and Christian texts). The fact that the participants cast their net so wide shows that, although the Jewish and Christian apocalypses have received the largest amount of attention, they stand as only a part of an international literature, study of which should make a contribution to the examination of the Jewish and Christian apocalypses.

For a long time scholars have recognized that Jewish apocalypticism was indebted to Persian/Iranian theology. The specific tenets usually mentioned are dualism and periodization of history. Persian/Iranian apocalypses are indeed an important comparative source (whatever problems there may be with their textual condition), but in recent times parallels to Jewish apocalypses from more ancient Mesopotamian sources have been noted. The so-called Akkadian Prophecies (or Apocalypses) have recently entered prominently into apocalyptic studies. These are five texts that range in date from the twelfth century BC to the Seleucid period; they are unified by the presence in them of 'predictions' of events that have already taken place – a feature that they share with the apocalypses which contain historical surveys. In their historical 'predictions' the contents are revealed to the recipients, but the individuals who figure in the revelations are not named. The 'predictions' draw heavily upon the language of omen apodoses (the clauses giving the consequences that will follow from the omen examined) and thus have a verbal and thematic connection with mantic wisdom. One of these texts, the Dynastic Prophecy (from the Late Babylonian period), resembles Daniel 2 and 7 in that it speaks of a series of rising and falling kingdoms – Assyria, Babylon, Elam and the Haneans (apparently the Greeks) are named. The Akkadian texts also attest features such as pseudonymity and commands to keep the contents of the disclosures secret; however, they do not speak of world-wide judgement and appear to lack eschatological teachings generally.[26]

These Akkadian Prophecies are one more piece of evidence that allows us to reconstruct more fully the international phenomenon and context of prophecy/apocalypticism. We now have texts that, in whole or in part, may be termed apocalypses from Greco-Roman Egypt (the Demotic Chronicle, the Lamb to Bocchoris, the Potter's Oracle and the Apocalypse of Asclepius) and from Persia (Zand-i Vohuman Yasn (= the Bahman Yasht), the Arda Viraf Nameh; the Oracle of Hystaspes contains apocalyptic material but is itself not an apocalypse); various works from Greece and Rome may be classed as apocalypses (e.g., Poimandres) or offer material that resembles apocalyptic teachings. All of these texts are, naturally, worthy of careful study in themselves, but for students of the larger apocalyptic phenomenon they provide not only comparative literary evidence but more possibilities for examining usage and social location. M. Hengel has argued that early Jewish apocalypses betray influences from varied quarters. In particular he writes that the frameworks of the 'universal history' that we find in the early Jewish apocalypses 'were largely drawn from the mythological conceptions of the Hellenistic oriental environment'.[27] He adds that we should be cautious in using terms such as 'Hellenistic' and 'oriental', since even originally oriental themes may have been transmitted to Jewish writers by Hellenistic sources.[28] If the first Jewish apocalypses appeared in the third and second centuries, the wide Hellenistic context provided their learned authors with opportunities to mine not only native but also international traditions and motifs of various kinds.

### CONCLUDING COMMENTS

The last quarter century has been a golden age in several respects for the study of apocalyptic literature. For one, we have witnessed publication of new texts of works previously known only through translations: a parade example is the Qumran Aramaic copies of the Book of Enoch. These fragmentary manuscripts have opened a new window on the earliest form of the Enochic booklets and raised important questions about the development of the present five-book collection that goes under the name 1 Enoch.[29] The very fragmentary copies of an Aramaic Levi work have had a similar if smaller effect on study of the Testament of Levi and its literary ancestry.[30] There are now extensive Hebrew fragments of the Book of Jubilees, including texts for a number of verses in the apocalyptic twenty-third chapter.[31] Besides pieces of ancient texts, modern translations and brief commentaries on large numbers of ancient Jewish and Christian apocalypses and related material have seen the light of day. Mention should be made of the ongoing German series 'Jüdische Schriften aus hellenistisch-römischer Zeit' and J. H. Charlesworth's two-volume *The Old Testament Pseudepigrapha*, the first of which is entirely devoted to apocalypses and testaments.[32] This latter volume greatly expands the number of apocalyptic and similar texts that are now readily available for reading and study.

A number of books that offer introductions to or summaries of the apocalypses have been published in recent decades. E. Schürer's *The History of the Jewish People in the Age of Jesus Christ (175 BC – AD 135)* has been revised and updated;[33] series such as 'Compendia rerum iudaicarum ad Novum Testamentum' have included substantial sections on apocalyptic literature.[34] Mention should also be made of three introductions: W. Schmithals, *The Apocalyptic Movement*;[35] J. Collins, *The Apocalyptic Imagination*;[36] and G. W. E. Nickelsburg, *Jewish Literature Between the Bible and the Mishnah*.[37] Of signal importance has been the work on extensive commentaries for non-biblical apocalyptic works. M. Stone has contributed a full commentary on 4 Ezra and others are in preparation.[38] It remains the case, however, that for most extra-biblical apocalypses there are no commentaries other than the scattered notes that translators add to their renditions. This fact points to an obvious desideratum: the sorts of commentaries on all apocalyptic texts that biblical scholars have long had on scriptural works.

Although scholars have assiduously studied the apocalyptic sources, there are still few reference works on them. There is no encyclopedia of apocalyptic literature, nor (perhaps for practical reasons, such as the variety of languages in which they are preserved) are there concordances to such texts. Production of reference works on the apocalypses is highly desirable and would facilitate study of them.

Among the topics that require further study are the social location of the various apocalyptists and their communities and the functions that the apocalypses served within them. The social locations of the seers remain elusive yet intriguing. In most cases the modern scholar has no evidence apart from what may be teased from the texts of the apocalypses themselves. To take only the most familiar example, John who received the visions now recorded in the book of Revelation was probably a prisoner on the island of Patmos; he was able to convey his message to seven churches in seven cities in the province of Asia. He seems to have held a position of some authority in those churches, as the seven letters in chapters 2–3 indicate. The text also leaves the reader with the impression that the members of these churches as well as John himself were enduring trying times. Perhaps more may be gleaned from the book but not much. When we turn to Enoch and the apocalypses associated with his name, we are sure about even less. We do not know who wrote any one of them, and we certainly have little evidence about communities that may have gathered around the authors in this tradition. We receive only vague hints: he speaks to the chosen of the latter days or he conveys his teachings to his children. Perhaps Enoch's epistle (chapters 91–107) allows us to infer that his followers were poor because the writer complains about and warns the rich and powerful. It is often claimed that apocalypses are the literature of the oppressed, and that is true in some documented cases like the Revelation. But does it hold in all cases? We really do not know, however reasonable it may appear to make this claim. At least we may say that there is always an inner and an outer group in such texts.

The Qumran community has seemed a prime candidate for disclosing information about apocalyptic communities in early Judaism. We have solid reasons for thinking that a group of people settled around Khirbet Qumran and that they were responsible for the scrolls found in the eleven nearby caves. Among the more than 800 texts, some fall into the apocalyptic category; the copies of Daniel and the Enoch texts are familiar examples. Moreover, various texts reveal that the group had a keen interest in the last times (e.g., the War Scroll, the commentaries) and the Serek ha-Yaḥad states that the group had withdrawn into the wilderness until God's arrival. The community of Qumran, therefore, shows the sorts of traits we might expect an apocalyptic community to have. Its members, however, seem not to have composed what we would call apocalypses, although they wrote related kinds of texts. Were there other communities that prized particular apocalypses and lived by them? We would like to know.

The apocalypses are learned compositions whose authors betray their acquaintance with a wide range of literature and traditional imagery. Perhaps this, too, says something about the social location of apocalyptists. The texts were not written, however, to demonstrate the education of the authors: they present their teachings as the results of extraordinary, intense and overwhelming experiences. It would be at least interesting if we could explain more about the nature of their revelatory experiences.[39]

## Notes

1 K. Koch, *The Rediscovery of Apocalyptic*, Studies in Biblical Theology 22 (Naperville, IL: Allenson, 1972), pp. 24–7.

2 *Ibid.*, p. 28.

3 *Ibid.*, pp. 28–33.

4 P. Hanson, *The Dawn of Apocalyptic* (Philadelphia: Fortress Press, 1975), pp. 11–12. See also his contributions 'Prolegomena to the Study of Jewish Apocalyptic', in F. M. Cross, W. E. Lemke and P. D. Miller (eds.), *Magnalia Dei: The Mighty Acts of God* (Garden City, NY: Doubleday, 1976), pp. 389–413; 'Apocalypticism', *Interpreter's Dictionary of the Bible Supplement* (New York:

Abingdon Press, 1976) 28–34; 'Apocalypses and Apocalypticism: the Genre, Introductory Overview', *Anchor Bible Dictionary* (New York, Doubleday, 1992) vol. 1, pp. 279–82.

5 J. J. Collins, 'Introduction: Towards the Morphology of a Genre', in J. J. Collins (ed.), *Apocalypse: The Morphology of a Genre*, Semeia 14 (Chico, CA: Scholars Press, 1979), p. 9.

6 Hanson (*The Dawn of Apocalyptic*, p. 8) terms it the dominant aspect.

7 M. E. Stone, 'Lists of Revealed Things in the Apocalyptic Literature' in Cross, Lemke and Miller (eds.), *Magnalia Dei*, pp. 414–52.

8 C. Rowland, *The Open Heaven* (New York: Crossroad, 1982). The Mishnaic passage is quoted from H. Danby, *The Mishnah* (London: Oxford University Press, 1933), p. 213.

9 See M. N. A. Bockmuehl, *Revelation and Mystery in Ancient Judaism and Pauline Christianity*, Wissenschaftliche Untersuchungen zum Neuen Testament 36 (Tübingen: J. C. B. Mohr (Paul Siebeck), 1990), pp. 24–41.

10 Collins, 'Introduction: Towards the Morphology of a Genre', p. 13.

11 J. J. Collins, 'Genre, Ideology and Social Movements', in J. J. Collins and J. H. Charlesworth (eds.), *Mysteries and Revelations: Apocalyptic Studies since the Uppsala Colloquium*, Journal for the Study of the Pseudepigrapha Supplements 9 (Sheffield: Sheffield Academic Press, 1991), p. 19. The wording of the additional line was first given in A. Yarbro Collins, 'Introduction: Early Christian Apocalypticism', in A. Yarbro Collins (ed.), *Early Christian Apocalypticism: Genre and Social Setting*, Semeia 36 (1986), p. 7.

12 F. M. Cross, *Canaanite Myth and Hebrew Epic* (Cambridge, MA: Harvard University Press, 1973), p. 343.

13 *Ibid.*, p. 346.

14 O. Plöger, *Theocracy and Eschatology* (Richmond: John Knox, 1968 (an English translation of the second German edition which appeared in 1962)). For Hanson's views, see *The Dawn of Apocalyptic*.

15 D. S. Russell, *The Method and Message of Jewish Apocalyptic* (Philadelphia: Westminster Press, 1964), p. 88.

16 G. von Rad, *Old Testament Theology*, 2 vols. (New York: Harper & Row, 1962–65), vol. II, p. 303.

17 G. von Rad, *Wisdom in Israel* (Nashville and New York: Abingdon Press, 1972), pp. 263–83.

18 This narrowing of his claim is found in G. von Rad, *Theologie des Alten Testaments*, vol. II: *Die Theologie der prophetischen Überlieferungen Israels*, 5th edn (Munich: Kaiser, 1968), p. 331.

19 See especially H. P. Müller, 'Mantische Weisheit und Apokalyptik', in *Congress Volume Uppsala 1971*, Supplements to Vetus Testamentum 22 (Leiden: Brill, 1972), pp. 268–93. Cf. J. C. VanderKam, *Enoch and the Growth of an Apocalyptic Tradition*, Catholic Biblical Quarterly Monograph Series 16 (Washington, DC: Catholic Biblical Association of America, 1984), pp. 3–8.

20 The details for these associations are given in VanderKam, *Enoch and the*

*Growth of an Apocalyptic Tradition*. See also H. S. Kvanvig, *Roots of Apocalyptic: The Mesopotamian Background of the Enoch Figure and of the Son of Man*, Wissenschaftliche Monographien zum Alten und Neuen Testament 61 (Neukirchen-Vluyn: Neukirchener, 1988).

21 See H. P. Müller, 'Magisch-mantische Weisheit und die Gestalt Daniels', *Ugarit-Forschungen* 1 (1969), pp. 79–94; J. J. Collins, 'The Court Tales in Daniel and the Development of Apocalyptic', *Journal of Biblical Literature* 94 (1975), pp. 218–34.

22 R. Bauckham has entitled his recent book on John's Revelation *The Climax of Prophecy* (Edinburgh: T. & T. Clark, 1993). The biblical citations given above are from the New Revised Standard Version.

23 On this point, see J. Barton, *Oracles of God: Perceptions of Ancient Prophecy in Israel after the Exile* (New York/Oxford: Oxford University Press, 1986), pp. 179–213.

24 For more details, see J. C. VanderKam, 'The Prophetic-Sapiential Origins of Apocalyptic Thought', in J. D. Martin and P. R. Davies (eds.), *A Word in Season: Essays in Honour of William McKane, Journal for the Study of the Old Testament Supplements* 42 (Sheffield: JSOT Press, 1986), pp. 163–76.

25 *Apocalypticism in the Mediterranean World and the Near East: Proceedings of the International Colloquium on Apocalypticism Uppsala, August 12–17, 1979*, ed. D. Hellholm (Tübingen: J. C. B. Mohr (Paul Siebeck), 1983; 2nd edn (with a supplementary bibliography) 1989).

26 For the Akkadian texts, see H. Ringgren, 'Akkadian Apocalypses', in *ibid.*, pp. 379–86. Ringgren with most others does not consider these texts apocalyptic in character but 'valuable comparative material ... some of the stones out of which the structure of apocalypticism is built up' (p. 386). See also VanderKam, *Enoch and the Growth of an Apocalyptic Tradition*, pp. 62–9.

27 M. Hengel, *Judaism and Hellenism*, 2 vols. (Philadelphia: Fortress Press, 1974), vol. I, p. 181.

28 He illustrates his point from the images of the four world empires in Daniel 2 and 7 for which there are parallels, more or less complete, in a variety of non-Jewish texts. See his entire presentation under the heading of 'The Hasidim and the First Climax of Jewish Apocalyptic' (*ibid.*, vol. I, pp. 175–218).

29 J. T. Milik, *The Books of Enoch: Aramaic Fragments of Qumrân Cave 4* (Oxford: Clarendon Press, 1976).

30 The official publication will be in a future volume of the Discoveries in the Judaean Desert series, but the texts are available. See, for example, K. Beyer, *Die aramäischen Texte vom Toten Meer: Ergänzungsband* (Göttingen: Vandenhoeck & Ruprecht, 1994), pp. 71–8; cf. pp. 78–82; M. E. Stone and J. C. Greenfield, 'The Prayer of Levi', *Journal of Biblical Literature* 112 (1993), pp. 247–66.

31 All of the cave 4 Jubilees fragments have now been published by J. T. Milik and J. C. VanderKam in *Qumran Cave 4, VIII: Parabiblical Texts Part I*, Discoveries in the Judaean Desert XIII (Oxford: Clarendon Press, 1994), pp. 1–140. For other fragments of Jubilees 23, see 2Q19 and 3Q5.

32 J. H. Charlesworth, *The Old Testament Pseudepigrapha*, 2 vols. (Garden City, NY: Doubleday, 1983, 1985).

33 The three volumes were revised and edited by G. Vermes and F. Millar (Edinburgh: T. & T. Clark, 1973–87). The third volume contains coverage of the apocalyptic literature.

34 See in particular M. E. Stone's section 'Apocalyptic Literature' in M. E. Stone (ed.), *Jewish Writings of the Second Temple Period: Apocrypha, Pseudepigrapha, Qumran Sectarian Writings, Philo, Josephus* (Assen: van Gorcum/Philadelphia: Fortress Press, 1984), pp. 383–441. Another volume in the series is devoted to another aspect of apocalypticism: J. C. VanderKam and W. Adler (eds.), *The Jewish Apocalyptic Heritage in Early Christianity* (Assen: van Gorcum/ Minneapolis: Fortress Press, 1996).

35 Subtitle: *Introduction & Interpretation* (Nashville/New York: Abingdon Press, 1975 (the German original was published in 1973)).

36 Subtitle: *An Introduction to the Jewish Matrix of Christianity* (New York: Crossroad, 1984, 1987).

37 Subtitle: *A Historical and Literary Introduction* (Philadelphia: Fortress Press, 1981; revised edn, 1987).

38 M. E. Stone, *Fourth Ezra*, Hermeneia (Minneapolis: Fortress Press, 1990). The editors of the Hermeneia series envision commentaries on 'important literary works in the categories of apocryphal and pseudepigraphal works relating to the Old and New Testaments, including some of Essene or Gnostic authorship' (from the Foreword). Nickelsburg's commentary on 1 Enoch is in an advanced state of preparation.

39 See Stone's comments in *Fourth Ezra*, pp. 30–5, 119–24.

## Further reading

Charlesworth, James H. (ed.), *The Old Testament Pseudepigrapha*, vol. 1: *Apocalyptic Literature and Testaments*, Garden City, NY: Doubleday, 1983.

Collins, John J. (ed.), *Apocalypse: The Morphology of a Genre*, Semeia 14, Chico, CA: Scholars Press, 1979.

   *Daniel with an Introduction to Apocalyptic Literature*, The Forms of Old Testament Literature xx, Grand Rapids, MI: Eerdmans, 1984.

   *The Apocalyptic Imagination: An Introduction to the Jewish Matrix of Christianity*, New York: Crossroad, 1984.

Hanson, Paul D., *The Dawn of Apocalyptic: The Historical and Sociological Roots of Jewish Apocalyptic Eschatology*, rev. edn, Philadelphia: Fortress Press, 1979 (first edn 1975).

   *Old Testament Apocalyptic*, Interpreting Biblical Texts, Nashville: Abingdon Press, 1987.

Nickelsburg, George W. E., *Jewish Literature Between the Bible and the Mishnah: A Historical and Literary Introduction*, Philadelphia: Fortress Press, 1981.

Rowland, Christopher, *The Open Heaven: A Study of Apocalyptic in Judaism and Early Christianity*, New York: Crossroad, 1982.

Sparks, H. F. D. (ed.), *The Apocryphal Old Testament*, Oxford: Clarendon Press, 1984.

VanderKam, James C., *Enoch and the Growth of an Apocalyptic Tradition*, Catholic Biblical Quarterly Monograph Series 16, Washington, DC: Catholic Biblical Association, 1984.

'Prophecy and Apocalyptics in the Ancient Near East', in J. Sasson (ed.), *Civilizations of the Ancient Near East*, New York: Scribners, 1995, vol. III, pp. 2083–94.

John J. Collins and Bernard McGinn are editing a multi-volume *Encyclopedia of Apocalypticism* which will contain articles covering apocalypticism in all periods in which it is attested. Volume I is entitled *Origins of Apocalypse in Judaism and Early Christianity*. The encyclopedia will be published by Continuum.

# General index

# Index of biblical references